The AMAZING SPIDER-MAN

W O R L D W I D E

DAN SLOTT & CHRISTOS GAGE
WRITERS

GIUSEPPE CAMUNCOLI
PENCILER

CAM SMITH
WITH **GIUSEPPE CAMUNCOLI** (#20) & **ROBERTO POGGI** (#21)
INKERS

JASON KEITH
COLORIST

VC'S JOE CARAMAGNA
LETTERER

ALEX ROSS
COVER ART

AMAZING SPIDER-MAN ANNUAL #1

"MASK OF DEATH"

HUMBERTO RAMOS & CHRISTOS GAGE
WRITERS

FRANCISCO HERRERA
ARTIST

FERNANDA RIZO
COLORIST

"NEON DRAGON"

JAMES ASMUS
WRITER

CORY SMITH
PENCILER

SCOTT HANNA, ROBERT POGGI & LORENZO RUGGIERO
INKERS

RAIN BEREDO
COLORIST

"WHOSE CRIME IS IT ANYWAY?"

WAYNE BRADY & JONATHAN MANGUM
WRITERS

BRUNO OLIVEIRA
ARTIST

LEE LOUGHRIDGE
COLORIST

VC'S TRAVIS LANHAM & JOE CARAMAGNA
LETTERERS

FRANCISCO HERRERA & FERNANDA RIZO
COVER ART

ALLISON STOCK
ASSISTANT EDITOR

DEVIN LEWIS
ASSOCIATE EDITOR

NICK LOWE
EDITOR

SPIDER-MAN CREATED BY
STAN LEE & STEVE DITKO

COLLECTION EDITOR: **JENNIFER GRÜNWALD**
ASSISTANT EDITOR: **CAITLIN O'CONNELL**
ASSOCIATE MANAGING EDITOR: **KATERI WOODY**

EDITOR, SPECIAL PROJECTS: **MARK D. BEAZLEY**
VP PRODUCTION & SPECIAL PROJECTS: **JEFF YOUNGQUIST**
SVP PRINT, SALES & MARKETING: **DAVID GABRIEL**

EDITOR IN CHIEF: **AXEL ALONSO**
CHIEF CREATIVE OFFICER: **JOE QUESADA**

PRESIDENT: **DAN BUCKLEY**
EXECUTIVE PRODUCER: **ALAN FINE**

PREVIOUSLY

IN ORDER TO ESCAPE DEATH, SPIDER-MAN'S GREATEST FOE, DOCTOR OCTOPUS, SWITCHED BODIES WITH PETER PARKER. PETER'S MIND ENDED UP BACK IN HIS BODY, SEEMINGLY SILENCING OTTO OCTAVIUS FOREVER.

AFTER BREAKING INTO THE HEADQUARTERS OF A MYSTERIOUS NEW PHARMACEUTICAL COMPANY CALLED NEW U, THE AMAZING SPIDER-MAN WAS HORRIFIED TO FIND HIS METAL-ARMED NEMESIS ALIVE AND WELL.

HOW OTTO SURVIVED REMAINS A MYSTERY...

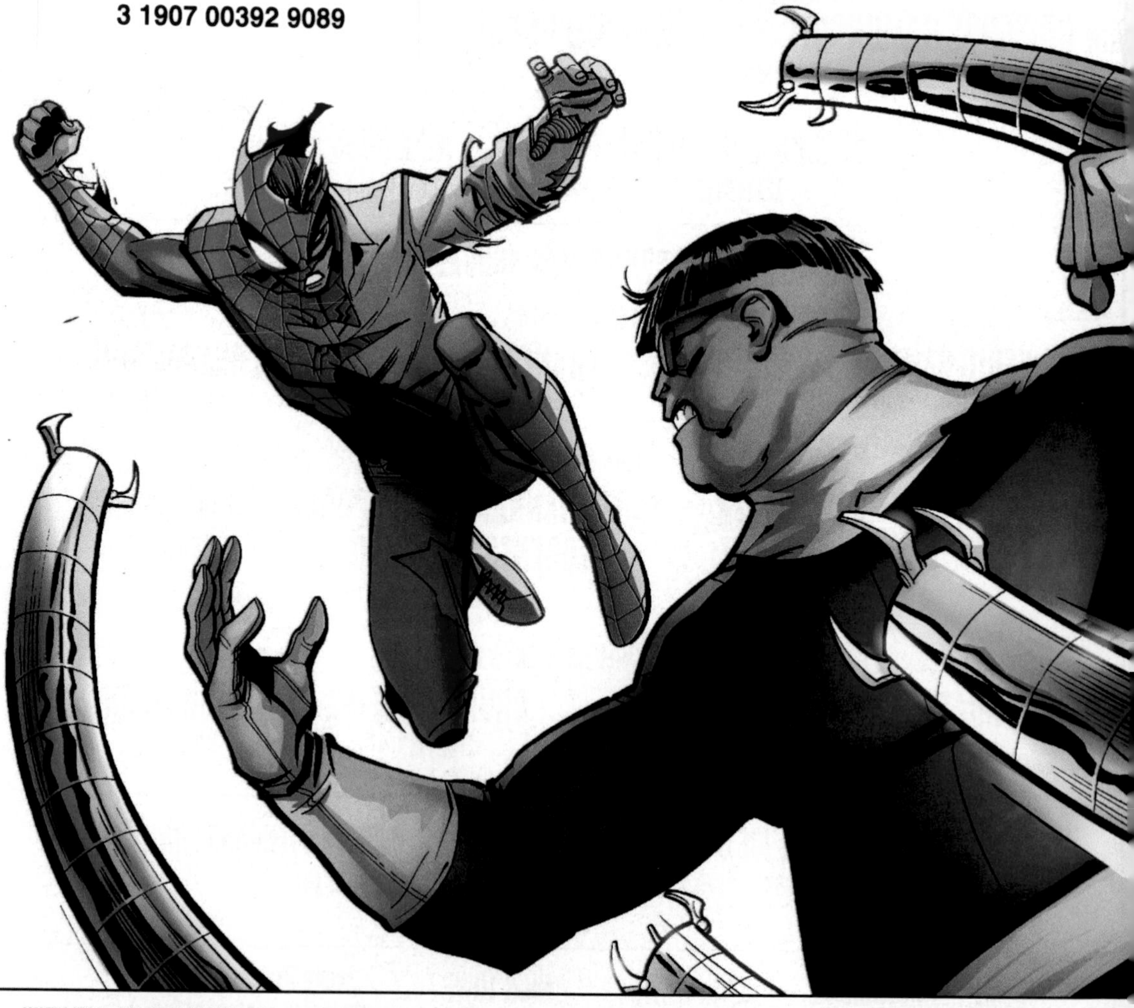

AMAZING SPIDER-MAN: WORLDWIDE VOL. 5. Contains material originally published in magazine form as AMAZING SPIDER-MAN #20-24 and ANNUAL #1. First printing 2017. ISBN# 978-1-302-90238-4. Published by MARVEL WORLD INC., a subsidiary of MARVEL ENTERTAINMENT, LLC. OFFICE OF PUBLICATION: 135 West 50th Street, New York, NY 10020. Copyright © 2017 MARVEL No similarity between any of the names, characters, persons, and/or institutions magazine with those of any living or dead person or institution is intended, and any such similarity which may exist is purely coincidental. **Printed in the U.S.A.** DAN BUCKLEY, President, Marvel Entertainment; JOE QUESADA, Chief Cr Officer; TOM BREVOORT, SVP of Publishing; DAVID BOGART, SVP of Business Affairs & Operations, Publishing & Partnership; C.B. CEBULSKI, VP of Brand Management & Development, Asia; DAVID GABRIEL, SVP of Sales & Marketing, Publi JEFF YOUNGQUIST, VP of Production & Special Projects; DAN CARR, Executive Director of Publishing Technology; ALEX MORALES, Director of Publishing Operations; SUSAN CRESPI, Production Manager; STAN LEE, Chairman Emeritu information regarding advertising in Marvel Comics or on Marvel.com, please contact Vit DeBellis, Integrated Sales Manager, at vdebellis@marvel.com. For Marvel subscription inquiries, please call 888-511-5480. **Manufactured bet 3/17/2017 and 4/17/2017 by QUAD/GRAPHICS WASECA, WASECA, MN, USA.**

10 9 8 7 6 5 4 3 2 1

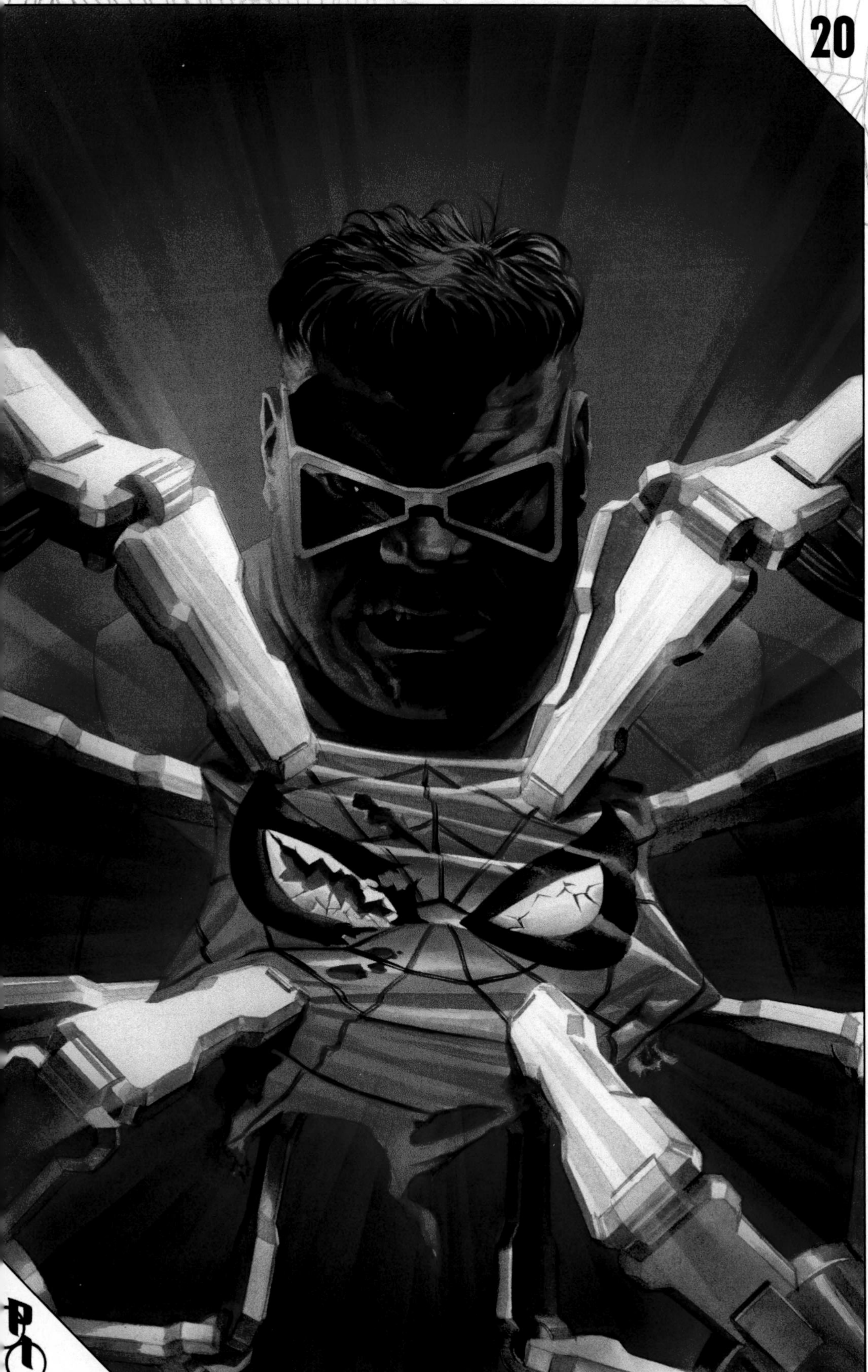

"SPIDER-MAN'S SUPERIOR"

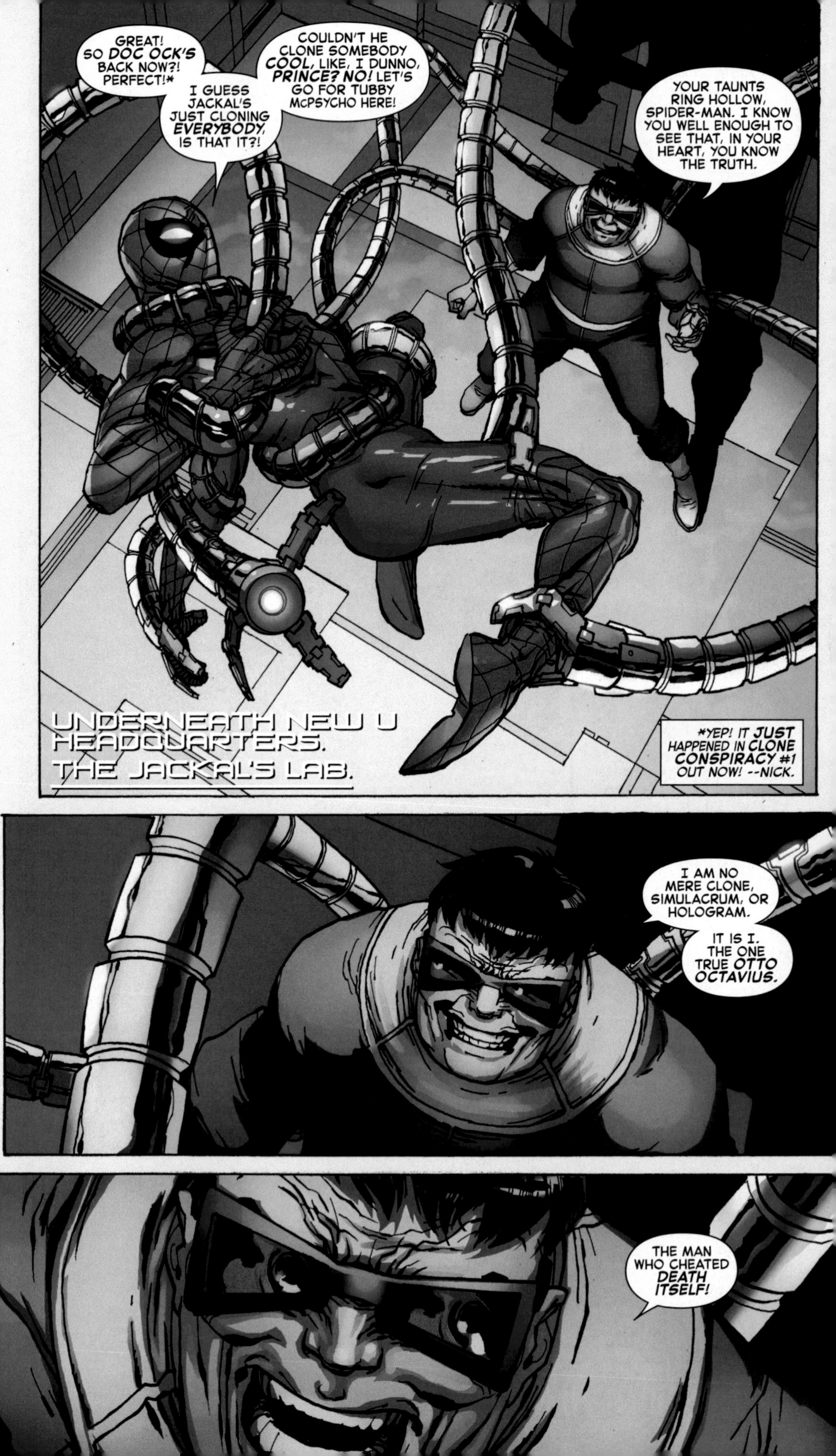
GREAT! SO DOC OCK'S BACK NOW?! PERFECT!*
I GUESS JACKAL'S JUST CLONING EVERYBODY, IS THAT IT?!
COULDN'T HE CLONE SOMEBODY COOL, LIKE, I DUNNO, PRINCE? NO! LET'S GO FOR TUBBY McPSYCHO HERE!
YOUR TAUNTS RING HOLLOW, SPIDER-MAN. I KNOW YOU WELL ENOUGH TO SEE THAT, IN YOUR HEART, YOU KNOW THE TRUTH.
UNDERNEATH NEW U HEADQUARTERS.
THE JACKAL'S LAB.
*YEP! IT JUST HAPPENED IN CLONE CONSPIRACY #1 OUT NOW! --NICK.
I AM NO MERE CLONE, SIMULACRUM, OR HOLOGRAM.
IT IS I. THE ONE TRUE OTTO OCTAVIUS.
THE MAN WHO CHEATED DEATH ITSELF!

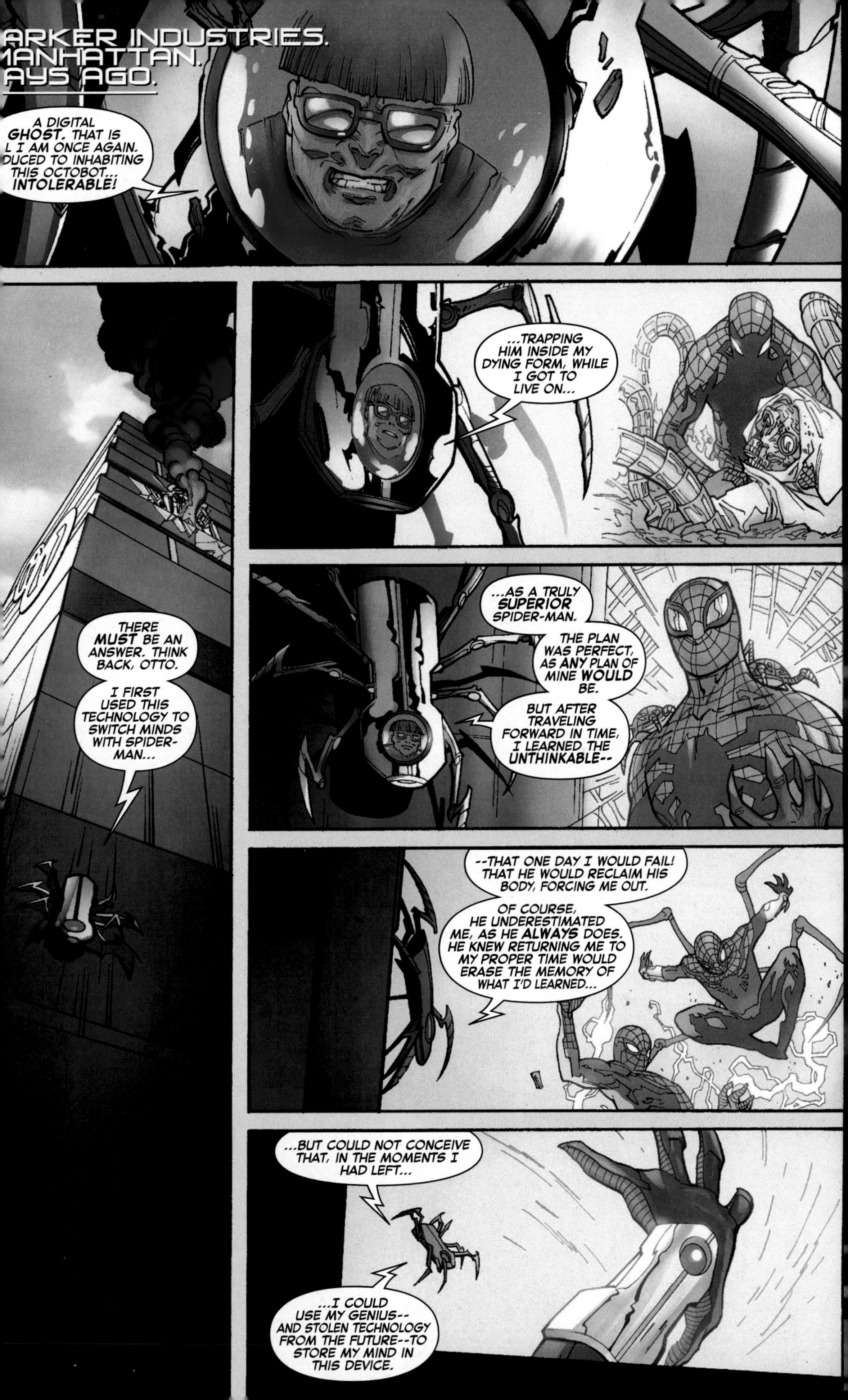
ARKER INDUSTRIES.
MANHATTAN.
AYS AGO.
A DIGITAL GHOST. THAT IS L I AM ONCE AGAIN. DUCED TO INHABITING THIS OCTOBOT... INTOLERABLE!
THERE MUST BE AN ANSWER. THINK BACK, OTTO.
I FIRST USED THIS TECHNOLOGY TO SWITCH MINDS WITH SPIDER-MAN...
...TRAPPING HIM INSIDE MY DYING FORM, WHILE I GOT TO LIVE ON...
...AS A TRULY SUPERIOR SPIDER-MAN.
THE PLAN WAS PERFECT, AS ANY PLAN OF MINE WOULD BE.
BUT AFTER TRAVELING FORWARD IN TIME, I LEARNED THE UNTHINKABLE--
--THAT ONE DAY I WOULD FAIL! THAT HE WOULD RECLAIM HIS BODY, FORCING ME OUT.
OF COURSE, HE UNDERESTIMATED ME, AS HE ALWAYS DOES. HE KNEW RETURNING ME TO MY PROPER TIME WOULD ERASE THE MEMORY OF WHAT I'D LEARNED...
...BUT COULD NOT CONCEIVE THAT, IN THE MOMENTS I HAD LEFT...
...I COULD USE MY GENIUS-- AND STOLEN TECHNOLOGY FROM THE FUTURE--TO STORE MY MIND IN THIS DEVICE.

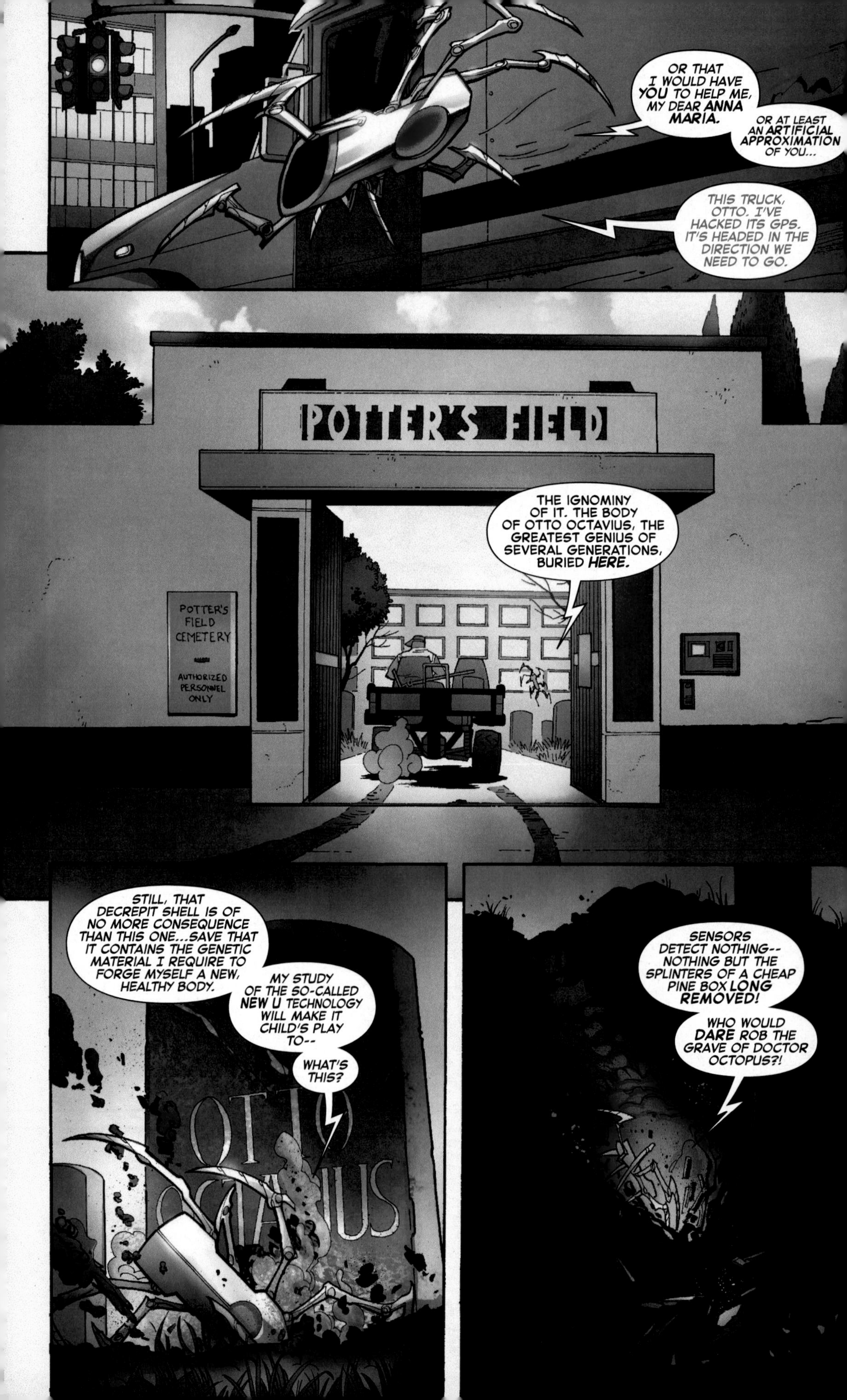
OR THAT I WOULD HAVE YOU TO HELP ME, MY DEAR ANNA MARIA.
OR AT LEAST AN ARTIFICIAL APPROXIMATION OF YOU...
THIS TRUCK, OTTO. I'VE HACKED ITS GPS. IT'S HEADED IN THE DIRECTION WE NEED TO GO.
POTTER'S FIELD
THE IGNOMINY OF IT. THE BODY OF OTTO OCTAVIUS, THE GREATEST GENIUS OF SEVERAL GENERATIONS, BURIED HERE.
POTTER'S FIELD CEMETERY
AUTHORIZED PERSONNEL ONLY
STILL, THAT DECREPIT SHELL IS OF NO MORE CONSEQUENCE THAN THIS ONE...SAVE THAT IT CONTAINS THE GENETIC MATERIAL I REQUIRE TO FORGE MYSELF A NEW, HEALTHY BODY.
MY STUDY OF THE SO-CALLED NEW U TECHNOLOGY WILL MAKE IT CHILD'S PLAY TO--
WHAT'S THIS?
OTTO OCTAVIUS
SENSORS DETECT NOTHING-- NOTHING BUT THE SPLINTERS OF A CHEAP PINE BOX LONG REMOVED!
WHO WOULD DARE ROB THE GRAVE OF DOCTOR OCTOPUS?!

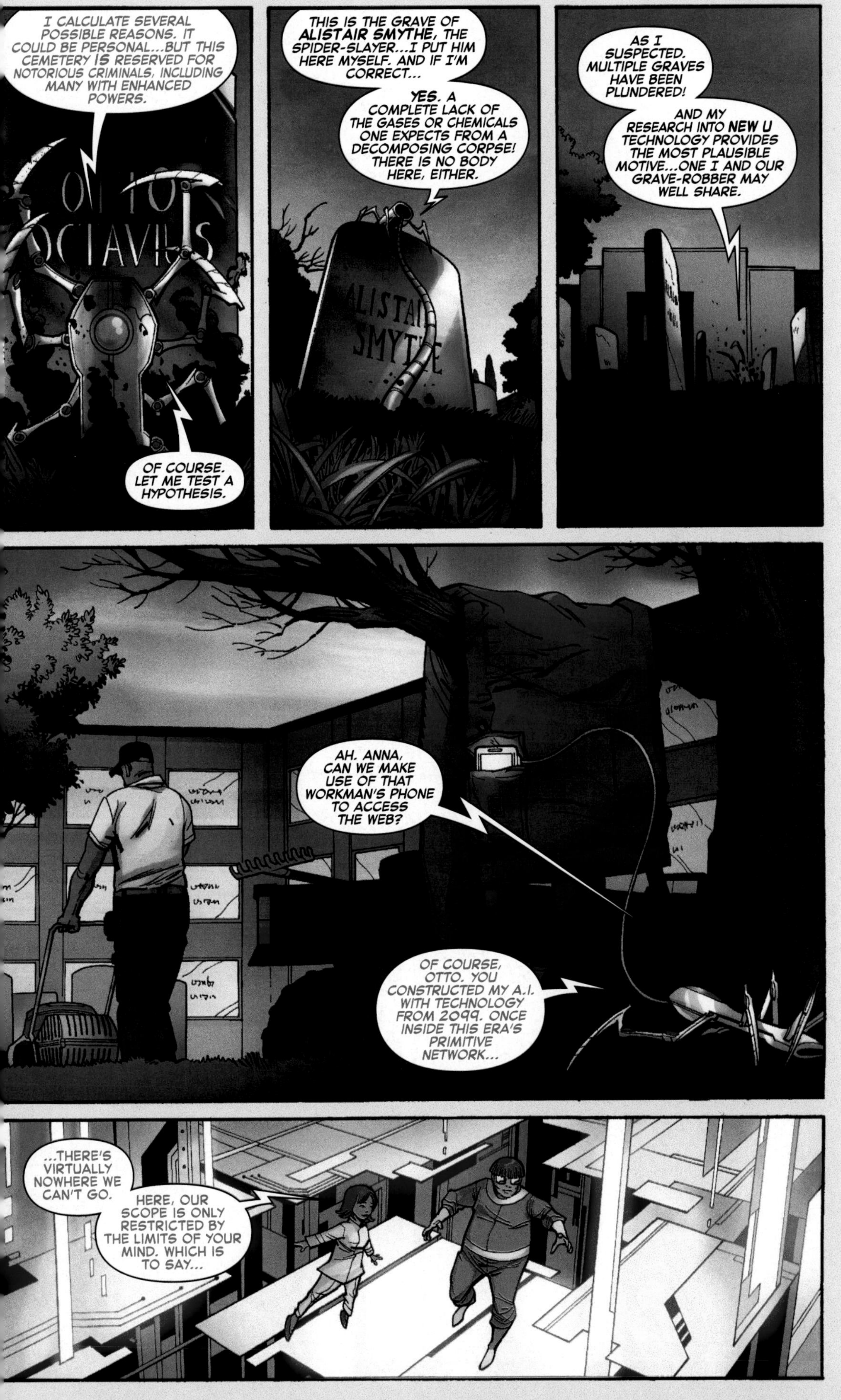

I CALCULATE SEVERAL POSSIBLE REASONS. IT COULD BE PERSONAL...BUT THIS CEMETERY IS RESERVED FOR NOTORIOUS CRIMINALS, INCLUDING MANY WITH ENHANCED POWERS.
OF COURSE. LET ME TEST A HYPOTHESIS.
THIS IS THE GRAVE OF ALISTAIR SMYTHE, THE SPIDER-SLAYER...I PUT HIM HERE MYSELF. AND IF I'M CORRECT...
YES. A COMPLETE LACK OF THE GASES OR CHEMICALS ONE EXPECTS FROM A DECOMPOSING CORPSE! THERE IS NO BODY HERE, EITHER.
AS I SUSPECTED. MULTIPLE GRAVES HAVE BEEN PLUNDERED!
AND MY RESEARCH INTO NEW U TECHNOLOGY PROVIDES THE MOST PLAUSIBLE MOTIVE...ONE I AND OUR GRAVE-ROBBER MAY WELL SHARE.
AH. ANNA, CAN WE MAKE USE OF THAT WORKMAN'S PHONE TO ACCESS THE WEB?
OF COURSE, OTTO. YOU CONSTRUCTED MY A.I. WITH TECHNOLOGY FROM 2099. ONCE INSIDE THIS ERA'S PRIMITIVE NETWORK...
...THERE'S VIRTUALLY NOWHERE WE CAN'T GO.
HERE, OUR SCOPE IS ONLY RESTRICTED BY THE LIMITS OF YOUR MIND. WHICH IS TO SAY...

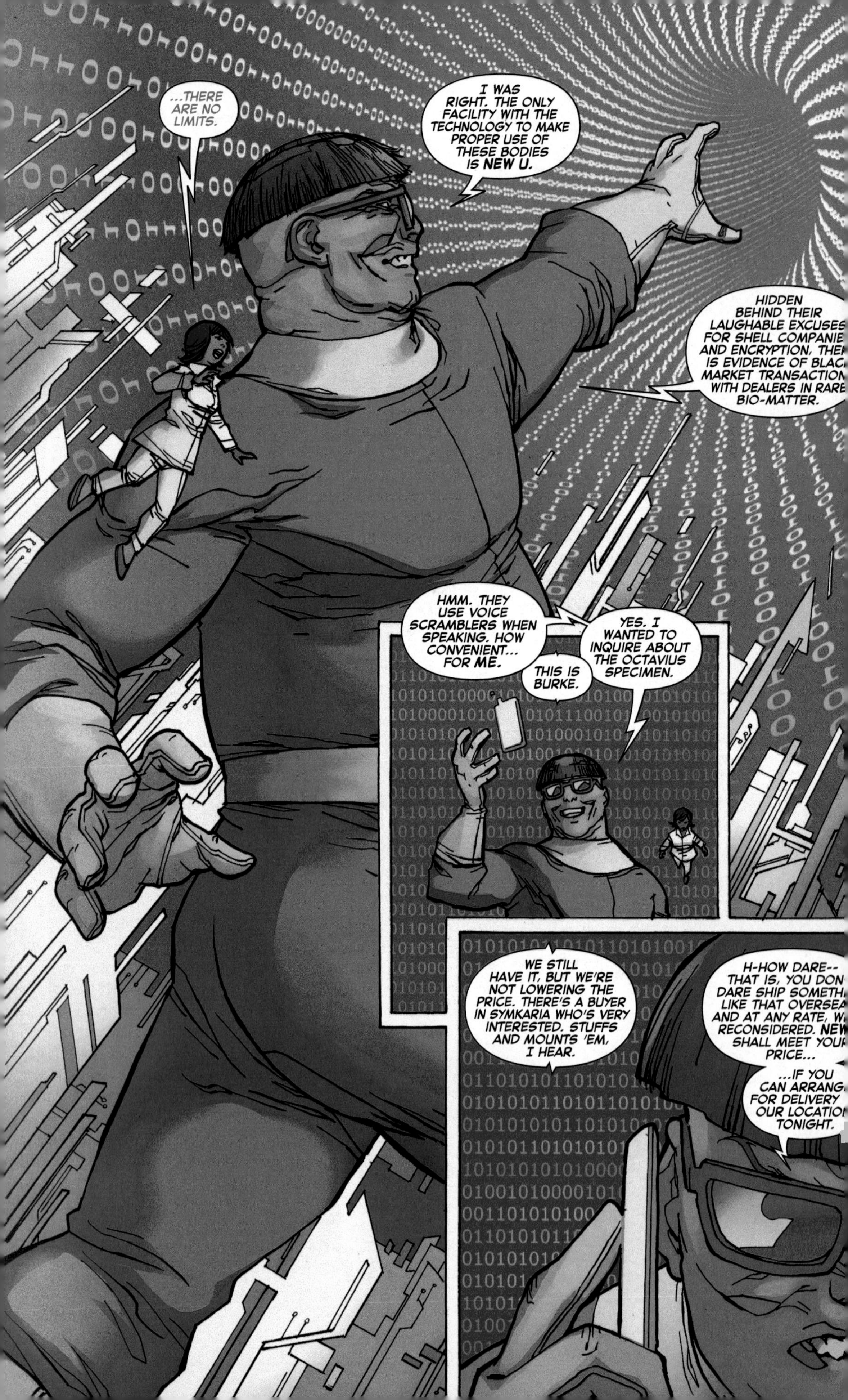
...THERE ARE NO LIMITS.
I WAS RIGHT. THE ONLY FACILITY WITH THE TECHNOLOGY TO MAKE PROPER USE OF THESE BODIES IS NEW U.
HIDDEN BEHIND THEIR LAUGHABLE EXCUSES FOR SHELL COMPANIE AND ENCRYPTION, THER IS EVIDENCE OF BLAC MARKET TRANSACTION WITH DEALERS IN RARE BIO-MATTER.
HMM. THEY USE VOICE SCRAMBLERS WHEN SPEAKING. HOW CONVENIENT... FOR ME.
THIS IS BURKE.
YES. I WANTED TO INQUIRE ABOUT THE OCTAVIUS SPECIMEN.
WE STILL HAVE IT, BUT WE'RE NOT LOWERING THE PRICE. THERE'S A BUYER IN SYMKARIA WHO'S VERY INTERESTED. STUFFS AND MOUNTS 'EM, I HEAR.
H-HOW DARE-- THAT IS, YOU DON DARE SHIP SOMETH LIKE THAT OVERSEA AND AT ANY RATE, W RECONSIDERED. NEW SHALL MEET YOUR PRICE...
...IF YOU CAN ARRANG FOR DELIVERY OUR LOCATIO TONIGHT.

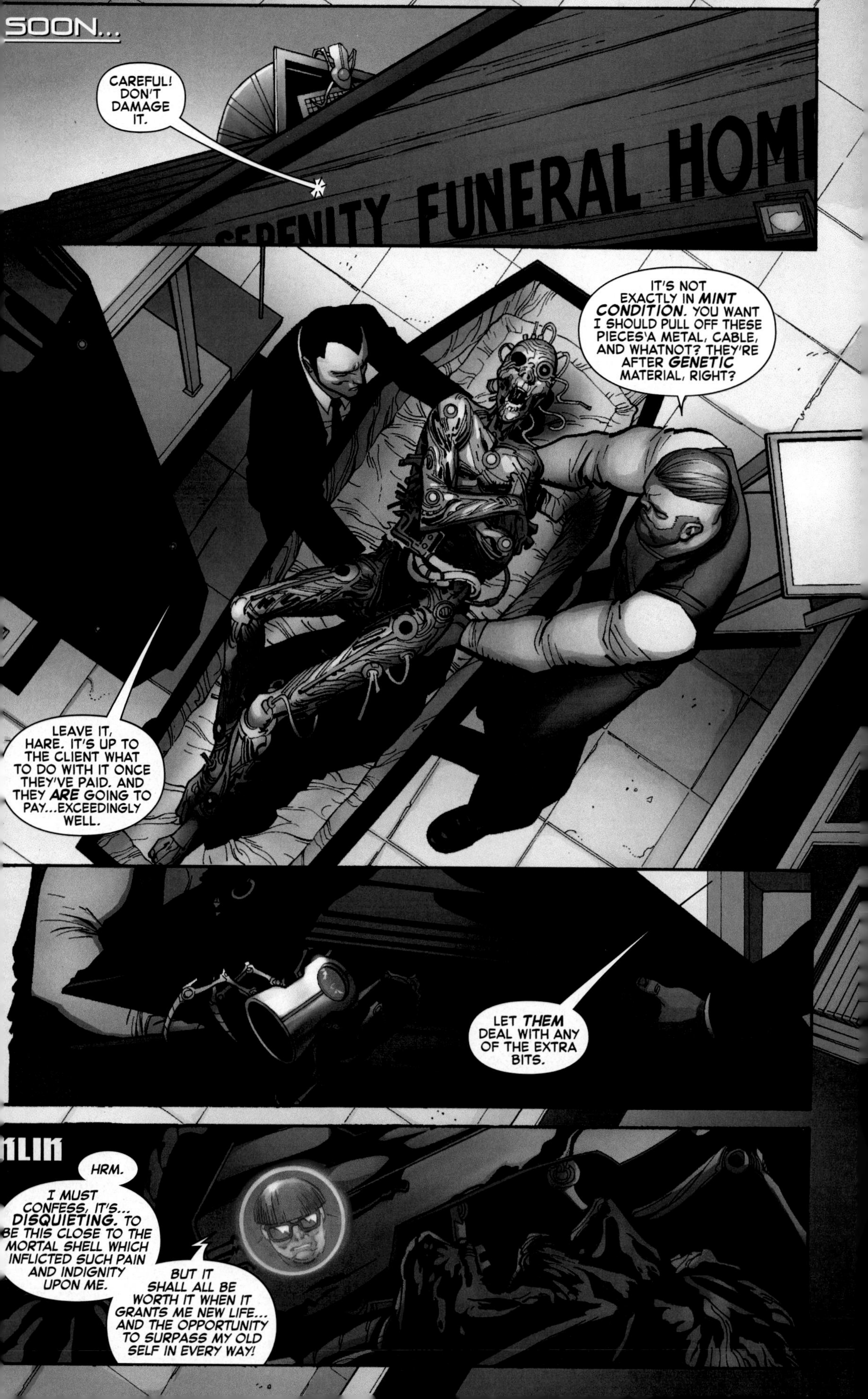
SOON...
CAREFUL! DON'T DAMAGE IT.
FUNERAL HOM
IT'S NOT EXACTLY IN MINT CONDITION. YOU WANT I SHOULD PULL OFF THESE PIECES'A METAL, CABLE, AND WHATNOT? THEY'RE AFTER GENETIC MATERIAL, RIGHT?
LEAVE IT, HARE. IT'S UP TO THE CLIENT WHAT TO DO WITH IT ONCE THEY'VE PAID. AND THEY ARE GOING TO PAY...EXCEEDINGLY WELL.
LET THEM DEAL WITH ANY OF THE EXTRA BITS.
HRM.
I MUST CONFESS, IT'S... DISQUIETING. TO BE THIS CLOSE TO THE MORTAL SHELL WHICH INFLICTED SUCH PAIN AND INDIGNITY UPON ME.
BUT IT SHALL ALL BE WORTH IT WHEN IT GRANTS ME NEW LIFE... AND THE OPPORTUNITY TO SURPASS MY OLD SELF IN EVERY WAY!

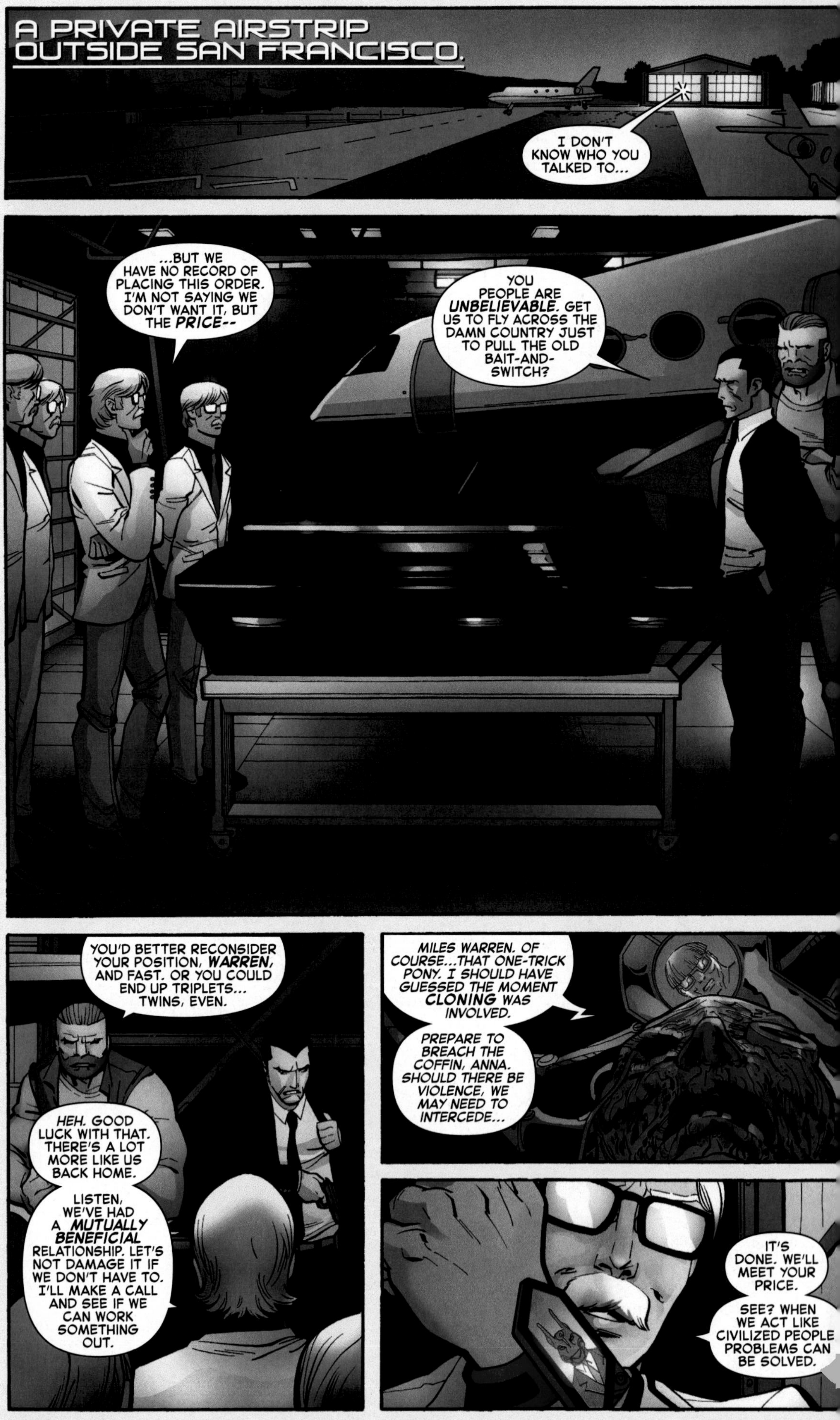
A PRIVATE AIRSTRIP OUTSIDE SAN FRANCISCO.
I DON'T KNOW WHO YOU TALKED TO...
...BUT WE HAVE NO RECORD OF PLACING THIS ORDER. I'M NOT SAYING WE DON'T WANT IT, BUT THE PRICE--
YOU PEOPLE ARE UNBELIEVABLE. GET US TO FLY ACROSS THE DAMN COUNTRY JUST TO PULL THE OLD BAIT-AND-SWITCH?
YOU'D BETTER RECONSIDER YOUR POSITION, WARREN, AND FAST. OR YOU COULD END UP TRIPLETS... TWINS, EVEN.
HEH. GOOD LUCK WITH THAT. THERE'S A LOT MORE LIKE US BACK HOME.
LISTEN, WE'VE HAD A MUTUALLY BENEFICIAL RELATIONSHIP. LET'S NOT DAMAGE IT IF WE DON'T HAVE TO. I'LL MAKE A CALL AND SEE IF WE CAN WORK SOMETHING OUT.
MILES WARREN. OF COURSE...THAT ONE-TRICK PONY. I SHOULD HAVE GUESSED THE MOMENT CLONING WAS INVOLVED.
PREPARE TO BREACH THE COFFIN, ANNA. SHOULD THERE BE VIOLENCE, WE MAY NEED TO INTERCEDE...
IT'S DONE. WE'LL MEET YOUR PRICE.
SEE? WHEN WE ACT LIKE CIVILIZED PEOPLE PROBLEMS CAN BE SOLVED.

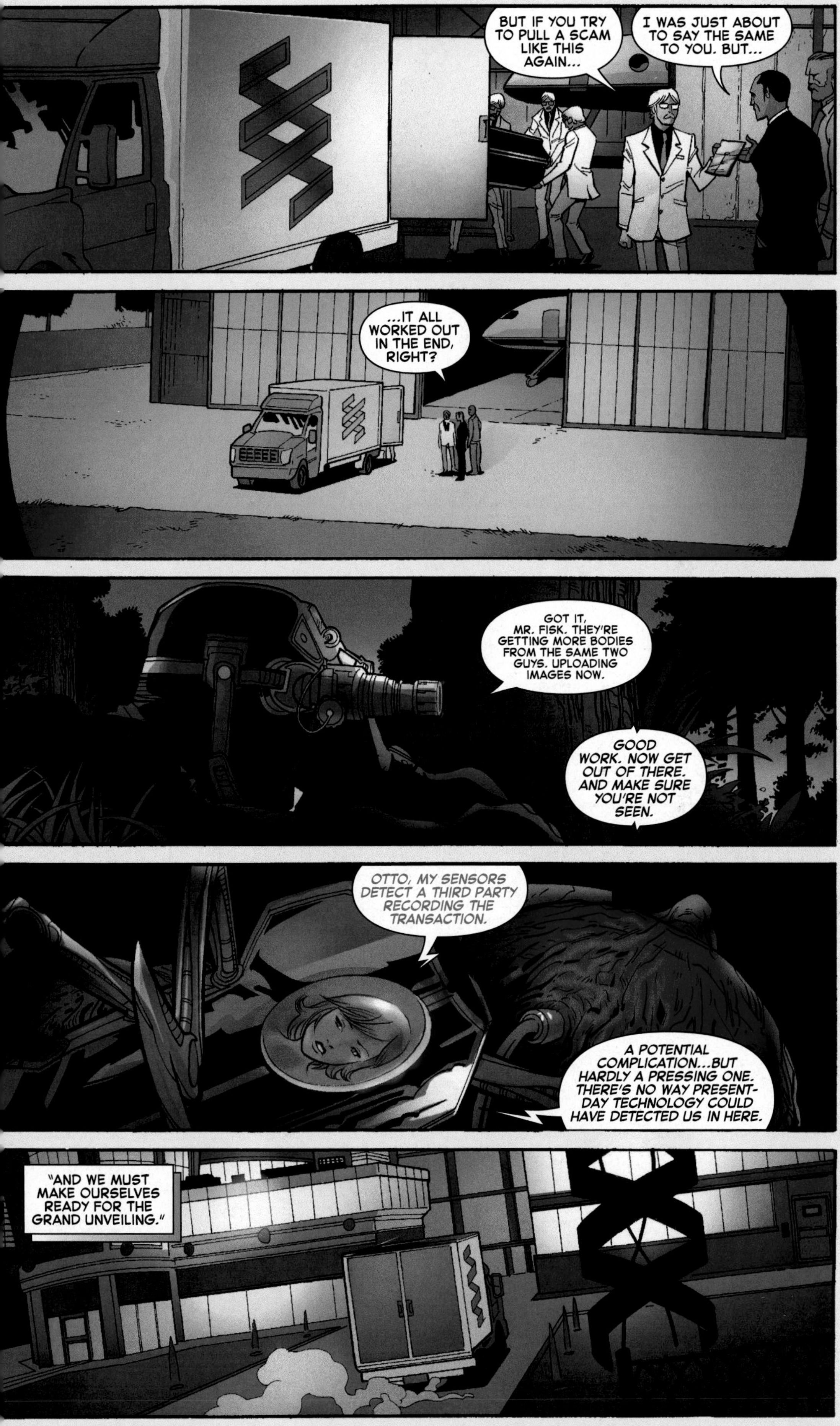
BUT IF YOU TRY TO PULL A SCAM LIKE THIS AGAIN...
I WAS JUST ABOUT TO SAY THE SAME TO YOU. BUT...
...IT ALL WORKED OUT IN THE END, RIGHT?
GOT IT, MR. FISK. THEY'RE GETTING MORE BODIES FROM THE SAME TWO GUYS. UPLOADING IMAGES NOW.
GOOD WORK. NOW GET OUT OF THERE. AND MAKE SURE YOU'RE NOT SEEN.
OTTO, MY SENSORS DETECT A THIRD PARTY RECORDING THE TRANSACTION.
A POTENTIAL COMPLICATION...BUT HARDLY A PRESSING ONE. THERE'S NO WAY PRESENT-DAY TECHNOLOGY COULD HAVE DETECTED US IN HERE.
"AND WE MUST MAKE OURSELVES READY FOR THE GRAND UNVEILING."

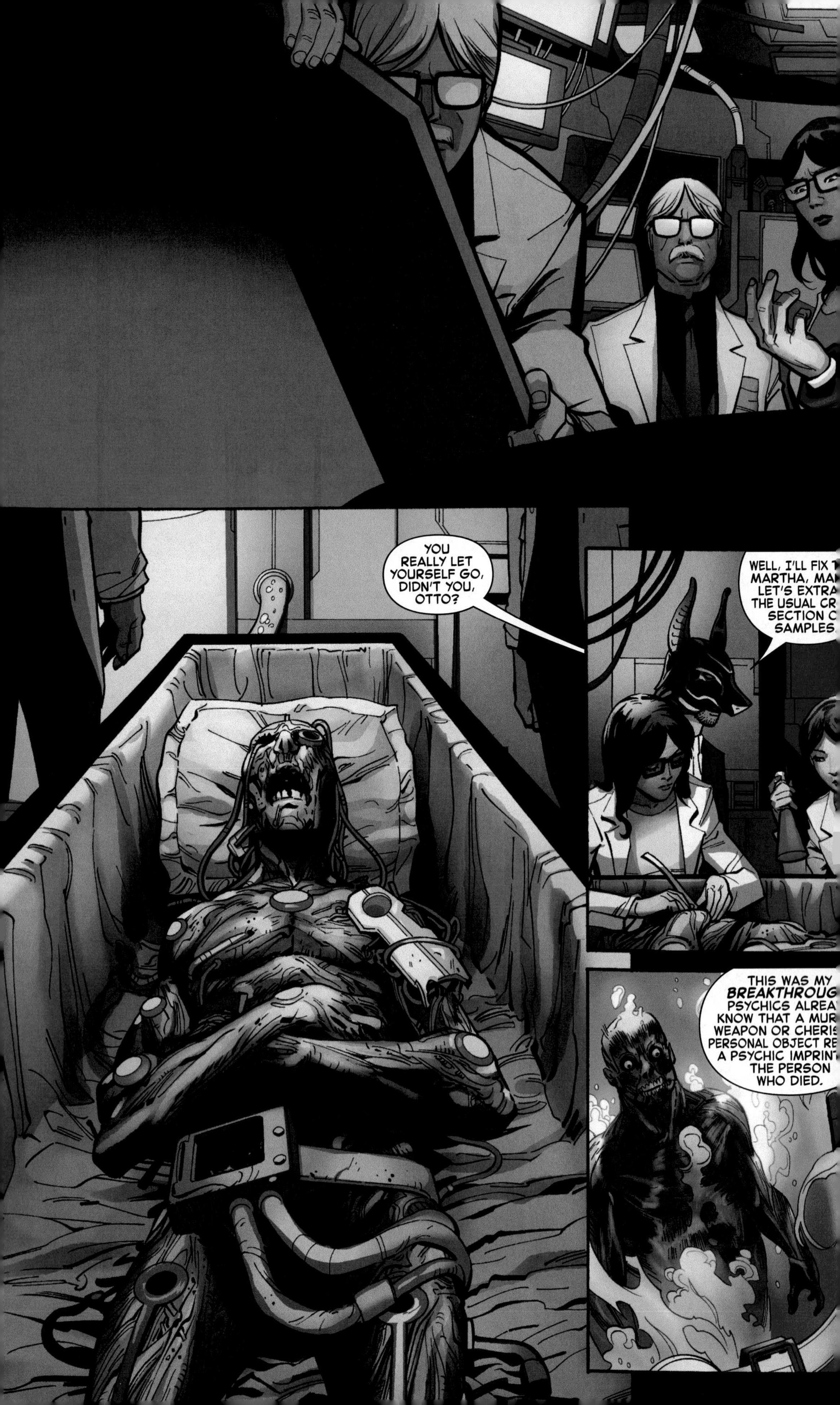
YOU REALLY LET YOURSELF GO, DIDN'T YOU, OTTO?
WELL, I'LL FIX
MARTHA, MA
LET'S EXTRA
THE USUAL CR
SECTION C
SAMPLES.
THIS WAS MY
BREAKTHROUG
PSYCHICS ALREA
KNOW THAT A MUR
WEAPON OR CHERIS
PERSONAL OBJECT RE
A PSYCHIC IMPRINT
THE PERSON
WHO DIED.

MY, OH MY. WILL YOU LOOK AT THAT.

THE DONOR BODY SUFFERED FROM A DEBILITATING ILLNESS, DR. CONNORS. PLEASE MAKE SURE IT, AND ANY OTHER ABNORMALITIES, ARE *WEEDED OUT.*

WE WANT ALL THE BUGS OUT OF DOCTOR OCTOPUS 2.0.

I STILL DON'T UNDERSTAND HOW THEY EMERGE WITH FULLY DEVELOPED PERSONALITIES. THERE AREN'T ANY BRAIN PATTERN RECORDINGS, OR--

OF COURSE, YOU'RE THE NEWEST MEMBER OF OUR LITTLE GROUP. WELL, DR. JAMESON, THANK YOU FOR THE OPPORTUNITY TO *SHOW OFF.*

YES, PLEASE DO, YOU CRETIN...

AND WHAT'S MORE PERSONAL AN THE BODY ITSELF? VE FOUND A WAY TO TORE, FROM GENETIC ERIAL, THE DECEASED'S SONA AND MEMORIES, RIGHT UP TO THE MOMENT OF DEATH!

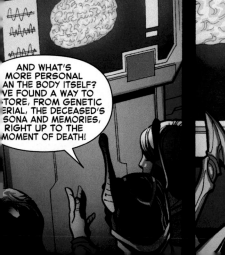

BUT...THOSE ARE NOT *MY* BRAIN PATTERNS! THERE CAN BE NO MISTAKE, I'VE STUDIED THEM THOROUGHLY. WHAT COULD--

NO. NO, IT CAN'T BE... AND YET...

WHEN MY OLD BODY DIED, IT WASN'T *MY* CONSCIOUSNESS INHABITING IT.

IT WAS *PARKER'S.*

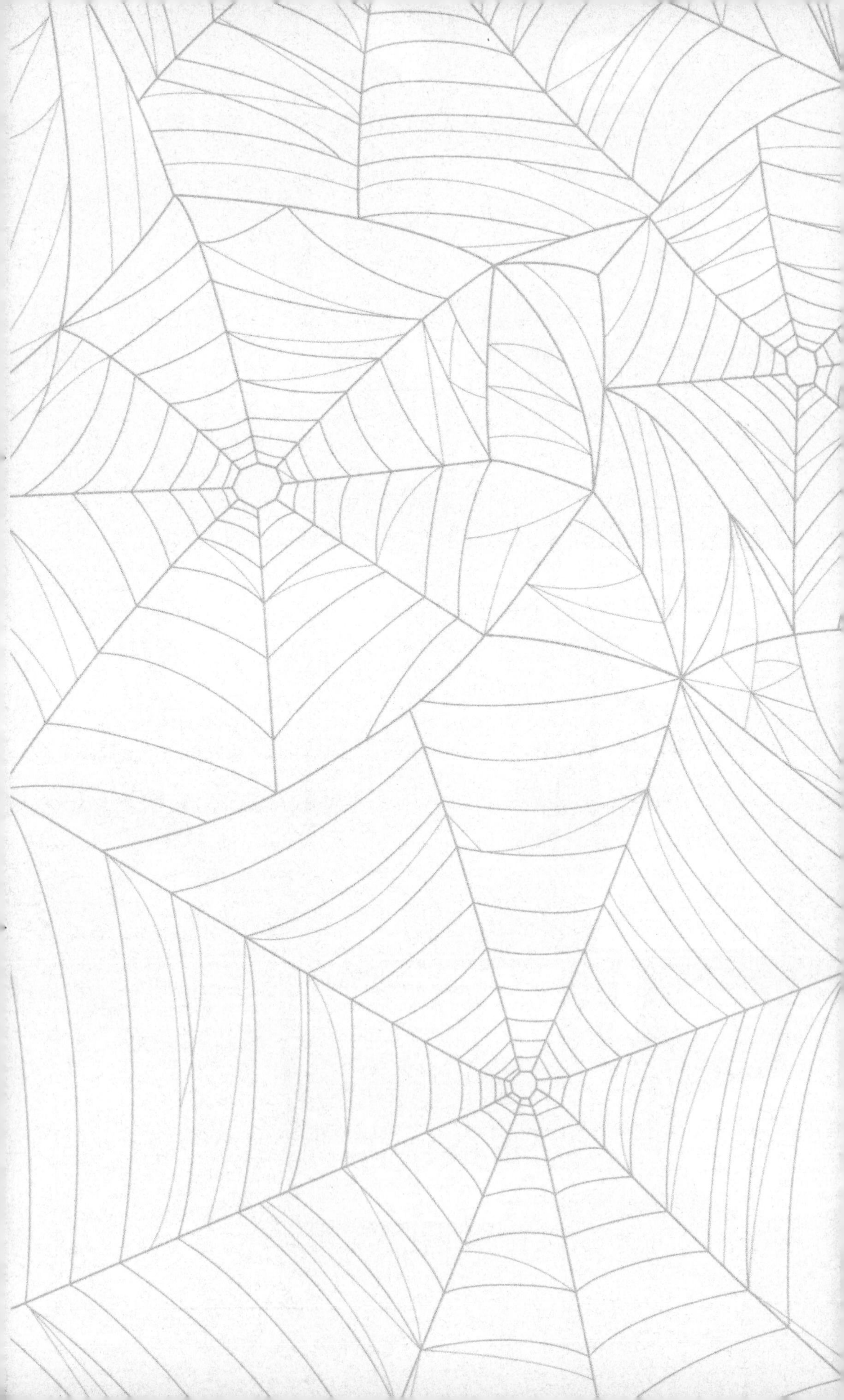

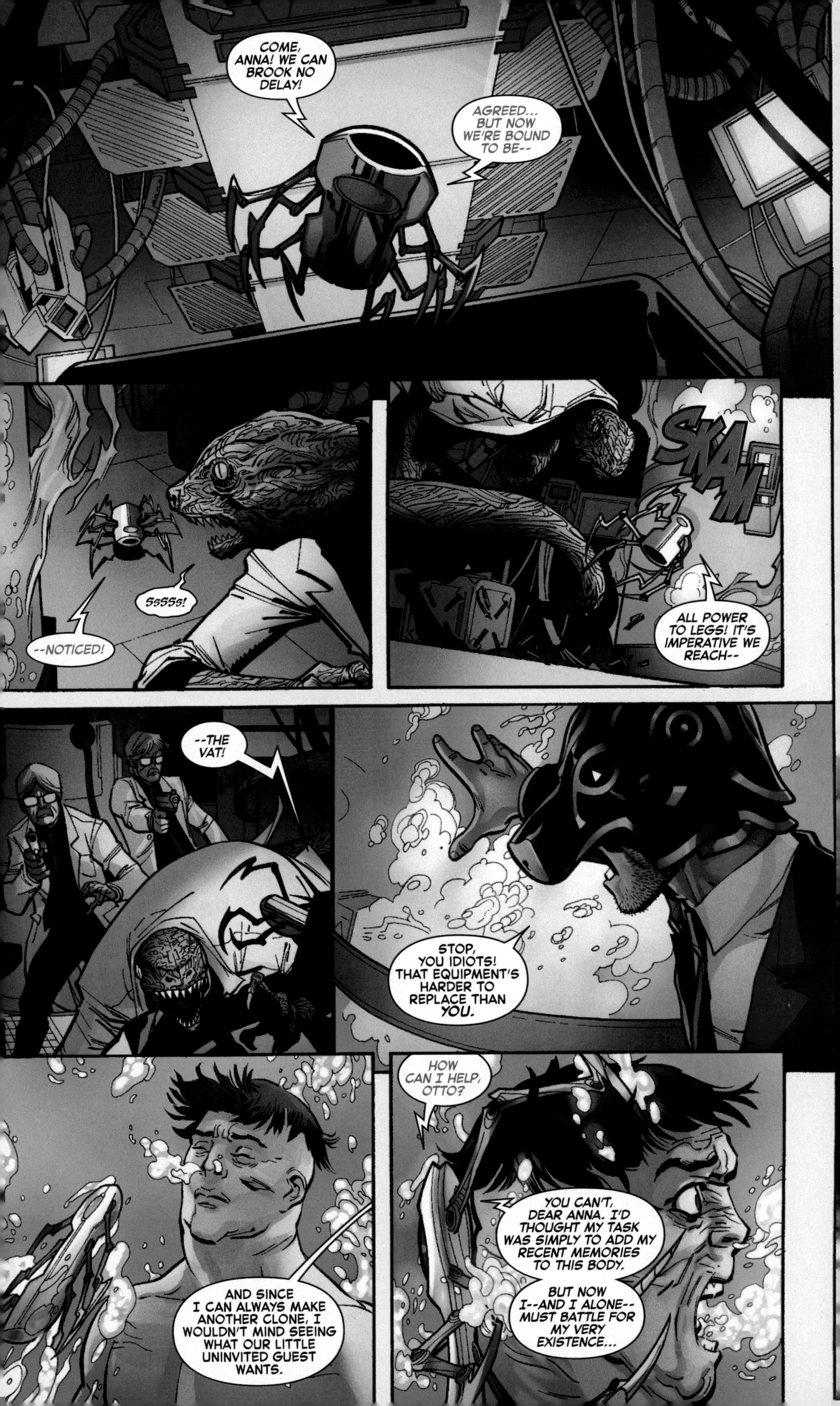
COME, ANNA! WE CAN BROOK NO DELAY!
AGREED... BUT NOW WE'RE BOUND TO BE--
SSSSS!
--NOTICED!
SKAM
ALL POWER TO LEGS! IT'S IMPERATIVE WE REACH--
--THE VAT!
STOP, YOU IDIOTS! THAT EQUIPMENT'S HARDER TO REPLACE THAN YOU.
AND SINCE I CAN ALWAYS MAKE ANOTHER CLONE, I WOULDN'T MIND SEEING WHAT OUR LITTLE UNINVITED GUEST WANTS.
HOW CAN I HELP, OTTO?
YOU CAN'T, DEAR ANNA. I'D THOUGHT MY TASK WAS SIMPLY TO ADD MY RECENT MEMORIES TO THIS BODY.
BUT NOW I--AND I ALONE--MUST BATTLE FOR MY VERY EXISTENCE...

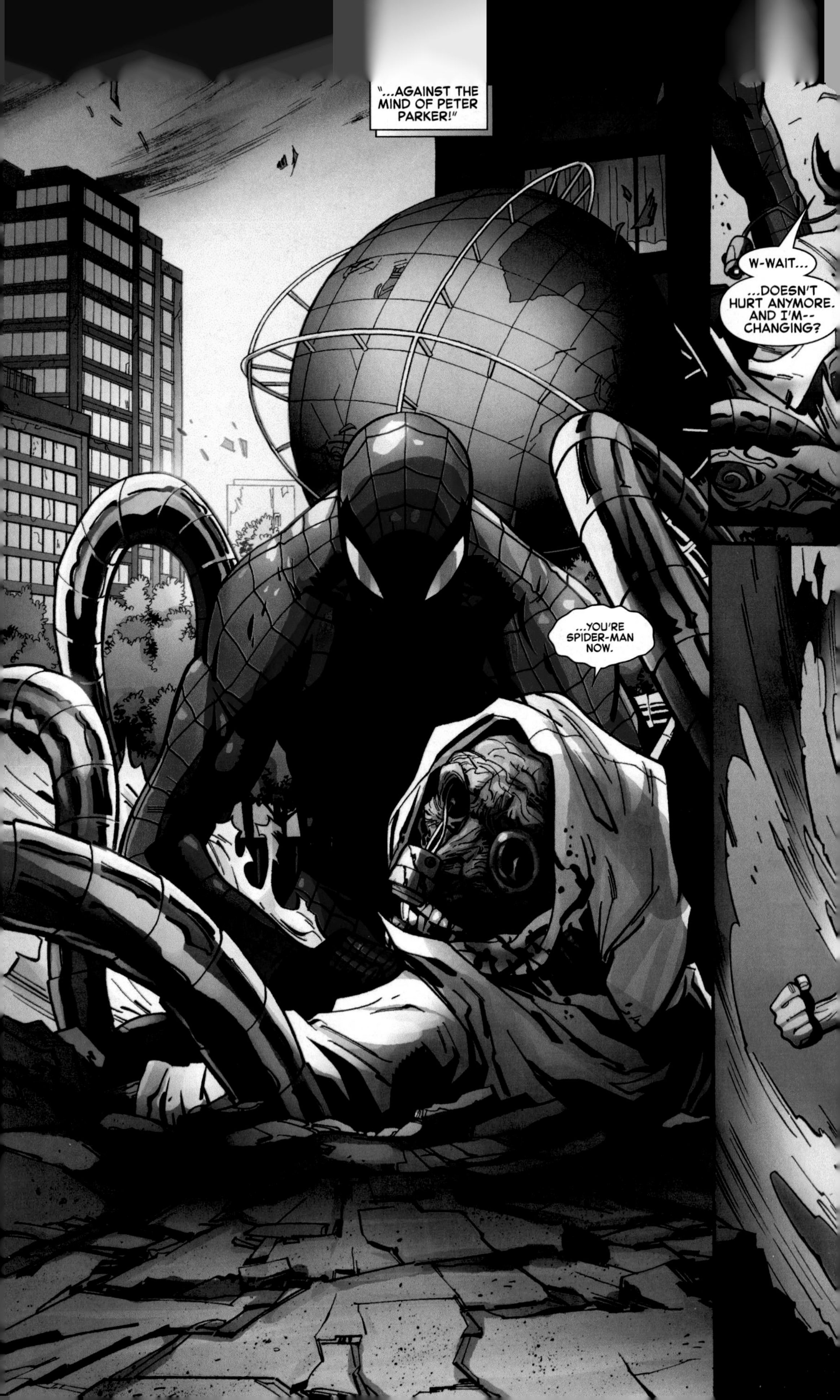
"...AGAINST THE MIND OF PETER PARKER!"
W-WAIT...
...DOESN'T HURT ANYMORE. AND I'M--CHANGING?
...YOU'RE SPIDER-MAN NOW.

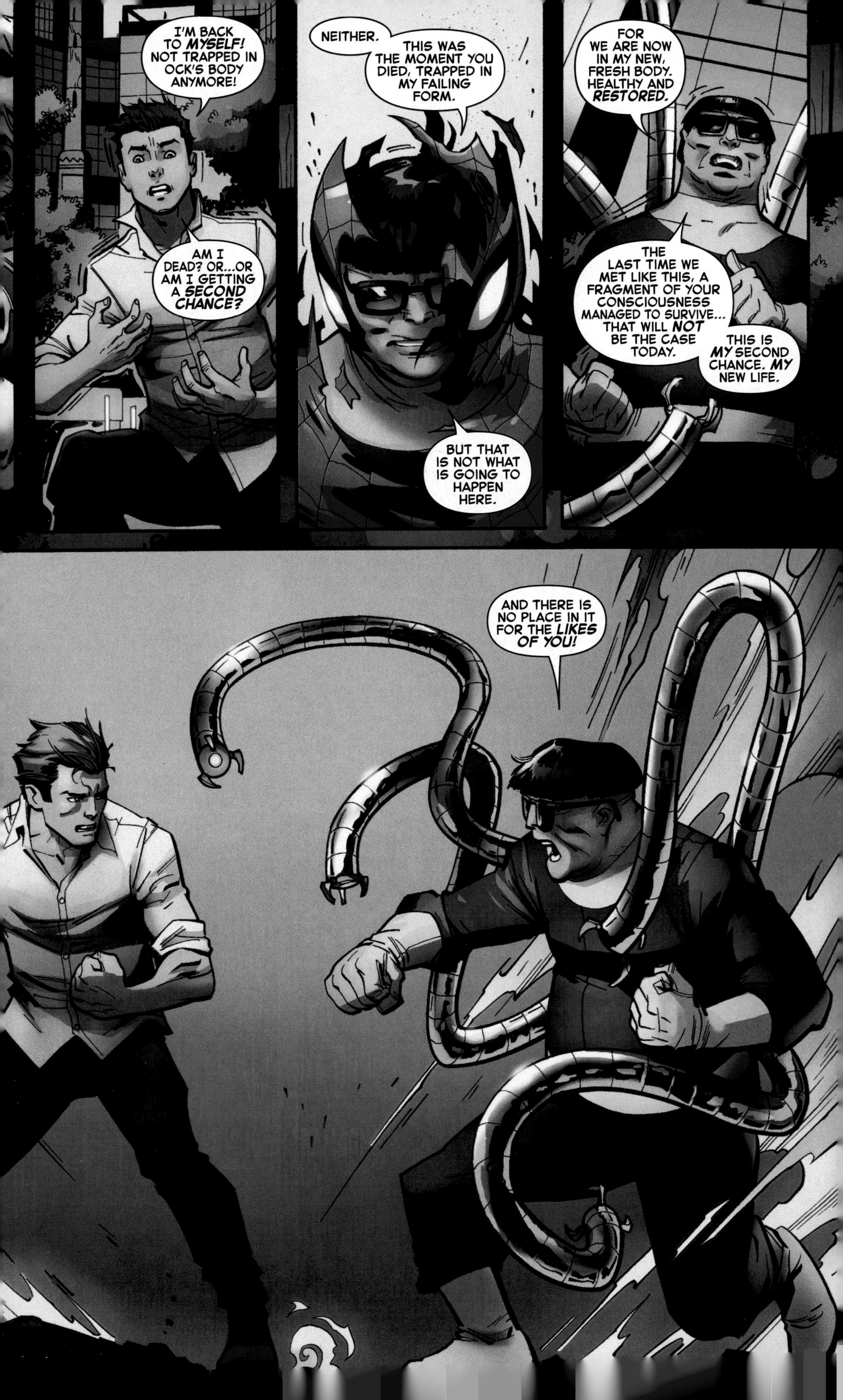
I'M BACK TO MYSELF! NOT TRAPPED IN OCK'S BODY ANYMORE!
AM I DEAD? OR...OR AM I GETTING A SECOND CHANCE?
NEITHER.
THIS WAS THE MOMENT YOU DIED, TRAPPED IN MY FAILING FORM.
BUT THAT IS NOT WHAT IS GOING TO HAPPEN HERE.
FOR WE ARE NOW IN MY NEW, FRESH BODY. HEALTHY AND RESTORED.
THE LAST TIME WE MET LIKE THIS, A FRAGMENT OF YOUR CONSCIOUSNESS MANAGED TO SURVIVE... THAT WILL NOT BE THE CASE TODAY.
THIS IS MY SECOND CHANCE. MY NEW LIFE.
AND THERE IS NO PLACE IN IT FOR THE LIKES OF YOU!

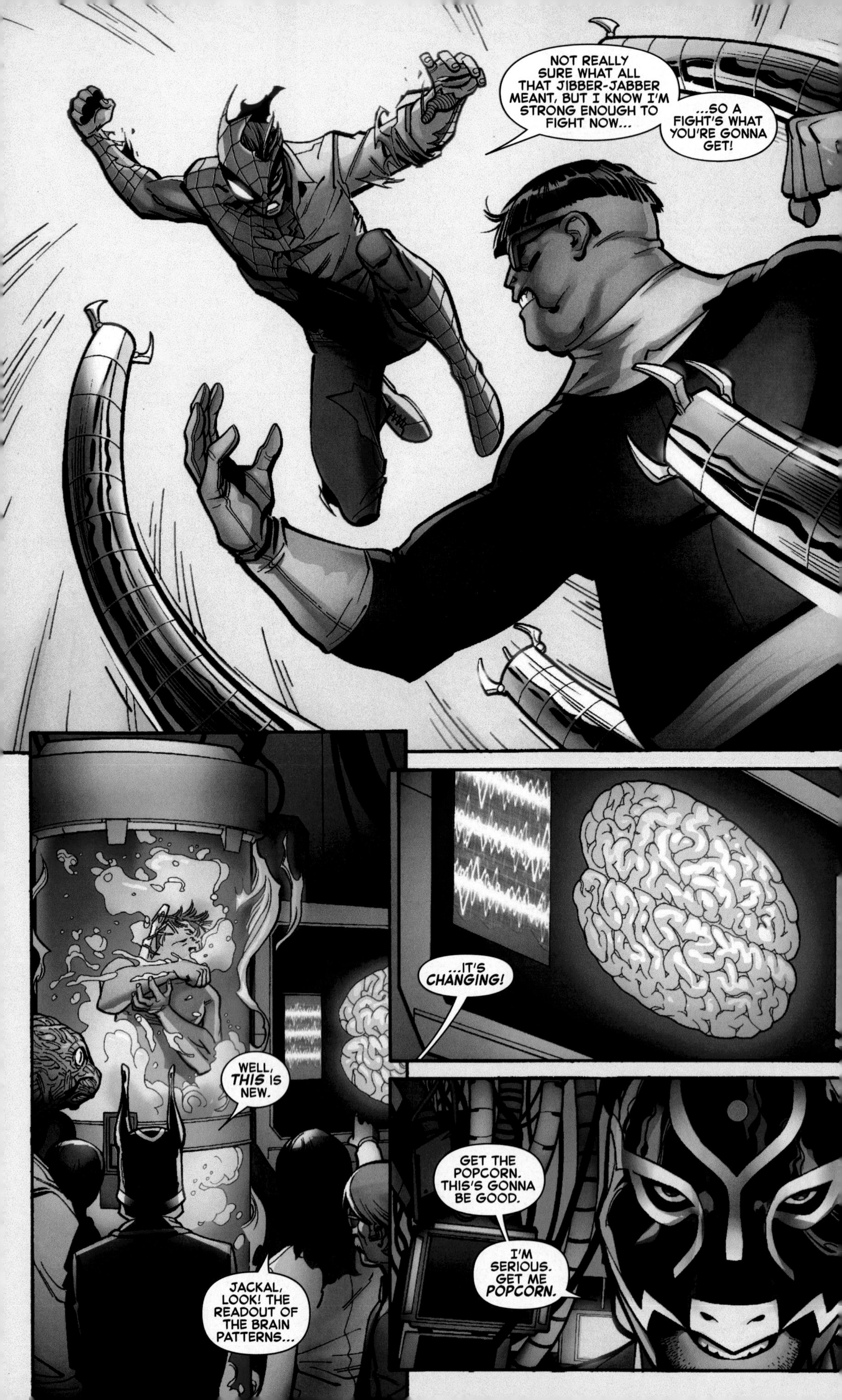

NOT REALLY SURE WHAT ALL THAT JIBBER-JABBER MEANT, BUT I KNOW I'M STRONG ENOUGH TO FIGHT NOW...
...SO A FIGHT'S WHAT YOU'RE GONNA GET!
WELL, *THIS* IS NEW.
JACKAL, LOOK! THE READOUT OF THE BRAIN PATTERNS...
...IT'S *CHANGING!*
GET THE POPCORN. THIS'S GONNA BE GOOD.
I'M SERIOUS. GET ME *POPCORN.*

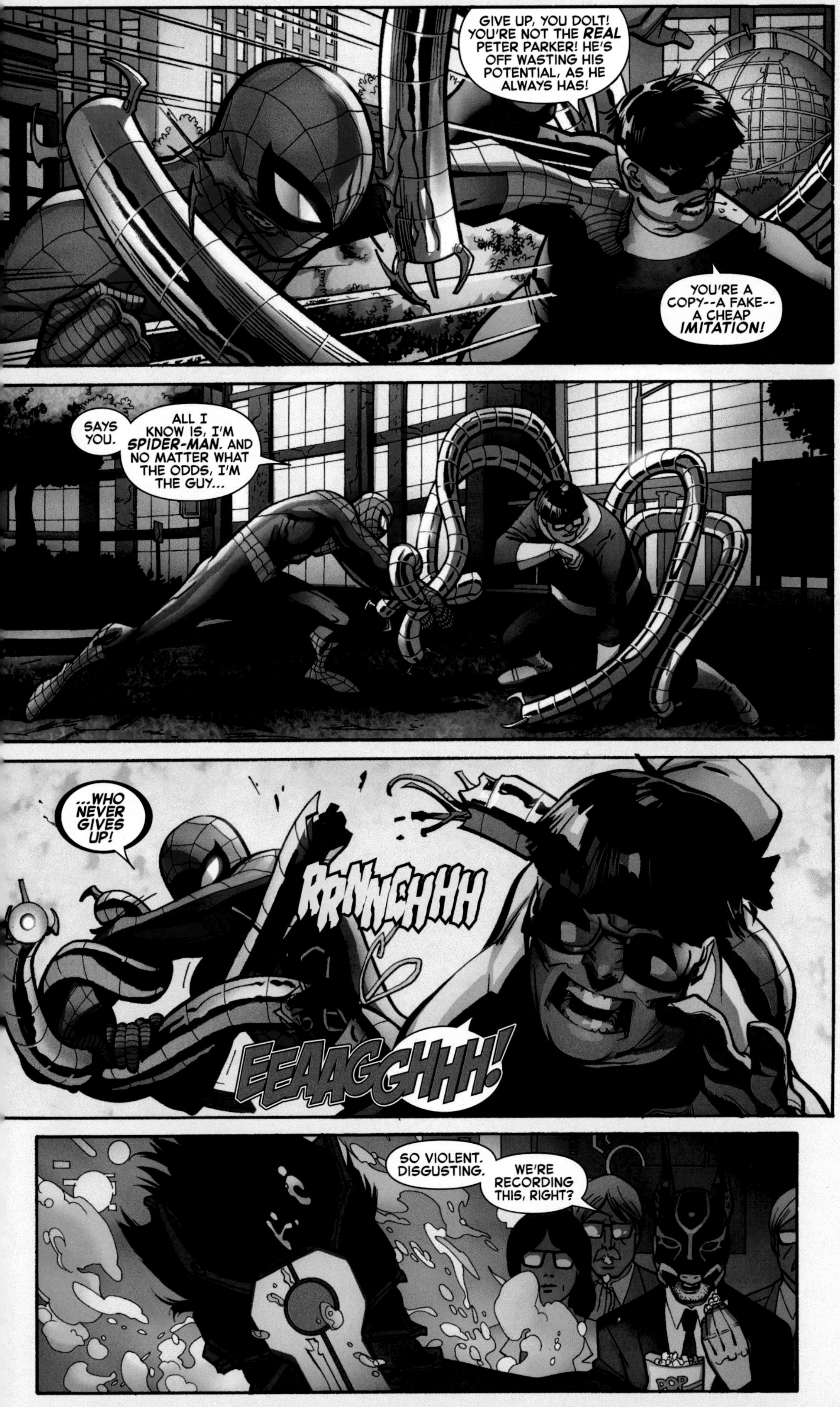
GIVE UP, YOU DOLT! YOU'RE NOT THE REAL PETER PARKER! HE'S OFF WASTING HIS POTENTIAL, AS HE ALWAYS HAS!
YOU'RE A COPY--A FAKE--A CHEAP IMITATION!
SAYS YOU.
ALL I KNOW IS, I'M SPIDER-MAN. AND NO MATTER WHAT THE ODDS, I'M THE GUY...
...WHO NEVER GIVES UP!
RRNNCHHH
EEAAGGHHH!
SO VIOLENT. DISGUSTING.
WE'RE RECORDING THIS, RIGHT?
POP

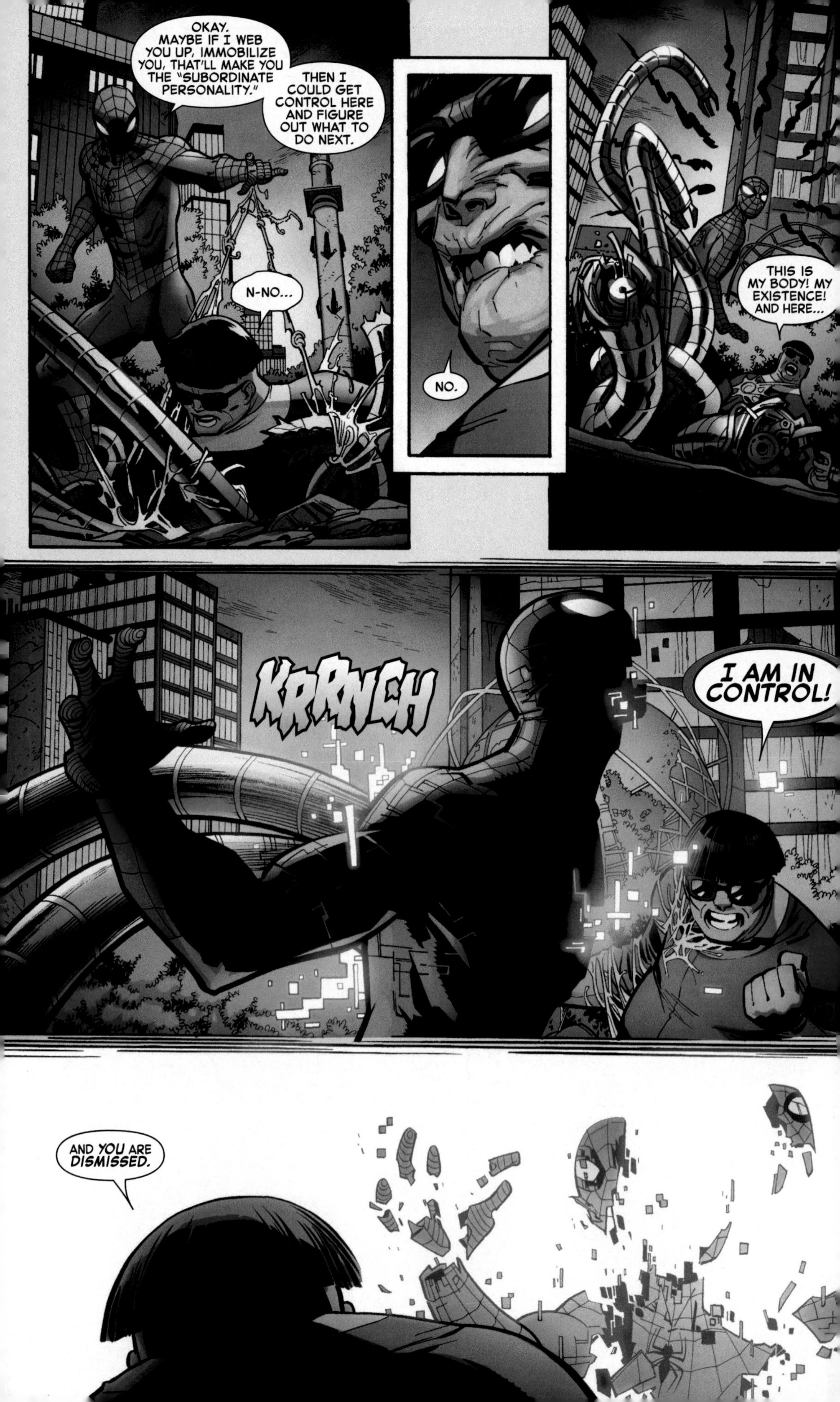
OKAY. MAYBE IF I WEB YOU UP, IMMOBILIZE YOU, THAT'LL MAKE YOU THE "SUBORDINATE PERSONALITY."
THEN I COULD GET CONTROL HERE AND FIGURE OUT WHAT TO DO NEXT.
N-NO...
NO.
THIS IS MY BODY! MY EXISTENCE! AND HERE...
KRRNCH
I AM IN CONTROL!
AND YOU ARE DISMISSED.

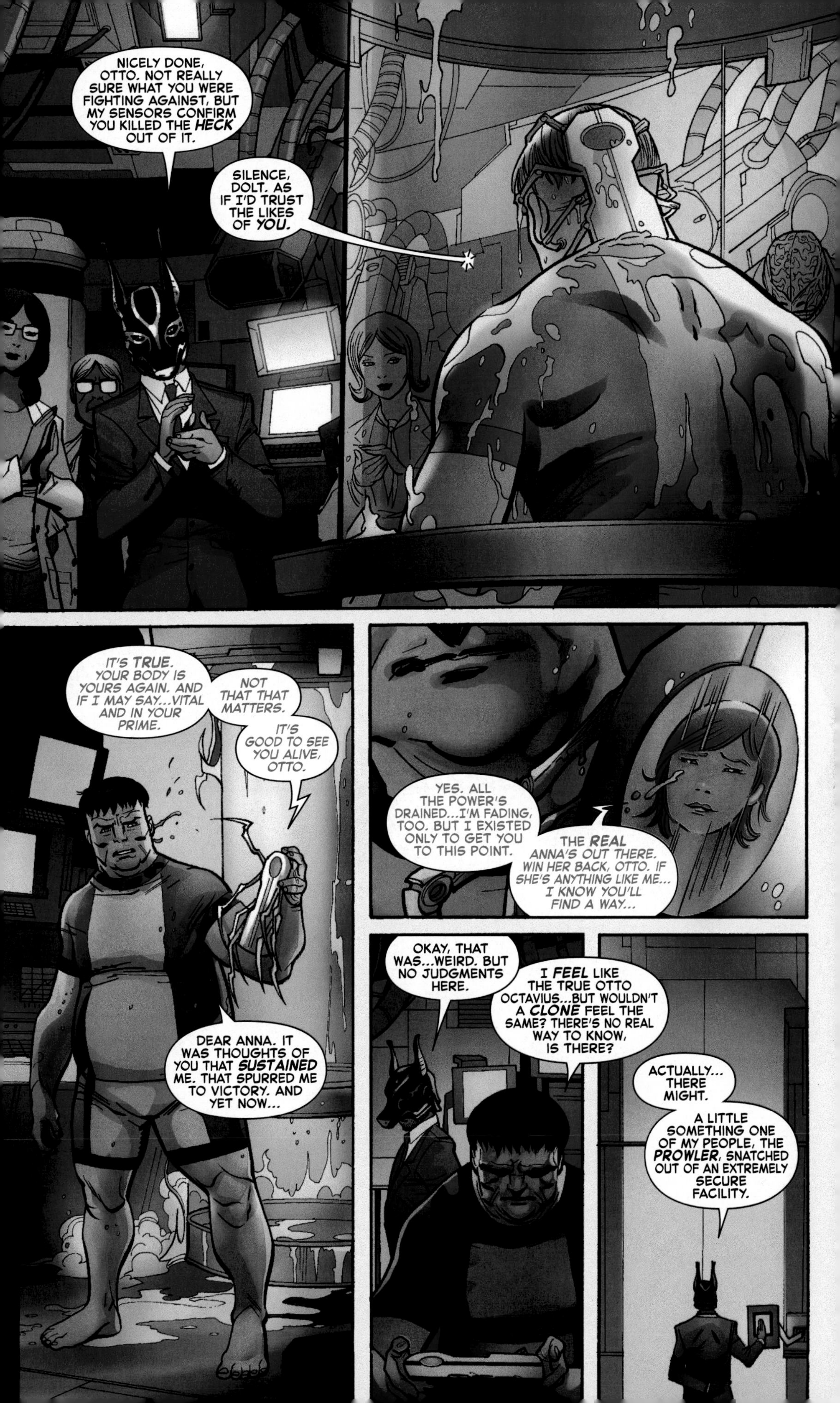
NICELY DONE, OTTO. NOT REALLY SURE WHAT YOU WERE FIGHTING AGAINST, BUT MY SENSORS CONFIRM YOU KILLED THE HECK OUT OF IT.
SILENCE, DOLT. AS IF I'D TRUST THE LIKES OF YOU.
IT'S TRUE. YOUR BODY IS YOURS AGAIN. AND IF I MAY SAY...VITAL AND IN YOUR PRIME.
NOT THAT THAT MATTERS.
IT'S GOOD TO SEE YOU ALIVE, OTTO.
DEAR ANNA. IT WAS THOUGHTS OF YOU THAT SUSTAINED ME. THAT SPURRED ME TO VICTORY. AND YET NOW...
YES. ALL THE POWER'S DRAINED...I'M FADING, TOO. BUT I EXISTED ONLY TO GET YOU TO THIS POINT.
THE REAL ANNA'S OUT THERE. WIN HER BACK, OTTO. IF SHE'S ANYTHING LIKE ME... I KNOW YOU'LL FIND A WAY...
OKAY, THAT WAS...WEIRD. BUT NO JUDGMENTS HERE.
I FEEL LIKE THE TRUE OTTO OCTAVIUS...BUT WOULDN'T A CLONE FEEL THE SAME? THERE'S NO REAL WAY TO KNOW, IS THERE?
ACTUALLY... THERE MIGHT.
A LITTLE SOMETHING ONE OF MY PEOPLE, THE PROWLER, SNATCHED OUT OF AN EXTREMELY SECURE FACILITY.

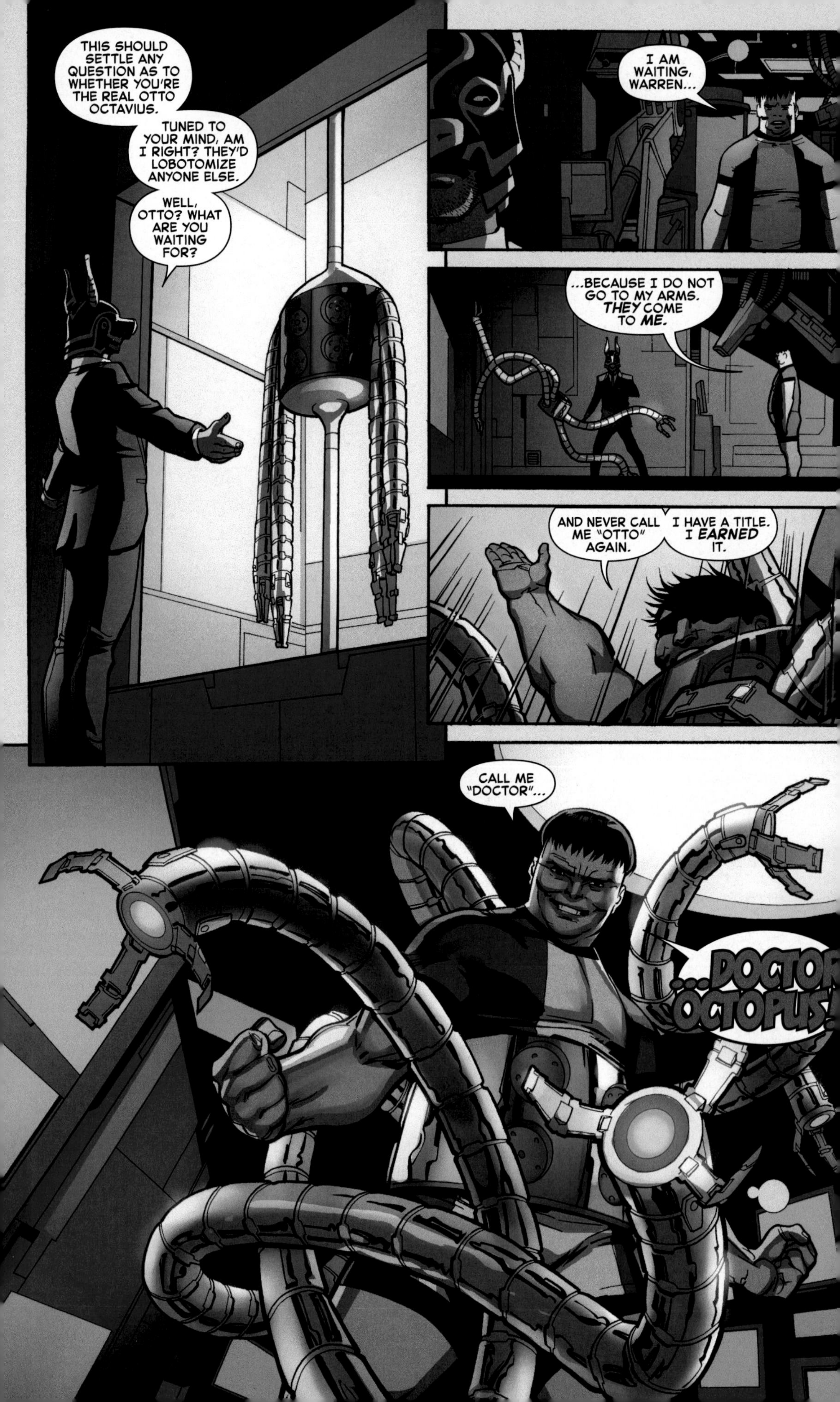

THIS SHOULD SETTLE ANY QUESTION AS TO WHETHER YOU'RE THE REAL OTTO OCTAVIUS.
TUNED TO YOUR MIND, AM I RIGHT? THEY'D LOBOTOMIZE ANYONE ELSE.
WELL, OTTO? WHAT ARE YOU WAITING FOR?
I AM WAITING, WARREN...
...BECAUSE I DO NOT GO TO MY ARMS. THEY COME TO ME.
AND NEVER CALL ME "OTTO" AGAIN.
I HAVE A TITLE. I EARNED IT.
CALL ME "DOCTOR"...
...DOCTOR OCTOPUS!

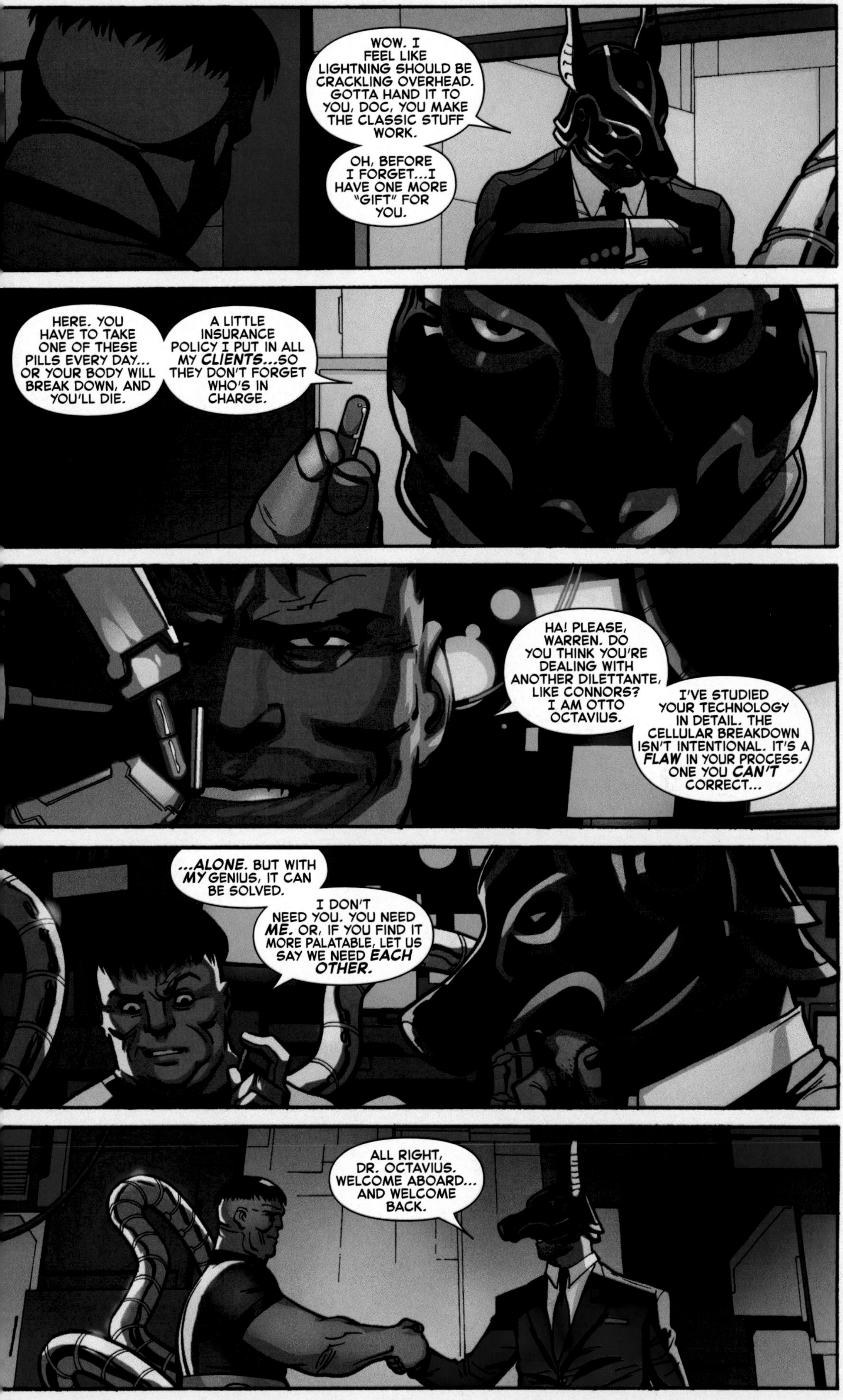
WOW. I FEEL LIKE LIGHTNING SHOULD BE CRACKLING OVERHEAD. GOTTA HAND IT TO YOU, DOC, YOU MAKE THE CLASSIC STUFF WORK.
OH, BEFORE I FORGET...I HAVE ONE MORE "GIFT" FOR YOU.
HERE. YOU HAVE TO TAKE ONE OF THESE PILLS EVERY DAY... OR YOUR BODY WILL BREAK DOWN, AND YOU'LL DIE.
A LITTLE INSURANCE POLICY I PUT IN ALL MY *CLIENTS*...SO THEY DON'T FORGET WHO'S IN CHARGE.
HA! PLEASE, WARREN. DO YOU THINK YOU'RE DEALING WITH ANOTHER DILETTANTE, LIKE CONNORS? I AM OTTO OCTAVIUS.
I'VE STUDIED YOUR TECHNOLOGY IN DETAIL. THE CELLULAR BREAKDOWN ISN'T INTENTIONAL. IT'S A *FLAW* IN YOUR PROCESS. ONE YOU *CAN'T* CORRECT...
...ALONE. BUT WITH *MY* GENIUS, IT CAN BE SOLVED.
I DON'T NEED YOU. YOU NEED *ME*. OR, IF YOU FIND IT MORE PALATABLE, LET US SAY WE NEED *EACH OTHER.*
ALL RIGHT, DR. OCTAVIUS. WELCOME ABOARD... AND WELCOME BACK.

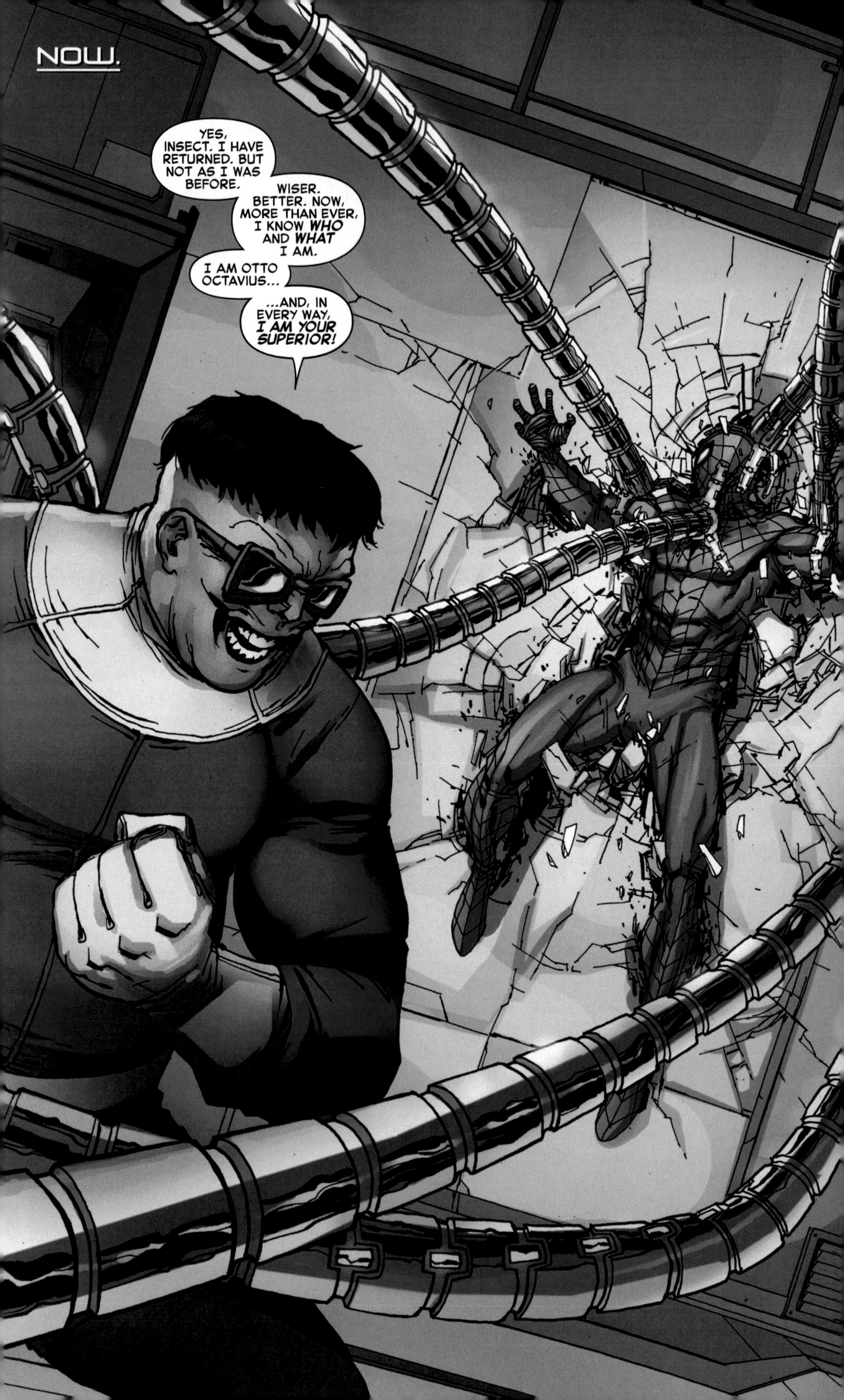
NOW.
YES, INSECT. I HAVE RETURNED. BUT NOT AS I WAS BEFORE.
WISER. BETTER. NOW, MORE THAN EVER, I KNOW WHO AND WHAT I AM.
I AM OTTO OCTAVIUS...
...AND, IN EVERY WAY, I AM YOUR SUPERIOR!

21

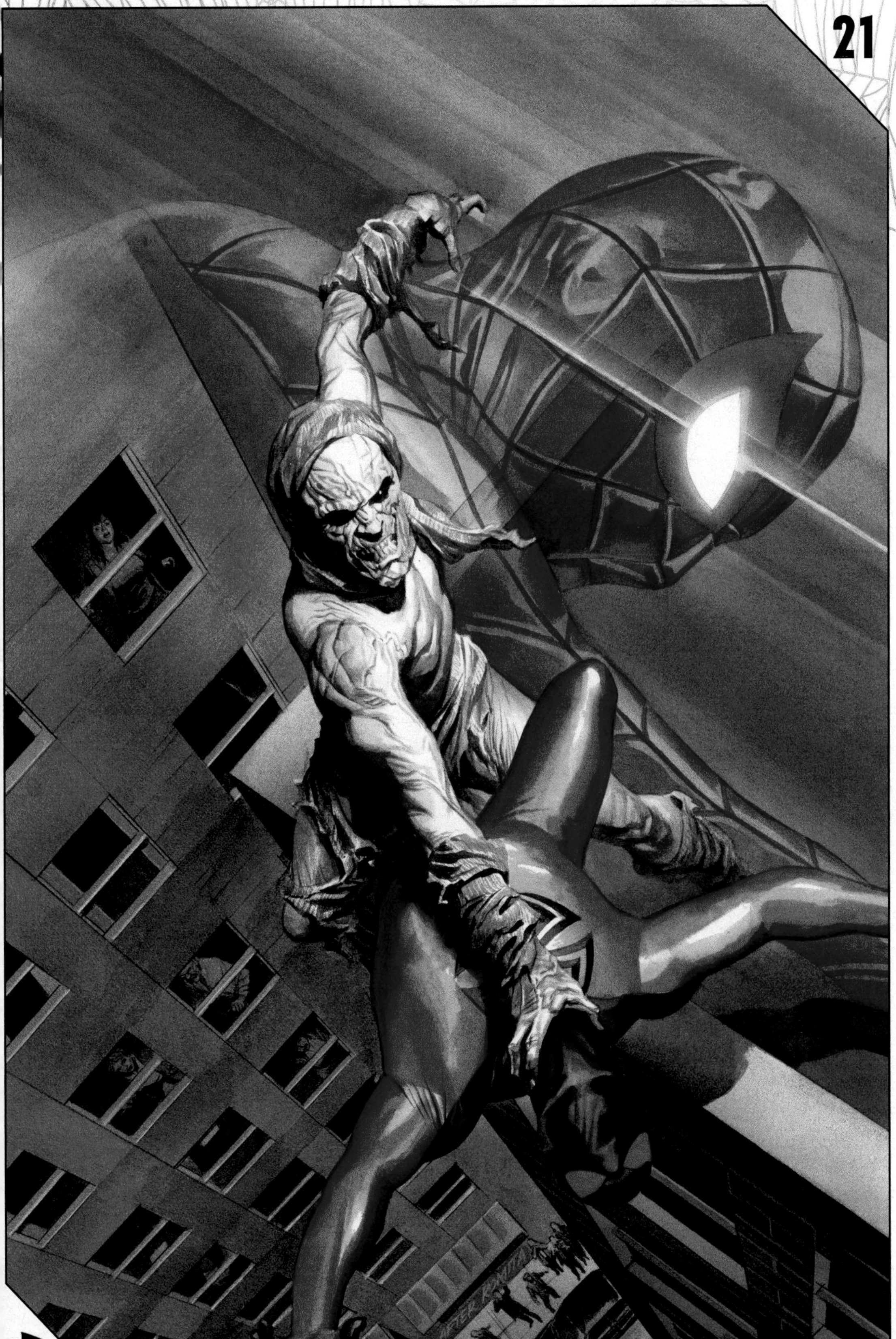

"LIVE ANOTHER DAY"

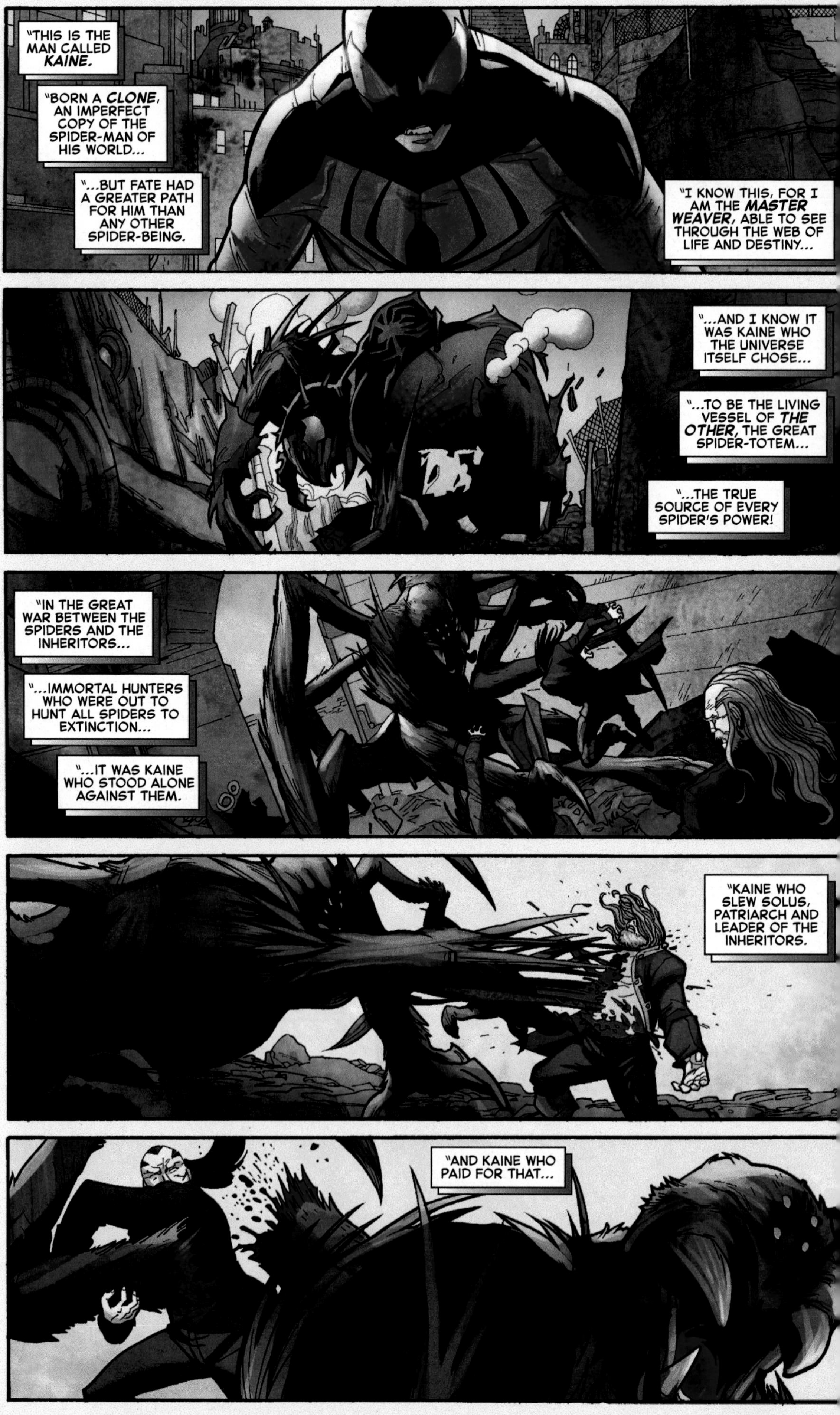

"THIS IS THE MAN CALLED KAINE.
"BORN A CLONE, AN IMPERFECT COPY OF THE SPIDER-MAN OF HIS WORLD...
"...BUT FATE HAD A GREATER PATH FOR HIM THAN ANY OTHER SPIDER-BEING.
"I KNOW THIS, FOR I AM THE MASTER WEAVER, ABLE TO SEE THROUGH THE WEB OF LIFE AND DESTINY...
"...AND I KNOW IT WAS KAINE WHO THE UNIVERSE ITSELF CHOSE...
"...TO BE THE LIVING VESSEL OF THE OTHER, THE GREAT SPIDER-TOTEM...
"...THE TRUE SOURCE OF EVERY SPIDER'S POWER!
"IN THE GREAT WAR BETWEEN THE SPIDERS AND THE INHERITORS...
"...IMMORTAL HUNTERS WHO WERE OUT TO HUNT ALL SPIDERS TO EXTINCTION...
"...IT WAS KAINE WHO STOOD ALONE AGAINST THEM.
"KAINE WHO SLEW SOLUS, PATRIARCH AND LEADER OF THE INHERITORS.
"AND KAINE WHO PAID FOR THAT...

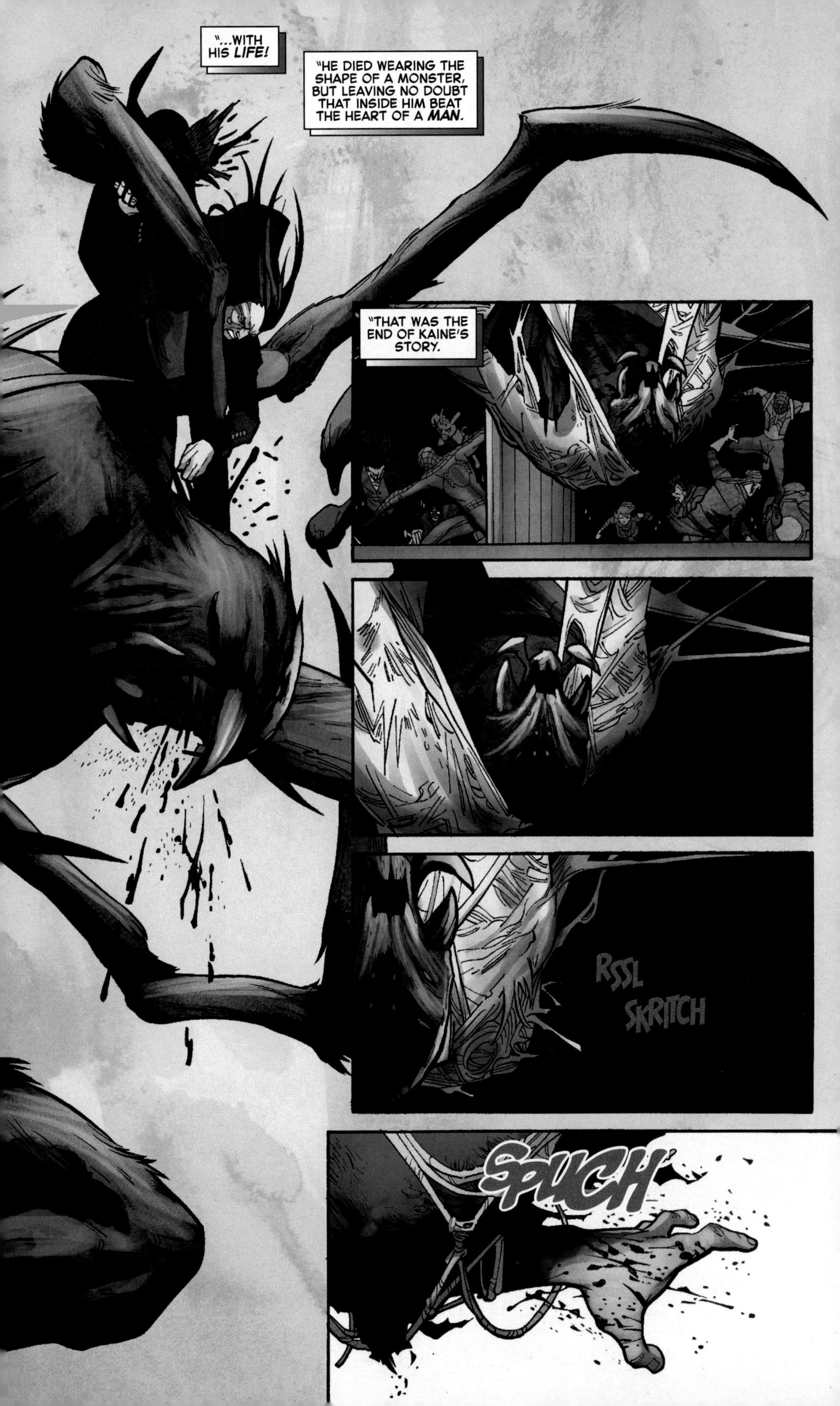
"...WITH HIS LIFE!
"HE DIED WEARING THE SHAPE OF A MONSTER, BUT LEAVING NO DOUBT THAT INSIDE HIM BEAT THE HEART OF A MAN.
"THAT WAS THE END OF KAINE'S STORY.
RSSL
SKRITCH
SPUCH

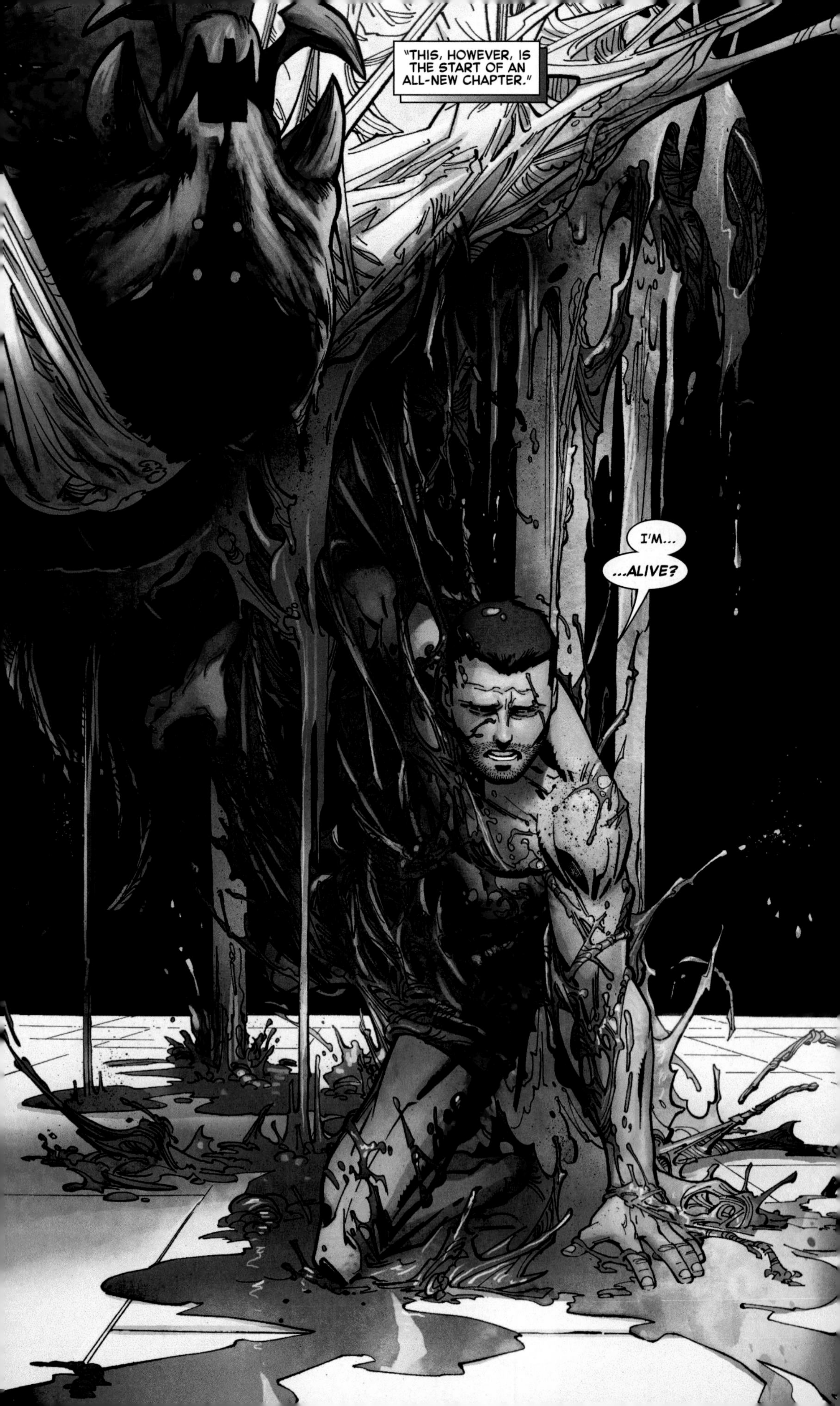
"THIS, HOWEVER, IS THE START OF AN ALL-NEW CHAPTER."
I'M...
...ALIVE?

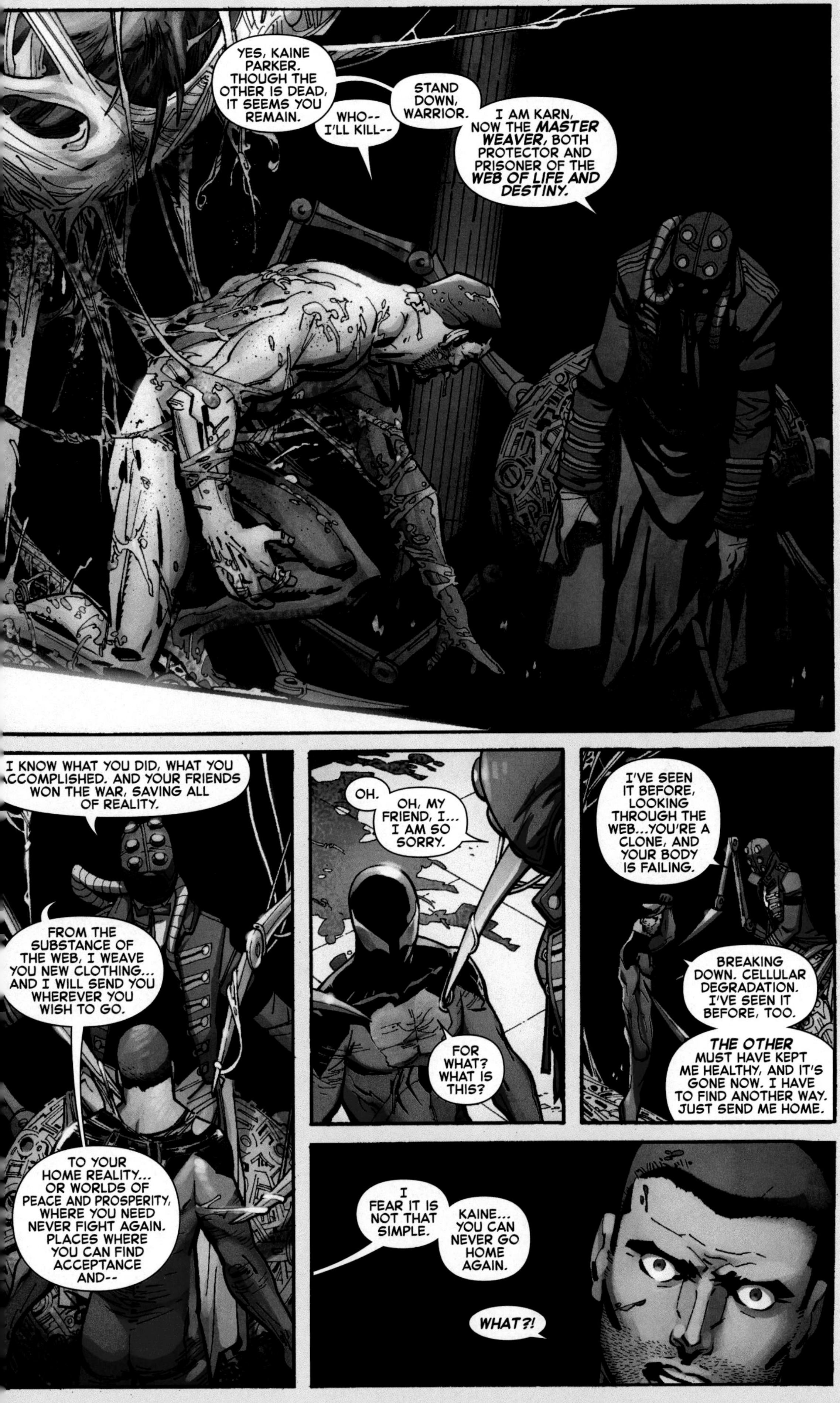
YES, KAINE PARKER. THOUGH THE OTHER IS DEAD, IT SEEMS YOU REMAIN.
WHO-- I'LL KILL--
STAND DOWN, WARRIOR.
I AM KARN, NOW THE MASTER WEAVER, BOTH PROTECTOR AND PRISONER OF THE WEB OF LIFE AND DESTINY.
I KNOW WHAT YOU DID, WHAT YOU ACCOMPLISHED. AND YOUR FRIENDS WON THE WAR, SAVING ALL OF REALITY.
FROM THE SUBSTANCE OF THE WEB, I WEAVE YOU NEW CLOTHING... AND I WILL SEND YOU WHEREVER YOU WISH TO GO.
TO YOUR HOME REALITY... OR WORLDS OF PEACE AND PROSPERITY, WHERE YOU NEED NEVER FIGHT AGAIN. PLACES WHERE YOU CAN FIND ACCEPTANCE AND--
OH.
OH, MY FRIEND, I... I AM SO SORRY.
FOR WHAT? WHAT IS THIS?
I'VE SEEN IT BEFORE, LOOKING THROUGH THE WEB...YOU'RE A CLONE, AND YOUR BODY IS FAILING.
BREAKING DOWN. CELLULAR DEGRADATION. I'VE SEEN IT BEFORE, TOO.
THE OTHER MUST HAVE KEPT ME HEALTHY, AND IT'S GONE NOW. I HAVE TO FIND ANOTHER WAY. JUST SEND ME HOME.
I FEAR IT IS NOT THAT SIMPLE.
KAINE... YOU CAN NEVER GO HOME AGAIN.
WHAT?!

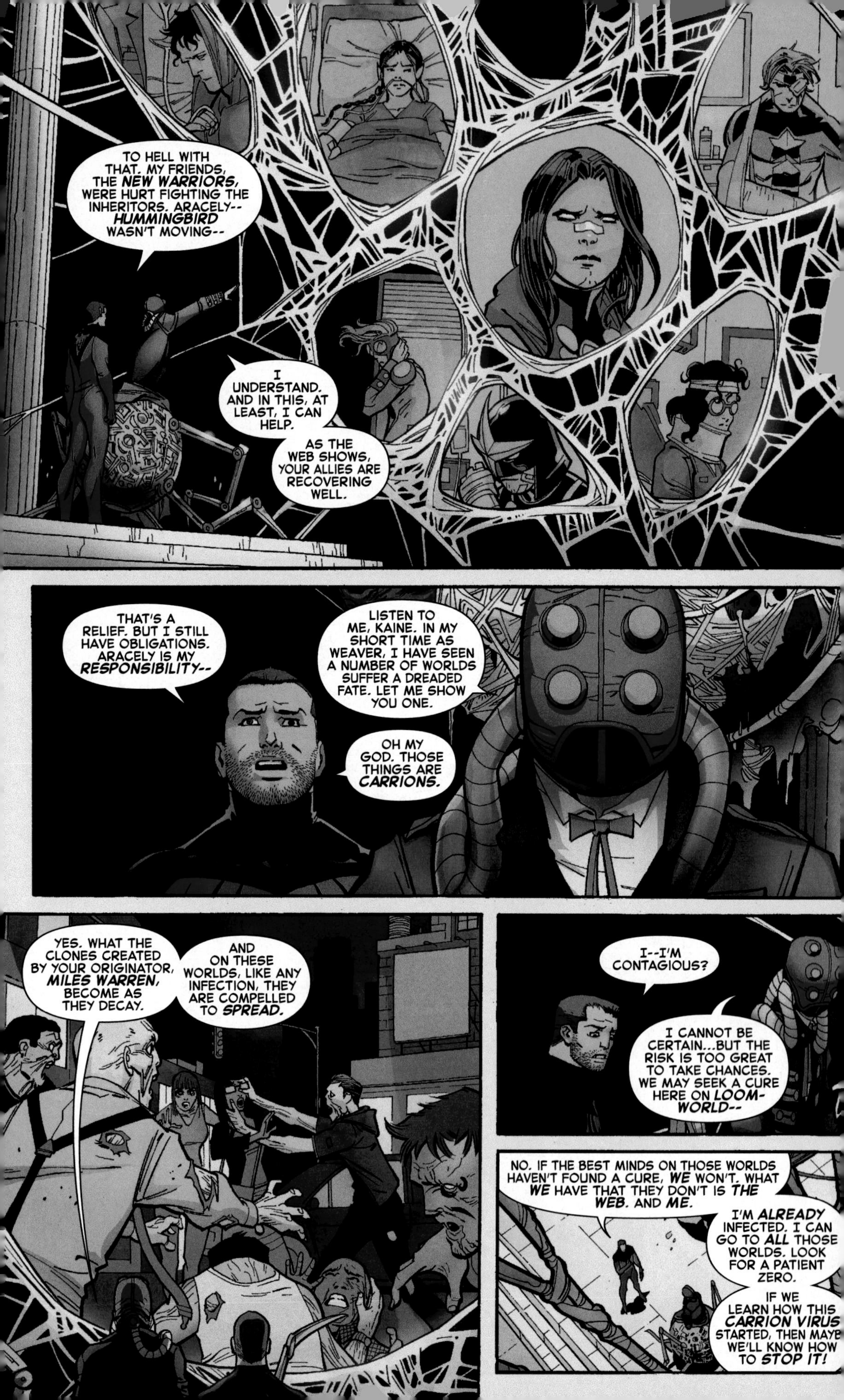
TO HELL WITH THAT. MY FRIENDS, THE NEW WARRIORS, WERE HURT FIGHTING THE INHERITORS. ARACELY-- HUMMINGBIRD WASN'T MOVING--
I UNDERSTAND. AND IN THIS, AT LEAST, I CAN HELP.
AS THE WEB SHOWS, YOUR ALLIES ARE RECOVERING WELL.
THAT'S A RELIEF. BUT I STILL HAVE OBLIGATIONS. ARACELY IS MY RESPONSIBILITY--
LISTEN TO ME, KAINE. IN MY SHORT TIME AS WEAVER, I HAVE SEEN A NUMBER OF WORLDS SUFFER A DREADED FATE. LET ME SHOW YOU ONE.
OH MY GOD. THOSE THINGS ARE CARRIONS.
YES. WHAT THE CLONES CREATED BY YOUR ORIGINATOR, MILES WARREN, BECOME AS THEY DECAY.
AND ON THESE WORLDS, LIKE ANY INFECTION, THEY ARE COMPELLED TO SPREAD.
I--I'M CONTAGIOUS?
I CANNOT BE CERTAIN...BUT THE RISK IS TOO GREAT TO TAKE CHANCES. WE MAY SEEK A CURE HERE ON LOOM-WORLD--
NO. IF THE BEST MINDS ON THOSE WORLDS HAVEN'T FOUND A CURE, WE WON'T. WHAT WE HAVE THAT THEY DON'T IS THE WEB. AND ME.
I'M ALREADY INFECTED. I CAN GO TO ALL THOSE WORLDS. LOOK FOR A PATIENT ZERO.
IF WE LEARN HOW THIS CARRION VIRUS STARTED, THEN MAYBE WE'LL KNOW HOW TO STOP IT!

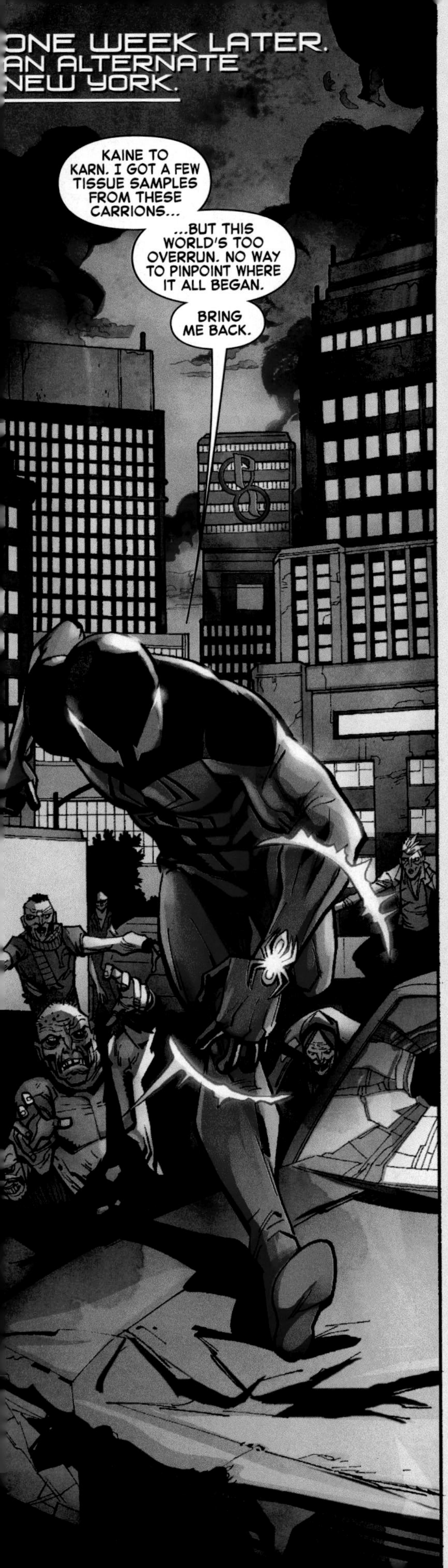
ONE WEEK LATER. AN ALTERNATE NEW YORK.
KAINE TO KARN. I GOT A FEW TISSUE SAMPLES FROM THESE CARRIONS...
...BUT THIS WORLD'S TOO OVERRUN. NO WAY TO PINPOINT WHERE IT ALL BEGAN.
BRING ME BACK.

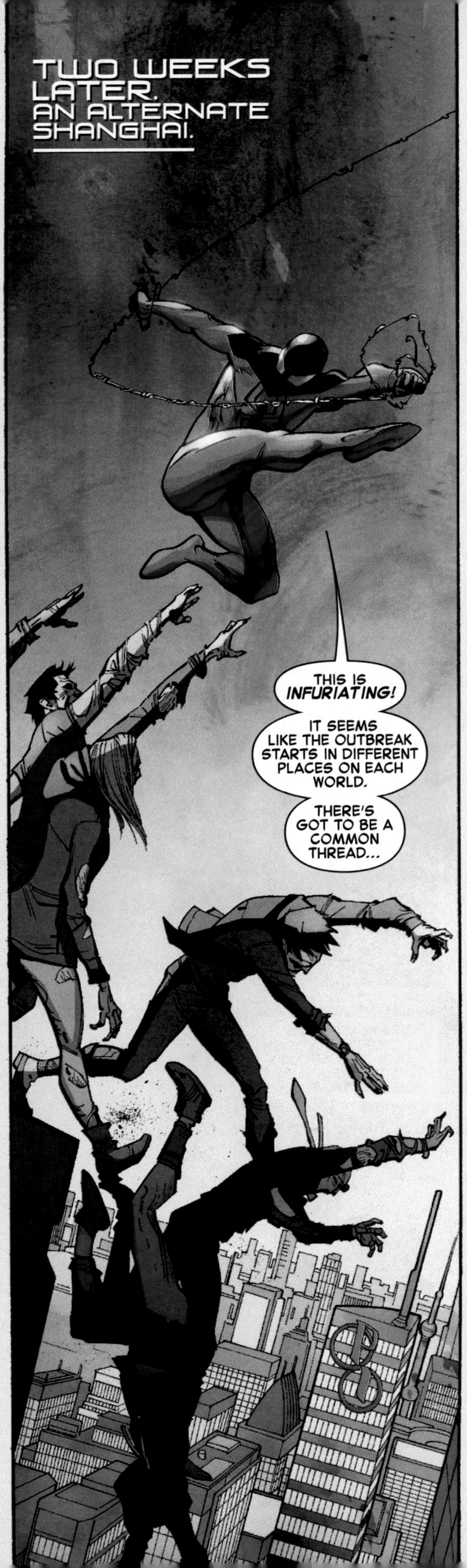
TWO WEEKS LATER. AN ALTERNATE SHANGHAI.
THIS IS *INFURIATING!*
IT SEEMS LIKE THE OUTBREAK STARTS IN DIFFERENT PLACES ON EACH WORLD.
THERE'S GOT TO BE A COMMON THREAD...

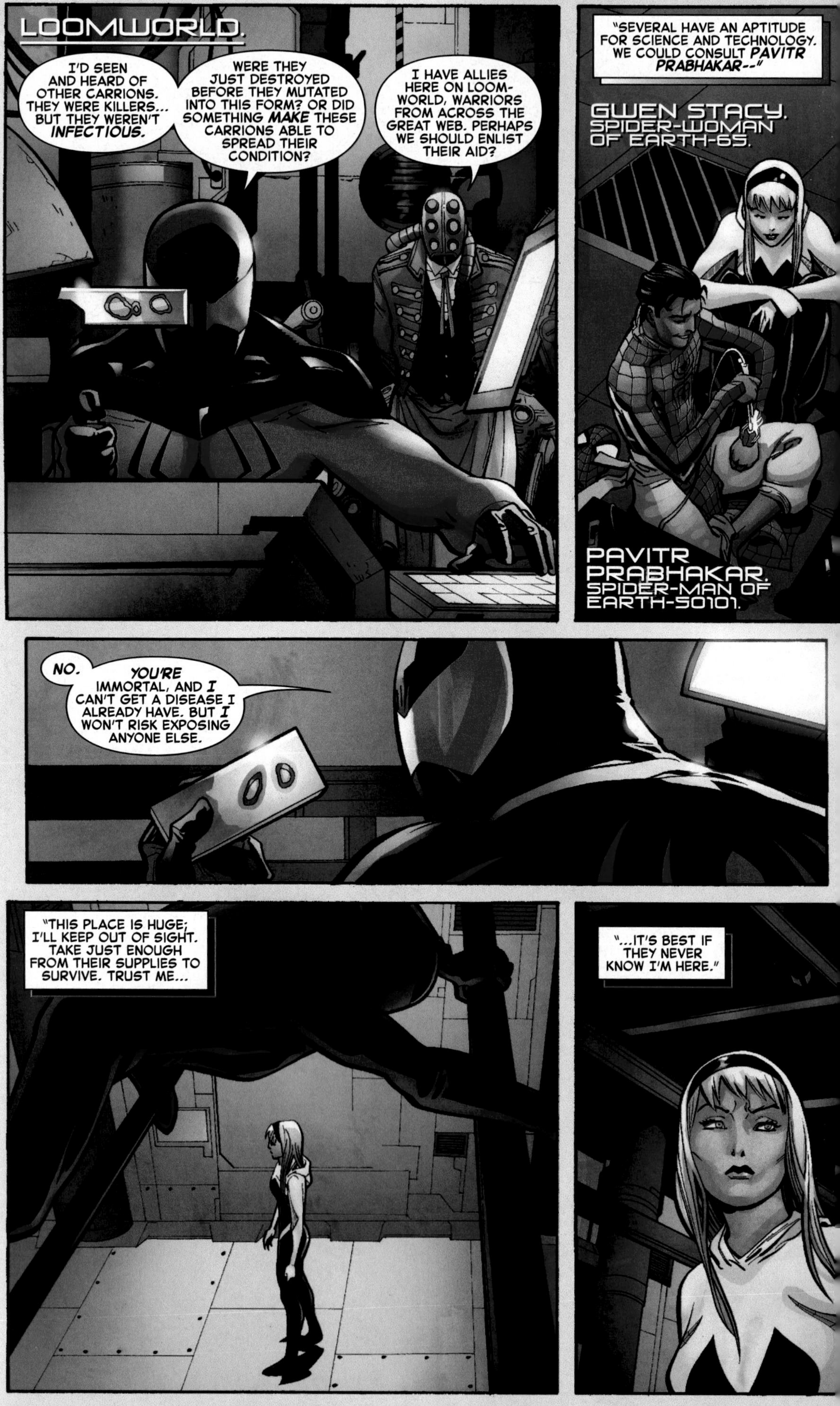

LOOMWORLD.
I'D SEEN AND HEARD OF OTHER CARRIONS. THEY WERE KILLERS... BUT THEY WEREN'T INFECTIOUS.
WERE THEY JUST DESTROYED BEFORE THEY MUTATED INTO THIS FORM? OR DID SOMETHING MAKE THESE CARRIONS ABLE TO SPREAD THEIR CONDITION?
I HAVE ALLIES HERE ON LOOMWORLD, WARRIORS FROM ACROSS THE GREAT WEB. PERHAPS WE SHOULD ENLIST THEIR AID?
"SEVERAL HAVE AN APTITUDE FOR SCIENCE AND TECHNOLOGY. WE COULD CONSULT PAVITR PRABHAKAR--"
GWEN STACY. SPIDER-WOMAN OF EARTH-65.
PAVITR PRABHAKAR. SPIDER-MAN OF EARTH-50101.
NO.
YOU'RE IMMORTAL, AND I CAN'T GET A DISEASE I ALREADY HAVE. BUT I WON'T RISK EXPOSING ANYONE ELSE.
"THIS PLACE IS HUGE; I'LL KEEP OUT OF SIGHT. TAKE JUST ENOUGH FROM THEIR SUPPLIES TO SURVIVE. TRUST ME...
"...IT'S BEST IF THEY NEVER KNOW I'M HERE."

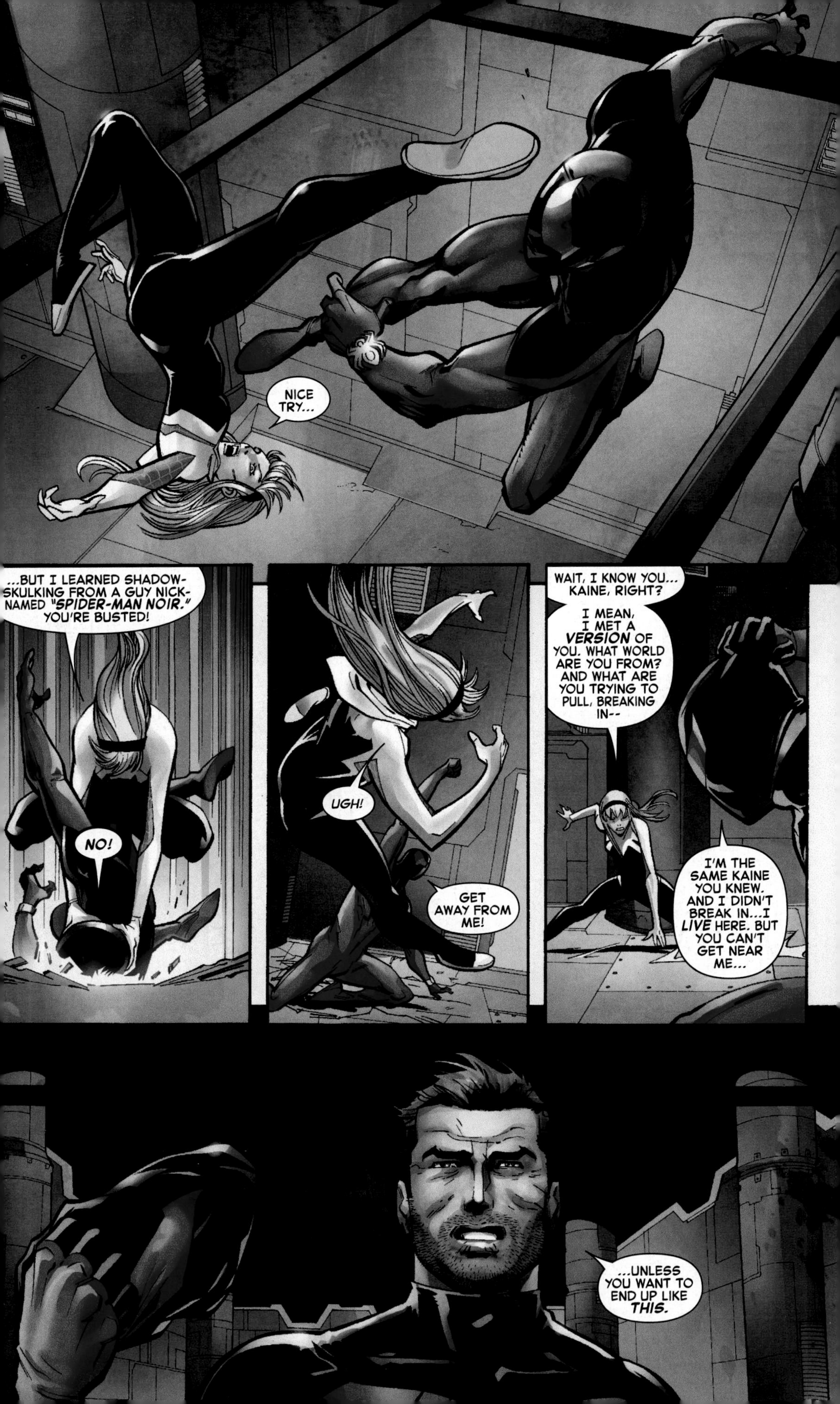
NICE TRY...
...BUT I LEARNED SHADOW-SKULKING FROM A GUY NICK-NAMED "SPIDER-MAN NOIR." YOU'RE BUSTED!
NO!
UGH!
GET AWAY FROM ME!
WAIT, I KNOW YOU... KAINE, RIGHT?
I MEAN, I MET A VERSION OF YOU. WHAT WORLD ARE YOU FROM? AND WHAT ARE YOU TRYING TO PULL, BREAKING IN--
I'M THE SAME KAINE YOU KNEW. AND I DIDN'T BREAK IN...I LIVE HERE. BUT YOU CAN'T GET NEAR ME...
...UNLESS YOU WANT TO END UP LIKE THIS.

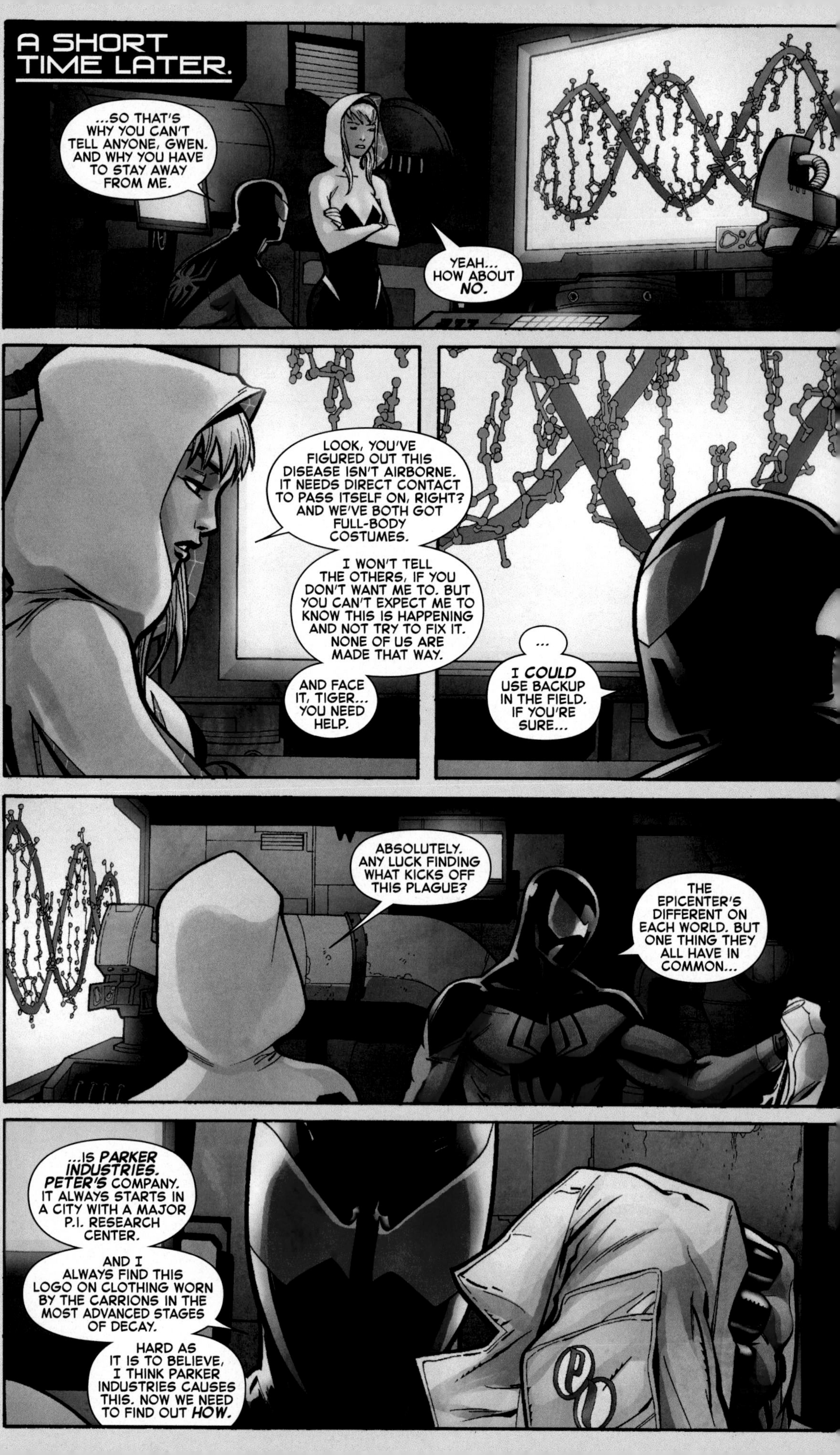
A SHORT TIME LATER.
...SO THAT'S WHY YOU CAN'T TELL ANYONE, GWEN. AND WHY YOU HAVE TO STAY AWAY FROM ME.
YEAH... HOW ABOUT NO.
LOOK, YOU'VE FIGURED OUT THIS DISEASE ISN'T AIRBORNE. IT NEEDS DIRECT CONTACT TO PASS ITSELF ON, RIGHT? AND WE'VE BOTH GOT FULL-BODY COSTUMES.
I WON'T TELL THE OTHERS, IF YOU DON'T WANT ME TO. BUT YOU CAN'T EXPECT ME TO KNOW THIS IS HAPPENING AND NOT TRY TO FIX IT. NONE OF US ARE MADE THAT WAY.
AND FACE IT, TIGER... YOU NEED HELP.
...
I COULD USE BACKUP IN THE FIELD. IF YOU'RE SURE...
ABSOLUTELY. ANY LUCK FINDING WHAT KICKS OFF THIS PLAGUE?
THE EPICENTER'S DIFFERENT ON EACH WORLD. BUT ONE THING THEY ALL HAVE IN COMMON...
...IS PARKER INDUSTRIES. PETER'S COMPANY. IT ALWAYS STARTS IN A CITY WITH A MAJOR P.I. RESEARCH CENTER.
AND I ALWAYS FIND THIS LOGO ON CLOTHING WORN BY THE CARRIONS IN THE MOST ADVANCED STAGES OF DECAY.
HARD AS IT IS TO BELIEVE, I THINK PARKER INDUSTRIES CAUSES THIS. NOW WE NEED TO FIND OUT HOW.

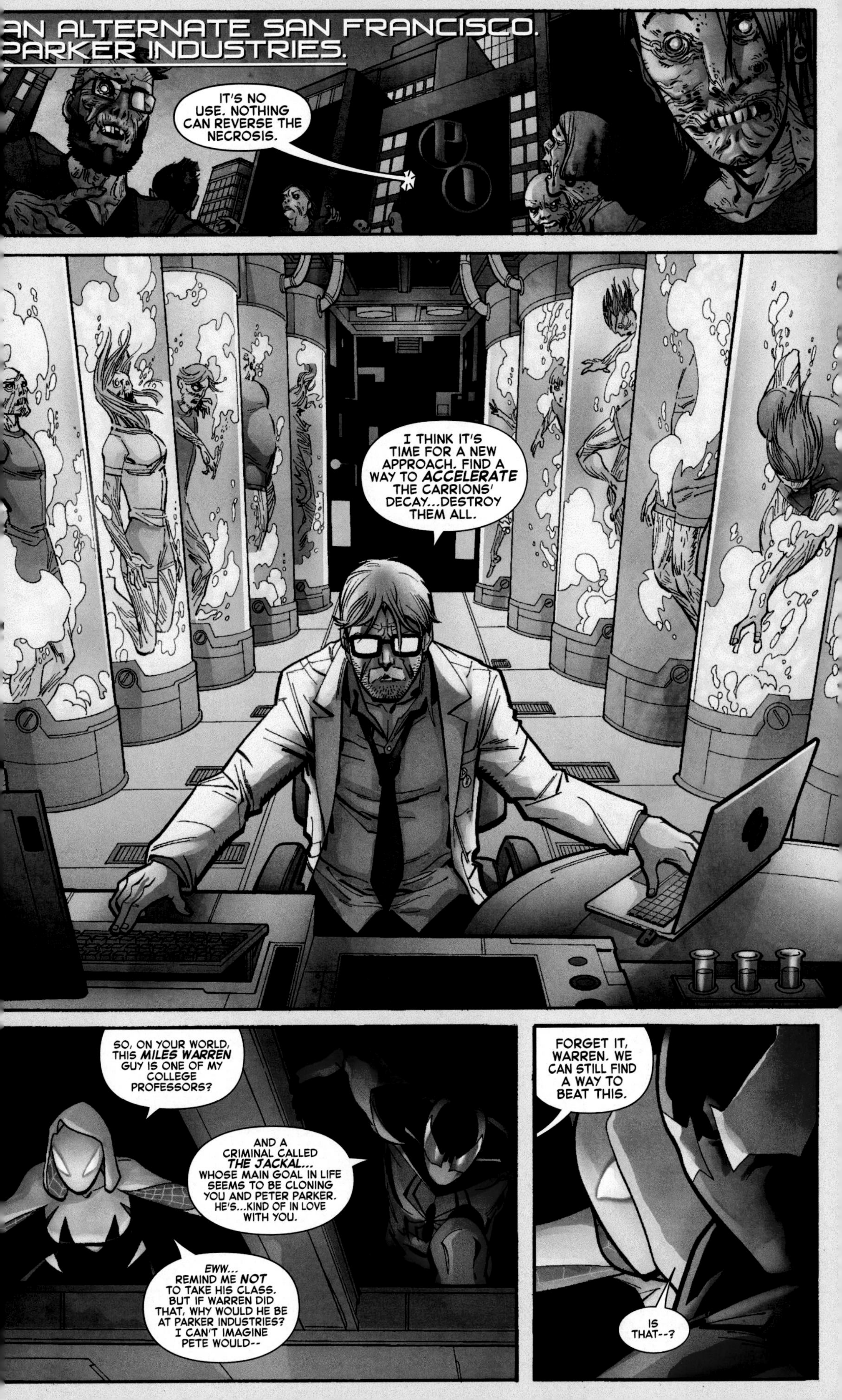
AN ALTERNATE SAN FRANCISCO.
PARKER INDUSTRIES.
IT'S NO USE. NOTHING CAN REVERSE THE NECROSIS.
I THINK IT'S TIME FOR A NEW APPROACH. FIND A WAY TO ACCELERATE THE CARRIONS' DECAY...DESTROY THEM ALL.
SO, ON YOUR WORLD, THIS MILES WARREN GUY IS ONE OF MY COLLEGE PROFESSORS?
AND A CRIMINAL CALLED THE JACKAL... WHOSE MAIN GOAL IN LIFE SEEMS TO BE CLONING YOU AND PETER PARKER. HE'S...KIND OF IN LOVE WITH YOU.
EWW... REMIND ME NOT TO TAKE HIS CLASS. BUT IF WARREN DID THAT, WHY WOULD HE BE AT PARKER INDUSTRIES? I CAN'T IMAGINE PETE WOULD--
FORGET IT, WARREN. WE CAN STILL FIND A WAY TO BEAT THIS.
IS THAT--?

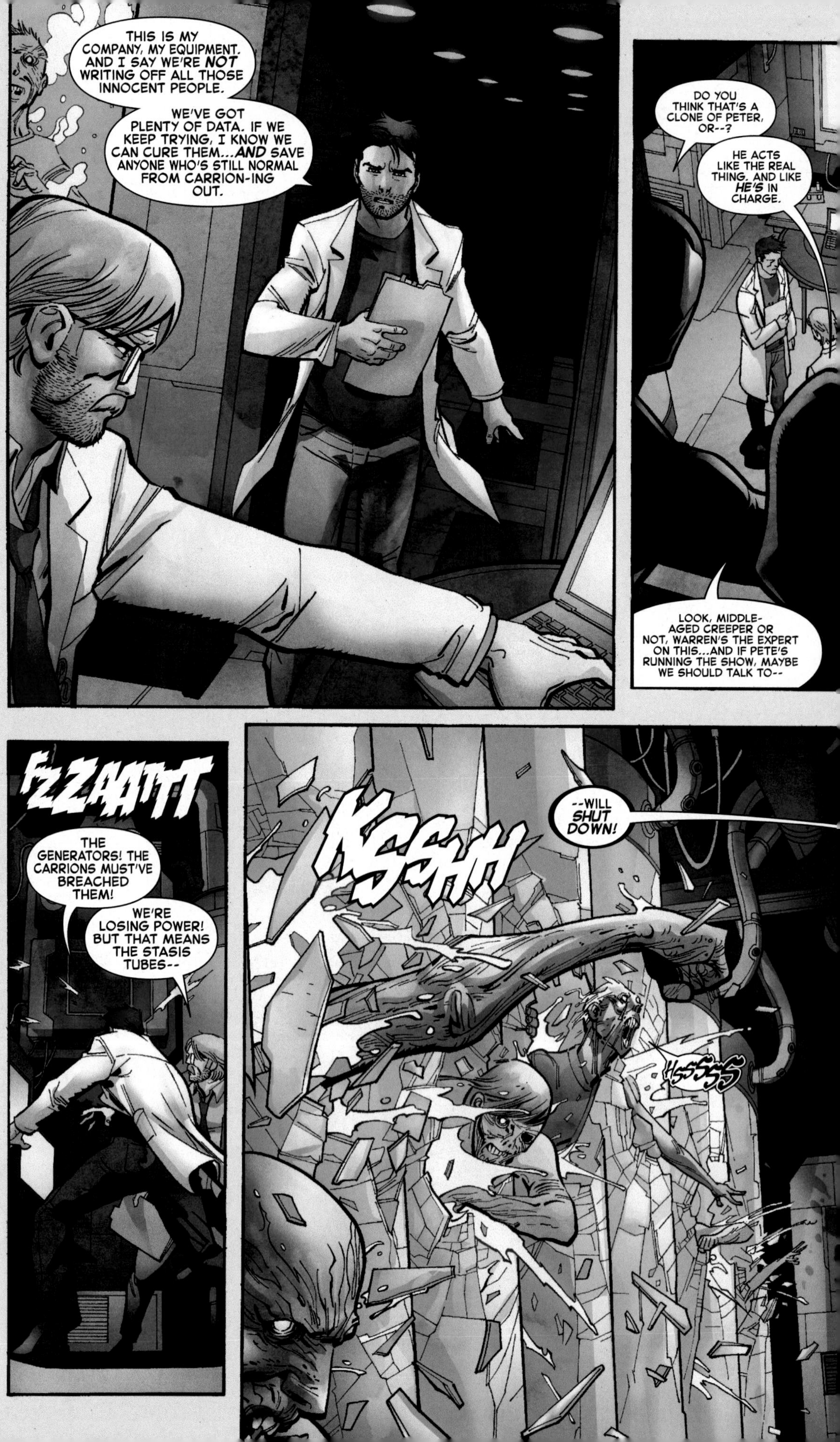

THIS IS MY COMPANY, MY EQUIPMENT. AND I SAY WE'RE *NOT* WRITING OFF ALL THOSE INNOCENT PEOPLE.
WE'VE GOT PLENTY OF DATA. IF WE KEEP TRYING, I KNOW WE CAN CURE THEM...*AND* SAVE ANYONE WHO'S STILL NORMAL FROM CARRION-ING OUT.
DO YOU THINK THAT'S A CLONE OF PETER, OR--?
HE ACTS LIKE THE REAL THING. AND LIKE *HE'S* IN CHARGE.
LOOK, MIDDLE-AGED CREEPER OR NOT, WARREN'S THE EXPERT ON THIS...AND IF PETE'S RUNNING THE SHOW, MAYBE WE SHOULD TALK TO--
FZZAATTT
THE GENERATORS! THE CARRIONS MUST'VE BREACHED THEM!
WE'RE LOSING POWER! BUT THAT MEANS THE STASIS TUBES--
KSSHH
--WILL *SHUT DOWN!*
HSSSSS

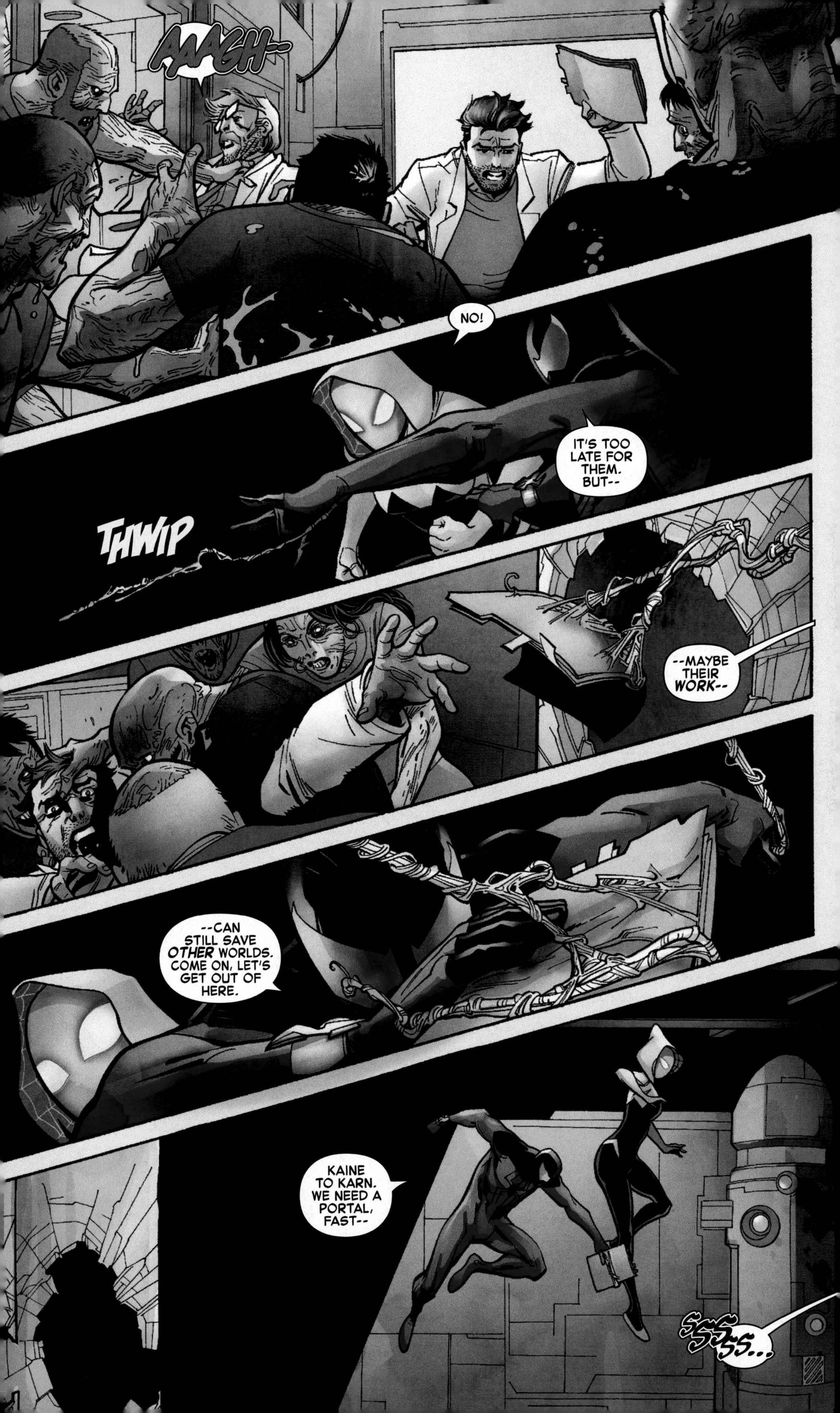
AAAGH--
NO!
IT'S TOO LATE FOR THEM. BUT--
THWIP
--MAYBE THEIR WORK--
--CAN STILL SAVE OTHER WORLDS. COME ON, LET'S GET OUT OF HERE.
KAINE TO KARN. WE NEED A PORTAL, FAST--
SSSSS...

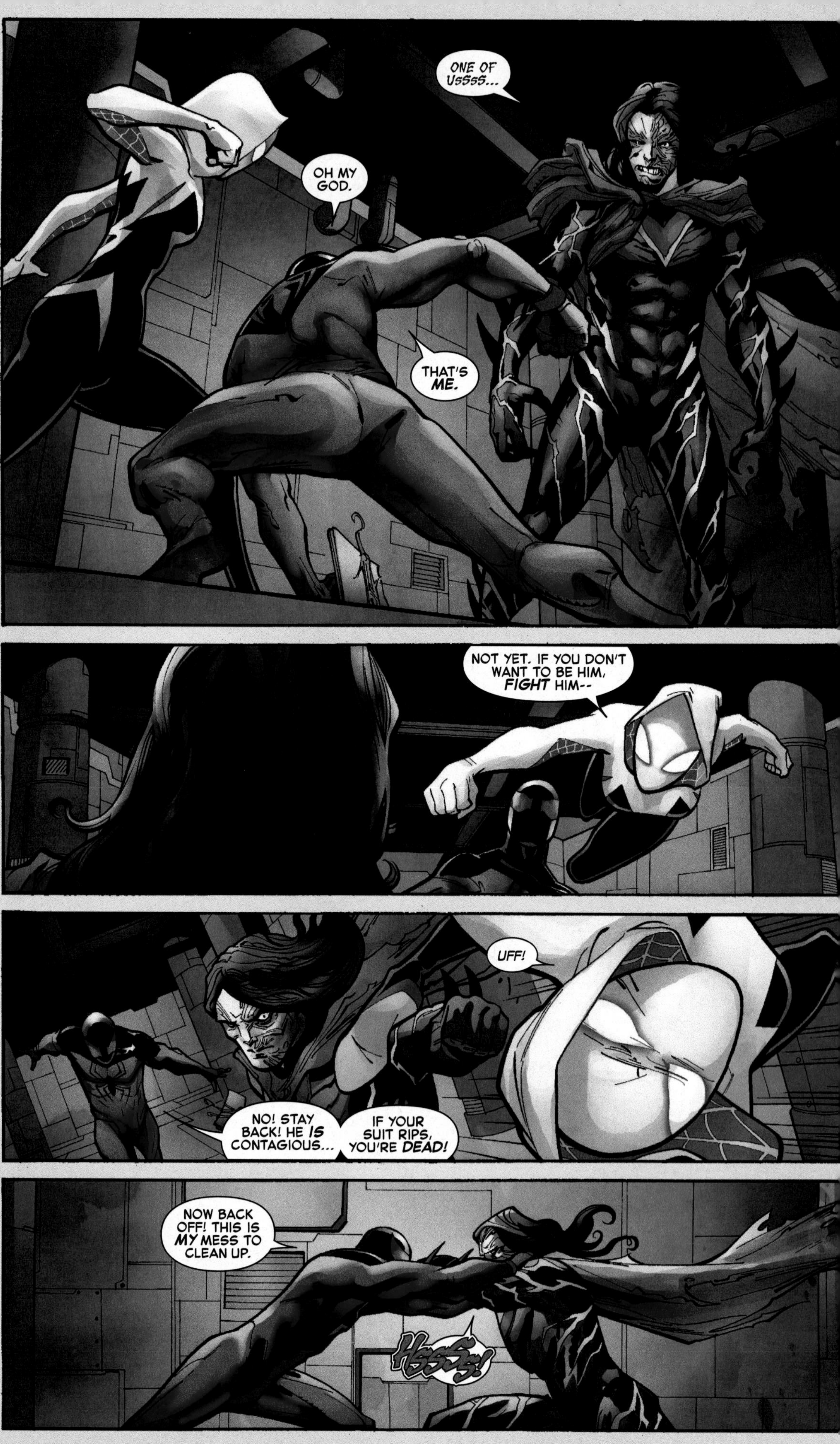
ONE OF USSSS...
OH MY GOD.
THAT'S ME.
NOT YET. IF YOU DON'T WANT TO BE HIM, FIGHT HIM--
UFF!
NO! STAY BACK! HE IS CONTAGIOUS...
IF YOUR SUIT RIPS, YOU'RE DEAD!
NOW BACK OFF! THIS IS MY MESS TO CLEAN UP.
HSSSS!

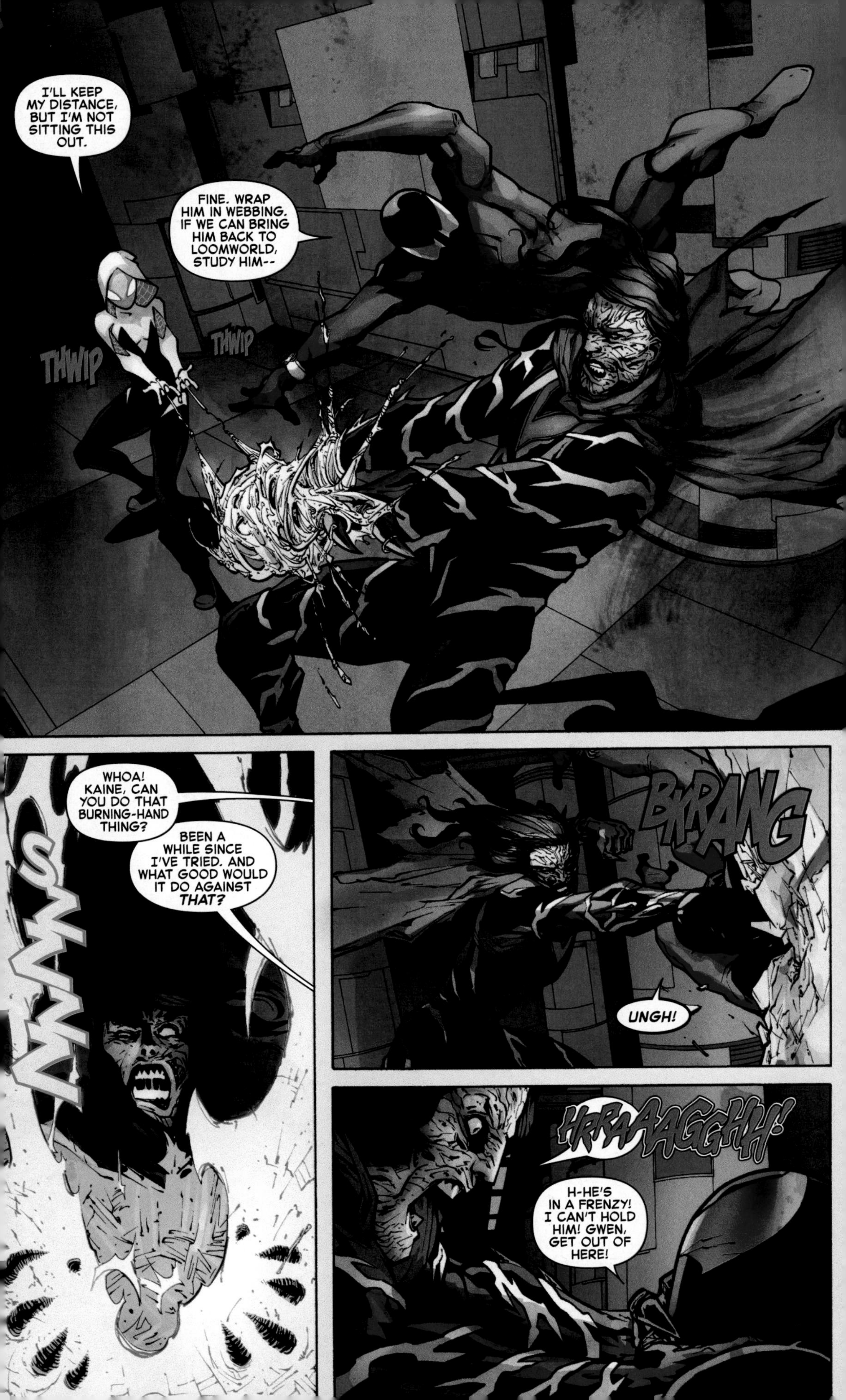
I'LL KEEP MY DISTANCE, BUT I'M NOT SITTING THIS OUT.
FINE. WRAP HIM IN WEBBING. IF WE CAN BRING HIM BACK TO LOOMWORLD, STUDY HIM--
THWIP
THWIP
WHOA! KAINE, CAN YOU DO THAT BURNING-HAND THING?
BEEN A WHILE SINCE I'VE TRIED. AND WHAT GOOD WOULD IT DO AGAINST THAT?
SWAMM
BKRANG
UNGH!
HRRAAAAGGHH!
H-HE'S IN A FRENZY! I CAN'T HOLD HIM! GWEN, GET OUT OF HERE!

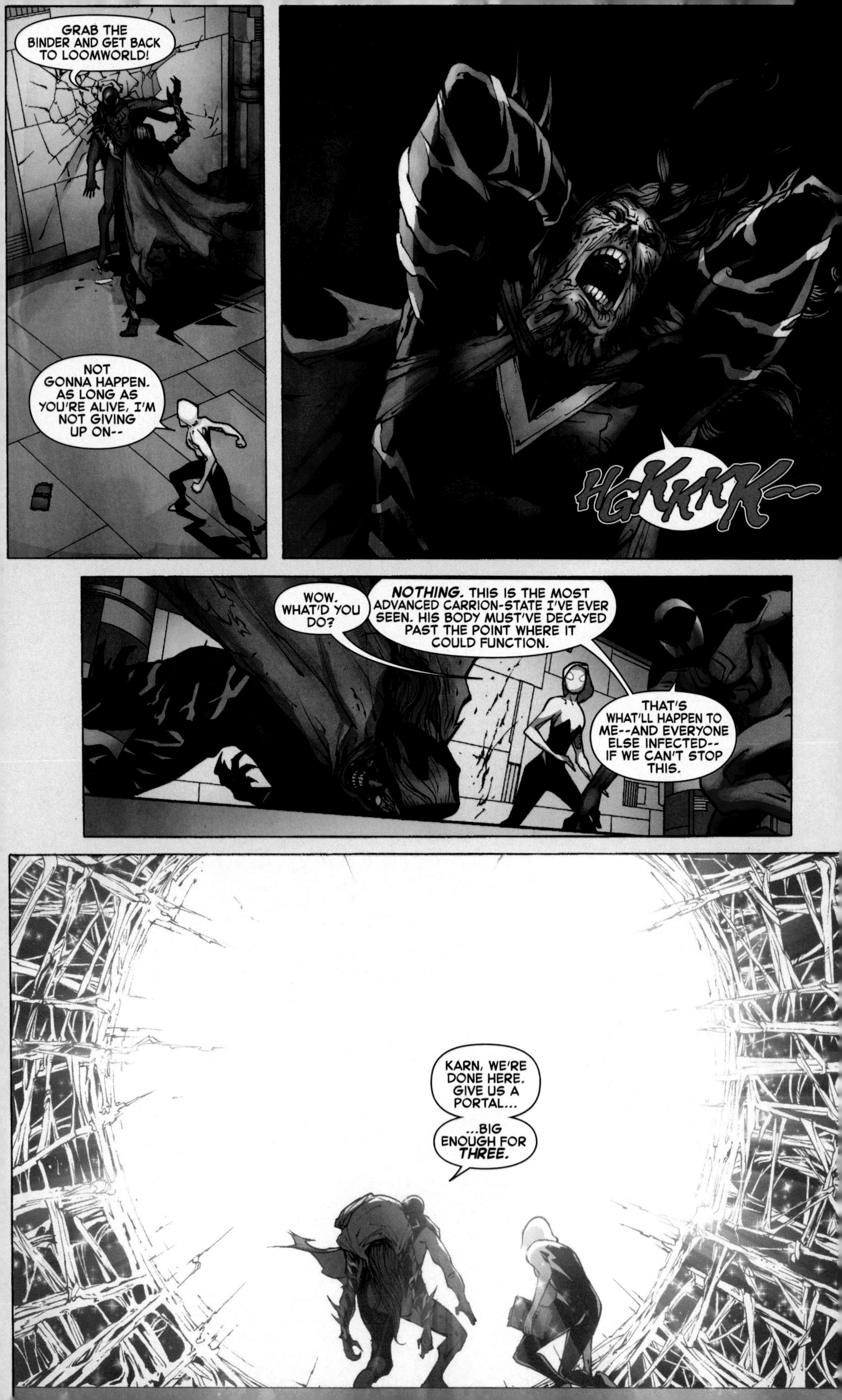
GRAB THE BINDER AND GET BACK TO LOOMWORLD!
NOT GONNA HAPPEN. AS LONG AS YOU'RE ALIVE, I'M NOT GIVING UP ON--
HGKKKK--
WOW. WHAT'D YOU DO?
NOTHING. THIS IS THE MOST ADVANCED CARRION-STATE I'VE EVER SEEN. HIS BODY MUST'VE DECAYED PAST THE POINT WHERE IT COULD FUNCTION.
THAT'S WHAT'LL HAPPEN TO ME--AND EVERYONE ELSE INFECTED--IF WE CAN'T STOP THIS.
KARN, WE'RE DONE HERE. GIVE US A PORTAL...
...BIG ENOUGH FOR THREE.

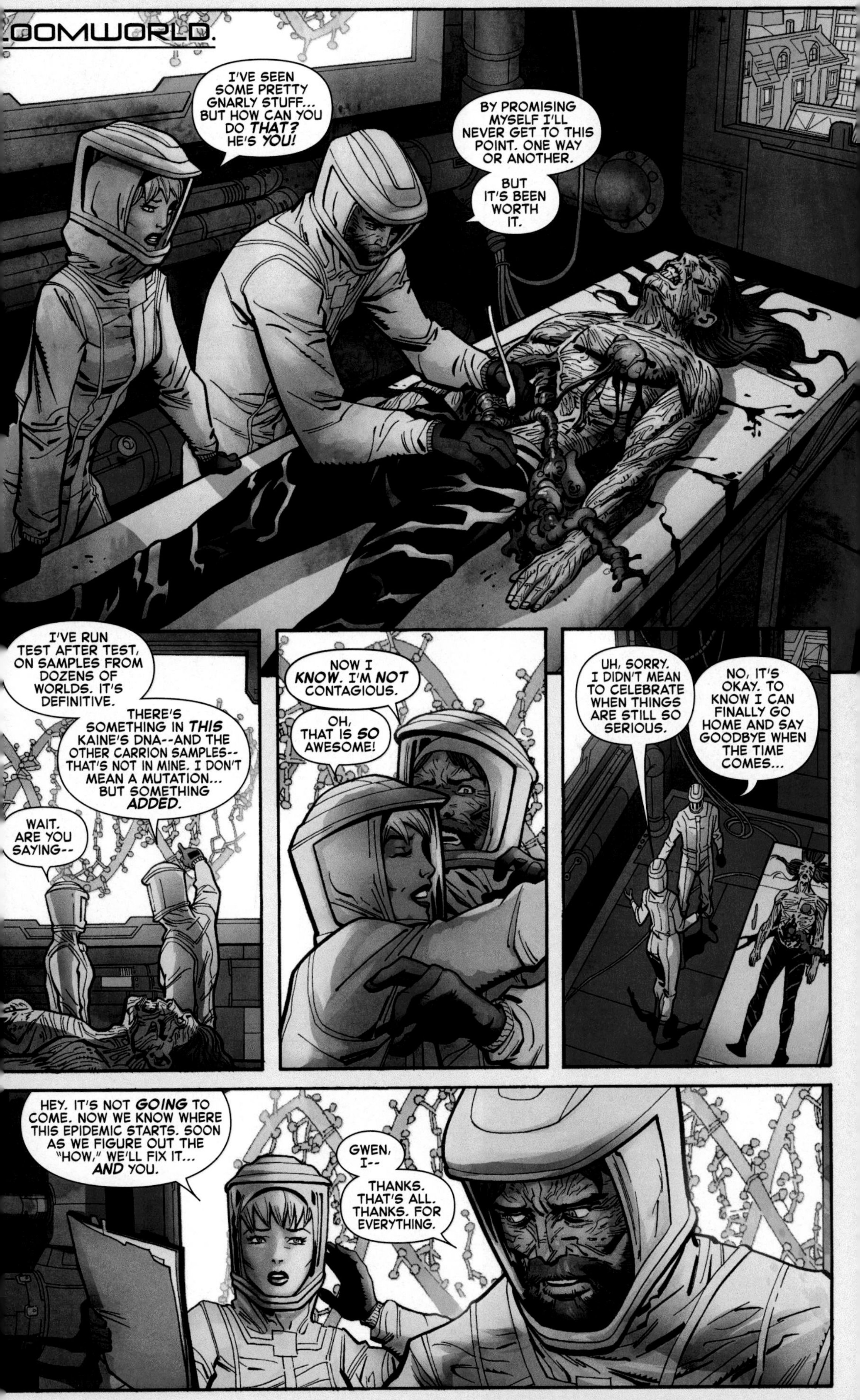

LOOMWORLD.
I'VE SEEN SOME PRETTY GNARLY STUFF... BUT HOW CAN YOU DO THAT? HE'S YOU!
BY PROMISING MYSELF I'LL NEVER GET TO THIS POINT. ONE WAY OR ANOTHER.
BUT IT'S BEEN WORTH IT.
I'VE RUN TEST AFTER TEST, ON SAMPLES FROM DOZENS OF WORLDS. IT'S DEFINITIVE.
THERE'S SOMETHING IN THIS KAINE'S DNA--AND THE OTHER CARRION SAMPLES--THAT'S NOT IN MINE. I DON'T MEAN A MUTATION... BUT SOMETHING ADDED.
WAIT. ARE YOU SAYING--
NOW I KNOW. I'M NOT CONTAGIOUS.
OH, THAT IS SO AWESOME!
UH, SORRY. I DIDN'T MEAN TO CELEBRATE WHEN THINGS ARE STILL SO SERIOUS.
NO, IT'S OKAY. TO KNOW I CAN FINALLY GO HOME AND SAY GOODBYE WHEN THE TIME COMES...
HEY. IT'S NOT GOING TO COME. NOW WE KNOW WHERE THIS EPIDEMIC STARTS. SOON AS WE FIGURE OUT THE "HOW," WE'LL FIX IT... AND YOU.
GWEN, I--
THANKS. THAT'S ALL. THANKS. FOR EVERYTHING.

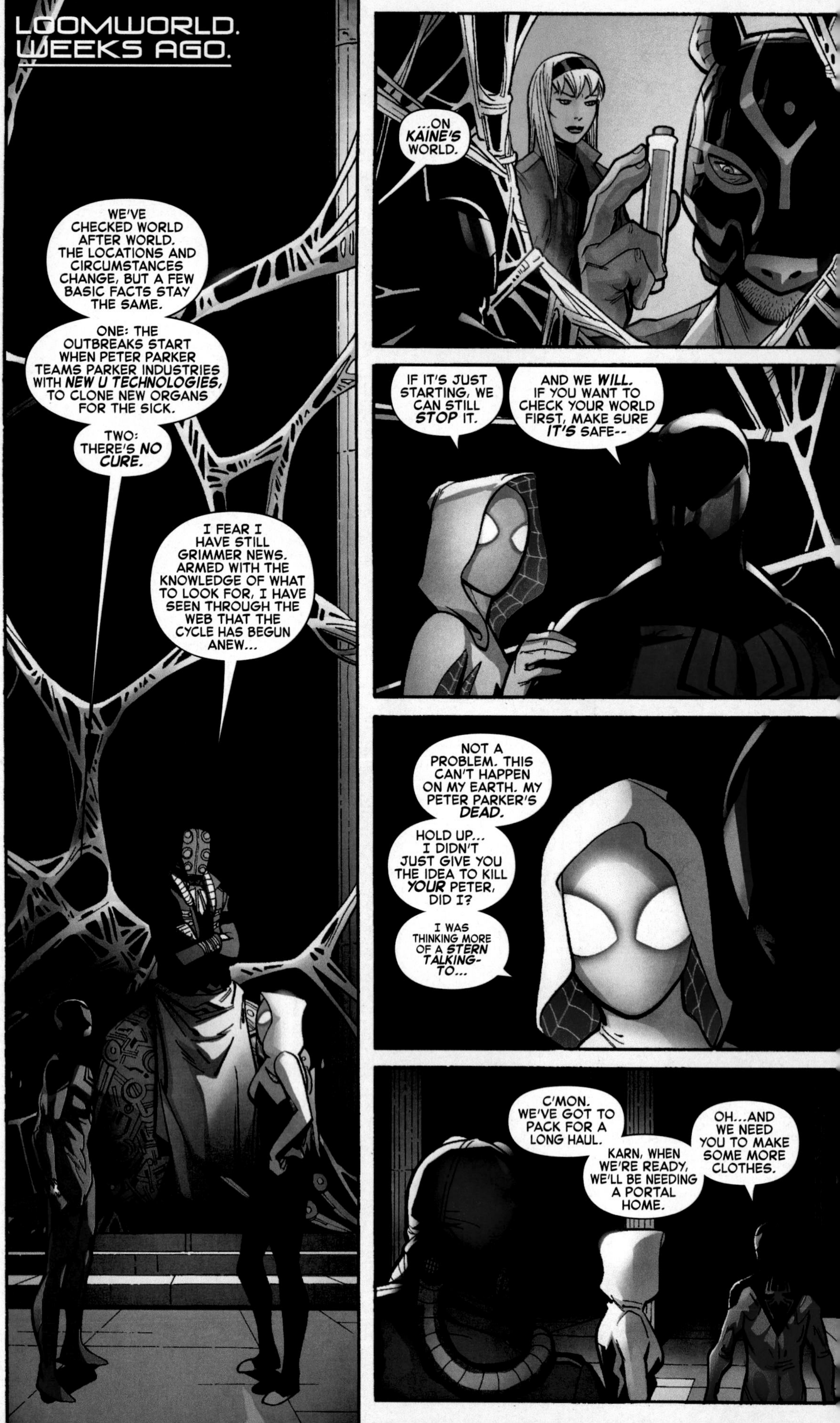

LOOMWORLD. WEEKS AGO.
WE'VE CHECKED WORLD AFTER WORLD. THE LOCATIONS AND CIRCUMSTANCES CHANGE, BUT A FEW BASIC FACTS STAY THE SAME.
ONE: THE OUTBREAKS START WHEN PETER PARKER TEAMS PARKER INDUSTRIES WITH NEW U TECHNOLOGIES, TO CLONE NEW ORGANS FOR THE SICK.
TWO: THERE'S NO CURE.
I FEAR I HAVE STILL GRIMMER NEWS. ARMED WITH THE KNOWLEDGE OF WHAT TO LOOK FOR, I HAVE SEEN THROUGH THE WEB THAT THE CYCLE HAS BEGUN ANEW...
...ON KAINE'S WORLD.
IF IT'S JUST STARTING, WE CAN STILL STOP IT.
AND WE WILL. IF YOU WANT TO CHECK YOUR WORLD FIRST, MAKE SURE IT'S SAFE--
NOT A PROBLEM. THIS CAN'T HAPPEN ON MY EARTH. MY PETER PARKER'S DEAD.
HOLD UP... I DIDN'T JUST GIVE YOU THE IDEA TO KILL YOUR PETER, DID I?
I WAS THINKING MORE OF A STERN TALKING-TO...
C'MON. WE'VE GOT TO PACK FOR A LONG HAUL.
KARN, WHEN WE'RE READY, WE'LL BE NEEDING A PORTAL HOME.
OH...AND WE NEED YOU TO MAKE SOME MORE CLOTHES.

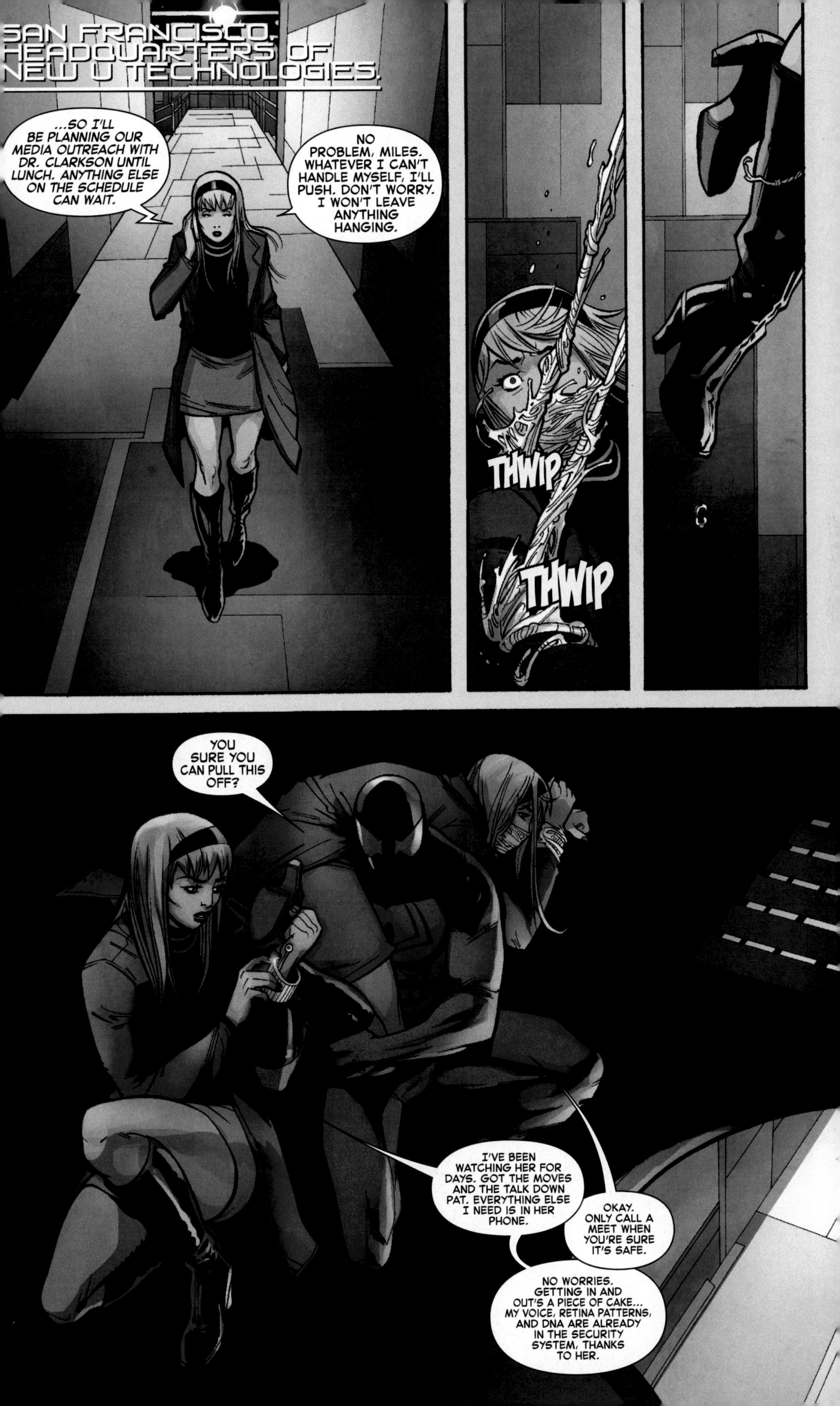
SAN FRANCISCO. HEADQUARTERS OF NEW U TECHNOLOGIES.
...SO I'LL BE PLANNING OUR MEDIA OUTREACH WITH DR. CLARKSON UNTIL LUNCH. ANYTHING ELSE ON THE SCHEDULE CAN WAIT.
NO PROBLEM, MILES. WHATEVER I CAN'T HANDLE MYSELF, I'LL PUSH. DON'T WORRY. I WON'T LEAVE ANYTHING HANGING.
THWIP
THWIP
YOU SURE YOU CAN PULL THIS OFF?
I'VE BEEN WATCHING HER FOR DAYS. GOT THE MOVES AND THE TALK DOWN PAT. EVERYTHING ELSE I NEED IS IN HER PHONE.
OKAY. ONLY CALL A MEET WHEN YOU'RE SURE IT'S SAFE.
NO WORRIES. GETTING IN AND OUT'S A PIECE OF CAKE... MY VOICE, RETINA PATTERNS, AND DNA ARE ALREADY IN THE SECURITY SYSTEM, THANKS TO HER.

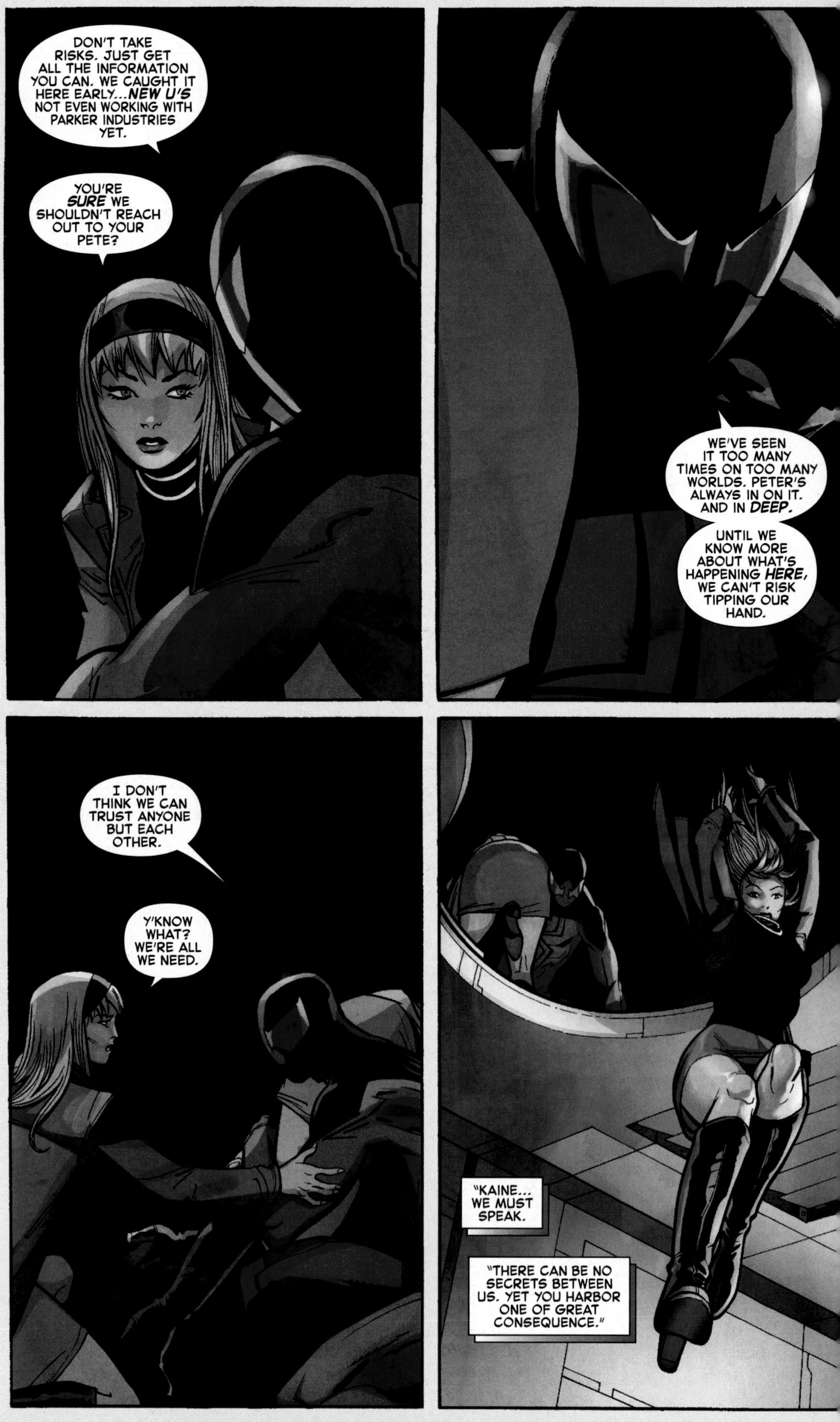

DON'T TAKE RISKS. JUST GET ALL THE INFORMATION YOU CAN. WE CAUGHT IT HERE EARLY...NEW U'S NOT EVEN WORKING WITH PARKER INDUSTRIES YET.
YOU'RE SURE WE SHOULDN'T REACH OUT TO YOUR PETE?
WE'VE SEEN IT TOO MANY TIMES ON TOO MANY WORLDS. PETER'S ALWAYS IN ON IT. AND IN DEEP.
UNTIL WE KNOW MORE ABOUT WHAT'S HAPPENING HERE, WE CAN'T RISK TIPPING OUR HAND.
I DON'T THINK WE CAN TRUST ANYONE BUT EACH OTHER.
Y'KNOW WHAT? WE'RE ALL WE NEED.
"KAINE... WE MUST SPEAK.
"THERE CAN BE NO SECRETS BETWEEN US. YET YOU HARBOR ONE OF GREAT CONSEQUENCE."

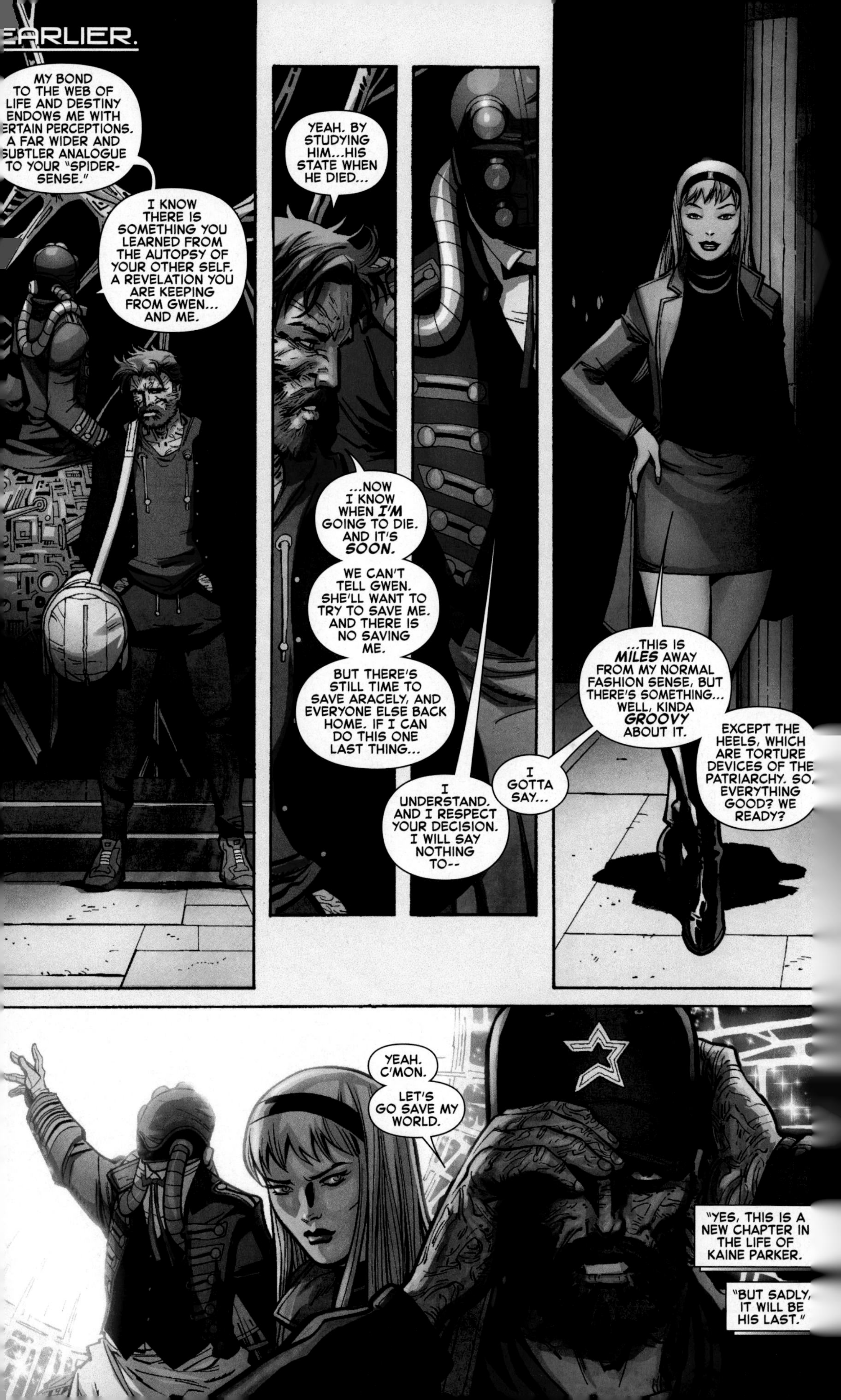

EARLIER.
MY BOND TO THE WEB OF LIFE AND DESTINY ENDOWS ME WITH CERTAIN PERCEPTIONS. A FAR WIDER AND SUBTLER ANALOGUE TO YOUR "SPIDER-SENSE."
I KNOW THERE IS SOMETHING YOU LEARNED FROM THE AUTOPSY OF YOUR OTHER SELF. A REVELATION YOU ARE KEEPING FROM GWEN... AND ME.
YEAH. BY STUDYING HIM...HIS STATE WHEN HE DIED...
...NOW I KNOW WHEN *I'M* GOING TO DIE. AND IT'S ***SOON.***
WE CAN'T TELL GWEN. SHE'LL WANT TO TRY TO SAVE ME. AND THERE IS NO SAVING ME.
BUT THERE'S STILL TIME TO SAVE ARACELY, AND EVERYONE ELSE BACK HOME. IF I CAN DO THIS ONE LAST THING...
I UNDERSTAND. AND I RESPECT YOUR DECISION. I WILL SAY NOTHING TO--
I GOTTA SAY...
...THIS IS ***MILES*** AWAY FROM MY NORMAL FASHION SENSE, BUT THERE'S SOMETHING... WELL, KINDA ***GROOVY*** ABOUT IT.
EXCEPT THE HEELS, WHICH ARE TORTURE DEVICES OF THE PATRIARCHY. SO, EVERYTHING GOOD? WE READY?
YEAH. C'MON.
LET'S GO SAVE MY WORLD.
"YES, THIS IS A NEW CHAPTER IN THE LIFE OF KAINE PARKER.
"BUT SADLY, IT WILL BE HIS LAST."

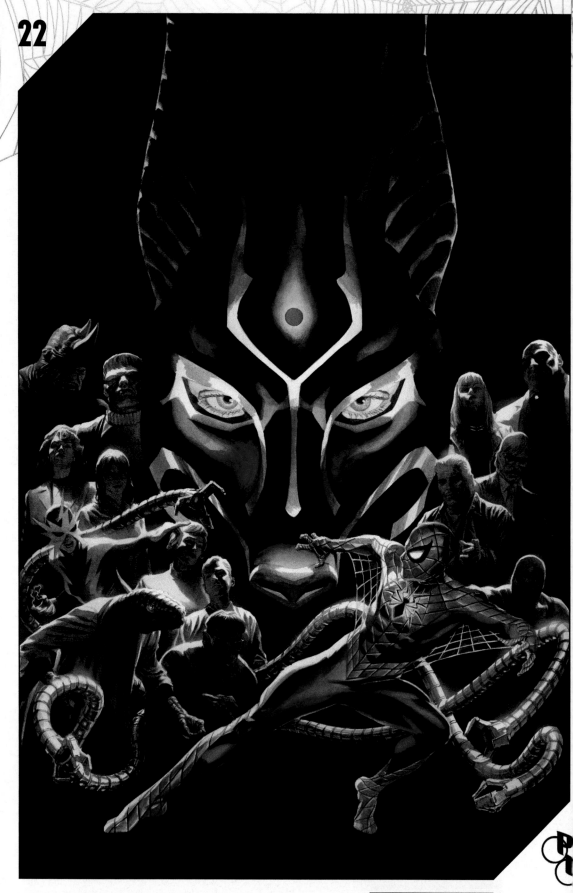

"SEEING RED"

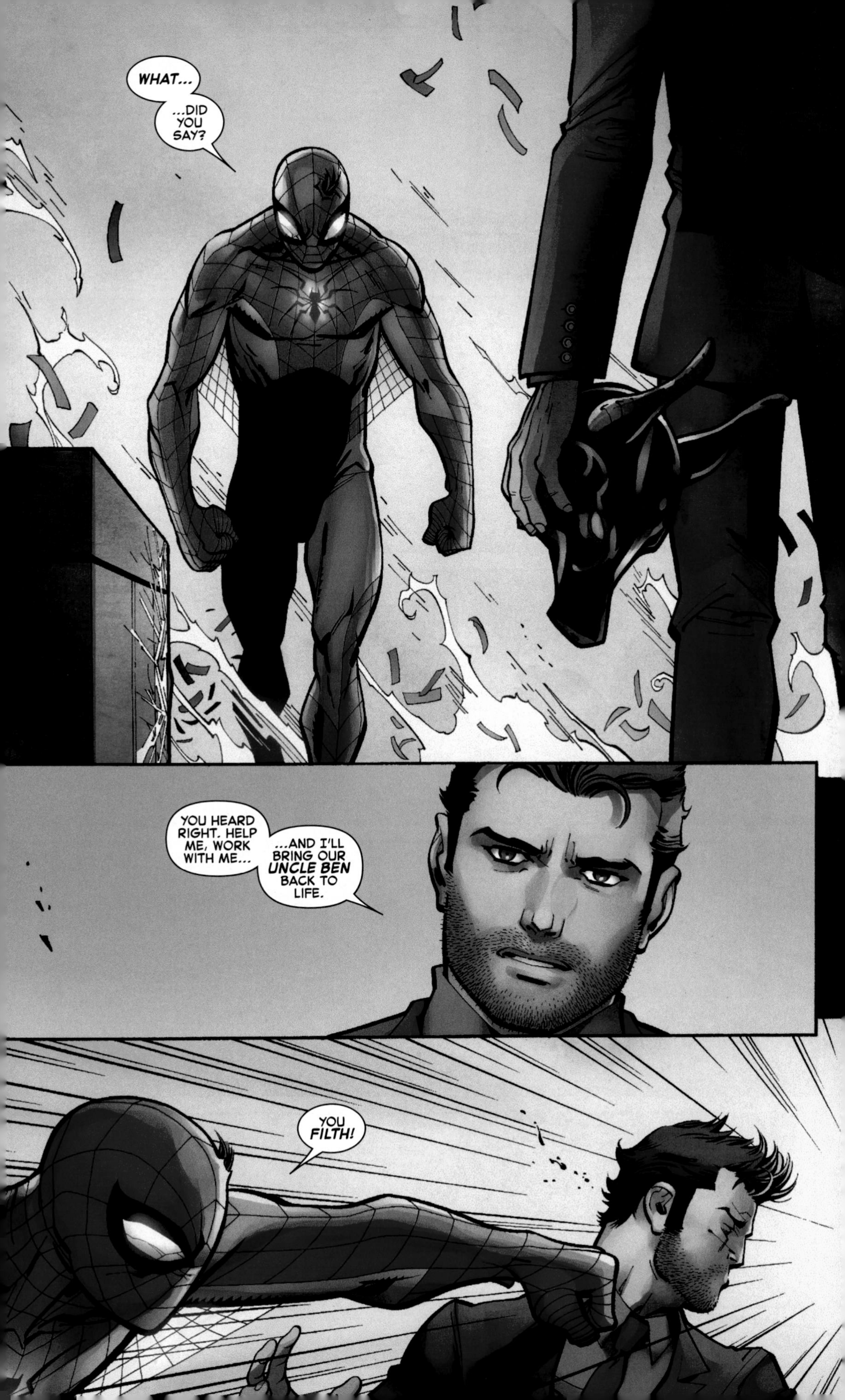
WHAT...
...DID YOU SAY?
YOU HEARD RIGHT. HELP ME, WORK WITH ME...
...AND I'LL BRING OUR UNCLE BEN BACK TO LIFE.
YOU FILTH!

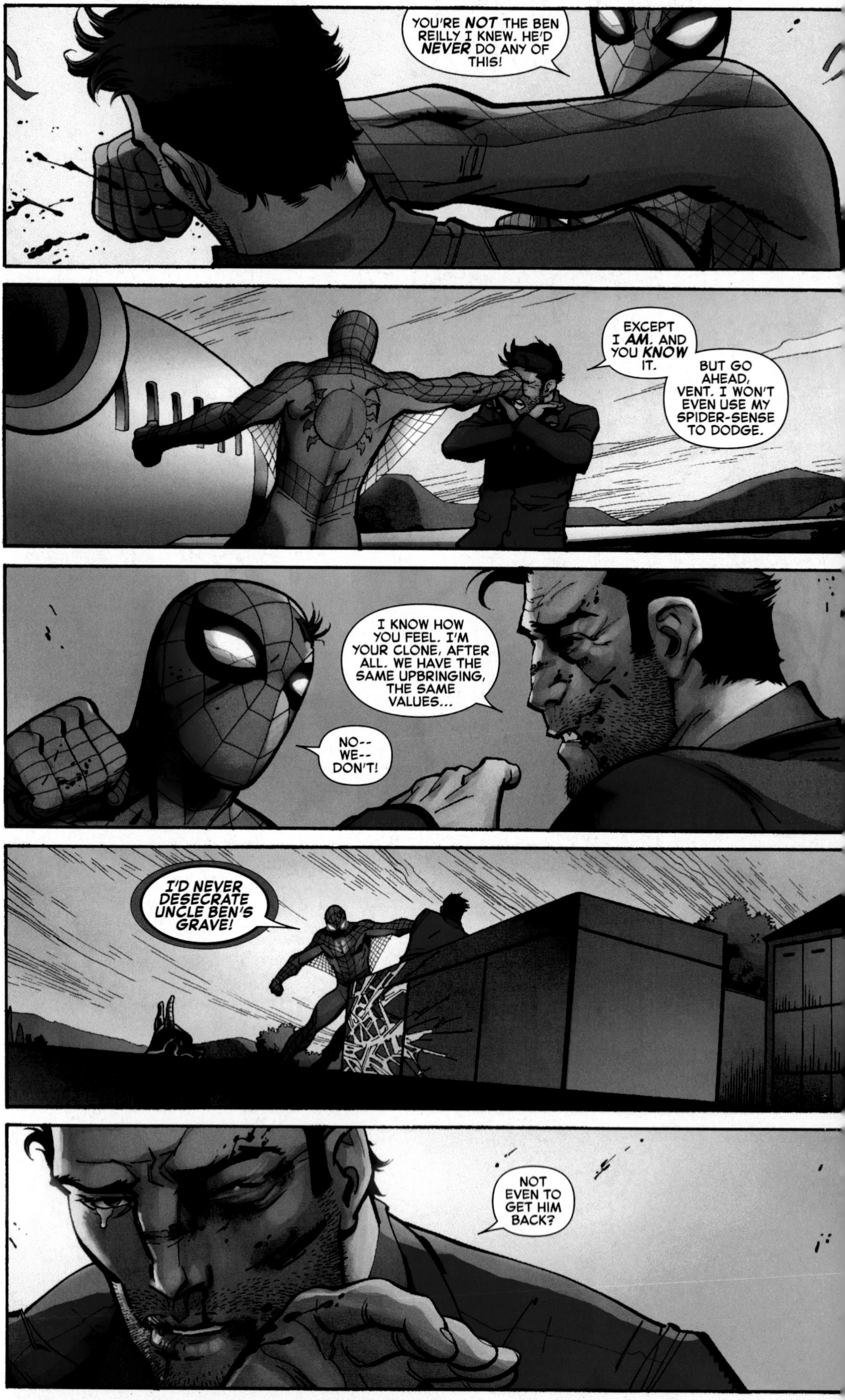
YOU'RE NOT THE BEN REILLY I KNEW. HE'D NEVER DO ANY OF THIS!
EXCEPT I AM. AND YOU KNOW IT.
BUT GO AHEAD, VENT. I WON'T EVEN USE MY SPIDER-SENSE TO DODGE.
I KNOW HOW YOU FEEL. I'M YOUR CLONE, AFTER ALL. WE HAVE THE SAME UPBRINGING, THE SAME VALUES...
NO-- WE-- DON'T!
I'D NEVER DESECRATE UNCLE BEN'S GRAVE!
NOT EVEN TO GET HIM BACK?

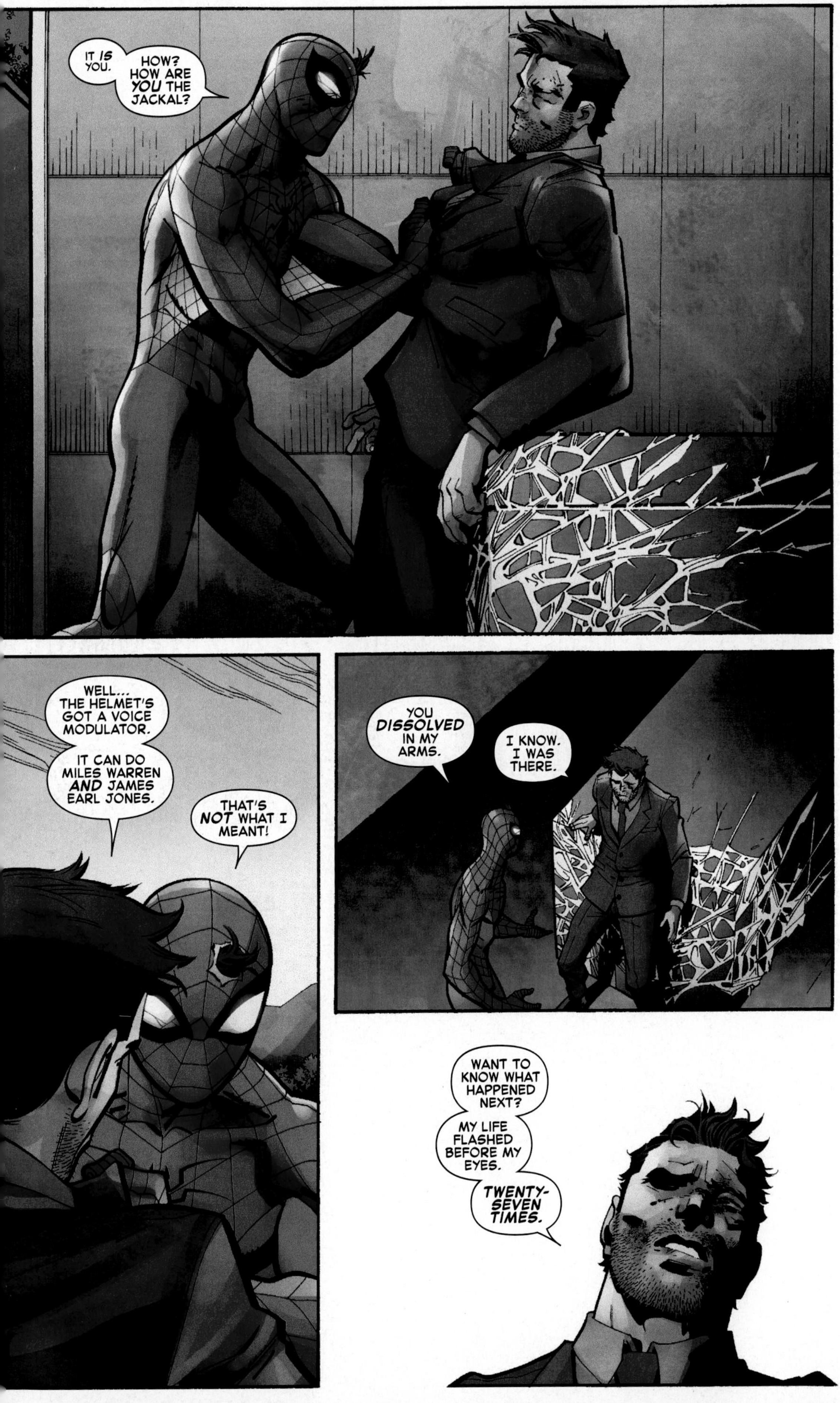
IT IS YOU.
HOW? HOW ARE YOU THE JACKAL?
WELL... THE HELMET'S GOT A VOICE MODULATOR.
IT CAN DO MILES WARREN AND JAMES EARL JONES.
THAT'S NOT WHAT I MEANT!
YOU DISSOLVED IN MY ARMS.
I KNOW. I WAS THERE.
WANT TO KNOW WHAT HAPPENED NEXT?
MY LIFE FLASHED BEFORE MY EYES.
TWENTY-SEVEN TIMES.

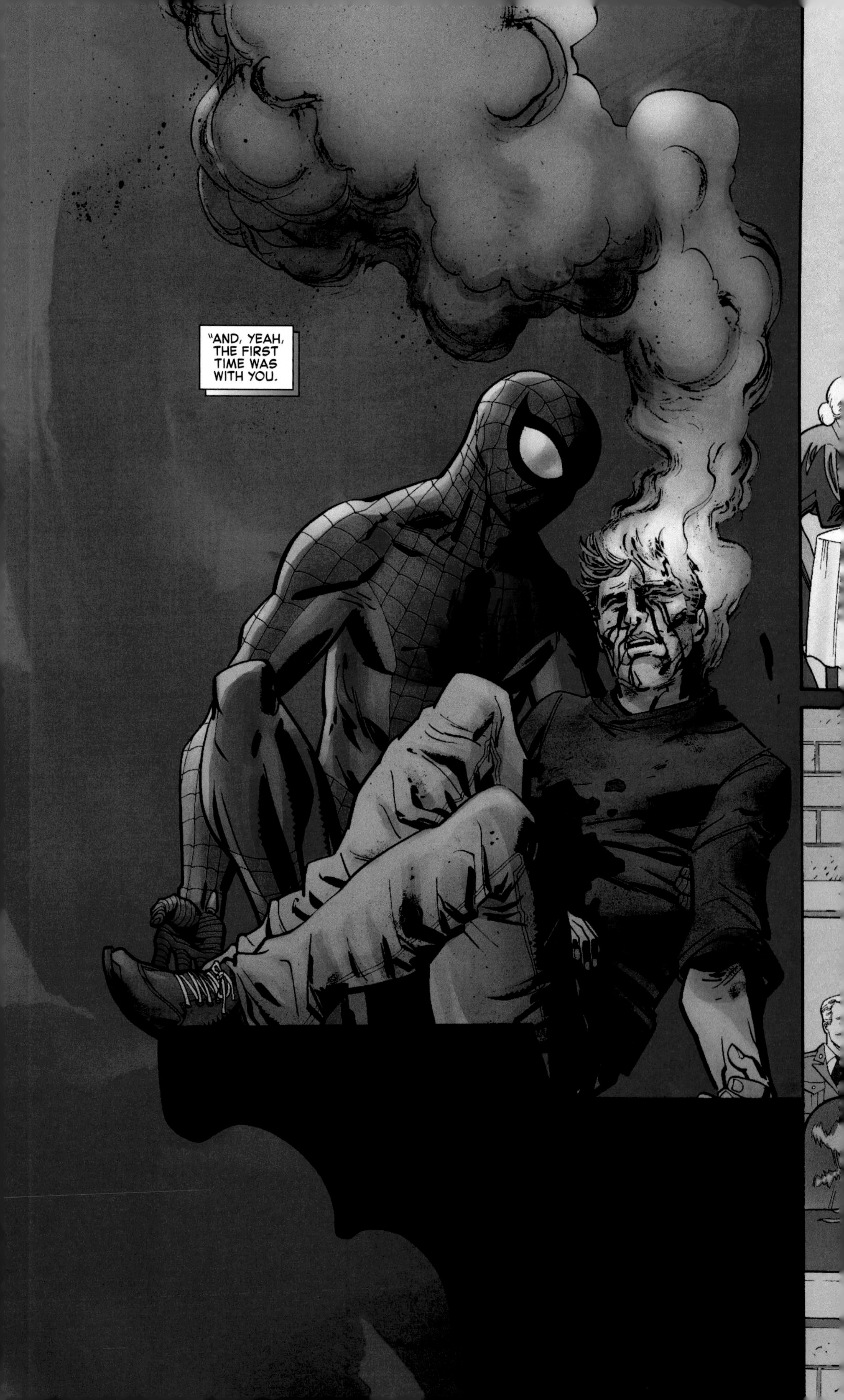
"AND, YEAH, THE FIRST TIME WAS WITH YOU.

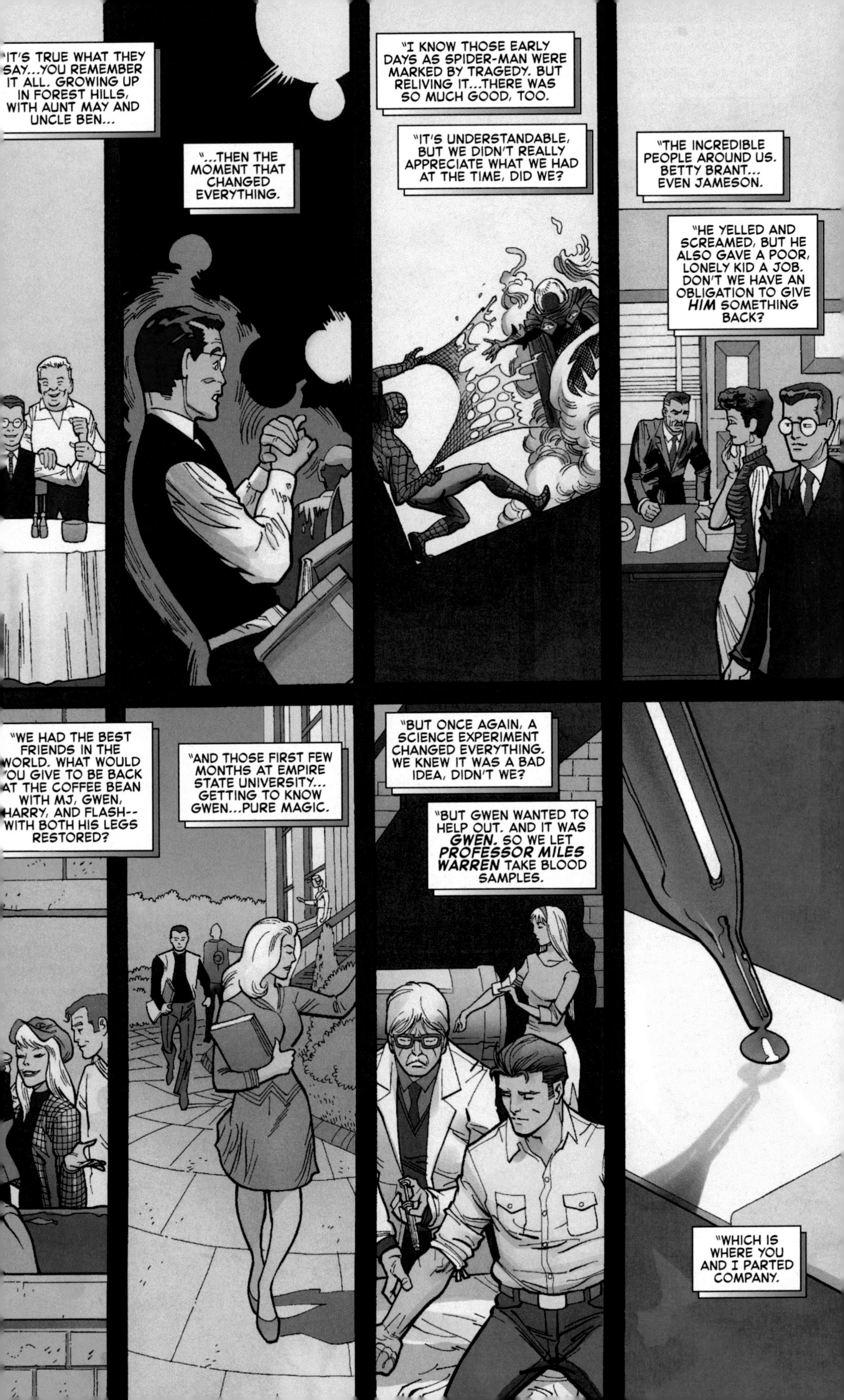
"IT'S TRUE WHAT THEY SAY...YOU REMEMBER IT ALL. GROWING UP IN FOREST HILLS, WITH AUNT MAY AND UNCLE BEN...
"...THEN THE MOMENT THAT CHANGED EVERYTHING.
"I KNOW THOSE EARLY DAYS AS SPIDER-MAN WERE MARKED BY TRAGEDY. BUT RELIVING IT...THERE WAS SO MUCH GOOD, TOO.
"IT'S UNDERSTANDABLE, BUT WE DIDN'T REALLY APPRECIATE WHAT WE HAD AT THE TIME, DID WE?
"THE INCREDIBLE PEOPLE AROUND US. BETTY BRANT... EVEN JAMESON.
"HE YELLED AND SCREAMED, BUT HE ALSO GAVE A POOR, LONELY KID A JOB. DON'T WE HAVE AN OBLIGATION TO GIVE *HIM* SOMETHING BACK?
"WE HAD THE BEST FRIENDS IN THE WORLD. WHAT WOULD YOU GIVE TO BE BACK AT THE COFFEE BEAN WITH MJ, GWEN, HARRY, AND FLASH-- WITH BOTH HIS LEGS RESTORED?
"AND THOSE FIRST FEW MONTHS AT EMPIRE STATE UNIVERSITY... GETTING TO KNOW GWEN...PURE MAGIC.
"BUT ONCE AGAIN, A SCIENCE EXPERIMENT CHANGED EVERYTHING. WE KNEW IT WAS A BAD IDEA, DIDN'T WE?
"BUT GWEN WANTED TO HELP OUT. AND IT WAS *GWEN.* SO WE LET *PROFESSOR MILES WARREN* TAKE BLOOD SAMPLES.
"WHICH IS WHERE YOU AND I PARTED COMPANY.

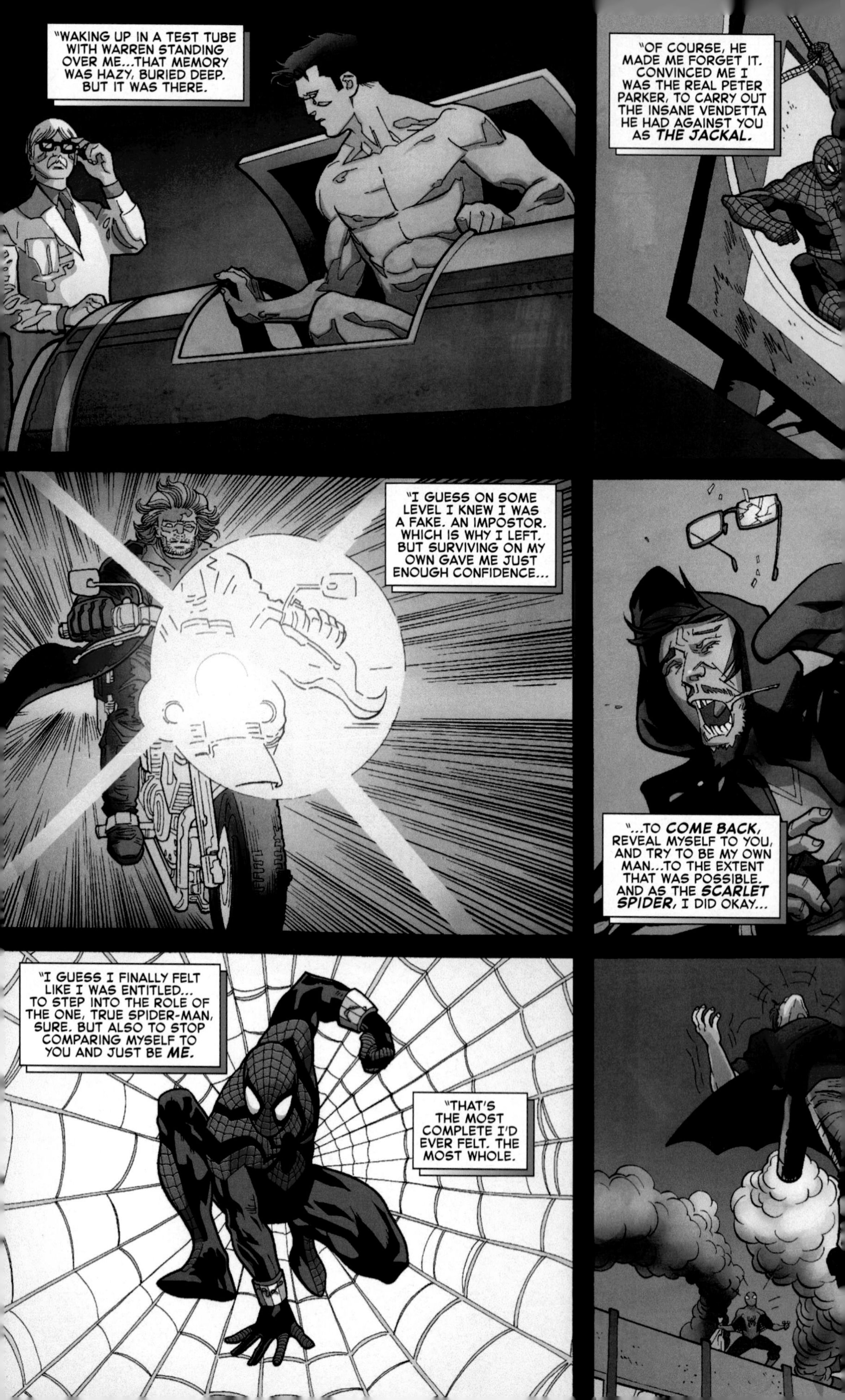

"WAKING UP IN A TEST TUBE WITH WARREN STANDING OVER ME...THAT MEMORY WAS HAZY, BURIED DEEP. BUT IT WAS THERE.
"OF COURSE, HE MADE ME FORGET IT. CONVINCED ME I WAS THE REAL PETER PARKER, TO CARRY OUT THE INSANE VENDETTA HE HAD AGAINST YOU AS THE JACKAL.
"I GUESS ON SOME LEVEL I KNEW I WAS A FAKE. AN IMPOSTOR. WHICH IS WHY I LEFT. BUT SURVIVING ON MY OWN GAVE ME JUST ENOUGH CONFIDENCE...
"...TO COME BACK, REVEAL MYSELF TO YOU, AND TRY TO BE MY OWN MAN...TO THE EXTENT THAT WAS POSSIBLE. AND AS THE SCARLET SPIDER, I DID OKAY...
"I GUESS I FINALLY FELT LIKE I WAS ENTITLED... TO STEP INTO THE ROLE OF THE ONE, TRUE SPIDER-MAN, SURE. BUT ALSO TO STOP COMPARING MYSELF TO YOU AND JUST BE ME.
"THAT'S THE MOST COMPLETE I'D EVER FELT. THE MOST WHOLE.

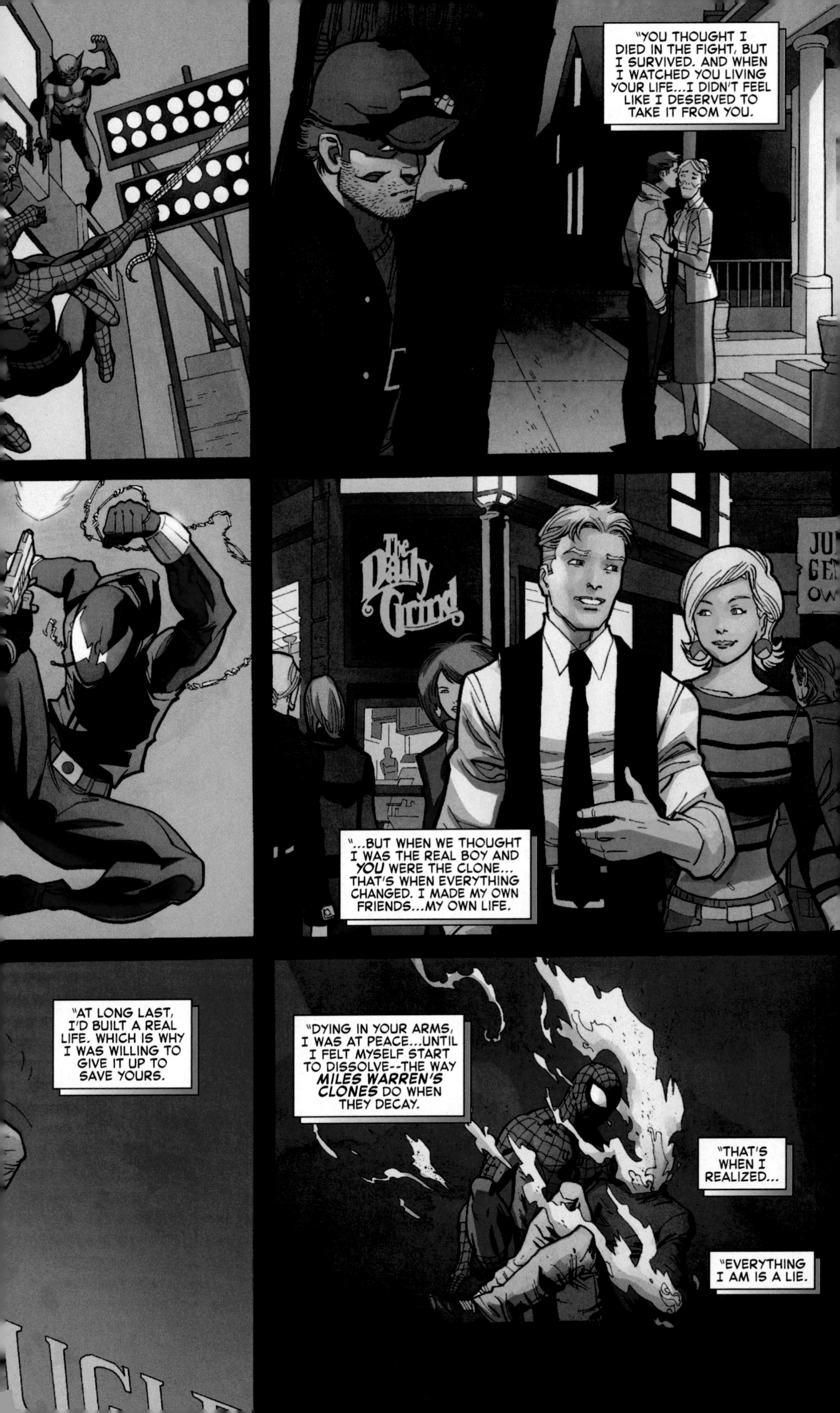
"YOU THOUGHT I DIED IN THE FIGHT, BUT I SURVIVED. AND WHEN I WATCHED YOU LIVING YOUR LIFE...I DIDN'T FEEL LIKE I DESERVED TO TAKE IT FROM YOU.
The Daily Grind
"...BUT WHEN WE THOUGHT I WAS THE REAL BOY AND *YOU* WERE THE CLONE... THAT'S WHEN EVERYTHING CHANGED. I MADE MY OWN FRIENDS...MY OWN LIFE.
"AT LONG LAST, I'D BUILT A REAL LIFE. WHICH IS WHY I WAS WILLING TO GIVE IT UP TO SAVE YOURS.
"DYING IN YOUR ARMS, I WAS AT PEACE...UNTIL I FELT MYSELF START TO DISSOLVE--THE WAY ***MILES WARREN'S CLONES*** DO WHEN THEY DECAY.
"THAT'S WHEN I REALIZED...
"EVERYTHING I AM IS A LIE.

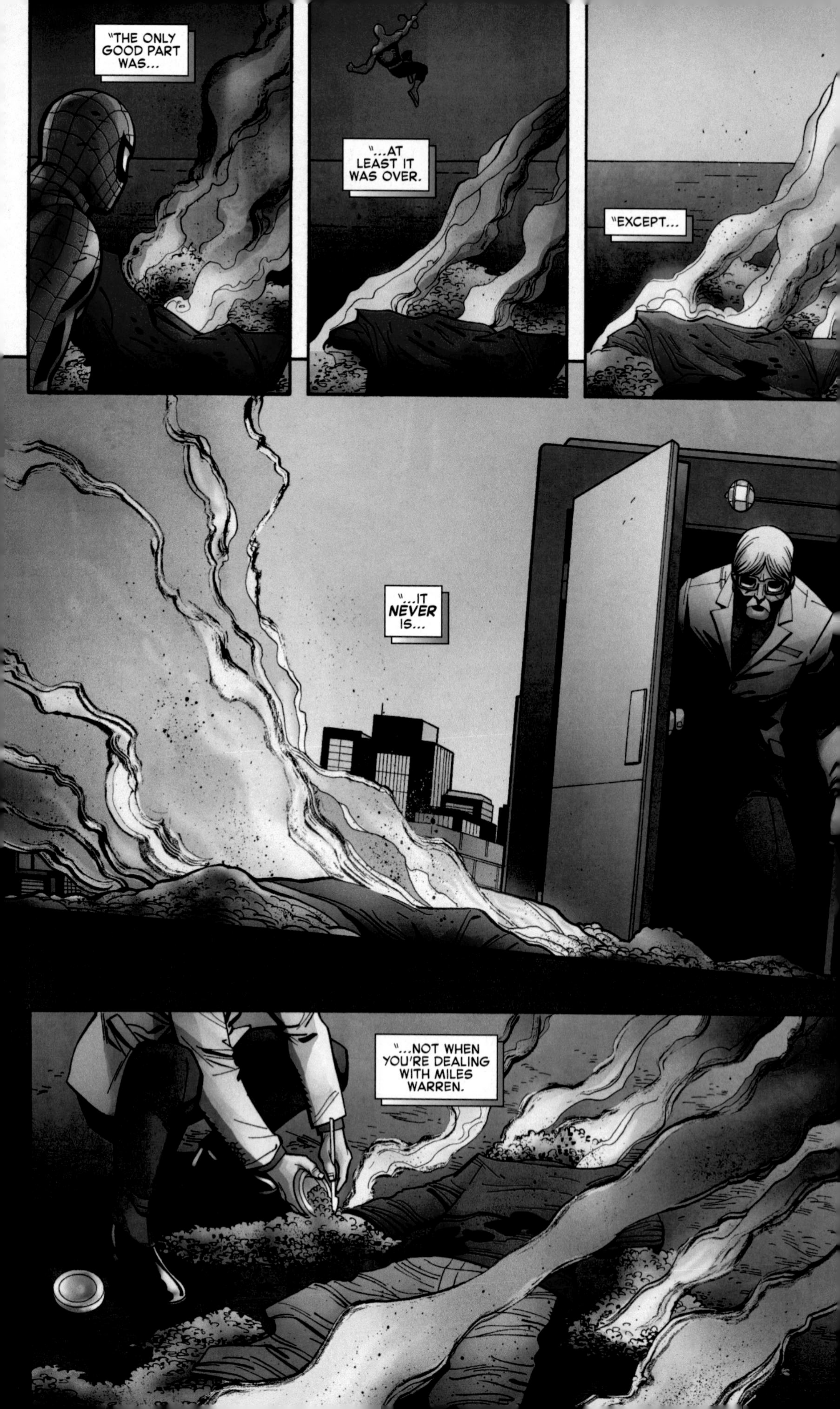
"THE ONLY GOOD PART WAS...
"...AT LEAST IT WAS OVER.
"EXCEPT...
"...IT NEVER IS...
"...NOT WHEN YOU'RE DEALING WITH MILES WARREN.

"NOT WHEN YOU'RE *ME*."

WHUH--

WHERE--

AH, MR. REILLY. PLEASE DON'T BOTHER TRYING TO BREAK LOOSE. I LITERALLY GREW YOU INTO THOSE SHACKLES.

I'VE SPENT YEARS STUDYING PARKER'S UPPER LIMITS. THERE'S ABSOLUTELY NO CHANCE OF YOU GETTING FREE.

H-HOW--? I DIED! DISSOLVED INTO *GOO!*

YOU REMEMBER? BUT THAT'S *WONDERFUL!* IF YOU CAN RETAIN YOUR OLD MEMORIES UP TO THE POINT OF DEATH, MY NEW PROCESS IS A RESOUNDING SUCCESS!

NO MORE IMPLANTING ARTIFICIAL MEMORIES. NO MORE AWKWARD GAPS. MY CLONES WILL BE *INDISTINGUISH-ABLE* FROM THE REAL--!

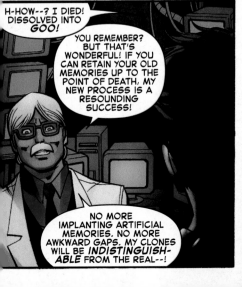

SO, LET'S SEE...

WELL, *THAT'S* A SHAME. THERE'S STILL A PROBLEM WITH CELLULAR DEGRADATION... IT'S AT THE MICROSCOPIC LEVEL NOW, BUT IT'S PROGRESSING QUICKLY.

I SIMPLY MUST CRACK IT. AND DO YOU KNOW WHAT THAT MEANS?

HOW THE HELL SHOULD I KNOW?

FAILING *MARKS,* MR. REILLY. WE'LL HAVE TO REPEAT THE SEMESTER, I'M AFRAID.

ZZRAKK

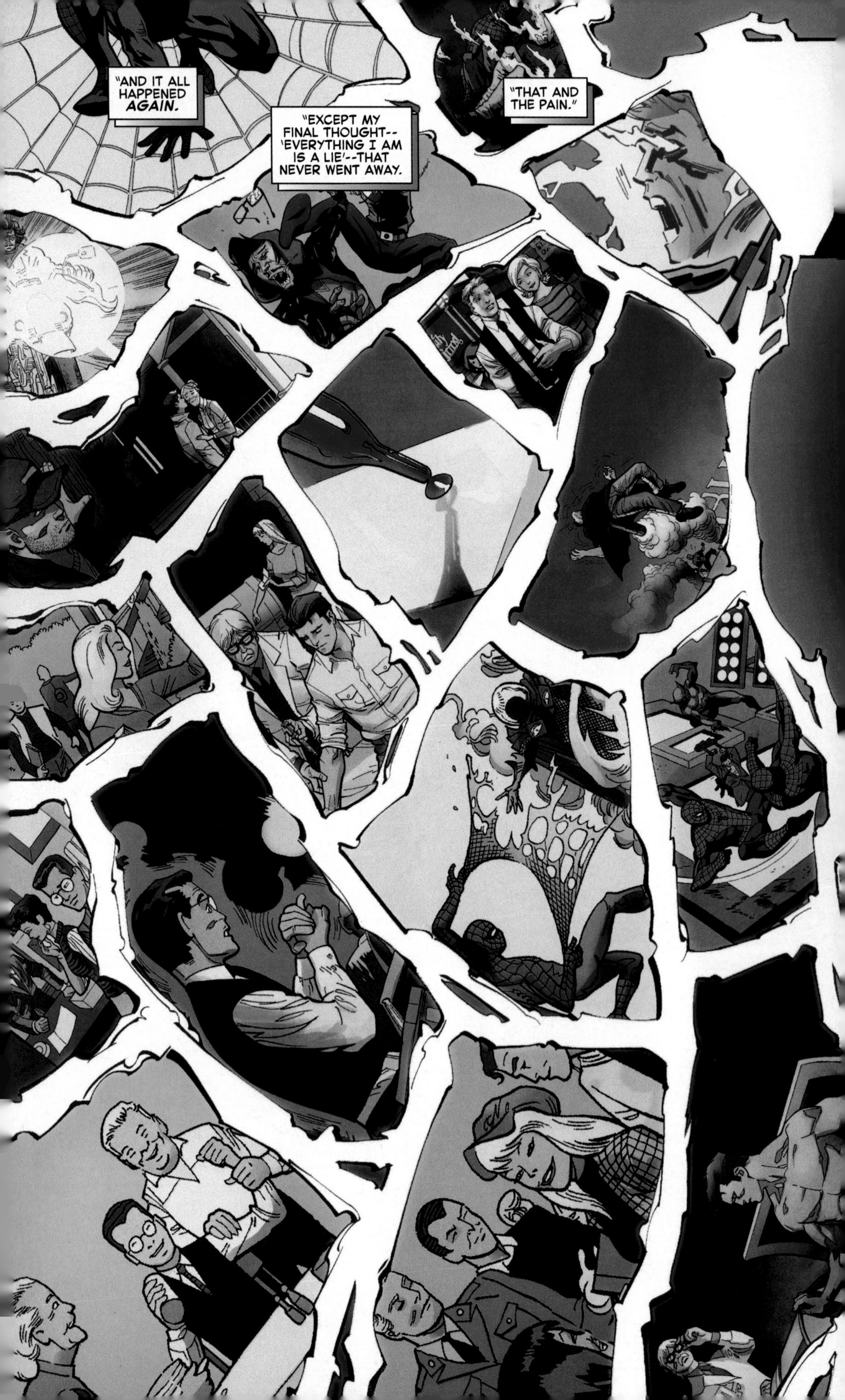
"AND IT ALL HAPPENED AGAIN.
"EXCEPT MY FINAL THOUGHT--'EVERYTHING I AM IS A LIE'--THAT NEVER WENT AWAY.
"THAT AND THE PAIN."

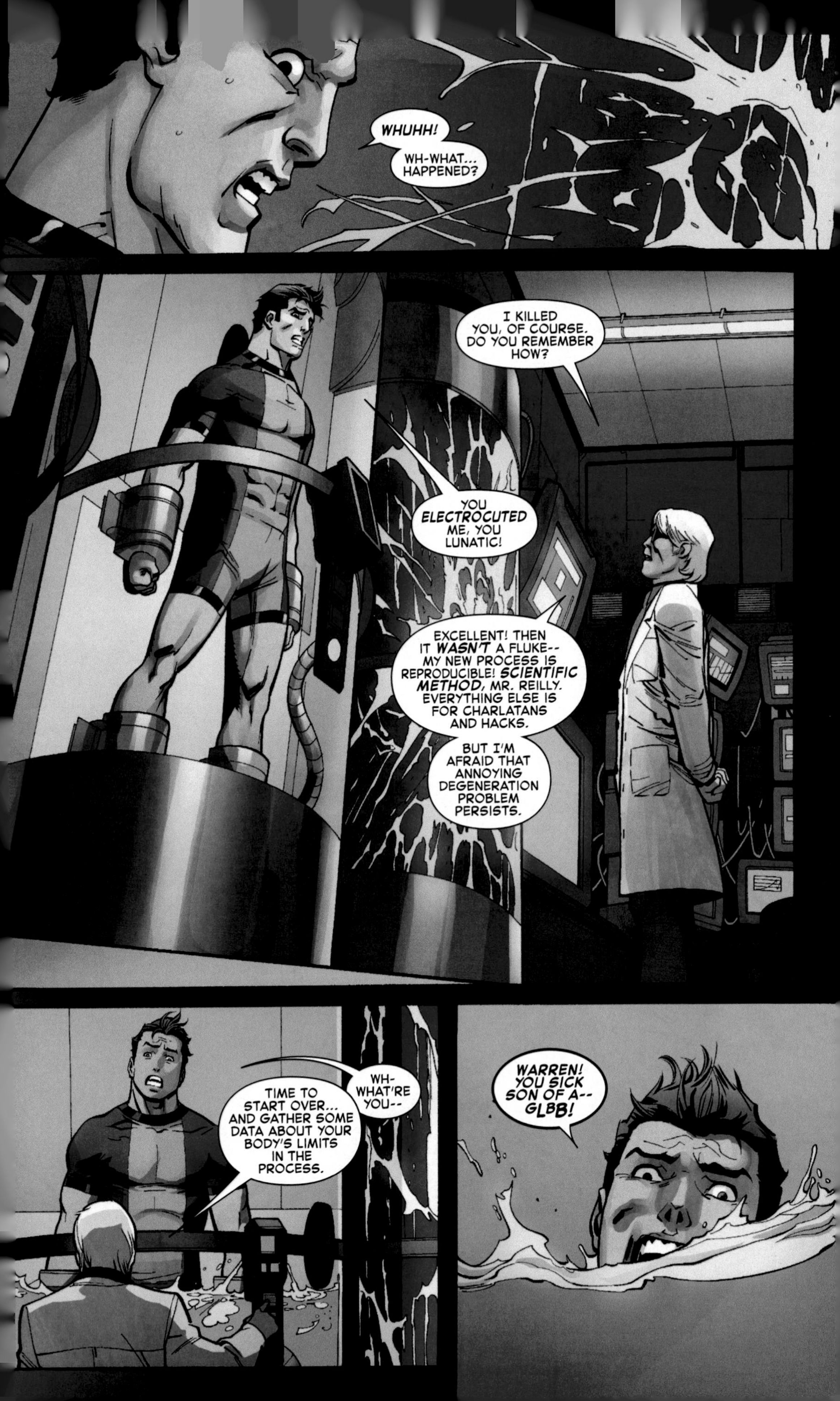
WHUHH!
WH-WHAT... HAPPENED?
I KILLED YOU, OF COURSE. DO YOU REMEMBER HOW?
YOU ELECTROCUTED ME, YOU LUNATIC!
EXCELLENT! THEN IT WASN'T A FLUKE-- MY NEW PROCESS IS REPRODUCIBLE! SCIENTIFIC METHOD, MR. REILLY. EVERYTHING ELSE IS FOR CHARLATANS AND HACKS.
BUT I'M AFRAID THAT ANNOYING DEGENERATION PROBLEM PERSISTS.
TIME TO START OVER... AND GATHER SOME DATA ABOUT YOUR BODY'S LIMITS IN THE PROCESS.
WH-WHAT'RE YOU--
WARREN! YOU SICK SON OF A-- GLBB!

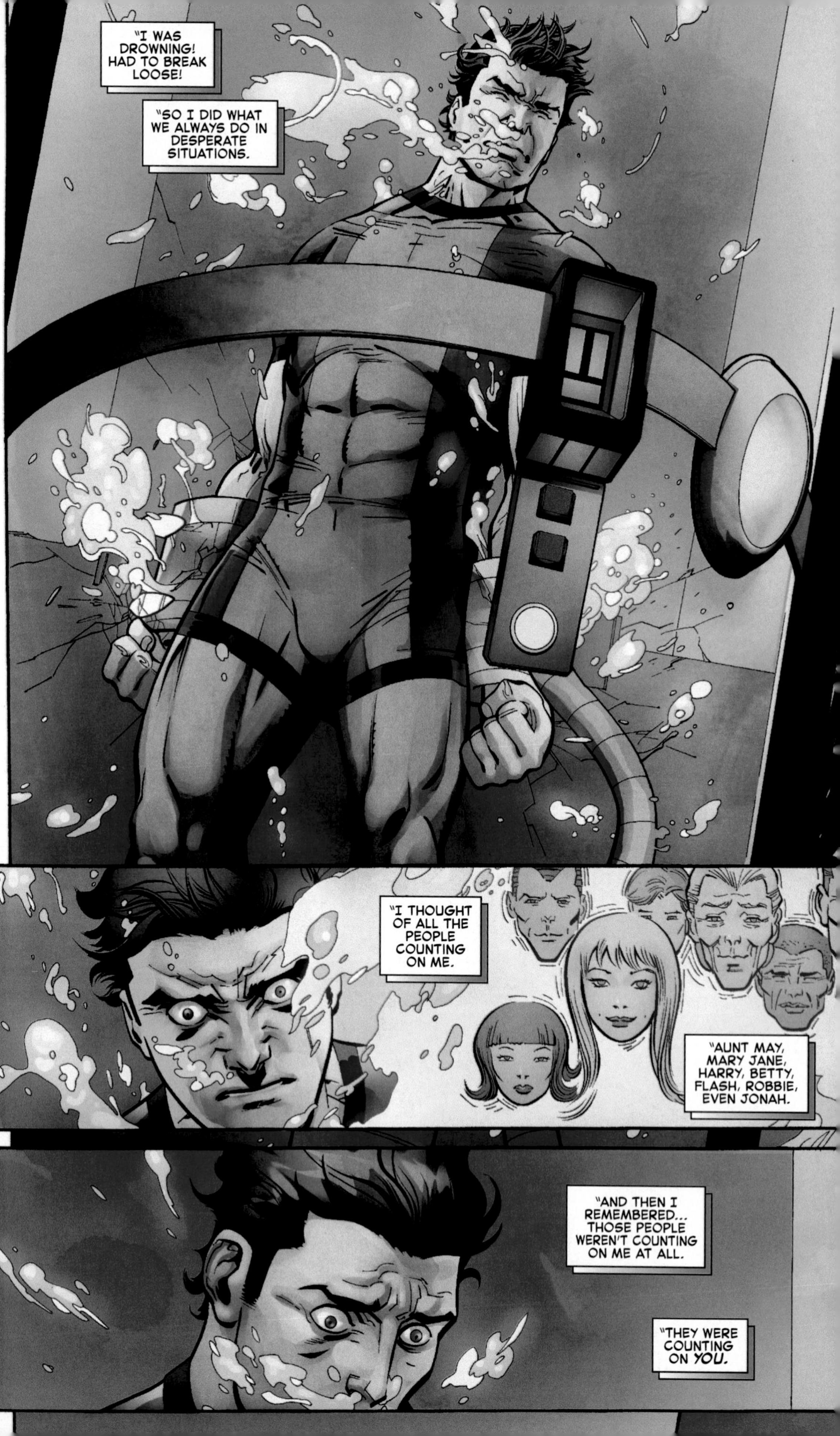
"I WAS DROWNING! HAD TO BREAK LOOSE!
"SO I DID WHAT WE ALWAYS DO IN DESPERATE SITUATIONS.
"I THOUGHT OF ALL THE PEOPLE COUNTING ON ME.
"AUNT MAY, MARY JANE, HARRY, BETTY, FLASH, ROBBIE, EVEN JONAH.
"AND THEN I REMEMBERED... THOSE PEOPLE WEREN'T COUNTING ON ME AT ALL.
"THEY WERE COUNTING ON *YOU*.

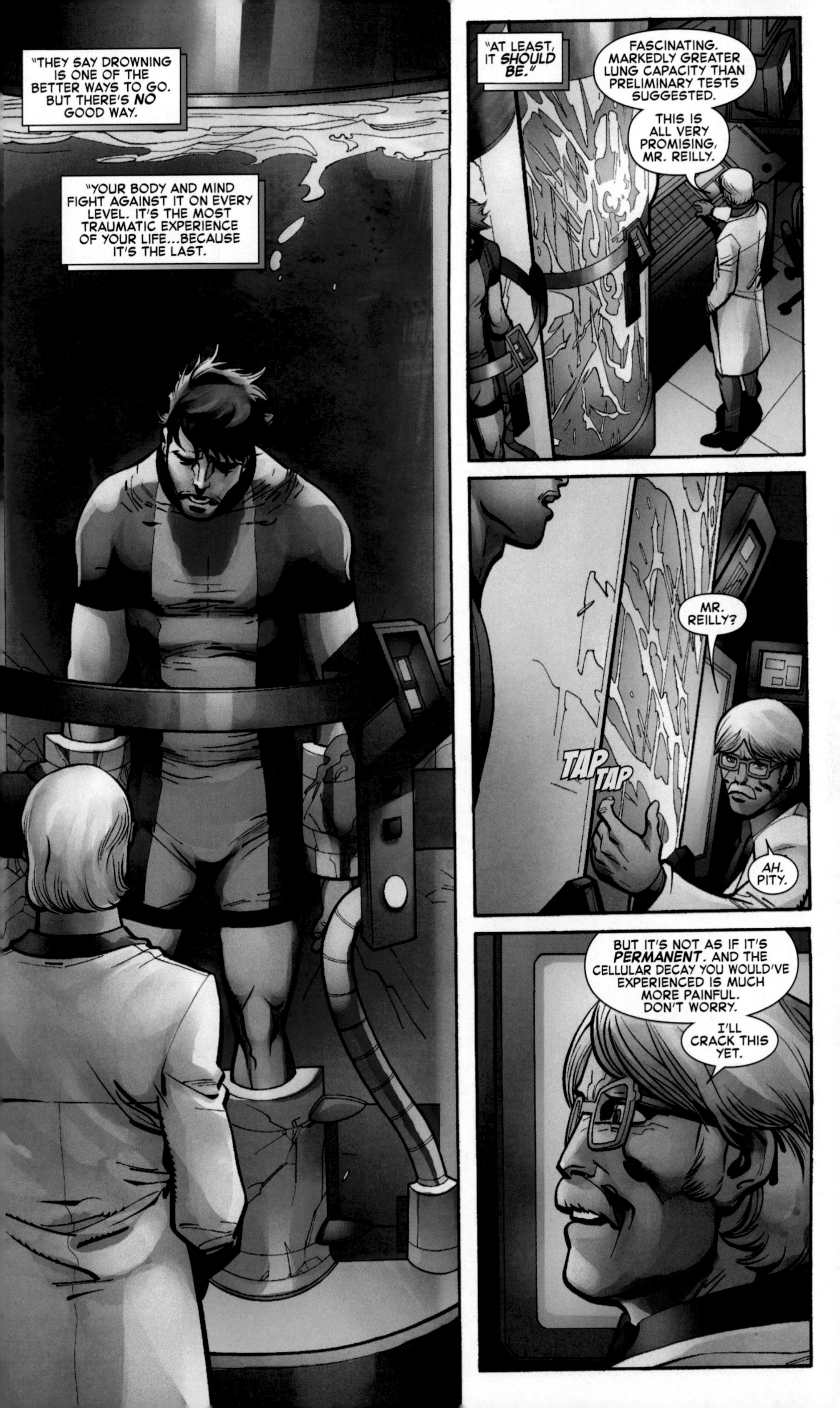

"THEY SAY DROWNING IS ONE OF THE BETTER WAYS TO GO. BUT THERE'S NO GOOD WAY.
"YOUR BODY AND MIND FIGHT AGAINST IT ON EVERY LEVEL. IT'S THE MOST TRAUMATIC EXPERIENCE OF YOUR LIFE...BECAUSE IT'S THE LAST.
"AT LEAST, IT SHOULD BE."
FASCINATING. MARKEDLY GREATER LUNG CAPACITY THAN PRELIMINARY TESTS SUGGESTED.
THIS IS ALL VERY PROMISING, MR. REILLY.
MR. REILLY?
TAP TAP
AH. PITY.
BUT IT'S NOT AS IF IT'S PERMANENT. AND THE CELLULAR DECAY YOU WOULD'VE EXPERIENCED IS MUCH MORE PAINFUL. DON'T WORRY.
I'LL CRACK THIS YET.

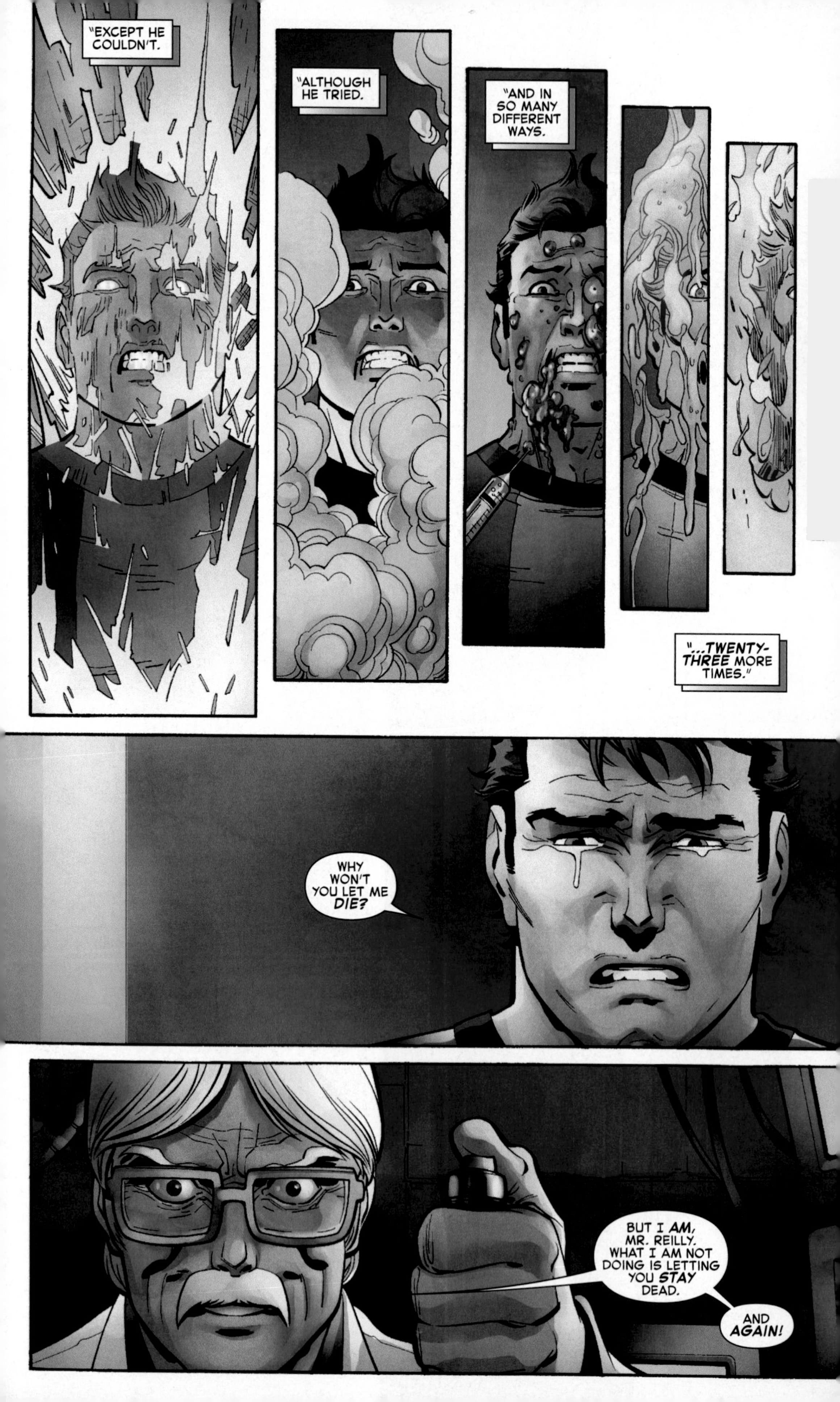
"EXCEPT HE COULDN'T.
"ALTHOUGH HE TRIED.
"AND IN SO MANY DIFFERENT WAYS.
"...TWENTY-THREE MORE TIMES."
WHY WON'T YOU LET ME DIE?
BUT I AM, MR. REILLY. WHAT I AM NOT DOING IS LETTING YOU STAY DEAD.
AND AGAIN!

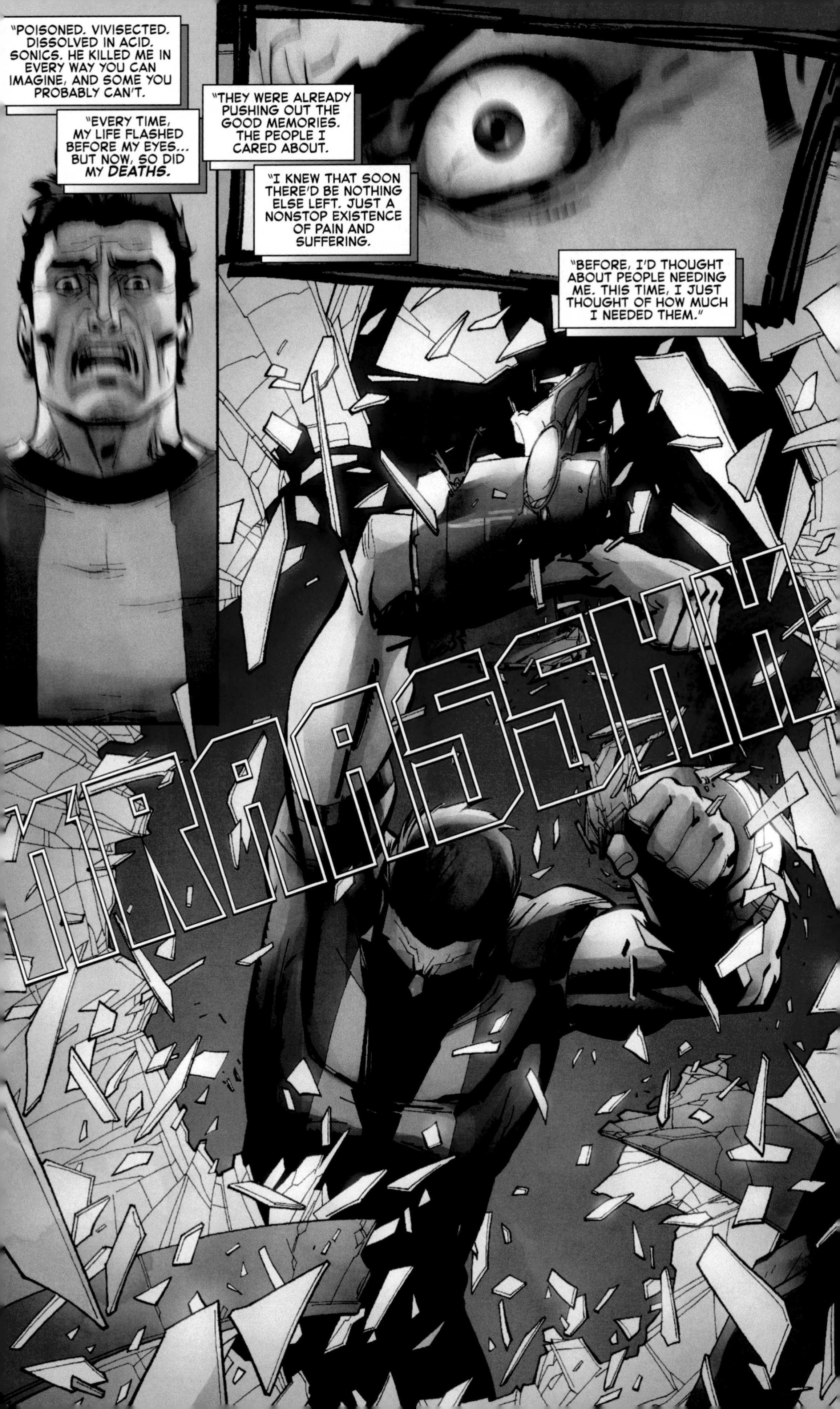
"POISONED. VIVISECTED. DISSOLVED IN ACID. SONICS. HE KILLED ME IN EVERY WAY YOU CAN IMAGINE, AND SOME YOU PROBABLY CAN'T.
"EVERY TIME, MY LIFE FLASHED BEFORE MY EYES... BUT NOW, SO DID MY *DEATHS.*
"THEY WERE ALREADY PUSHING OUT THE GOOD MEMORIES. THE PEOPLE I CARED ABOUT.
"I KNEW THAT SOON THERE'D BE NOTHING ELSE LEFT. JUST A NONSTOP EXISTENCE OF PAIN AND SUFFERING.
"BEFORE, I'D THOUGHT ABOUT PEOPLE NEEDING ME. THIS TIME, I JUST THOUGHT OF HOW MUCH I NEEDED THEM."
KRASSHH

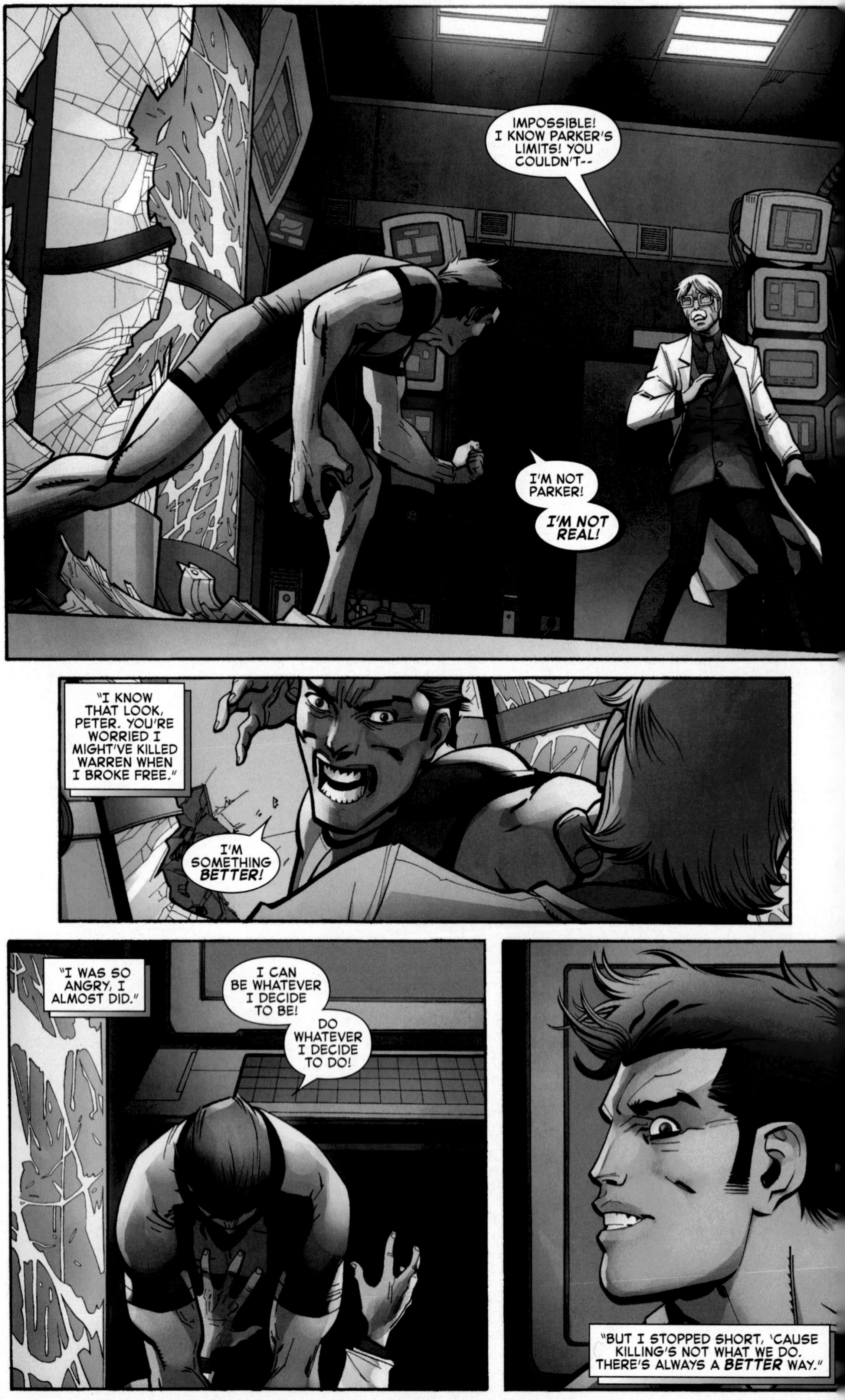
IMPOSSIBLE! I KNOW PARKER'S LIMITS! YOU COULDN'T--
I'M NOT PARKER!
I'M NOT REAL!
"I KNOW THAT LOOK, PETER. YOU'RE WORRIED I MIGHT'VE KILLED WARREN WHEN I BROKE FREE."
I'M SOMETHING BETTER!
"I WAS SO ANGRY, I ALMOST DID."
I CAN BE WHATEVER I DECIDE TO BE!
DO WHATEVER I DECIDE TO DO!
"BUT I STOPPED SHORT, 'CAUSE KILLING'S NOT WHAT WE DO. THERE'S ALWAYS A BETTER WAY."

HELLO, MILES. WELCOME BACK TO THE LAND OF THE LIVING. YEP--YOU'RE IN THE CLONE CLUB NOW.

YOU'LL BE GLAD TO HEAR I FIXED THE PROBLEM YOU COULDN'T. FOUND A WAY TO STOP THE CELLULAR DEGRADATION.

NOT PERMANENTLY. YOU HAVE TO TAKE THIS PILL EVERY DAY. IF YOU MISBEHAVE, I'LL STOP GIVING IT TO YOU, AND...WELL, I DON'T HAVE TO TELL YOU THAT WOULD BE BAD.

YOU'RE JUST TRYING TO MANIPULATE ME. I-I DON'T BELIEVE YOU.

THAT'S OKAY.

HE DOES.

THEY ALL DO.

TH-THE REAL ME... WHICH ONE IS--

THE ORIGINAL? I DON'T KNOW. IN FACT, I'M PRETTY SURE I'VE FORGOTTEN.

IF YOU THINK IT *IS* YOU? HEY, DON'T TAKE THE PILL. BUT IF YOU'RE WRONG, WELL...

"THERE'S ALWAYS A BETTER WAY."

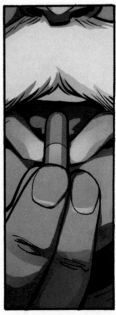

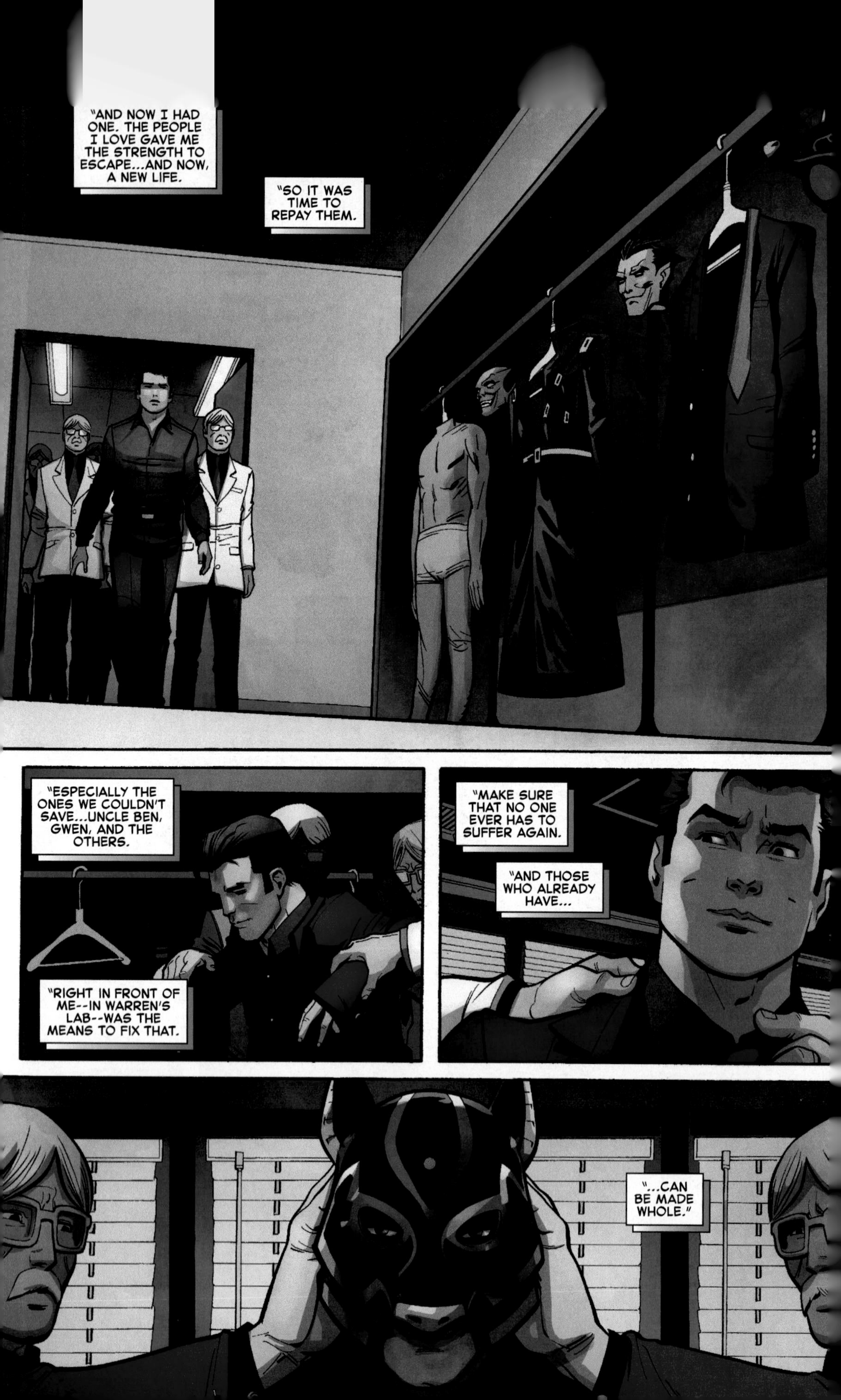
"AND NOW I HAD ONE. THE PEOPLE I LOVE GAVE ME THE STRENGTH TO ESCAPE...AND NOW, A NEW LIFE.
"SO IT WAS TIME TO REPAY THEM.
"ESPECIALLY THE ONES WE COULDN'T SAVE...UNCLE BEN, GWEN, AND THE OTHERS.
"RIGHT IN FRONT OF ME--IN WARREN'S LAB--WAS THE MEANS TO FIX THAT.
"MAKE SURE THAT NO ONE EVER HAS TO SUFFER AGAIN.
"AND THOSE WHO ALREADY HAVE...
"...CAN BE MADE WHOLE."

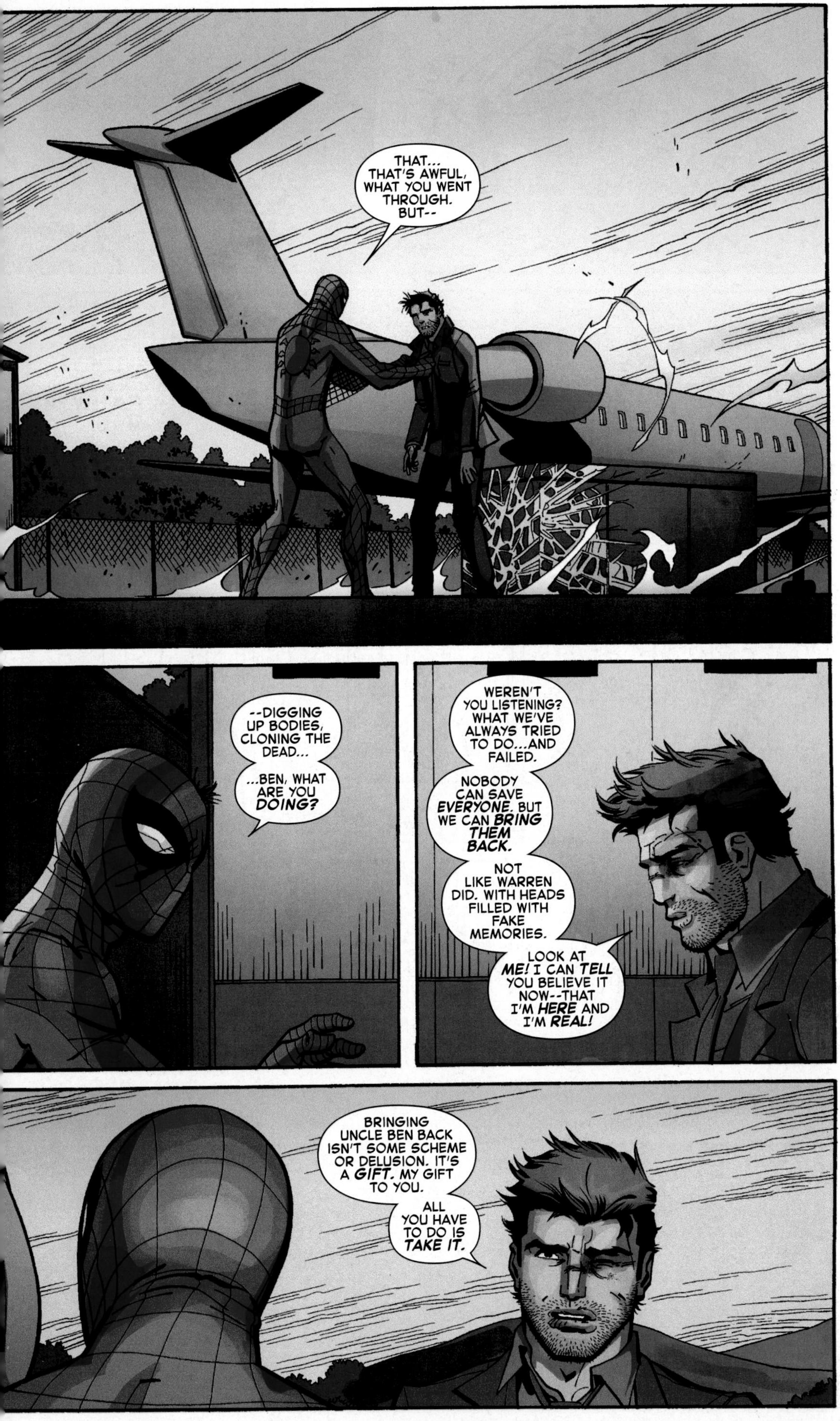

THAT... THAT'S AWFUL, WHAT YOU WENT THROUGH. BUT--
--DIGGING UP BODIES, CLONING THE DEAD...
...BEN, WHAT ARE YOU **DOING?**
WEREN'T YOU LISTENING? WHAT WE'VE ALWAYS TRIED TO DO...AND FAILED.
NOBODY CAN SAVE **EVERYONE.** BUT WE CAN **BRING THEM BACK.**
NOT LIKE WARREN DID. WITH HEADS FILLED WITH FAKE MEMORIES.
LOOK AT **ME!** I CAN **TELL** YOU BELIEVE IT NOW--THAT I'M **HERE** AND I'M **REAL!**
BRINGING UNCLE BEN BACK ISN'T SOME SCHEME OR DELUSION. IT'S A **GIFT.** MY GIFT TO YOU.
ALL YOU HAVE TO DO IS **TAKE IT.**

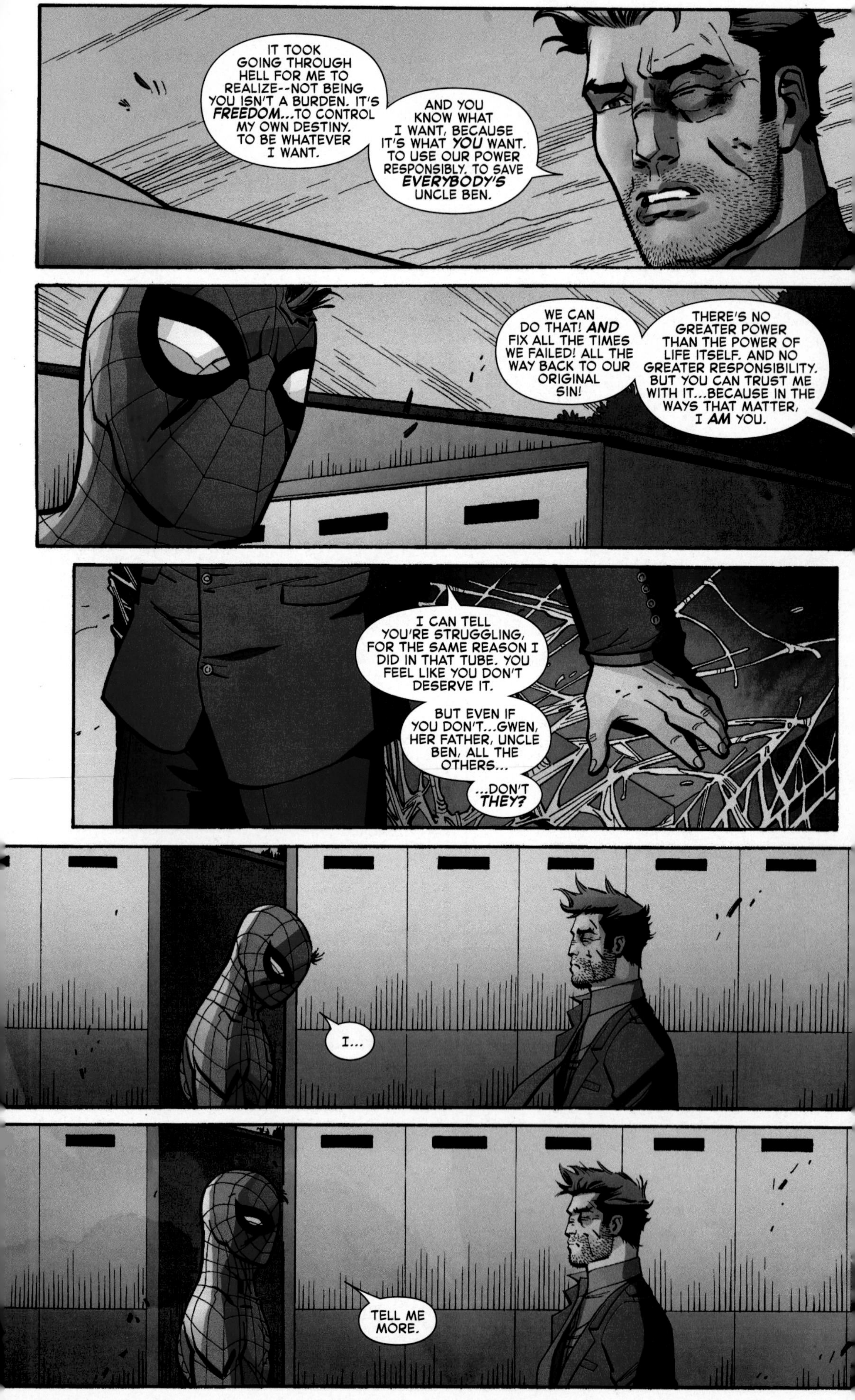
IT TOOK GOING THROUGH HELL FOR ME TO REALIZE--NOT BEING YOU ISN'T A BURDEN. IT'S FREEDOM...TO CONTROL MY OWN DESTINY. TO BE WHATEVER I WANT.
AND YOU KNOW WHAT I WANT, BECAUSE IT'S WHAT YOU WANT. TO USE OUR POWER RESPONSIBLY. TO SAVE EVERYBODY'S UNCLE BEN.
WE CAN DO THAT! AND FIX ALL THE TIMES WE FAILED! ALL THE WAY BACK TO OUR ORIGINAL SIN!
THERE'S NO GREATER POWER THAN THE POWER OF LIFE ITSELF. AND NO GREATER RESPONSIBILITY. BUT YOU CAN TRUST ME WITH IT...BECAUSE IN THE WAYS THAT MATTER, I AM YOU.
I CAN TELL YOU'RE STRUGGLING, FOR THE SAME REASON I DID IN THAT TUBE. YOU FEEL LIKE YOU DON'T DESERVE IT.
BUT EVEN IF YOU DON'T...GWEN, HER FATHER, UNCLE BEN, ALL THE OTHERS...
...DON'T THEY?
I...
TELL ME MORE.

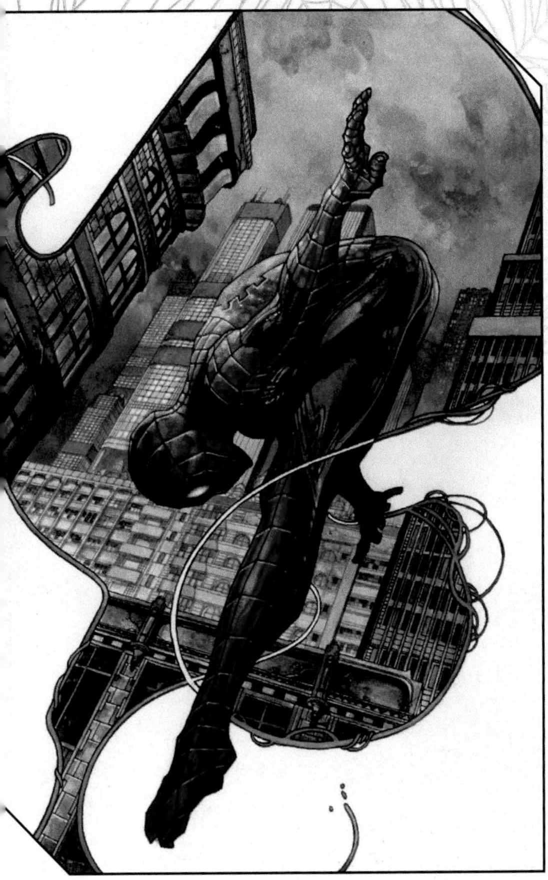

#20 VARIANT BY **SIMONE BIANCHI**

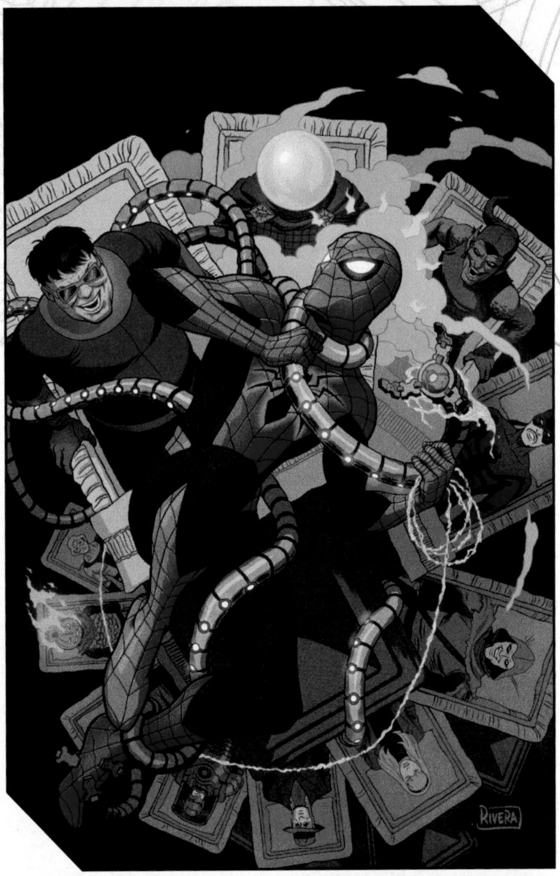
RIVERA

#21 VARIANT BY **PAOLO RIVERA**

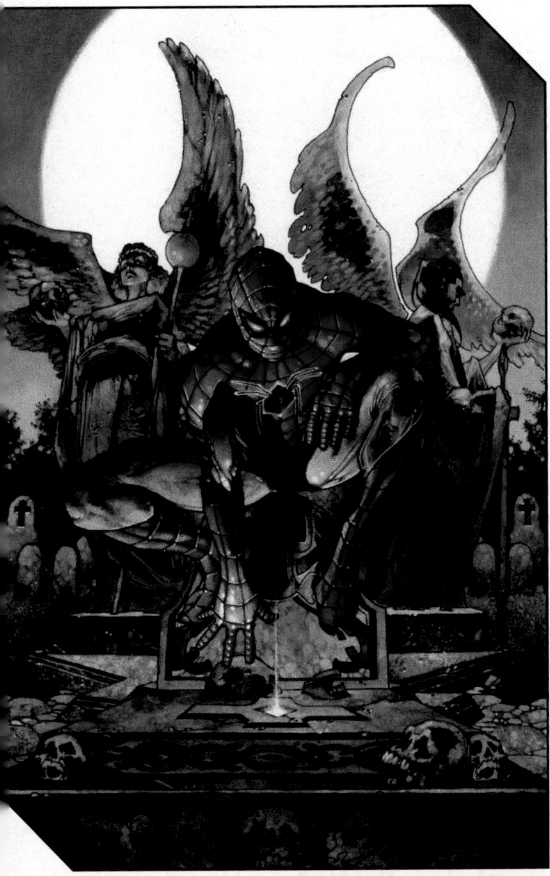

#22 VARIANT BY **SIMONE BIANCHI**

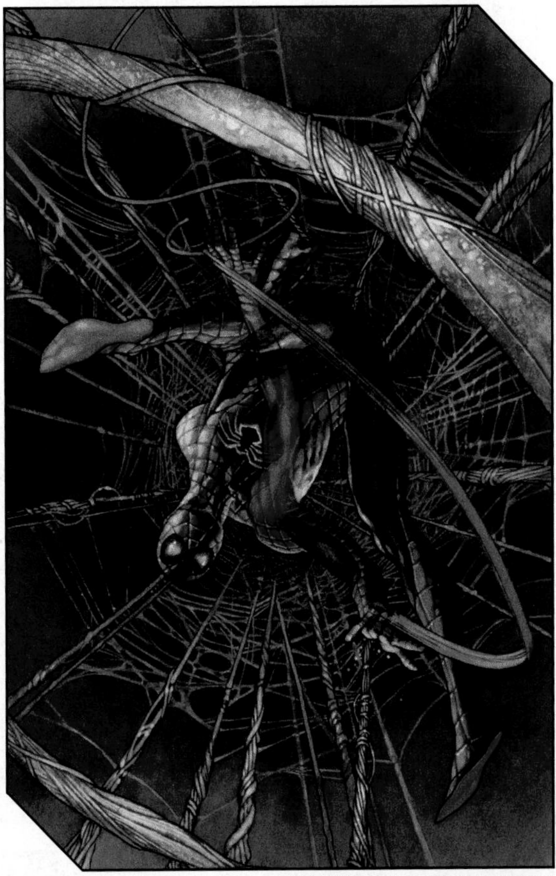

#23 VARIANT BY **SIMONE BIANCHI**

23

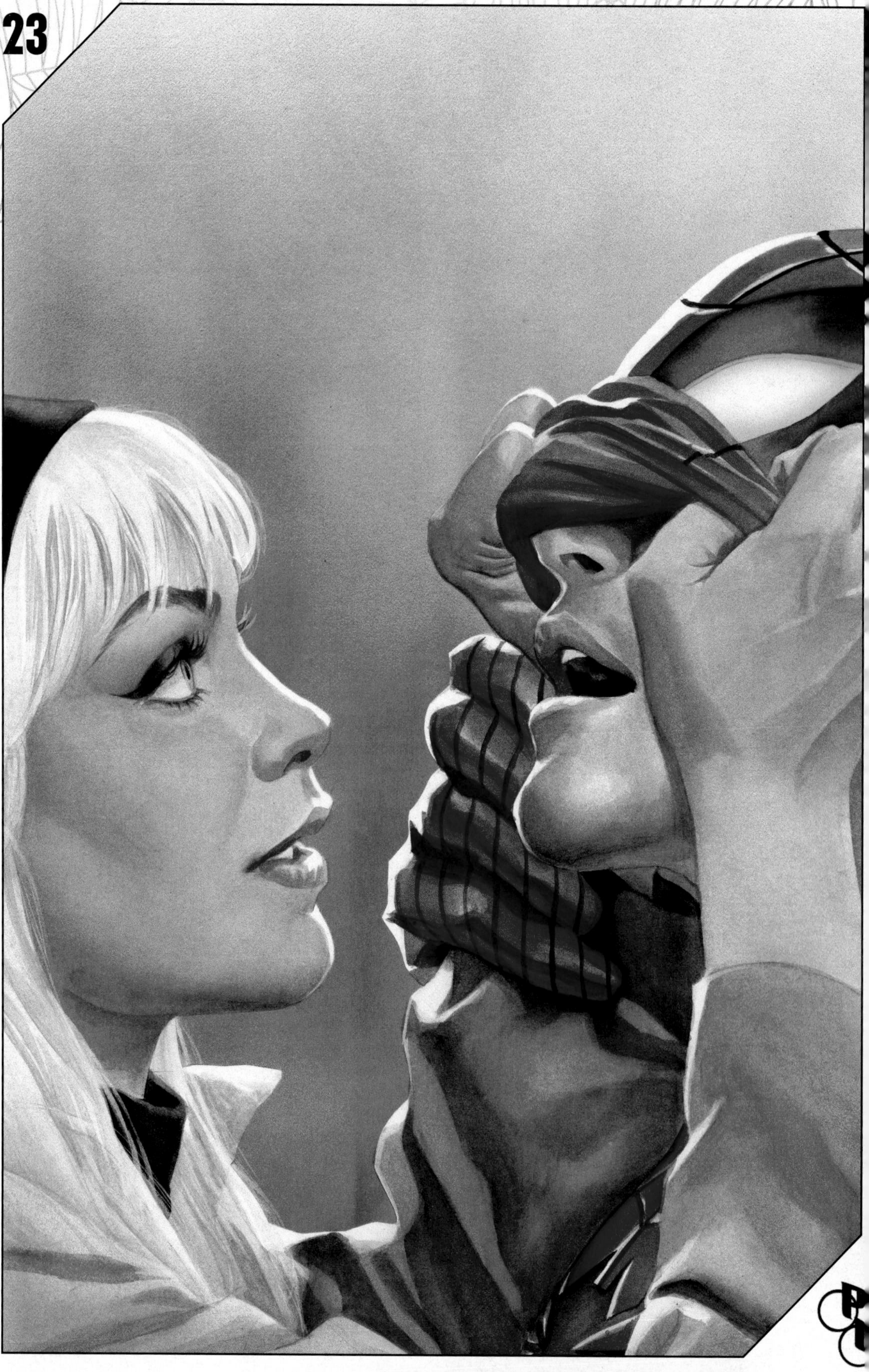

"THE MOMENT YOU KNOW"

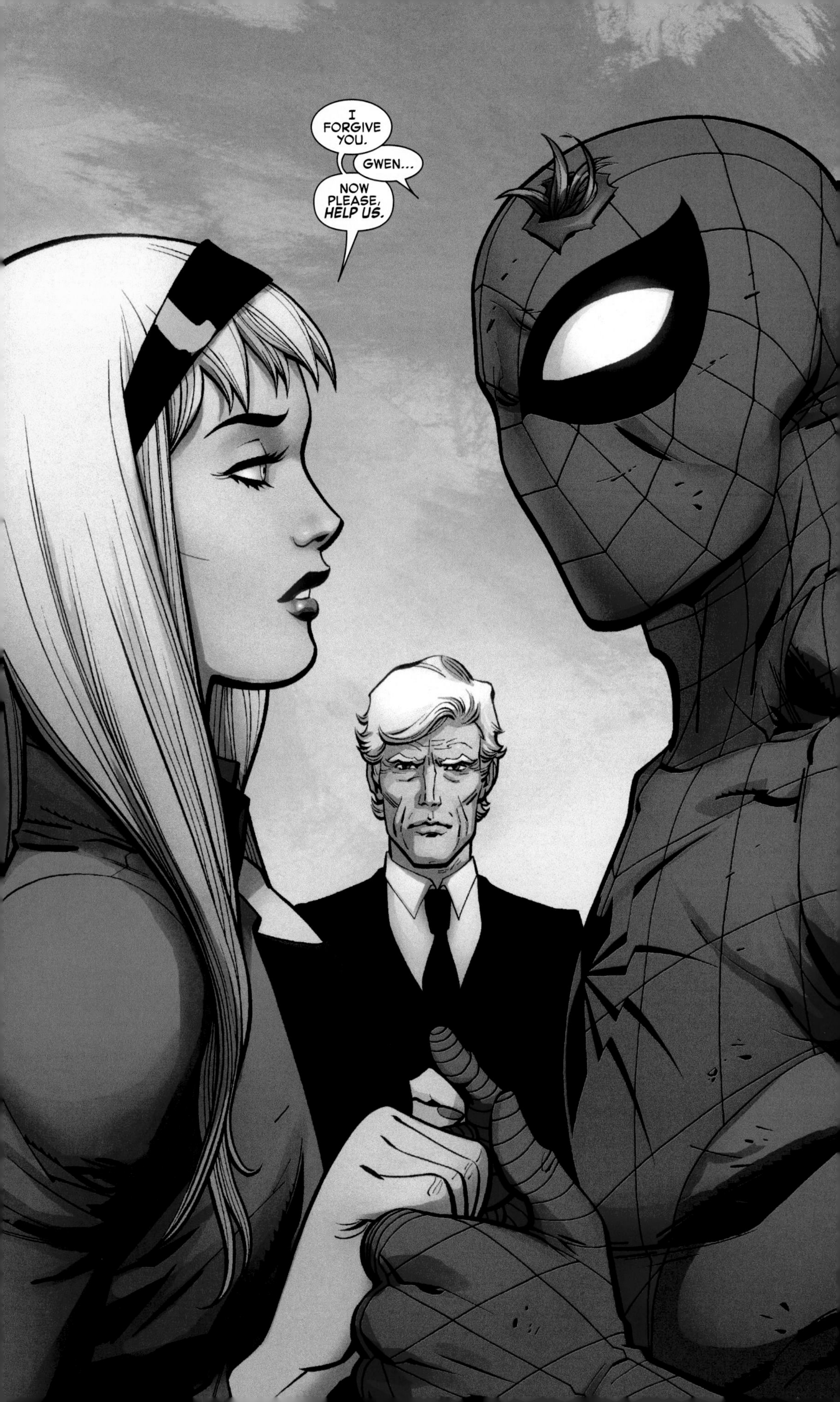
I FORGIVE YOU.
GWEN...
NOW PLEASE, HELP US.

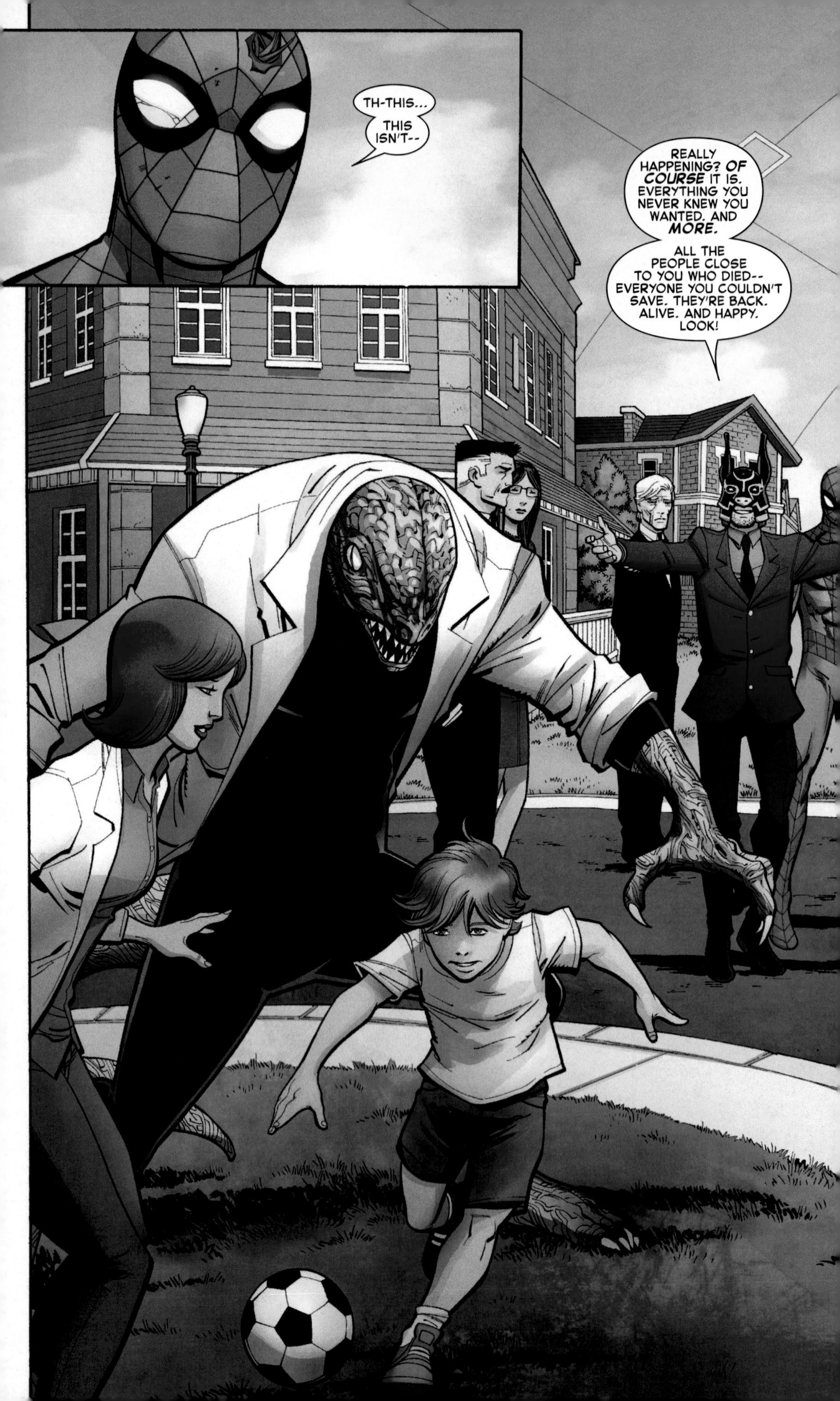
TH-THIS... THIS ISN'T--
REALLY HAPPENING? OF COURSE IT IS. EVERYTHING YOU NEVER KNEW YOU WANTED. AND MORE.
ALL THE PEOPLE CLOSE TO YOU WHO DIED-- EVERYONE YOU COULDN'T SAVE. THEY'RE BACK. ALIVE. AND HAPPY. LOOK!

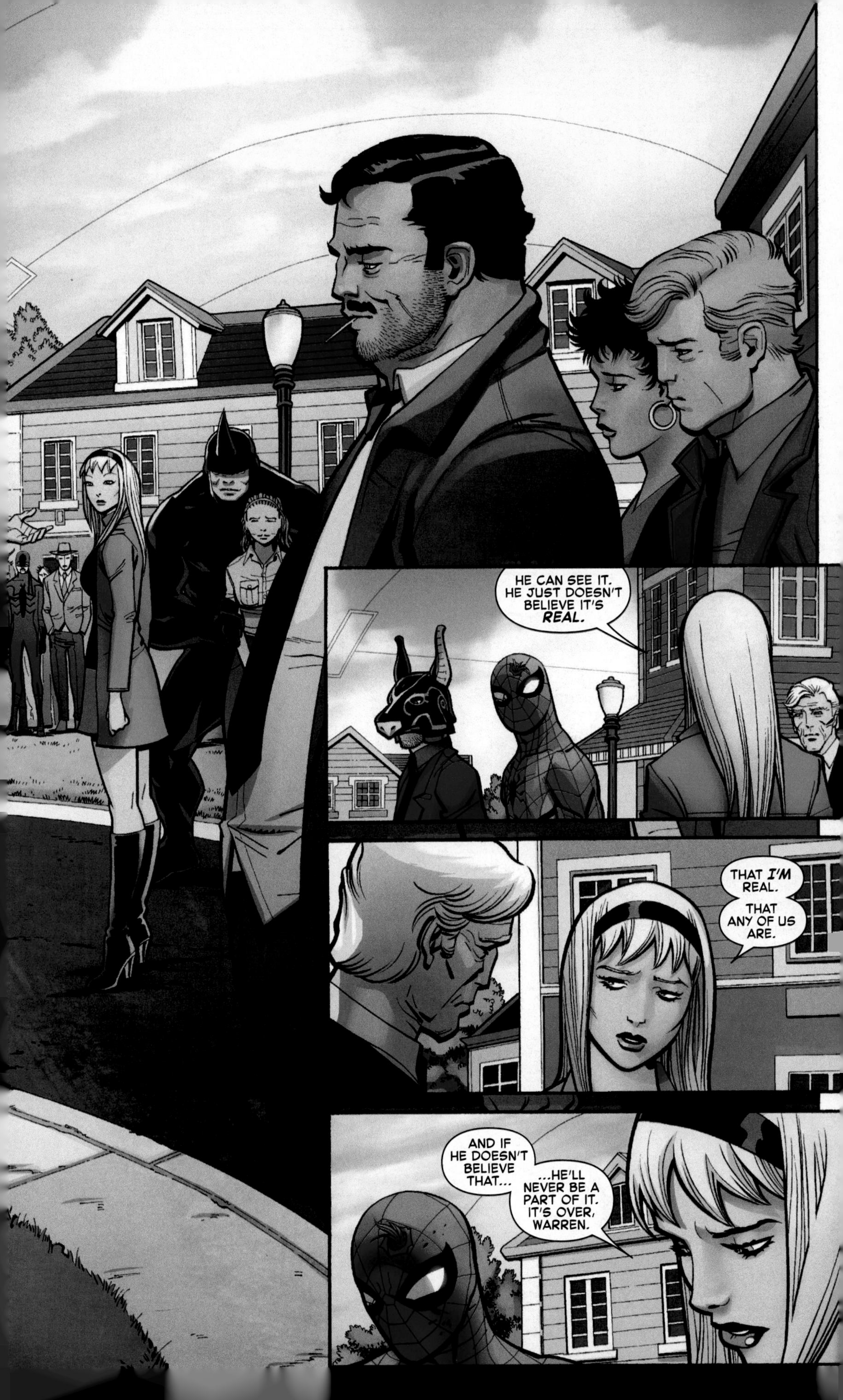

HE CAN SEE IT. HE JUST DOESN'T BELIEVE IT'S REAL.
THAT I'M REAL.
THAT ANY OF US ARE.
AND IF HE DOESN'T BELIEVE THAT...
...HE'LL NEVER BE A PART OF IT. IT'S OVER, WARREN.

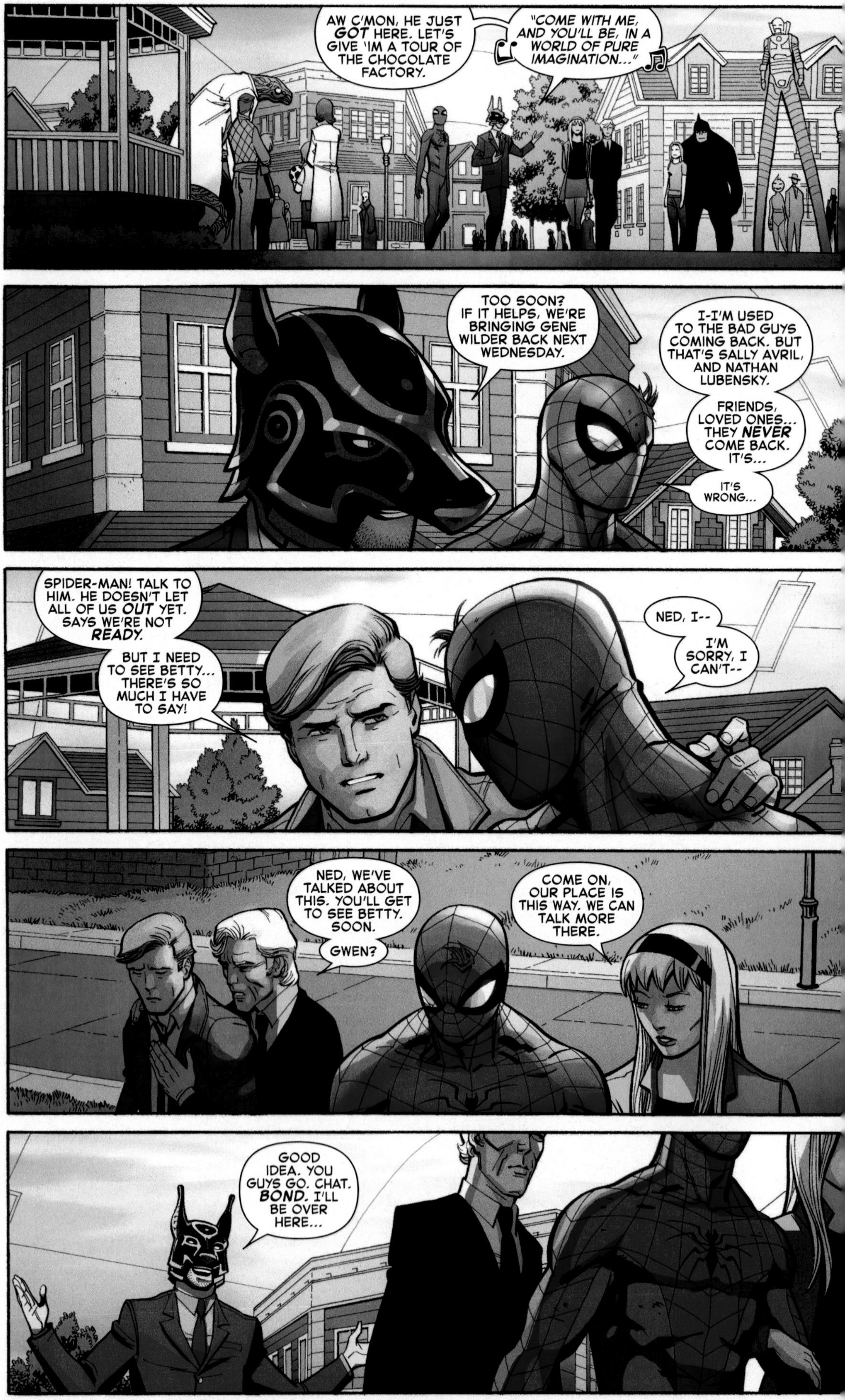

AW C'MON, HE JUST GOT HERE. LET'S GIVE 'IM A TOUR OF THE CHOCOLATE FACTORY.
"COME WITH ME, AND YOU'LL BE, IN A WORLD OF PURE IMAGINATION..."
TOO SOON? IF IT HELPS, WE'RE BRINGING GENE WILDER BACK NEXT WEDNESDAY.
I-I'M USED TO THE BAD GUYS COMING BACK. BUT THAT'S SALLY AVRIL, AND NATHAN LUBENSKY.
FRIENDS, LOVED ONES... THEY NEVER COME BACK. IT'S...
IT'S WRONG...
SPIDER-MAN! TALK TO HIM. HE DOESN'T LET ALL OF US OUT YET. SAYS WE'RE NOT READY.
BUT I NEED TO SEE BETTY... THERE'S SO MUCH I HAVE TO SAY!
NED, I--
I'M SORRY, I CAN'T--
NED, WE'VE TALKED ABOUT THIS. YOU'LL GET TO SEE BETTY. SOON.
GWEN?
COME ON, OUR PLACE IS THIS WAY. WE CAN TALK MORE THERE.
GOOD IDEA. YOU GUYS GO. CHAT. BOND. I'LL BE OVER HERE...

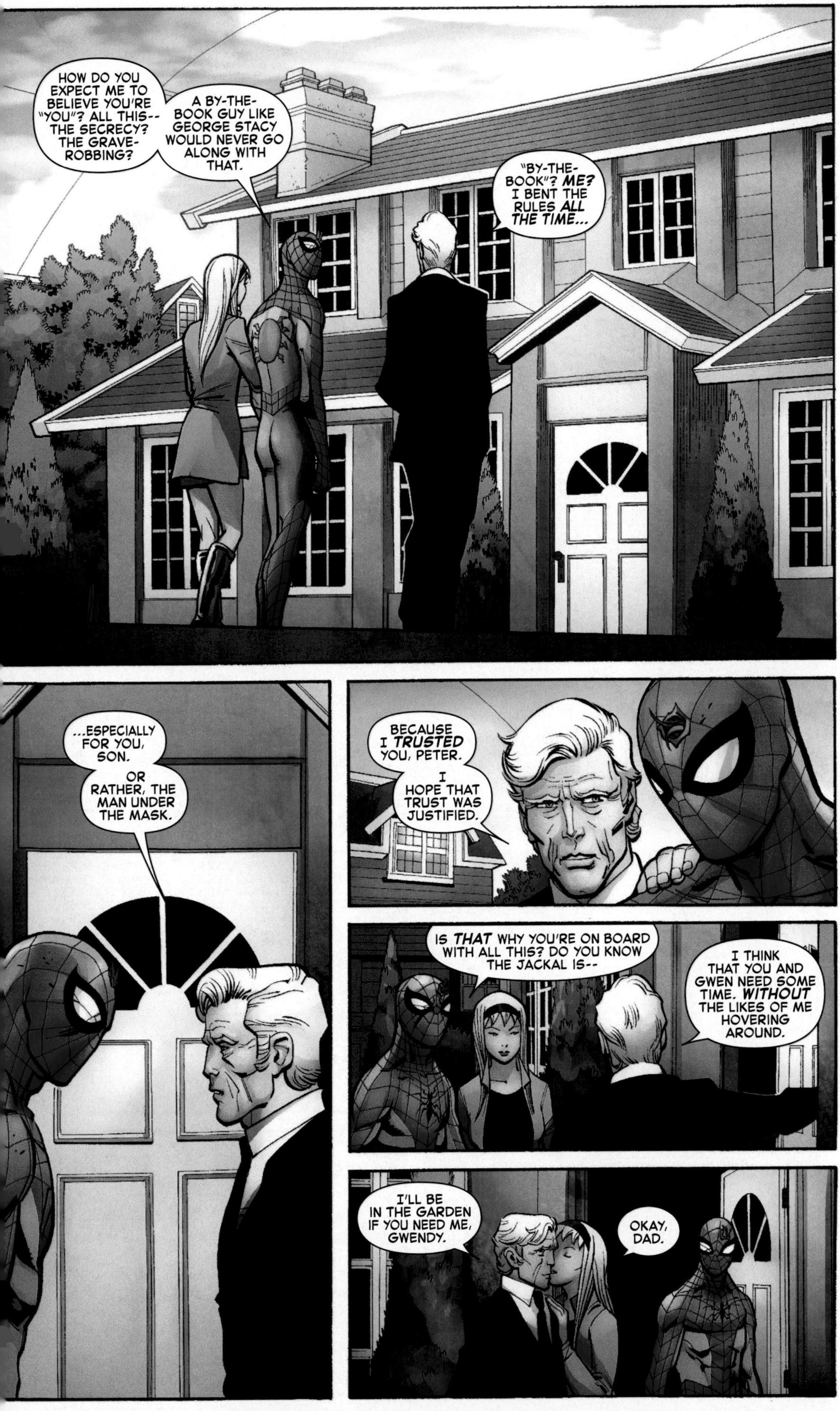

HOW DO YOU EXPECT ME TO BELIEVE YOU'RE "YOU"? ALL THIS-- THE SECRECY? THE GRAVE-ROBBING?
A BY-THE-BOOK GUY LIKE GEORGE STACY WOULD NEVER GO ALONG WITH THAT.
"BY-THE-BOOK"? ME? I BENT THE RULES ALL THE TIME...
...ESPECIALLY FOR YOU, SON.
OR RATHER, THE MAN UNDER THE MASK.
BECAUSE I TRUSTED YOU, PETER.
I HOPE THAT TRUST WAS JUSTIFIED.
IS THAT WHY YOU'RE ON BOARD WITH ALL THIS? DO YOU KNOW THE JACKAL IS--
I THINK THAT YOU AND GWEN NEED SOME TIME. WITHOUT THE LIKES OF ME HOVERING AROUND.
I'LL BE IN THE GARDEN IF YOU NEED ME, GWENDY.
OKAY, DAD.

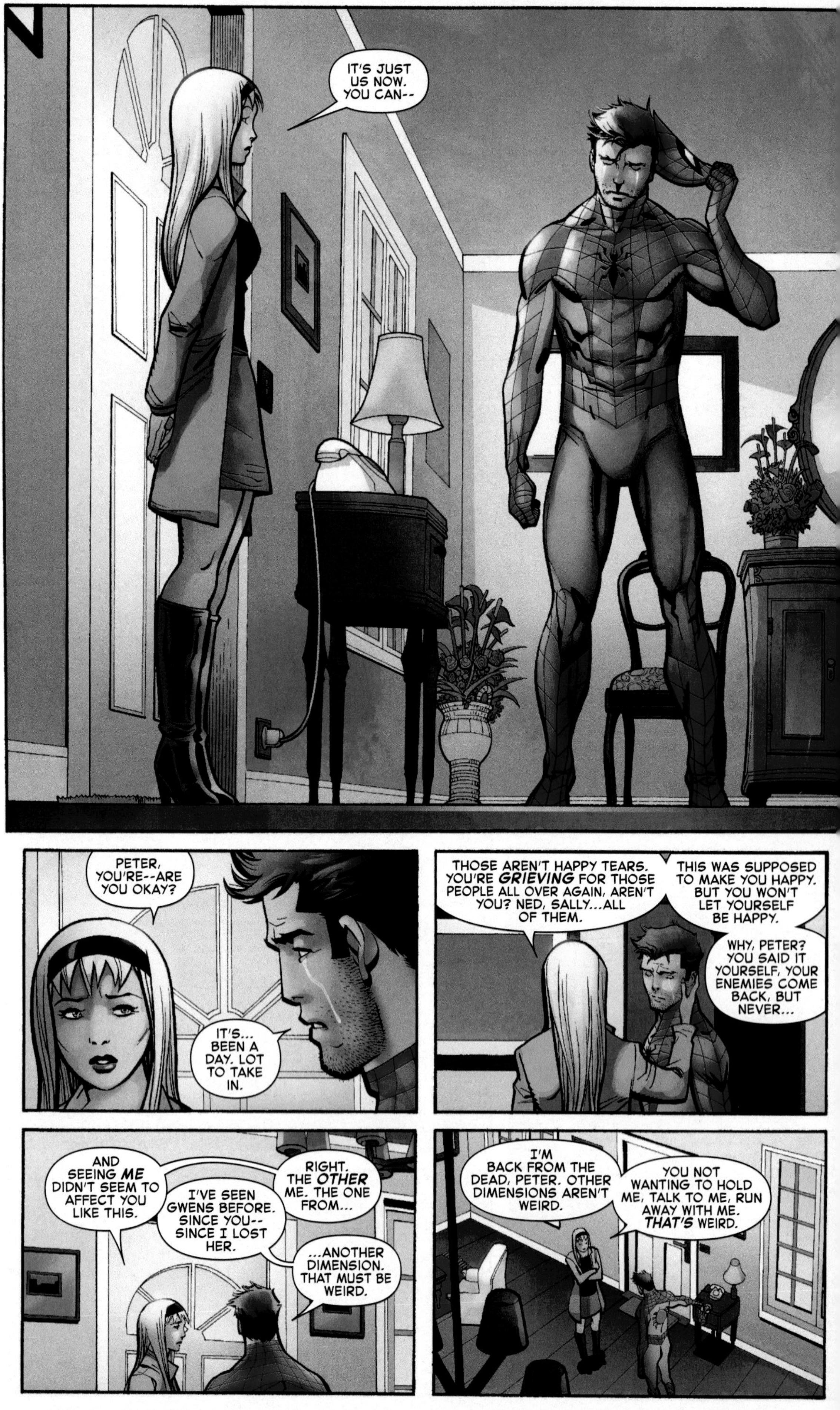
IT'S JUST US NOW. YOU CAN--
PETER, YOU'RE--ARE YOU OKAY?
IT'S... BEEN A DAY. LOT TO TAKE IN.
THOSE AREN'T HAPPY TEARS. YOU'RE GRIEVING FOR THOSE PEOPLE ALL OVER AGAIN, AREN'T YOU? NED, SALLY...ALL OF THEM.
THIS WAS SUPPOSED TO MAKE YOU HAPPY. BUT YOU WON'T LET YOURSELF BE HAPPY.
WHY, PETER? YOU SAID IT YOURSELF, YOUR ENEMIES COME BACK, BUT NEVER...
AND SEEING ME DIDN'T SEEM TO AFFECT YOU LIKE THIS.
I'VE SEEN GWENS BEFORE. SINCE YOU--SINCE I LOST HER.
RIGHT. THE OTHER ME. THE ONE FROM...
...ANOTHER DIMENSION. THAT MUST BE WEIRD.
I'M BACK FROM THE DEAD, PETER. OTHER DIMENSIONS AREN'T WEIRD.
YOU NOT WANTING TO HOLD ME, TALK TO ME, RUN AWAY WITH ME. THAT'S WEIRD.

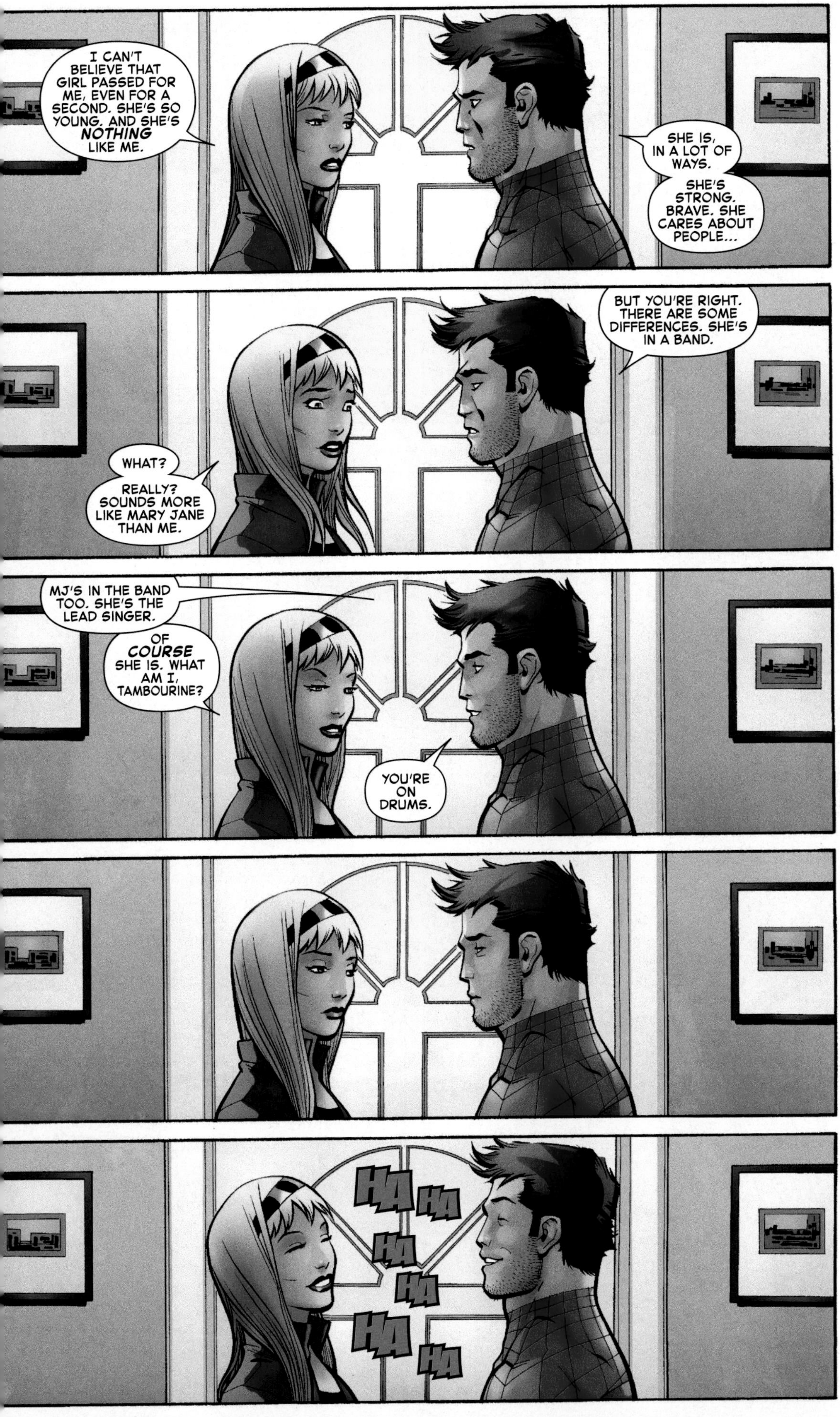
I CAN'T BELIEVE THAT GIRL PASSED FOR ME, EVEN FOR A SECOND. SHE'S SO YOUNG. AND SHE'S *NOTHING* LIKE ME.
SHE IS, IN A LOT OF WAYS.
SHE'S STRONG. BRAVE. SHE CARES ABOUT PEOPLE...
BUT YOU'RE RIGHT. THERE ARE SOME DIFFERENCES. SHE'S IN A BAND.
WHAT?
REALLY? SOUNDS MORE LIKE MARY JANE THAN ME.
MJ'S IN THE BAND TOO. SHE'S THE LEAD SINGER.
OF *COURSE* SHE IS. WHAT AM I, TAMBOURINE?
YOU'RE ON DRUMS.
HA HA HA HA HA HA

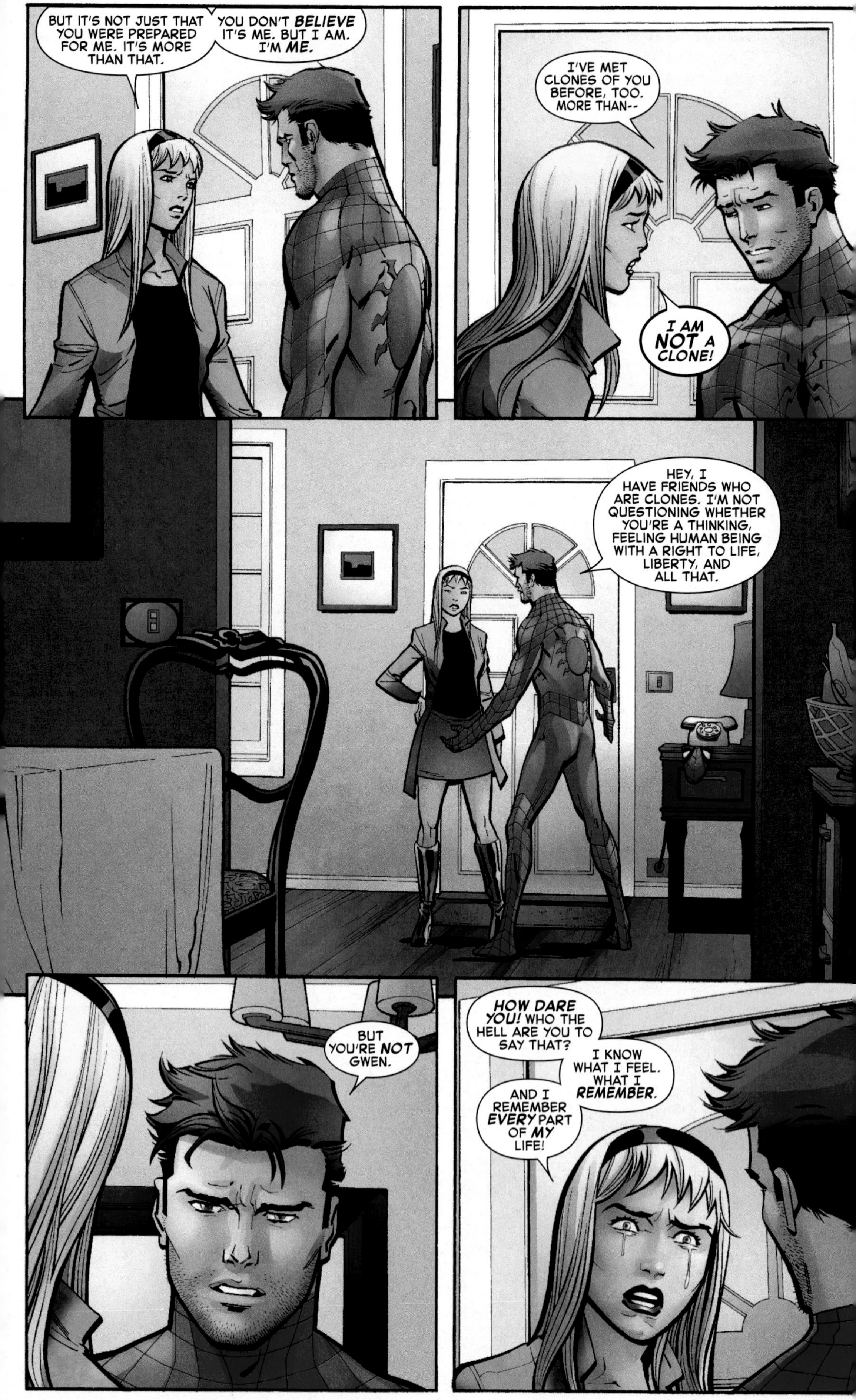
BUT IT'S NOT JUST THAT YOU WERE PREPARED FOR ME. IT'S MORE THAN THAT.
YOU DON'T BELIEVE IT'S ME. BUT I AM. I'M ME.
I'VE MET CLONES OF YOU BEFORE, TOO. MORE THAN--
I AM NOT A CLONE!
HEY, I HAVE FRIENDS WHO ARE CLONES. I'M NOT QUESTIONING WHETHER YOU'RE A THINKING, FEELING HUMAN BEING WITH A RIGHT TO LIFE, LIBERTY, AND ALL THAT.
BUT YOU'RE NOT GWEN.
HOW DARE YOU! WHO THE HELL ARE YOU TO SAY THAT?
I KNOW WHAT I FEEL. WHAT I REMEMBER.
AND I REMEMBER EVERY PART OF MY LIFE!

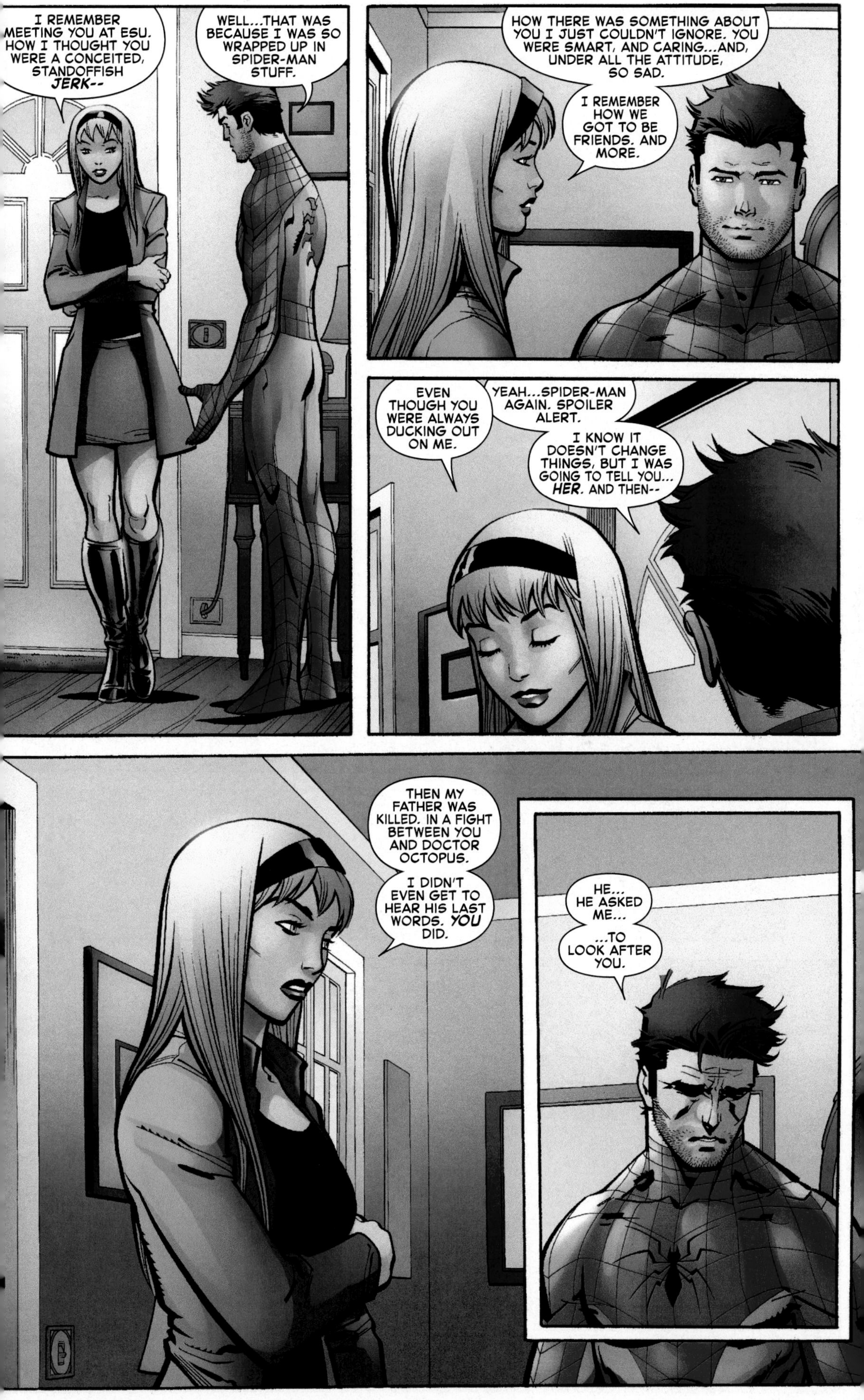
I REMEMBER MEETING YOU AT ESU. HOW I THOUGHT YOU WERE A CONCEITED, STANDOFFISH *JERK*--
WELL...THAT WAS BECAUSE I WAS SO WRAPPED UP IN SPIDER-MAN STUFF.
HOW THERE WAS SOMETHING ABOUT YOU I JUST COULDN'T IGNORE. YOU WERE SMART, AND CARING...AND, UNDER ALL THE ATTITUDE, SO SAD.
I REMEMBER HOW WE GOT TO BE FRIENDS. AND MORE.
EVEN THOUGH YOU WERE ALWAYS DUCKING OUT ON ME.
YEAH...SPIDER-MAN AGAIN. SPOILER ALERT.
I KNOW IT DOESN'T CHANGE THINGS, BUT I WAS GOING TO TELL YOU... *HER*. AND THEN--
THEN MY FATHER WAS KILLED. IN A FIGHT BETWEEN YOU AND DOCTOR OCTOPUS.
I DIDN'T EVEN GET TO HEAR HIS LAST WORDS. *YOU* DID.
HE... HE ASKED ME...
...TO LOOK AFTER YOU.

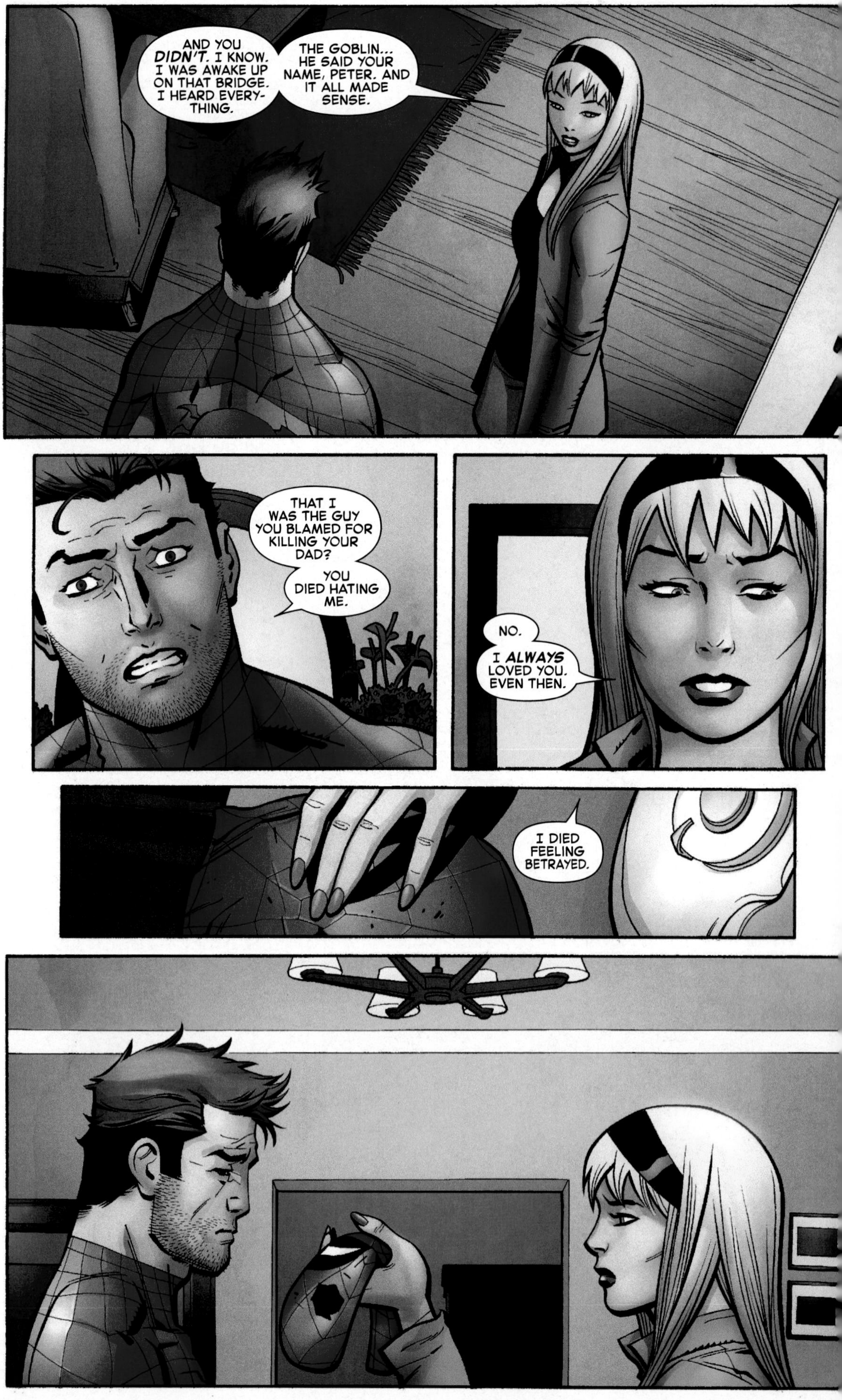

AND YOU DIDN'T. I KNOW. I WAS AWAKE UP ON THAT BRIDGE. I HEARD EVERY-THING.
THE GOBLIN... HE SAID YOUR NAME, PETER. AND IT ALL MADE SENSE.
THAT I WAS THE GUY YOU BLAMED FOR KILLING YOUR DAD?
YOU DIED HATING ME.
NO.
I ALWAYS LOVED YOU. EVEN THEN.
I DIED FEELING BETRAYED.

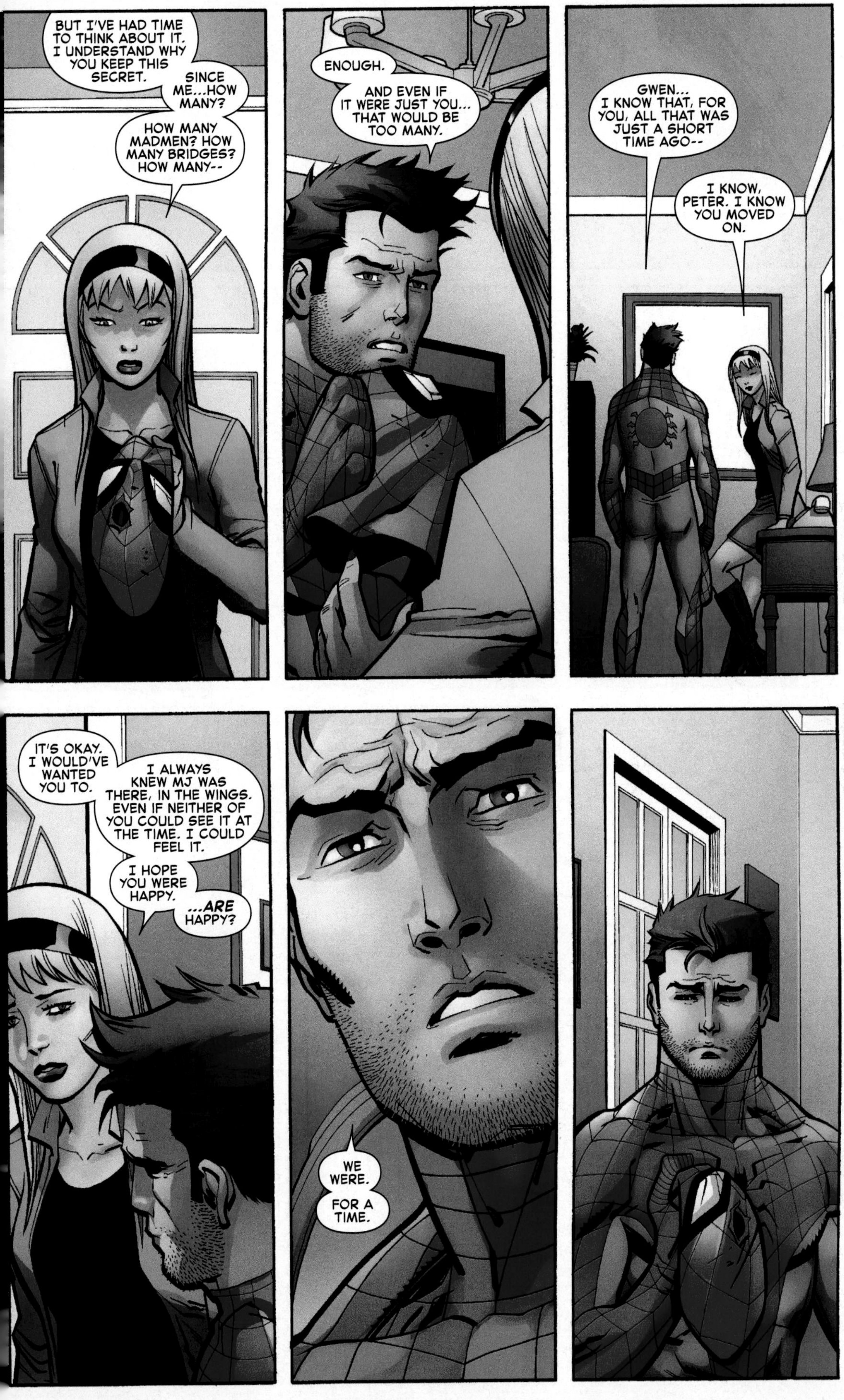
BUT I'VE HAD TIME TO THINK ABOUT IT. I UNDERSTAND WHY YOU KEEP THIS SECRET.
SINCE ME...HOW MANY?
HOW MANY MADMEN? HOW MANY BRIDGES? HOW MANY--
ENOUGH.
AND EVEN IF IT WERE JUST YOU... THAT WOULD BE TOO MANY.
GWEN... I KNOW THAT, FOR YOU, ALL THAT WAS JUST A SHORT TIME AGO--
I KNOW, PETER. I KNOW YOU MOVED ON.
IT'S OKAY. I WOULD'VE WANTED YOU TO.
I ALWAYS KNEW MJ WAS THERE, IN THE WINGS. EVEN IF NEITHER OF YOU COULD SEE IT AT THE TIME. I COULD FEEL IT.
I HOPE YOU WERE HAPPY.
...ARE HAPPY?
WE WERE.
FOR A TIME.

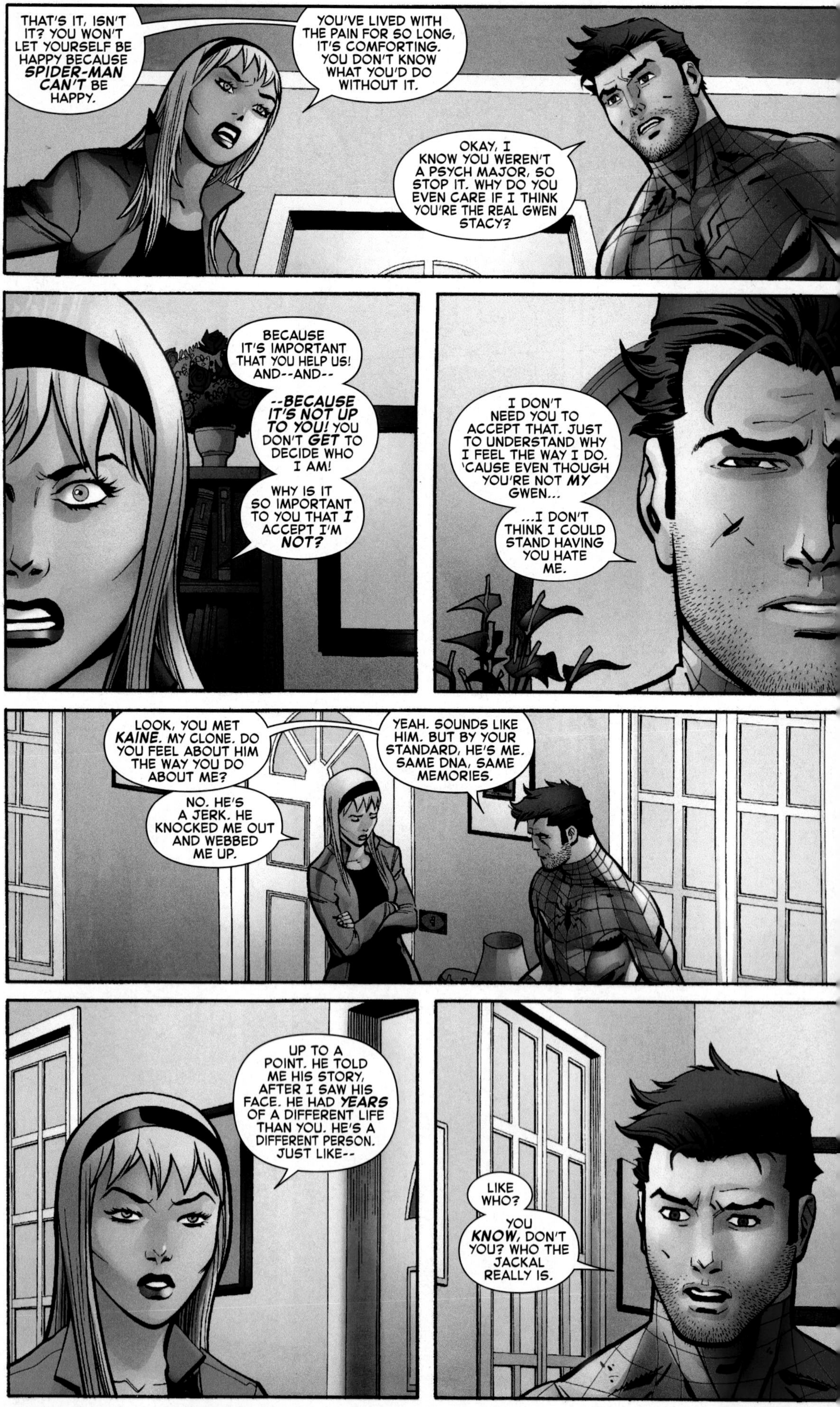

THAT'S IT, ISN'T IT? YOU WON'T LET YOURSELF BE HAPPY BECAUSE SPIDER-MAN CAN'T BE HAPPY.
YOU'VE LIVED WITH THE PAIN FOR SO LONG, IT'S COMFORTING. YOU DON'T KNOW WHAT YOU'D DO WITHOUT IT.
OKAY, I KNOW YOU WEREN'T A PSYCH MAJOR, SO STOP IT. WHY DO YOU EVEN CARE IF I THINK YOU'RE THE REAL GWEN STACY?
BECAUSE IT'S IMPORTANT THAT YOU HELP US! AND--AND--
--BECAUSE IT'S NOT UP TO YOU! YOU DON'T GET TO DECIDE WHO I AM!
WHY IS IT SO IMPORTANT TO YOU THAT I ACCEPT I'M NOT?
I DON'T NEED YOU TO ACCEPT THAT. JUST TO UNDERSTAND WHY I FEEL THE WAY I DO. 'CAUSE EVEN THOUGH YOU'RE NOT MY GWEN...
...I DON'T THINK I COULD STAND HAVING YOU HATE ME.
LOOK, YOU MET KAINE. MY CLONE. DO YOU FEEL ABOUT HIM THE WAY YOU DO ABOUT ME?
NO. HE'S A JERK. HE KNOCKED ME OUT AND WEBBED ME UP.
YEAH. SOUNDS LIKE HIM. BUT BY YOUR STANDARD, HE'S ME. SAME DNA, SAME MEMORIES.
UP TO A POINT. HE TOLD ME HIS STORY, AFTER I SAW HIS FACE. HE HAD YEARS OF A DIFFERENT LIFE THAN YOU. HE'S A DIFFERENT PERSON. JUST LIKE--
LIKE WHO?
YOU KNOW, DON'T YOU? WHO THE JACKAL REALLY IS.

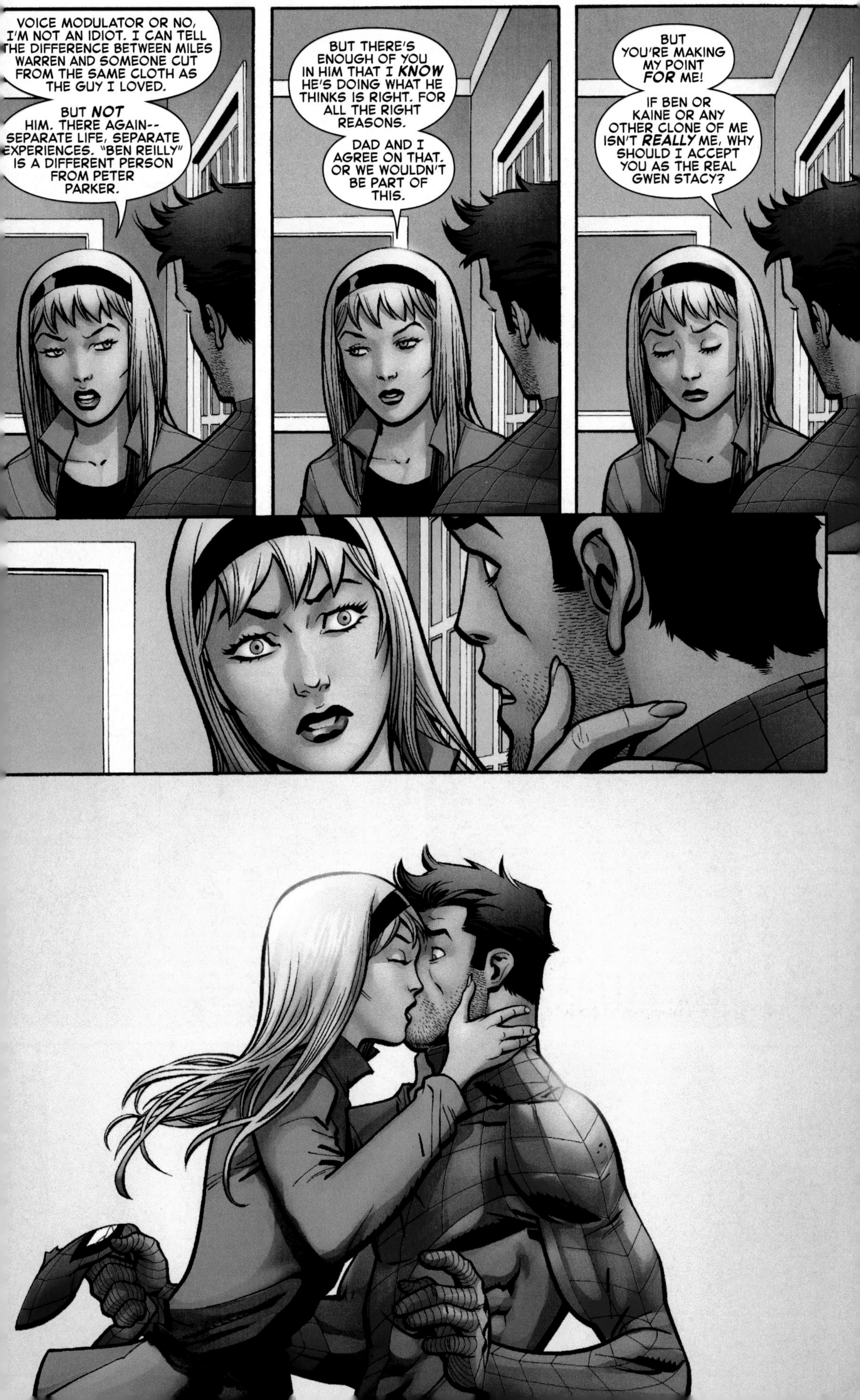

VOICE MODULATOR OR NO, I'M NOT AN IDIOT. I CAN TELL THE DIFFERENCE BETWEEN MILES WARREN AND SOMEONE CUT FROM THE SAME CLOTH AS THE GUY I LOVED.
BUT NOT HIM. THERE AGAIN-- SEPARATE LIFE, SEPARATE EXPERIENCES. "BEN REILLY" IS A DIFFERENT PERSON FROM PETER PARKER.
BUT THERE'S ENOUGH OF YOU IN HIM THAT I KNOW HE'S DOING WHAT HE THINKS IS RIGHT. FOR ALL THE RIGHT REASONS.
DAD AND I AGREE ON THAT. OR WE WOULDN'T BE PART OF THIS.
BUT YOU'RE MAKING MY POINT FOR ME!
IF BEN OR KAINE OR ANY OTHER CLONE OF ME ISN'T REALLY ME, WHY SHOULD I ACCEPT YOU AS THE REAL GWEN STACY?

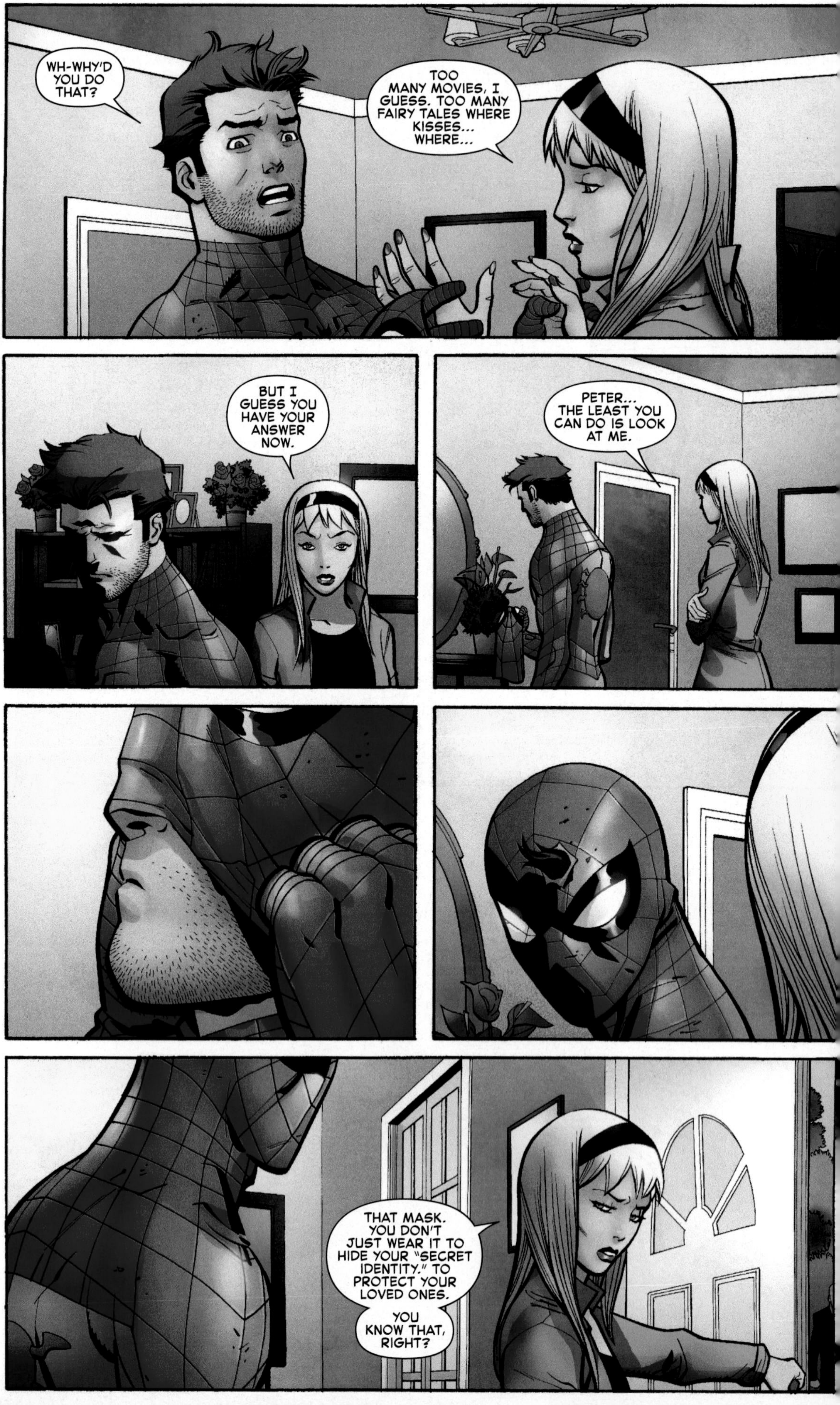

WH-WHY'D YOU DO THAT?
TOO MANY MOVIES, I GUESS. TOO MANY FAIRY TALES WHERE KISSES... WHERE...
BUT I GUESS YOU HAVE YOUR ANSWER NOW.
PETER... THE LEAST YOU CAN DO IS LOOK AT ME.
THAT MASK. YOU DON'T JUST WEAR IT TO HIDE YOUR "SECRET IDENTITY." TO PROTECT YOUR LOVED ONES.
YOU KNOW THAT, RIGHT?

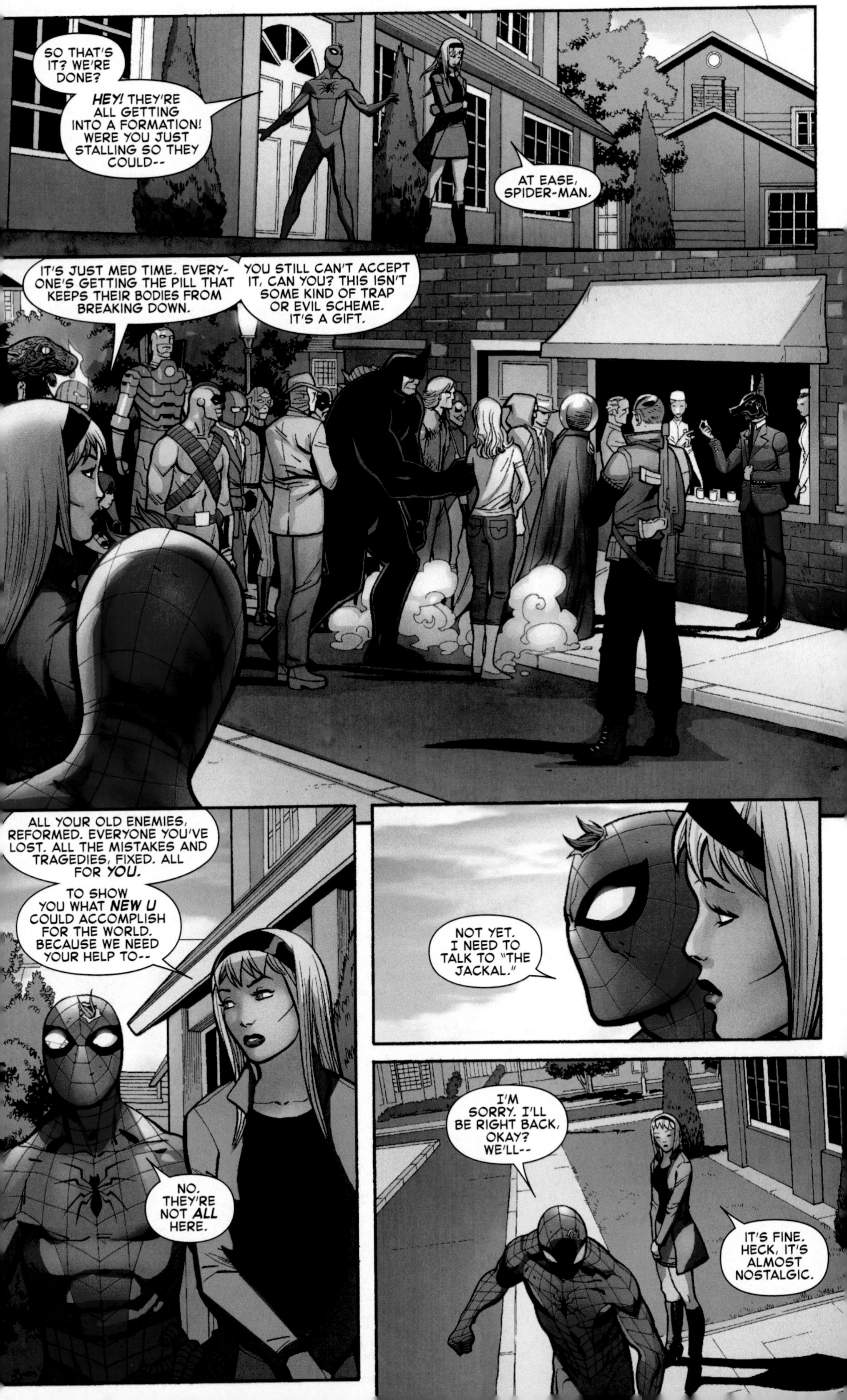
SO THAT'S IT? WE'RE DONE?
HEY! THEY'RE ALL GETTING INTO A FORMATION! WERE YOU JUST STALLING SO THEY COULD--
AT EASE, SPIDER-MAN.
IT'S JUST MED TIME. EVERYONE'S GETTING THE PILL THAT KEEPS THEIR BODIES FROM BREAKING DOWN.
YOU STILL CAN'T ACCEPT IT, CAN YOU? THIS ISN'T SOME KIND OF TRAP OR EVIL SCHEME. IT'S A GIFT.
ALL YOUR OLD ENEMIES, REFORMED. EVERYONE YOU'VE LOST. ALL THE MISTAKES AND TRAGEDIES, FIXED. ALL FOR YOU.
TO SHOW YOU WHAT NEW U COULD ACCOMPLISH FOR THE WORLD. BECAUSE WE NEED YOUR HELP TO--
NO. THEY'RE NOT ALL HERE.
NOT YET. I NEED TO TALK TO "THE JACKAL."
I'M SORRY. I'LL BE RIGHT BACK, OKAY? WE'LL--
IT'S FINE. HECK, IT'S ALMOST NOSTALGIC.

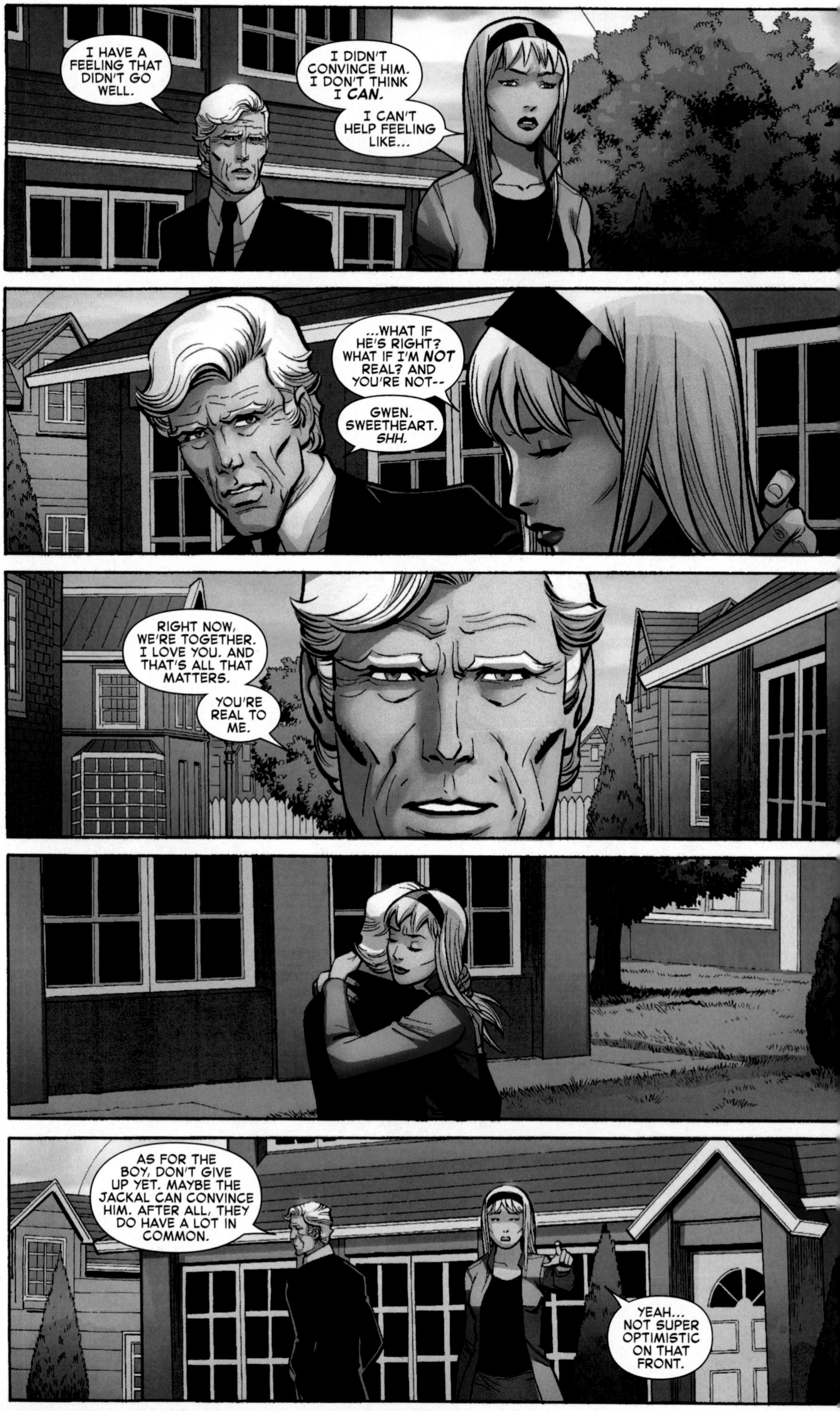

I HAVE A FEELING THAT DIDN'T GO WELL.
I DIDN'T CONVINCE HIM. I DON'T THINK I CAN.
I CAN'T HELP FEELING LIKE...
...WHAT IF HE'S RIGHT? WHAT IF I'M NOT REAL? AND YOU'RE NOT--
GWEN. SWEETHEART. SHH.
RIGHT NOW, WE'RE TOGETHER. I LOVE YOU. AND THAT'S ALL THAT MATTERS.
YOU'RE REAL TO ME.
AS FOR THE BOY, DON'T GIVE UP YET. MAYBE THE JACKAL CAN CONVINCE HIM. AFTER ALL, THEY DO HAVE A LOT IN COMMON.
YEAH... NOT SUPER OPTIMISTIC ON THAT FRONT.

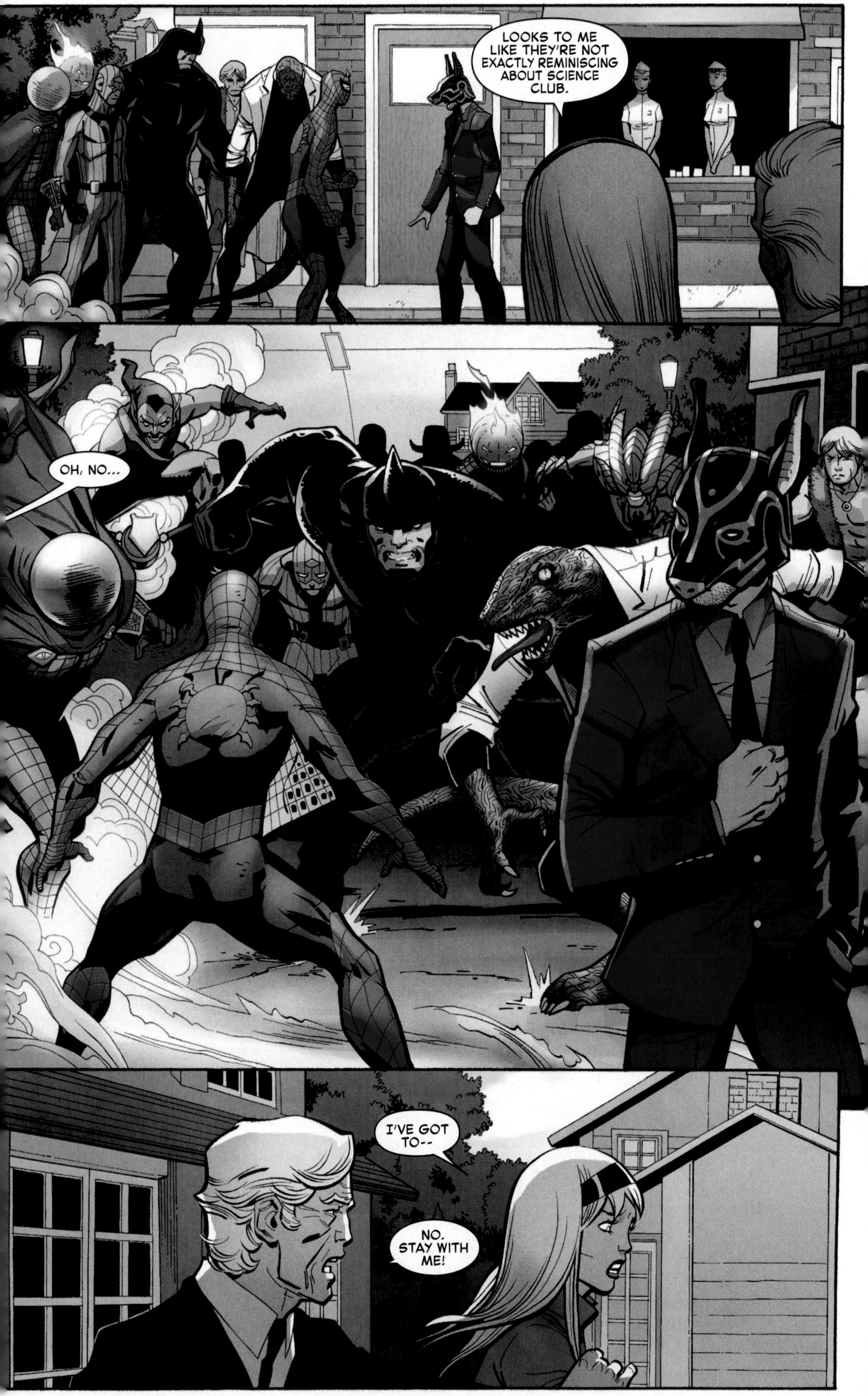
LOOKS TO ME LIKE THEY'RE NOT EXACTLY REMINISCING ABOUT SCIENCE CLUB.
OH, NO...
I'VE GOT TO--
NO. STAY WITH ME!

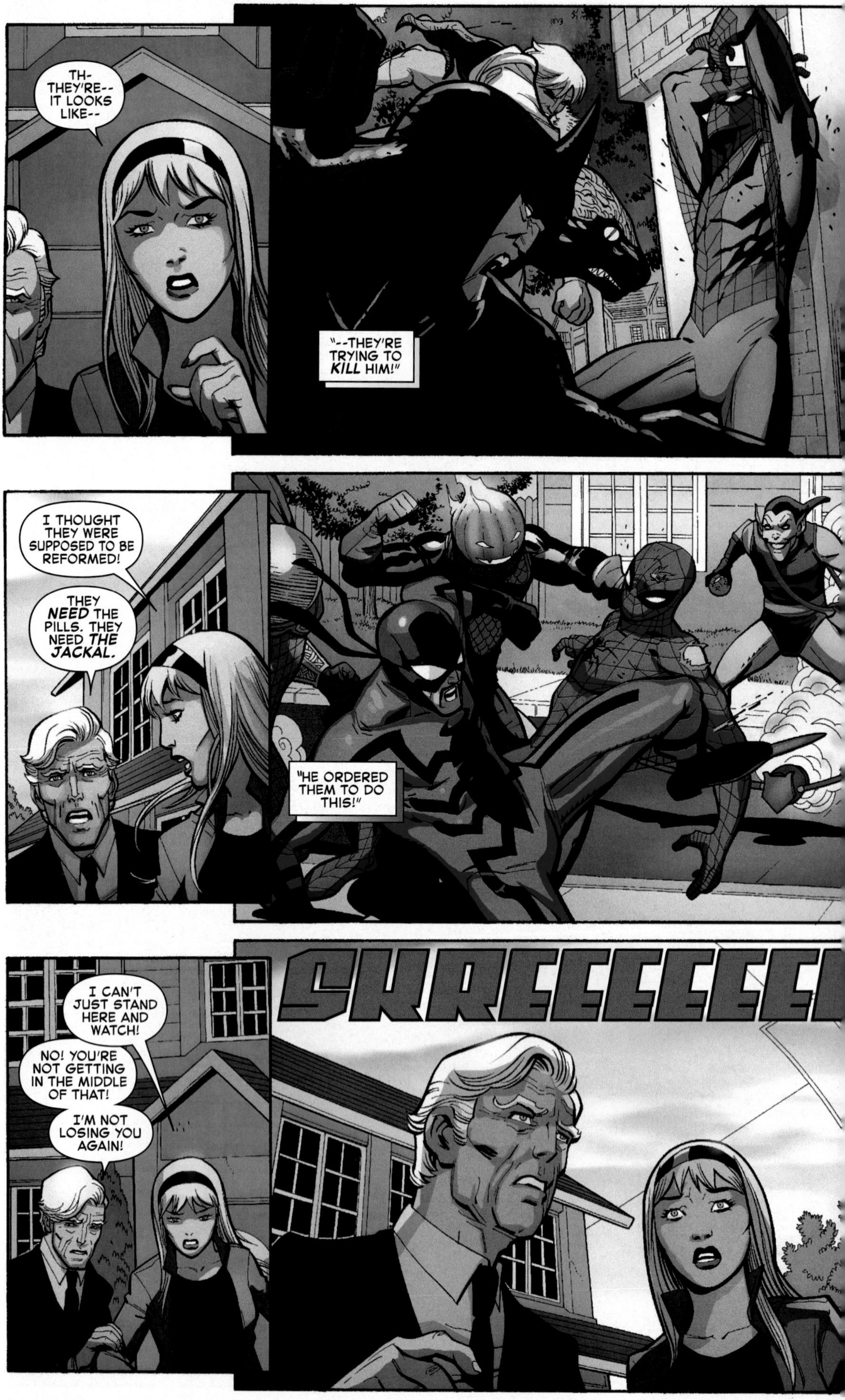
TH- THEY'RE-- IT LOOKS LIKE--
"--THEY'RE TRYING TO KILL HIM!"
I THOUGHT THEY WERE SUPPOSED TO BE REFORMED!
THEY NEED THE PILLS. THEY NEED THE JACKAL.
"HE ORDERED THEM TO DO THIS!"
I CAN'T JUST STAND HERE AND WATCH!
NO! YOU'RE NOT GETTING IN THE MIDDLE OF THAT!
I'M NOT LOSING YOU AGAIN!
SHREEEEEEE

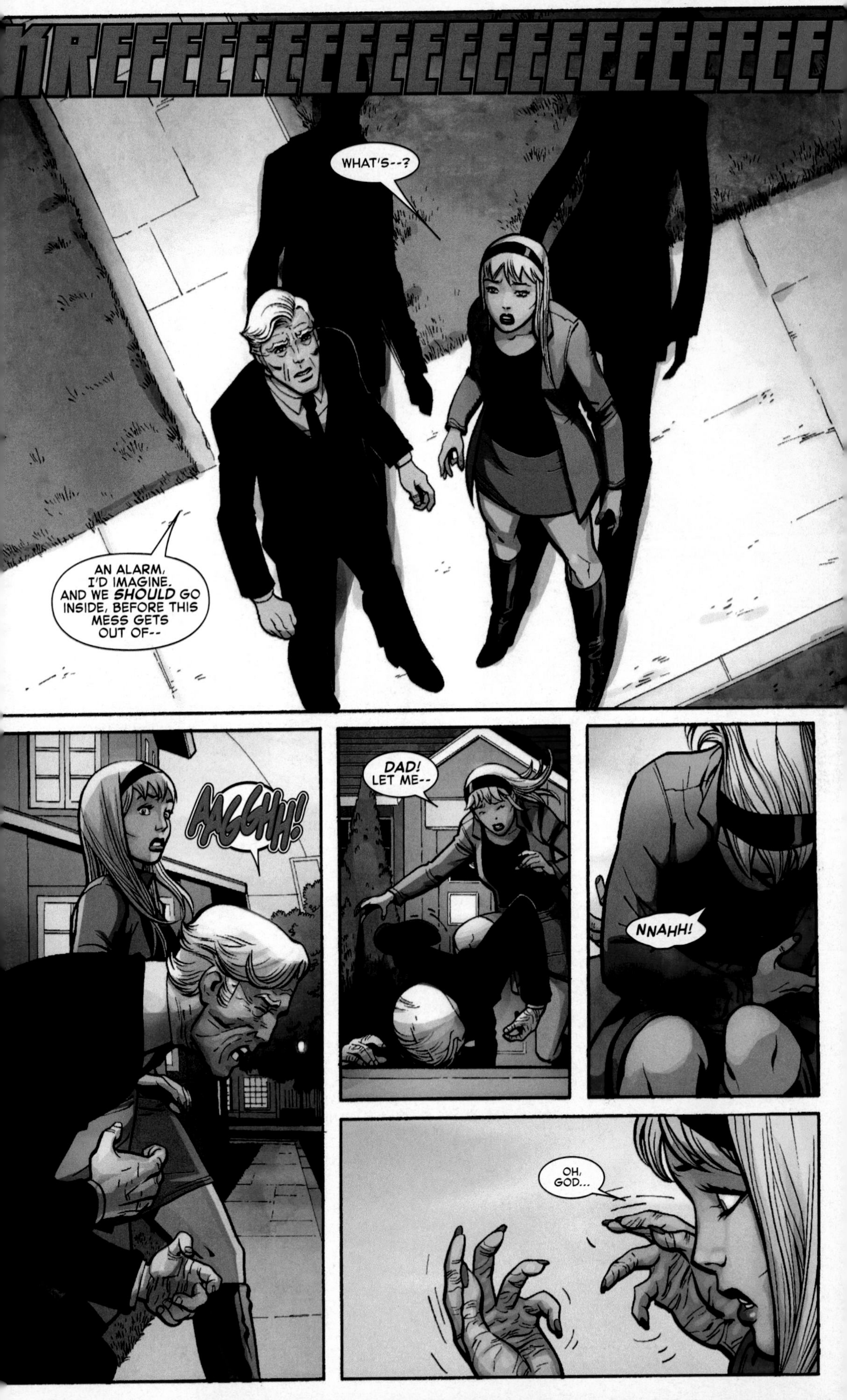
KREEEEEEEEEEEEEEEEEEEEEEE
WHAT'S--?
AN ALARM, I'D IMAGINE. AND WE SHOULD GO INSIDE, BEFORE THIS MESS GETS OUT OF--
AAGGHH!
DAD! LET ME--
NNAHH!
OH, GOD...

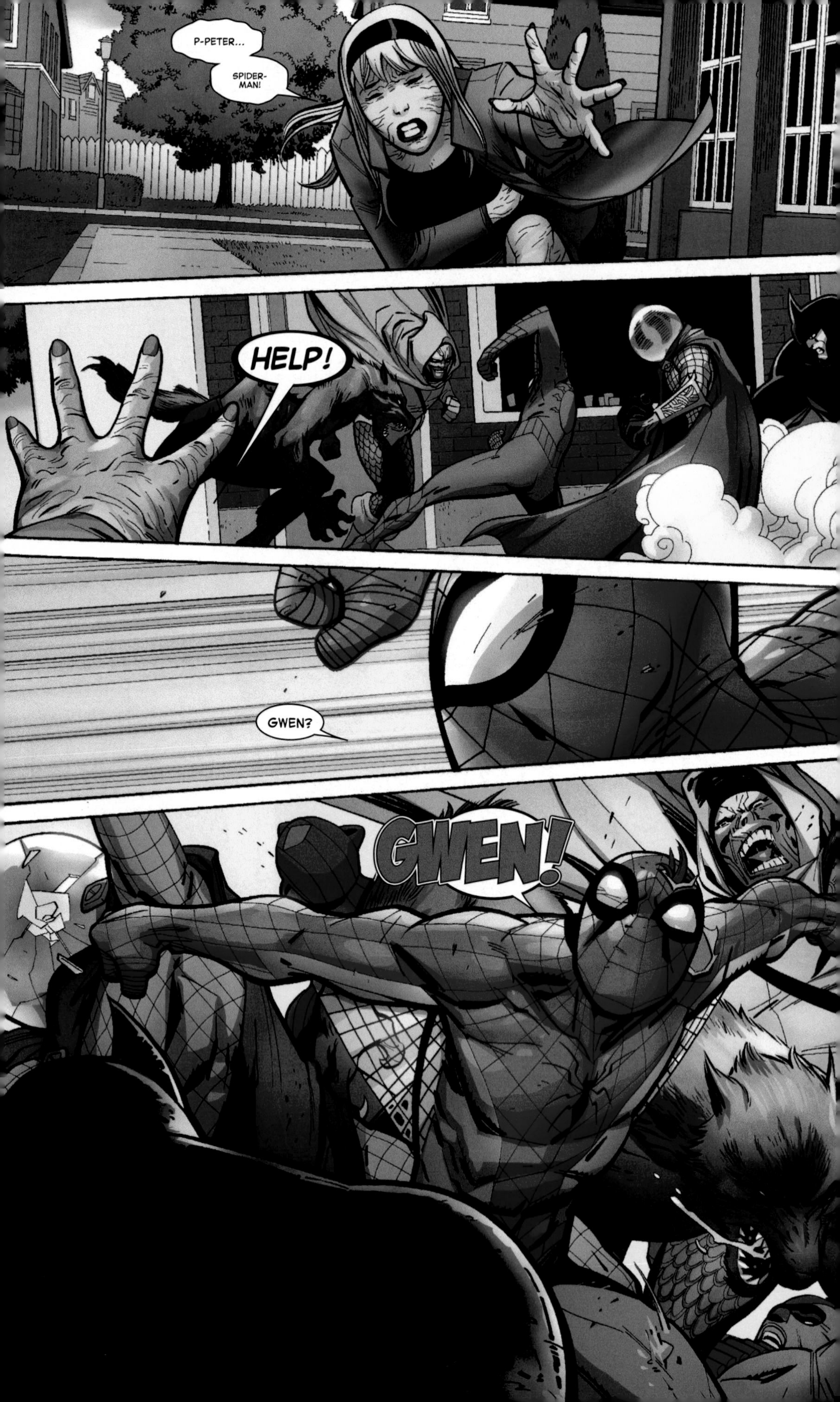
P-PETER...
SPIDER-MAN!
HELP!
GWEN?
GWEN!

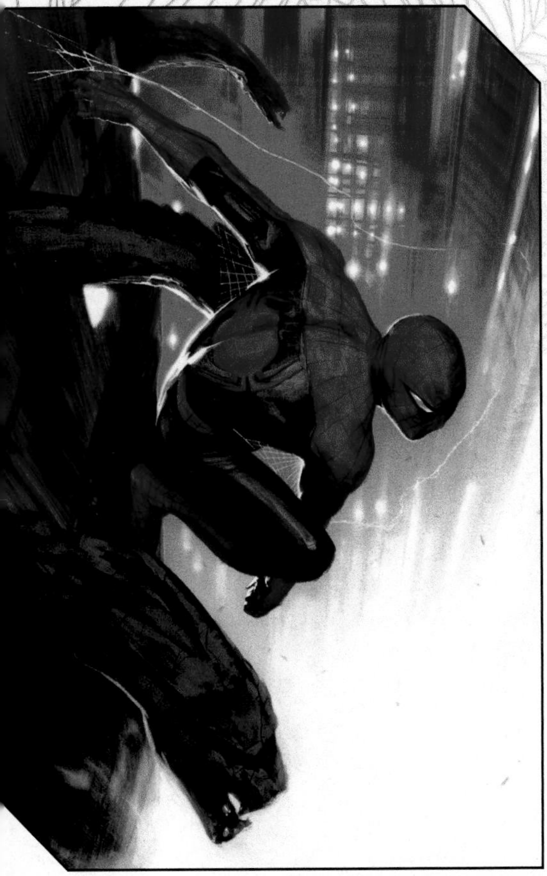

#24 VARIANT BY **GABRIELE DELL'OTTO**

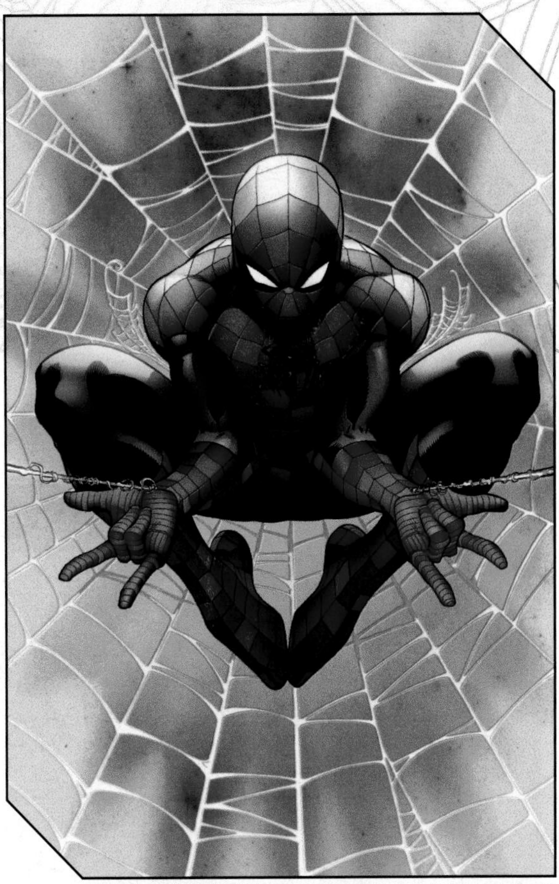

ANNUAL #1 VARIANT BY **ED McGUINNESS & TEO GONZALES**

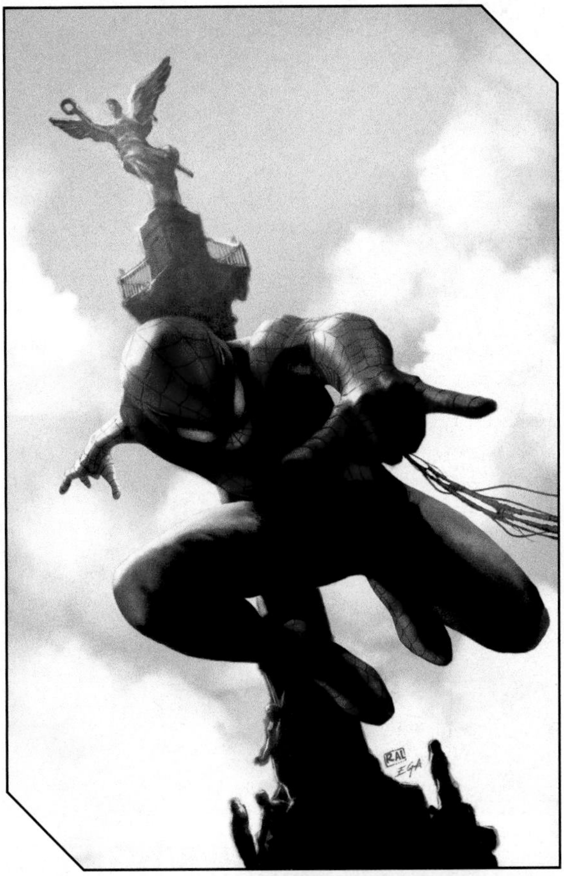

ANNUAL #1 VARIANT BY **RAUL VALDES**

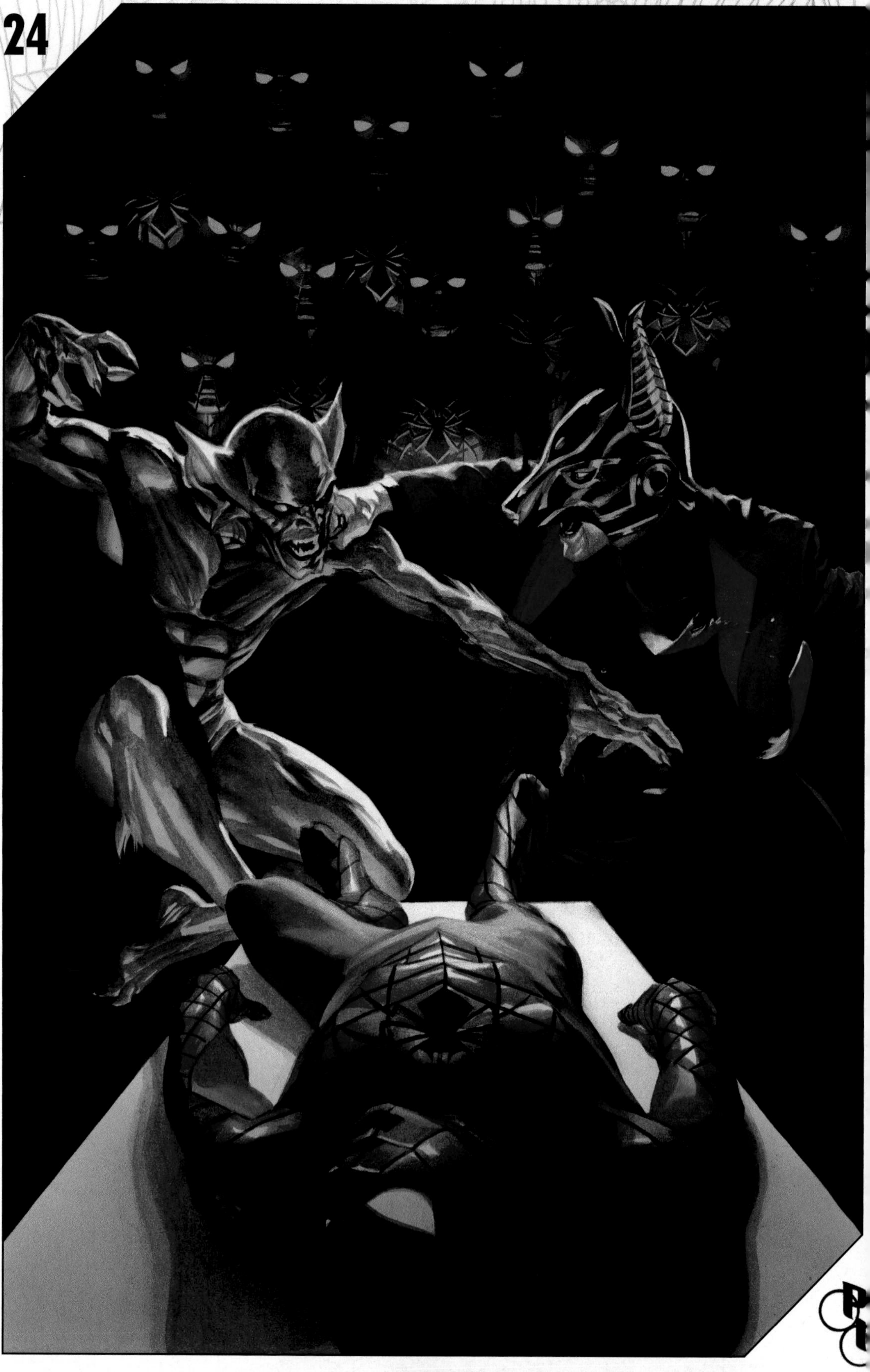

"NIGHT OF THE JACKALS"

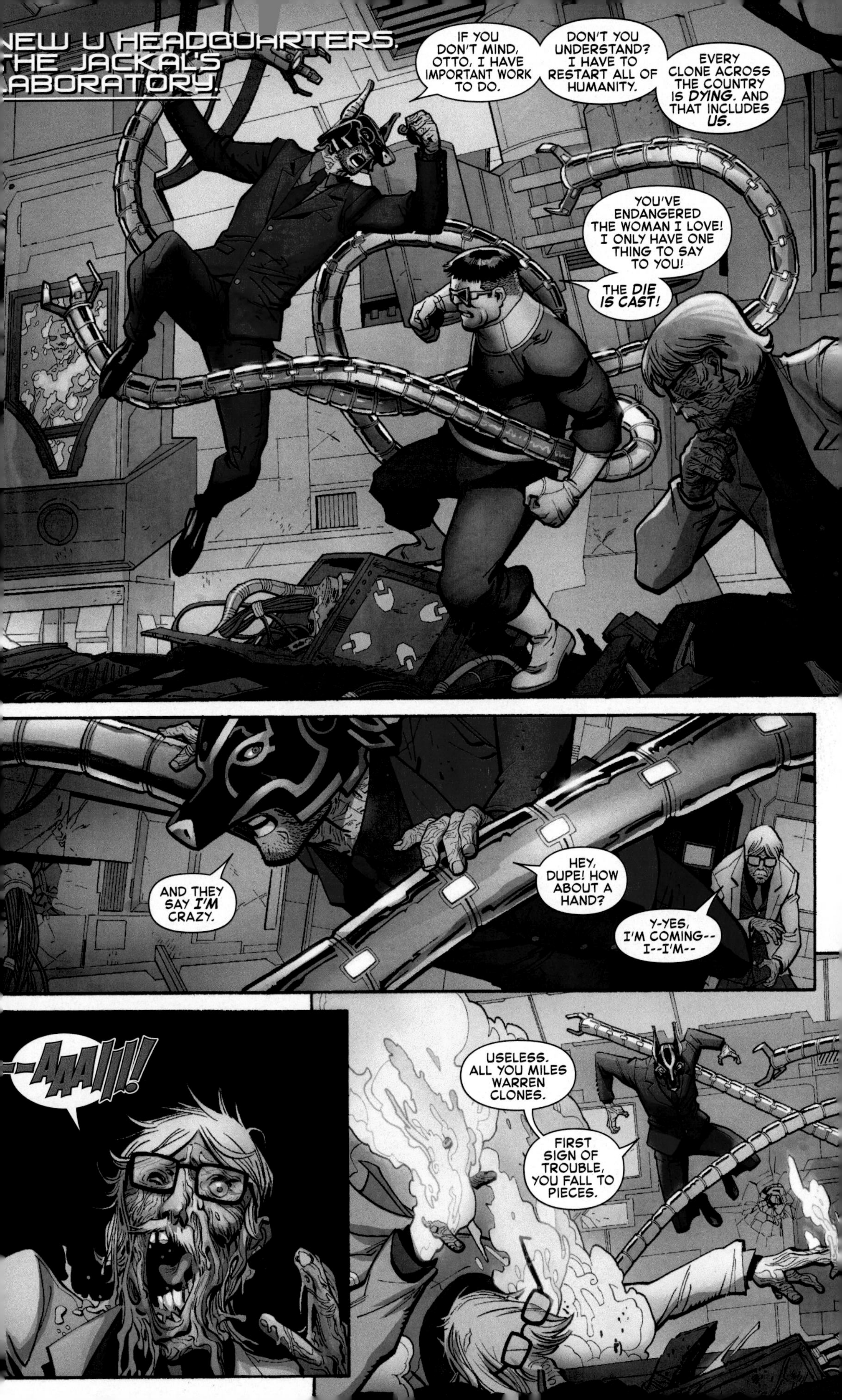

NEW U HEADQUARTERS. THE JACKAL'S LABORATORY.
IF YOU DON'T MIND, OTTO, I HAVE IMPORTANT WORK TO DO.
DON'T YOU UNDERSTAND? I HAVE TO RESTART ALL OF HUMANITY.
EVERY CLONE ACROSS THE COUNTRY IS DYING. AND THAT INCLUDES US.
YOU'VE ENDANGERED THE WOMAN I LOVE! I ONLY HAVE ONE THING TO SAY TO YOU!
THE DIE IS CAST!
AND THEY SAY I'M CRAZY.
HEY, DUPE! HOW ABOUT A HAND?
Y-YES, I'M COMING-- I--I'M--
--AAAIII!
USELESS. ALL YOU MILES WARREN CLONES.
FIRST SIGN OF TROUBLE, YOU FALL TO PIECES.

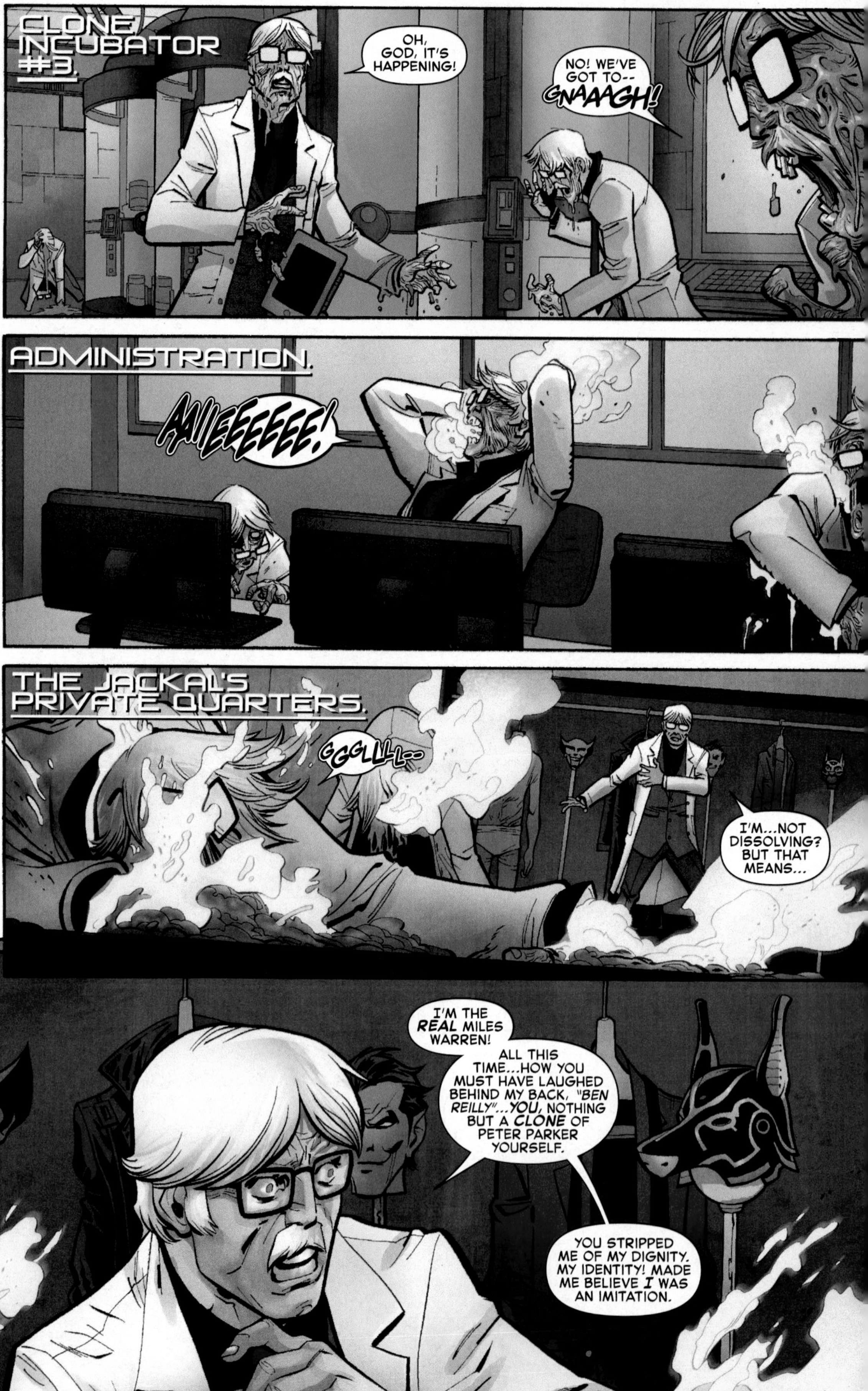
CLONE INCUBATOR #3.
OH, GOD, IT'S HAPPENING!
NO! WE'VE GOT TO-- GNAAAGH!
ADMINISTRATION.
AAIIEEEEEEE!
THE JACKAL'S PRIVATE QUARTERS.
GGGLLLL--
I'M...NOT DISSOLVING? BUT THAT MEANS...
I'M THE REAL MILES WARREN!
ALL THIS TIME...HOW YOU MUST HAVE LAUGHED BEHIND MY BACK, "BEN REILLY"...YOU, NOTHING BUT A CLONE OF PETER PARKER YOURSELF.
YOU STRIPPED ME OF MY DIGNITY. MY IDENTITY! MADE ME BELIEVE I WAS AN IMITATION.

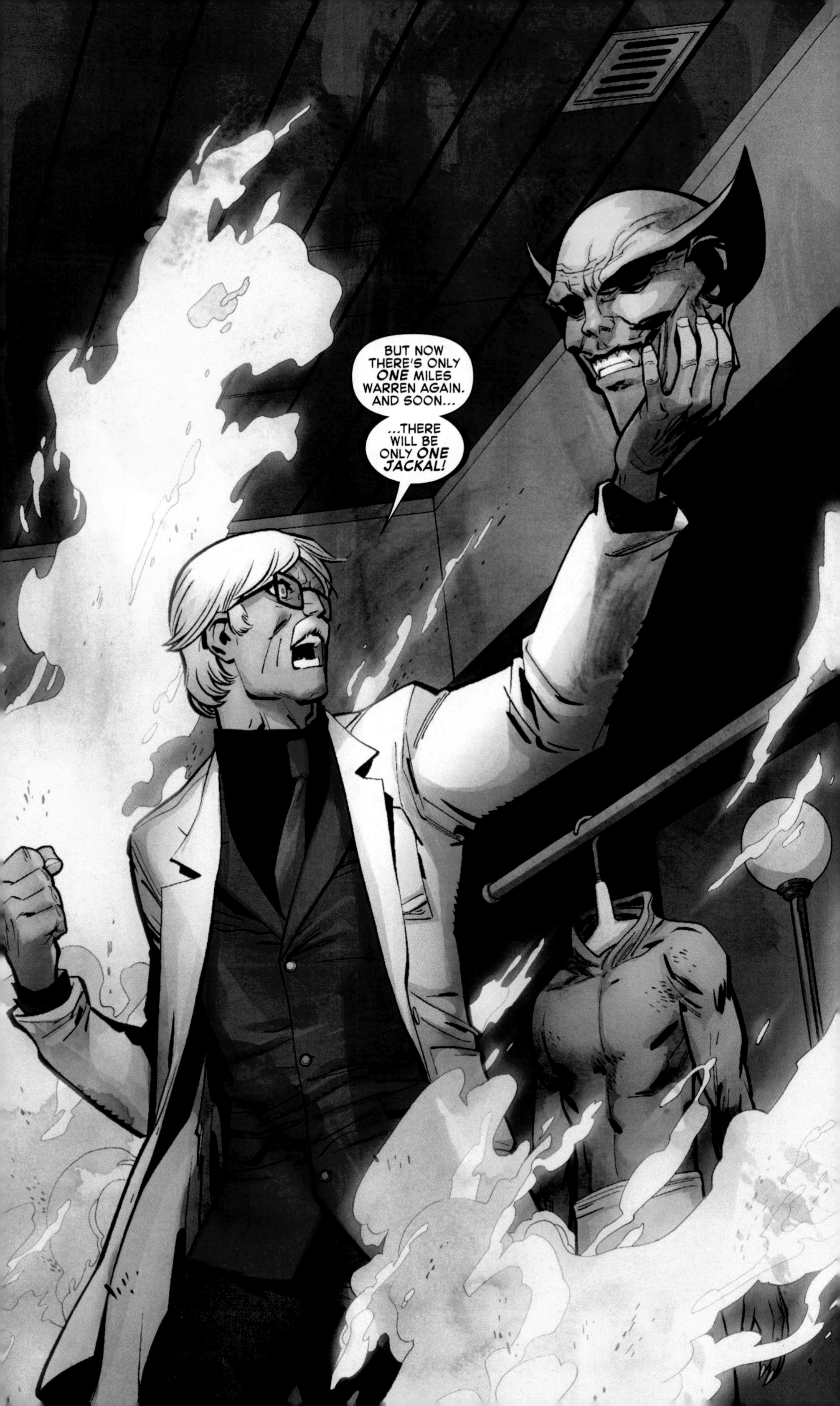
BUT NOW THERE'S ONLY *ONE* MILES WARREN AGAIN. AND SOON...
...THERE WILL BE ONLY *ONE JACKAL!*

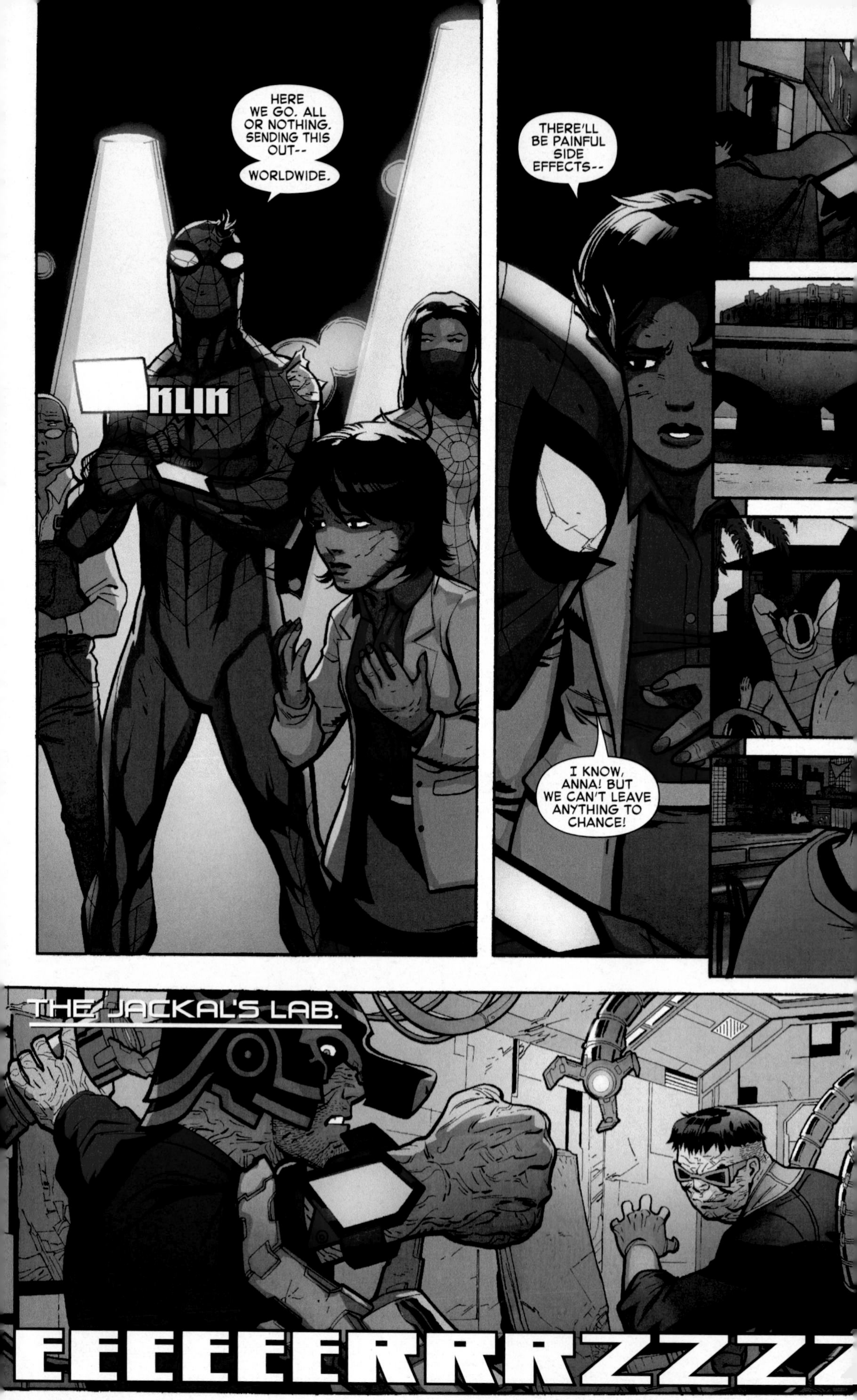
HERE WE GO. ALL OR NOTHING. SENDING THIS OUT--
WORLDWIDE.
KLIK
THERE'LL BE PAINFUL SIDE EFFECTS--
I KNOW, ANNA! BUT WE CAN'T LEAVE ANYTHING TO CHANCE!
THE JACKAL'S LAB.
EEEEEERRRRZZZZ

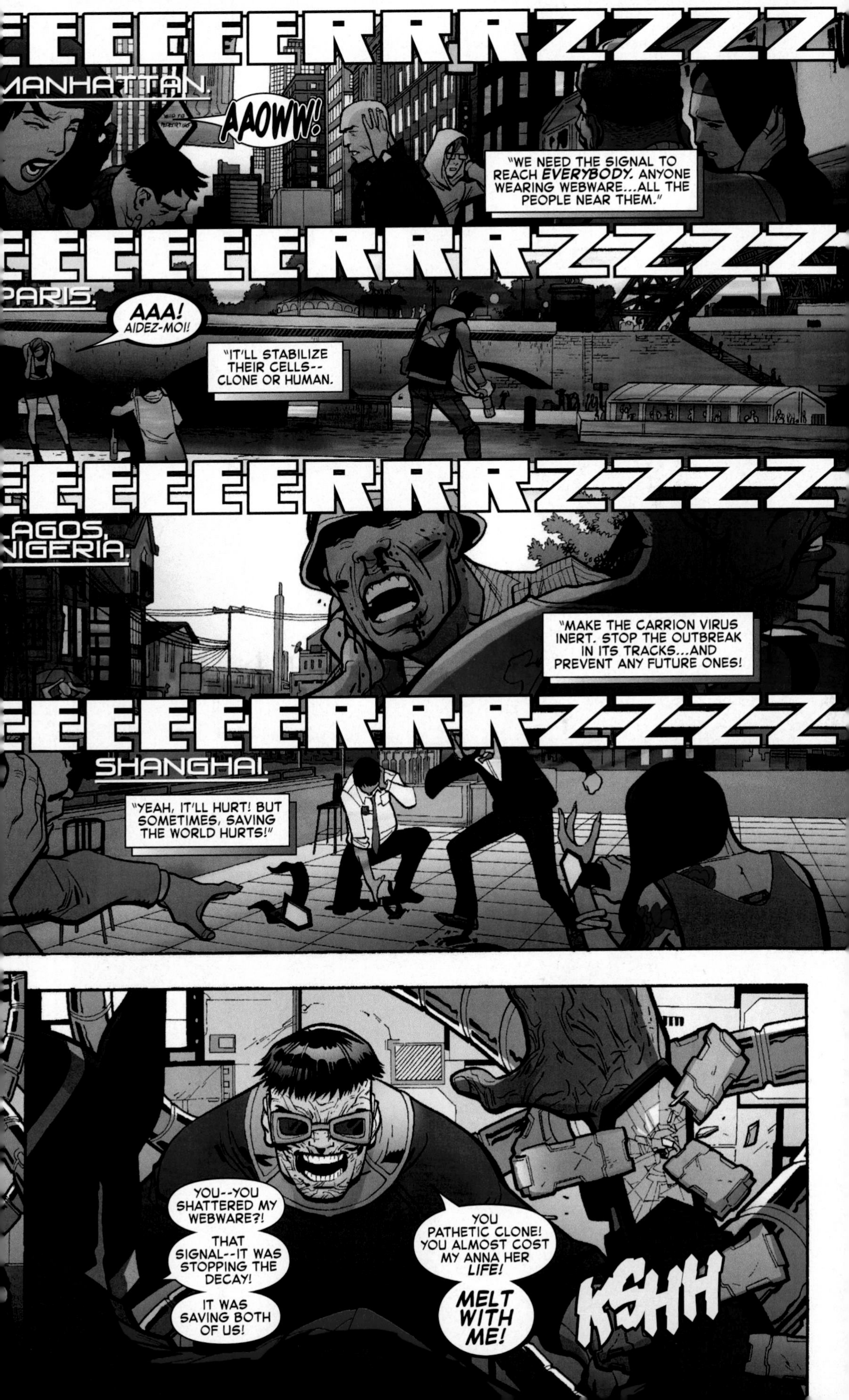
EEEEEERRRRZZZZ
MANHATTAN.
AAOWW!
"WE NEED THE SIGNAL TO REACH EVERYBODY. ANYONE WEARING WEBWARE...ALL THE PEOPLE NEAR THEM."
EEEEEERRRRZZZZ
PARIS.
AAA! AIDEZ-MOI!
"IT'LL STABILIZE THEIR CELLS-- CLONE OR HUMAN.
EEEEEERRRRZZZZ
LAGOS, NIGERIA.
"MAKE THE CARRION VIRUS INERT. STOP THE OUTBREAK IN ITS TRACKS...AND PREVENT ANY FUTURE ONES!
EEEEEERRRRZZZZ
SHANGHAI.
"YEAH, IT'LL HURT! BUT SOMETIMES, SAVING THE WORLD HURTS!"
YOU--YOU SHATTERED MY WEBWARE?!
THAT SIGNAL--IT WAS STOPPING THE DECAY!
IT WAS SAVING BOTH OF US!
YOU PATHETIC CLONE! YOU ALMOST COST MY ANNA HER LIFE!
MELT WITH ME!
KSHH

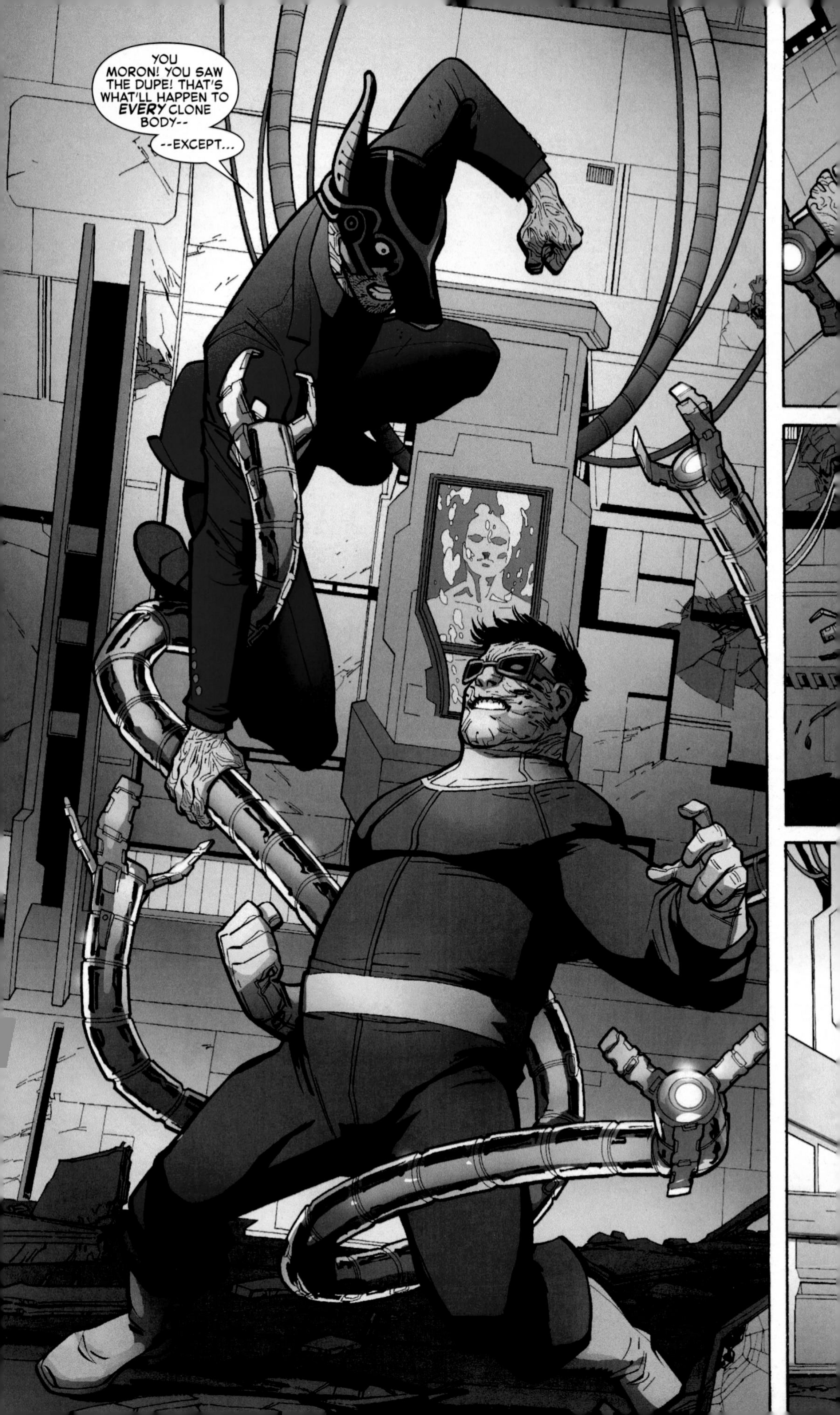
YOU MORON! YOU SAW THE DUPE! THAT'S WHAT'LL HAPPEN TO EVERY CLONE BODY--
--EXCEPT...

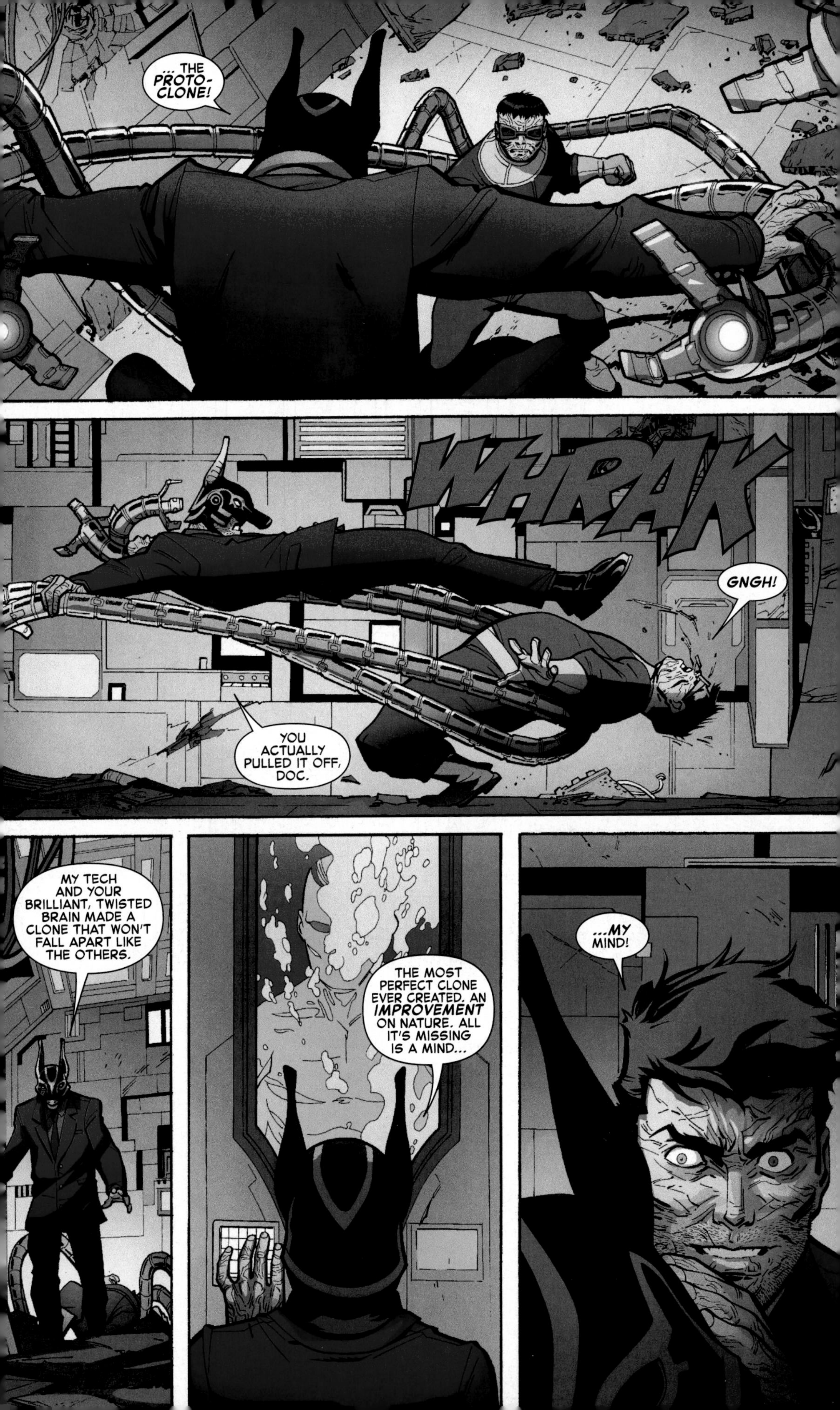

... THE PROTO-CLONE!
WHRAK
GNGH!
YOU ACTUALLY PULLED IT OFF, DOC.
MY TECH AND YOUR BRILLIANT, TWISTED BRAIN MADE A CLONE THAT WON'T FALL APART LIKE THE OTHERS.
THE MOST PERFECT CLONE EVER CREATED. AN *IMPROVEMENT* ON NATURE. ALL IT'S MISSING IS A MIND...
...MY MIND!

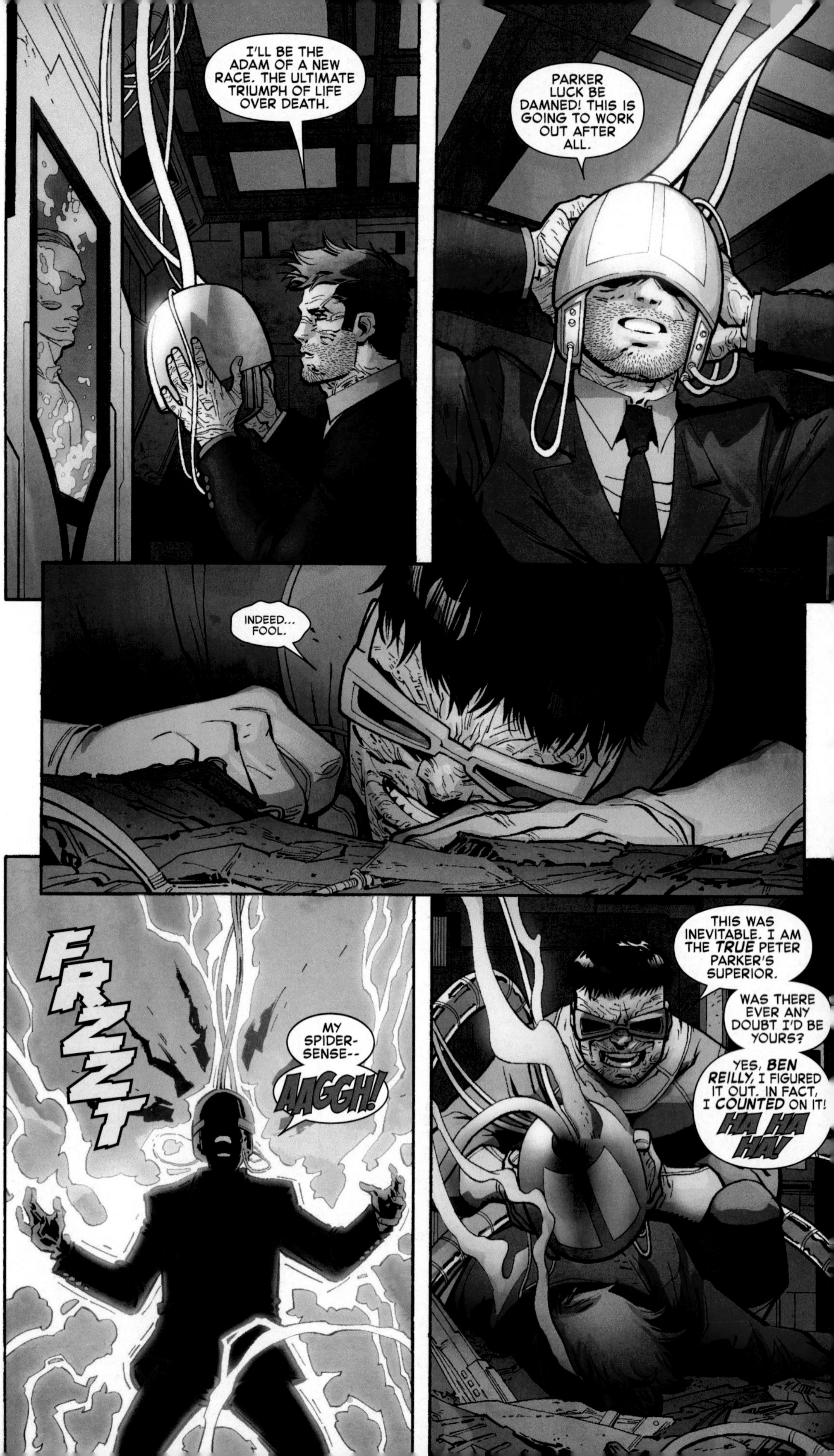

I'LL BE THE ADAM OF A NEW RACE. THE ULTIMATE TRIUMPH OF LIFE OVER DEATH.
PARKER LUCK BE DAMNED! THIS IS GOING TO WORK OUT AFTER ALL.
INDEED... FOOL.
FRZZZT
MY SPIDER-SENSE--
AAGGH!
THIS WAS INEVITABLE. I AM THE TRUE PETER PARKER'S SUPERIOR.
WAS THERE EVER ANY DOUBT I'D BE YOURS?
YES, BEN REILLY, I FIGURED IT OUT. IN FACT, I COUNTED ON IT!
HA HA HA!

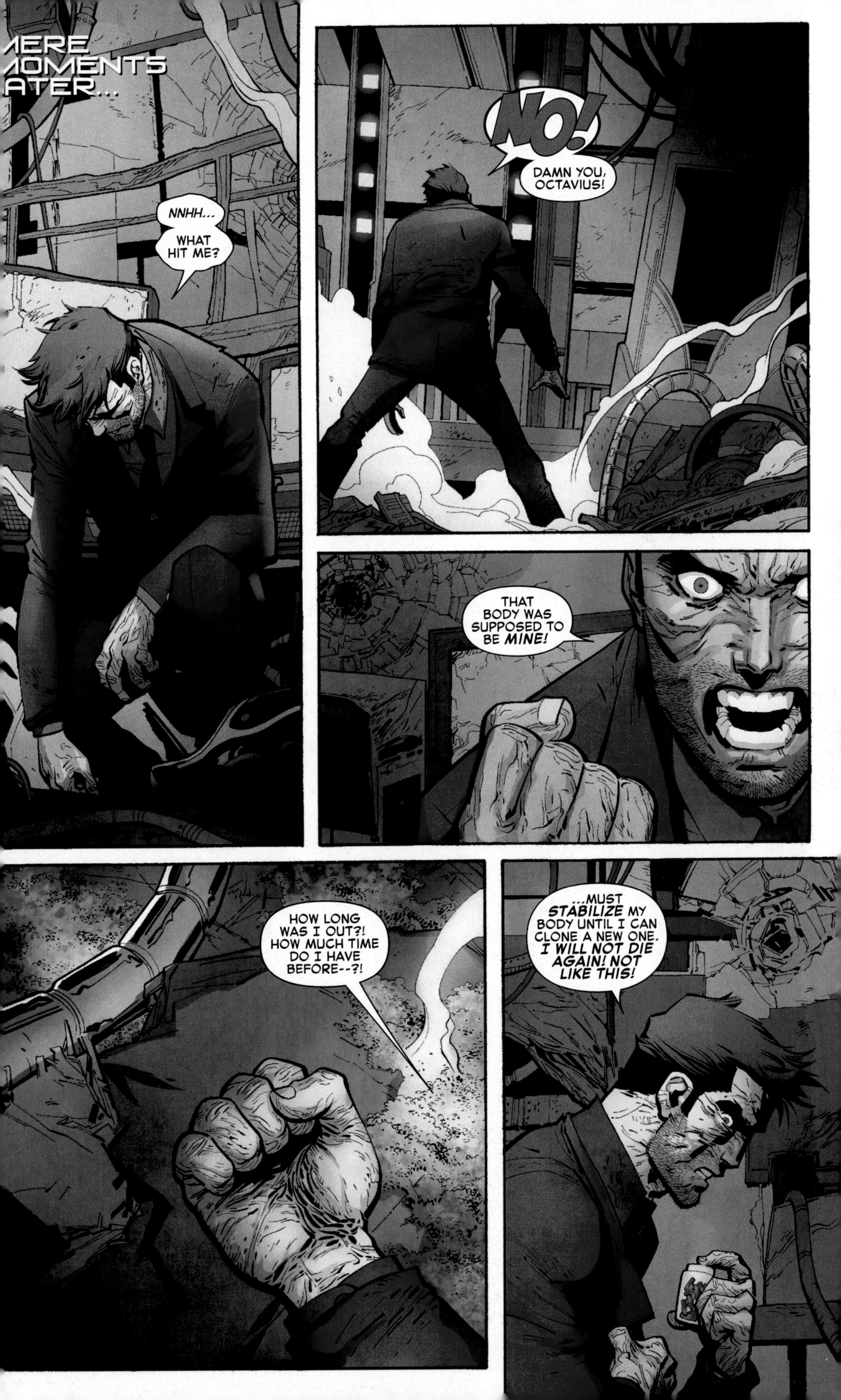

MERE
MOMENTS
LATER...
NNHH...
WHAT HIT ME?
NO!
DAMN YOU, OCTAVIUS!
THAT BODY WAS SUPPOSED TO BE MINE!
HOW LONG WAS I OUT?! HOW MUCH TIME DO I HAVE BEFORE--?!
...MUST STABILIZE MY BODY UNTIL I CAN CLONE A NEW ONE. I WILL NOT DIE AGAIN! NOT LIKE THIS!

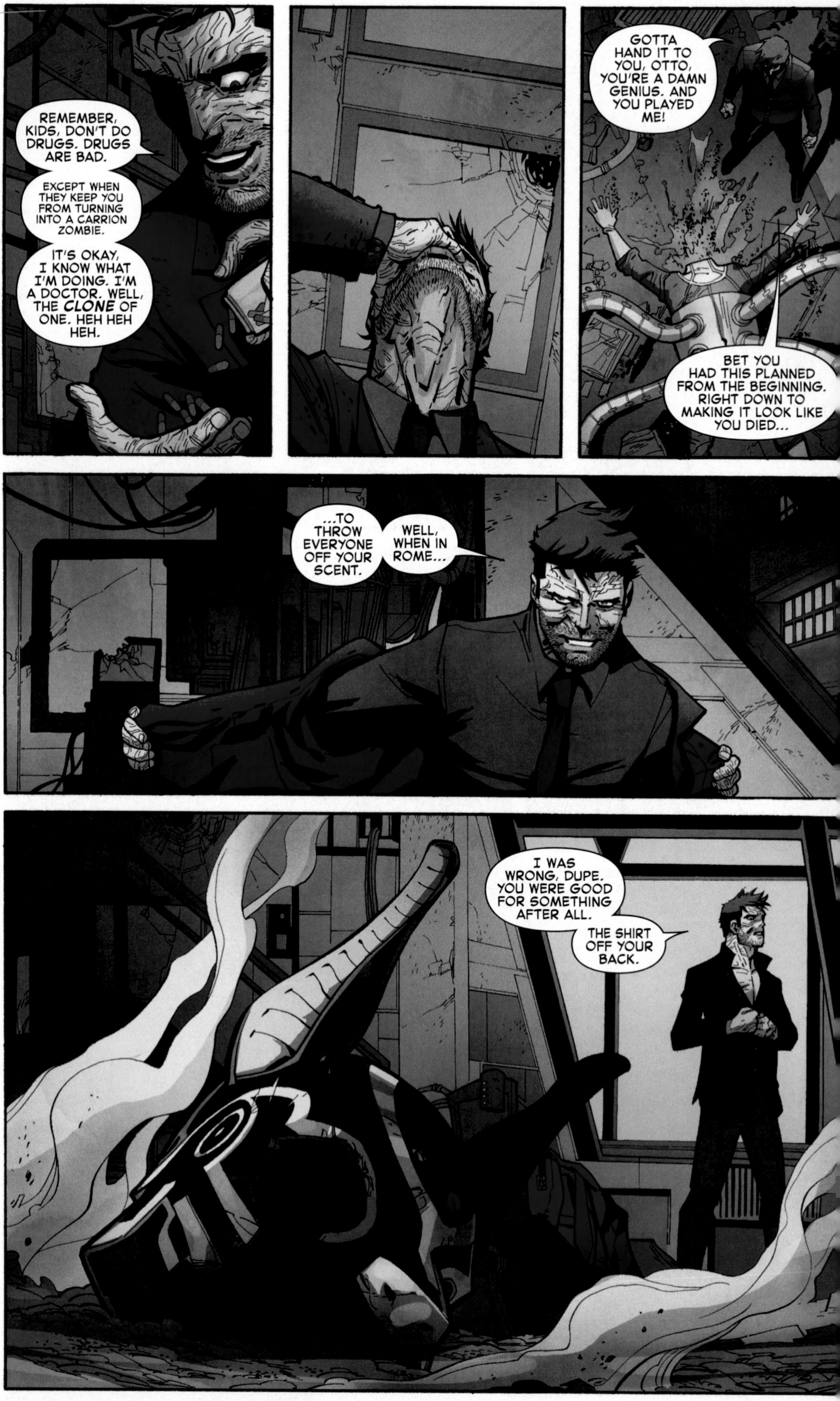
REMEMBER, KIDS, DON'T DO DRUGS. DRUGS ARE BAD.
EXCEPT WHEN THEY KEEP YOU FROM TURNING INTO A CARRION ZOMBIE.
IT'S OKAY, I KNOW WHAT I'M DOING. I'M A DOCTOR. WELL, THE CLONE OF ONE. HEH HEH HEH.
GOTTA HAND IT TO YOU, OTTO, YOU'RE A DAMN GENIUS. AND YOU PLAYED ME!
BET YOU HAD THIS PLANNED FROM THE BEGINNING. RIGHT DOWN TO MAKING IT LOOK LIKE YOU DIED...
...TO THROW EVERYONE OFF YOUR SCENT.
WELL, WHEN IN ROME...
I WAS WRONG, DUPE. YOU WERE GOOD FOR SOMETHING AFTER ALL.
THE SHIRT OFF YOUR BACK.

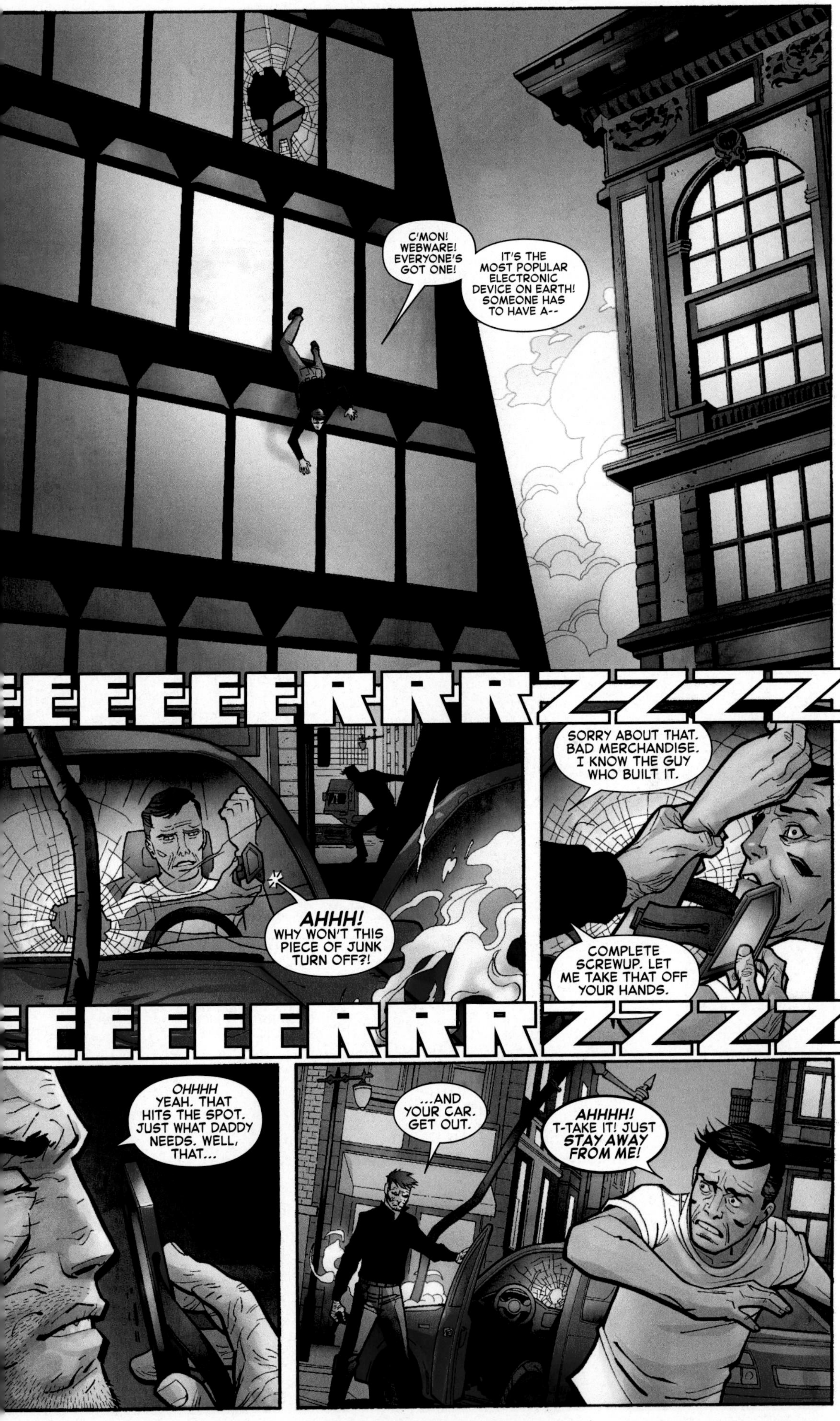
C'MON! WEBWARE! EVERYONE'S GOT ONE!
IT'S THE MOST POPULAR ELECTRONIC DEVICE ON EARTH! SOMEONE HAS TO HAVE A--
EEEEEERRRRZ-Z-Z-Z
AHHH! WHY WON'T THIS PIECE OF JUNK TURN OFF?!
SORRY ABOUT THAT. BAD MERCHANDISE. I KNOW THE GUY WHO BUILT IT.
COMPLETE SCREWUP. LET ME TAKE THAT OFF YOUR HANDS.
EEEEEERRRRZZZZ
OHHHH YEAH. THAT HITS THE SPOT. JUST WHAT DADDY NEEDS. WELL, THAT...
...AND YOUR CAR. GET OUT.
AHHHH! T-TAKE IT! JUST STAY AWAY FROM ME!

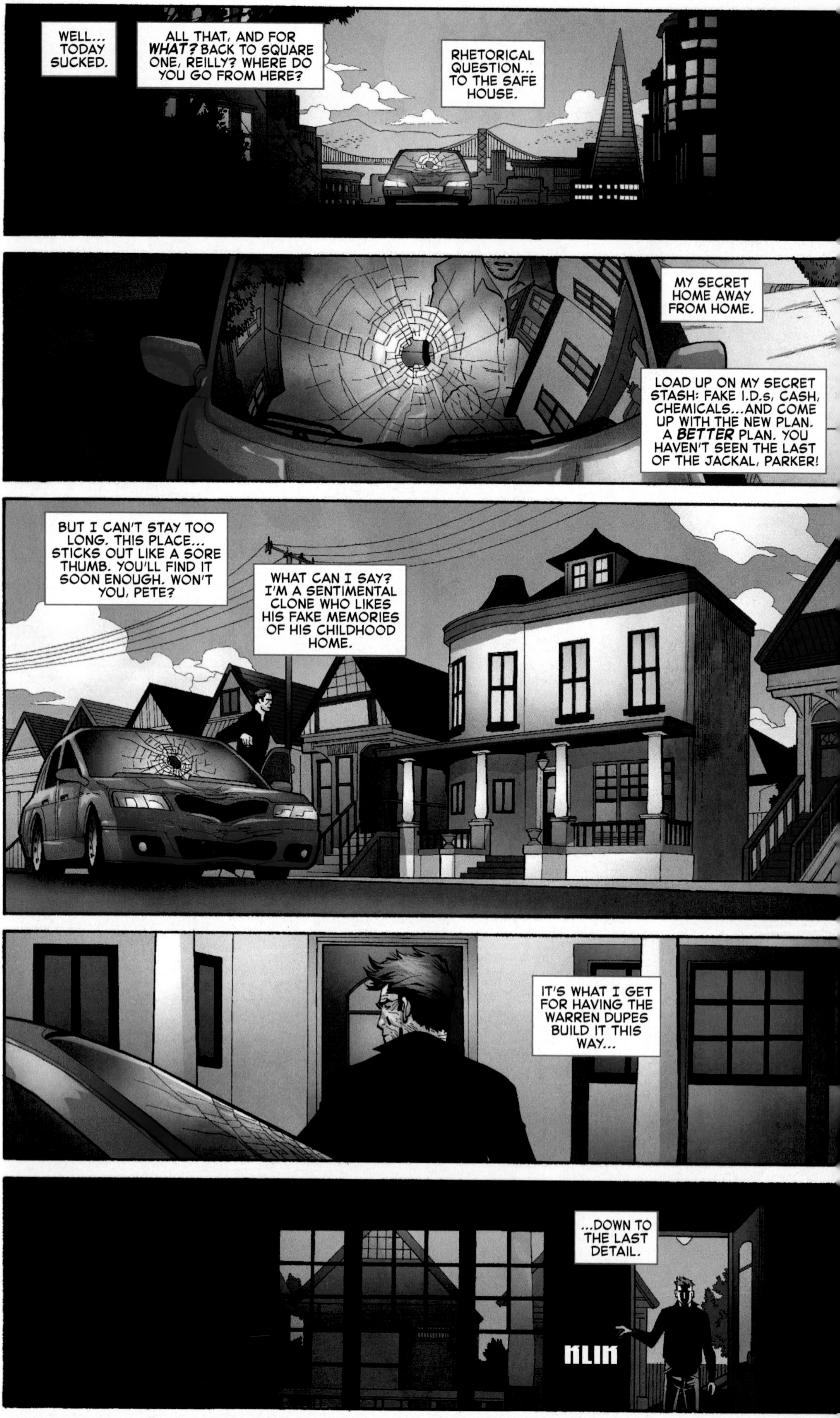

WELL... TODAY SUCKED.
ALL THAT, AND FOR WHAT? BACK TO SQUARE ONE, REILLY? WHERE DO YOU GO FROM HERE?
RHETORICAL QUESTION... TO THE SAFE HOUSE.
MY SECRET HOME AWAY FROM HOME.
LOAD UP ON MY SECRET STASH: FAKE I.D.s, CASH, CHEMICALS...AND COME UP WITH THE NEW PLAN. A BETTER PLAN. YOU HAVEN'T SEEN THE LAST OF THE JACKAL, PARKER!
BUT I CAN'T STAY TOO LONG. THIS PLACE... STICKS OUT LIKE A SORE THUMB. YOU'LL FIND IT SOON ENOUGH. WON'T YOU, PETE?
WHAT CAN I SAY? I'M A SENTIMENTAL CLONE WHO LIKES HIS FAKE MEMORIES OF HIS CHILDHOOD HOME.
IT'S WHAT I GET FOR HAVING THE WARREN DUPES BUILD IT THIS WAY...
...DOWN TO THE LAST DETAIL.
KLIK

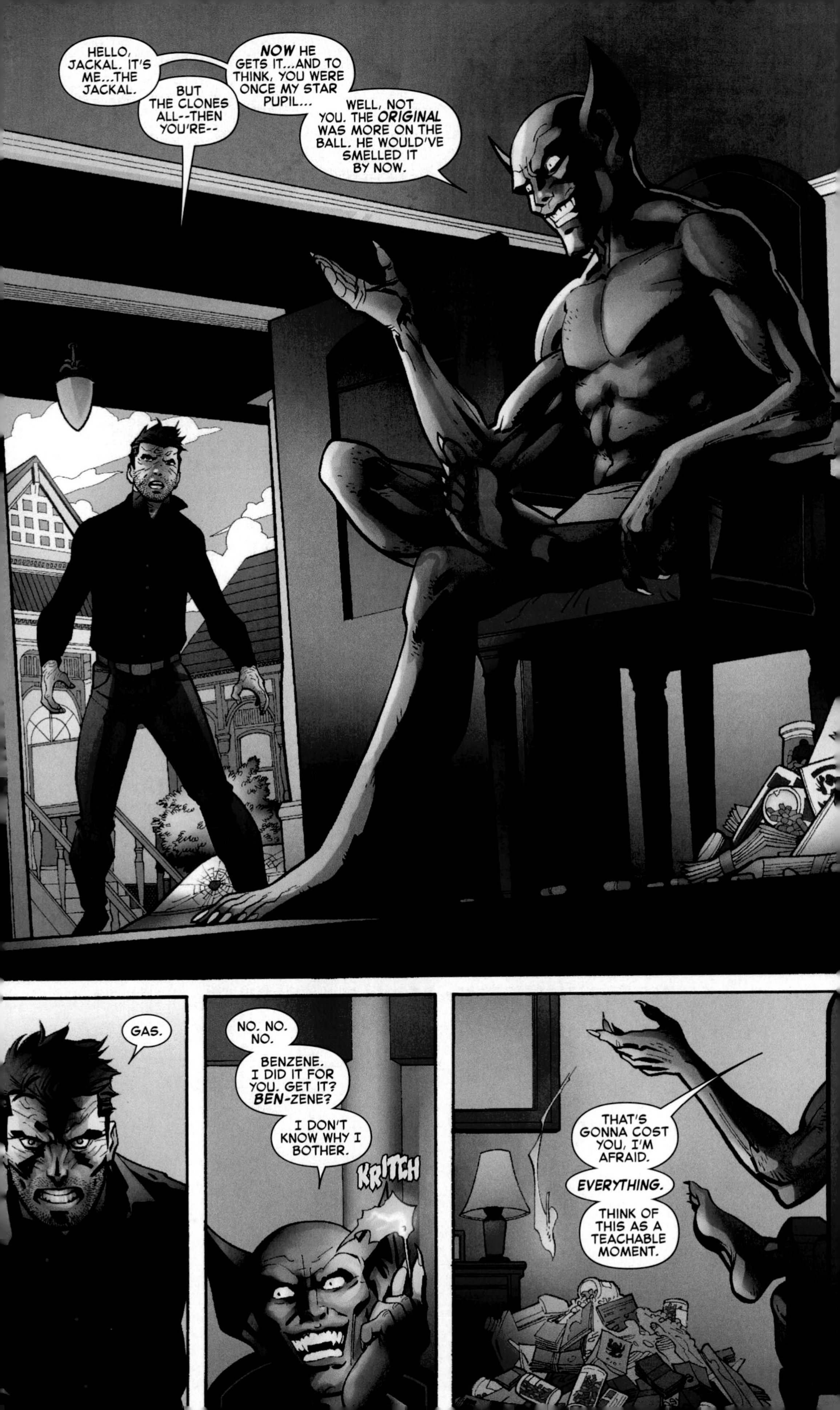
HELLO, JACKAL. IT'S ME...THE JACKAL.
BUT THE CLONES ALL--THEN YOU'RE--
NOW HE GETS IT...AND TO THINK, YOU WERE ONCE MY STAR PUPIL...
WELL, NOT YOU. THE ORIGINAL WAS MORE ON THE BALL. HE WOULD'VE SMELLED IT BY NOW.
GAS.
NO. NO. NO.
BENZENE. I DID IT FOR YOU. GET IT? BEN-ZENE?
I DON'T KNOW WHY I BOTHER.
KRITCH
THAT'S GONNA COST YOU, I'M AFRAID.
EVERYTHING.
THINK OF THIS AS A TEACHABLE MOMENT.

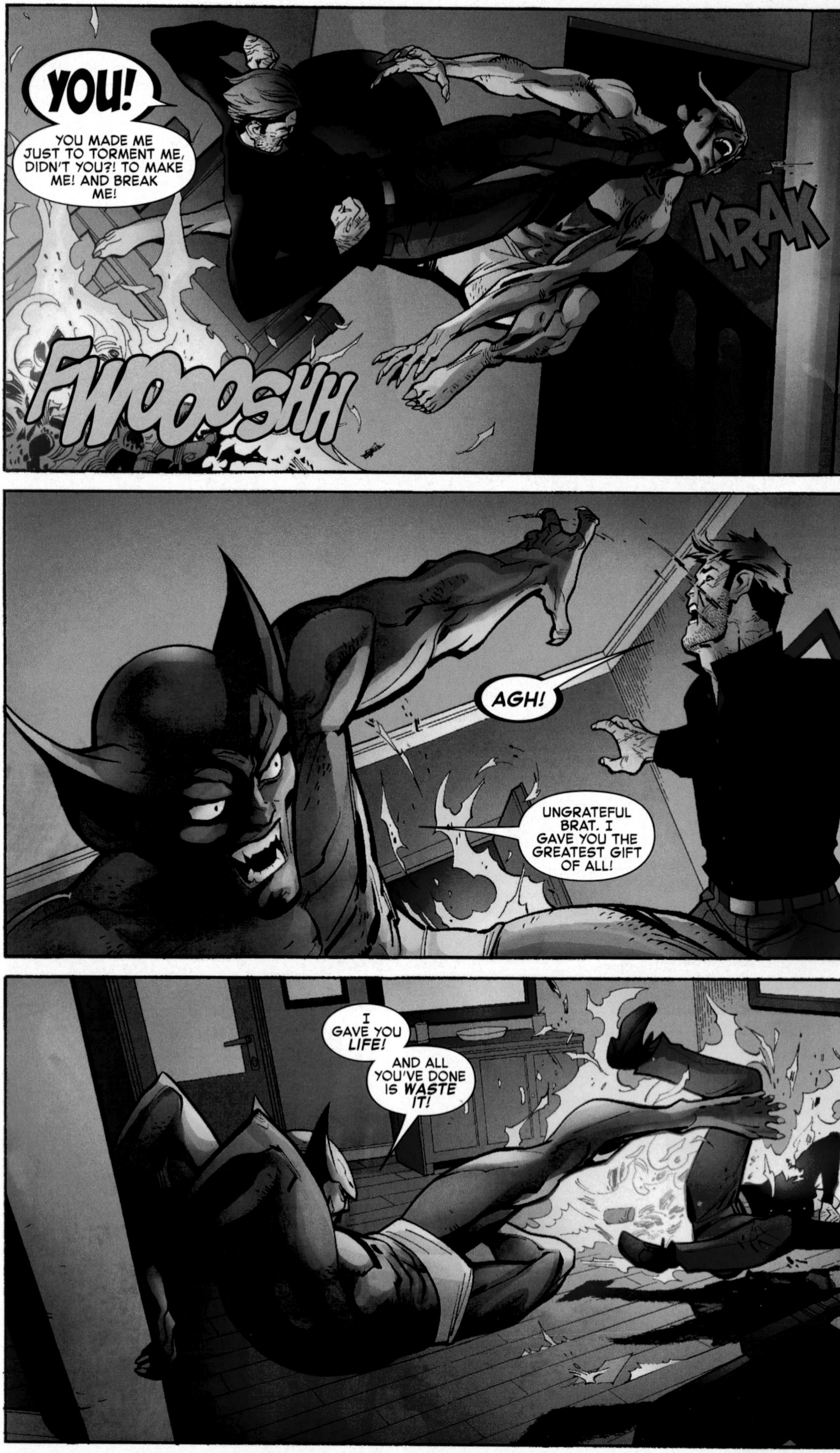
YOU!
YOU MADE ME JUST TO TORMENT ME, DIDN'T YOU?! TO MAKE ME! AND BREAK ME!
KRAK
FWOOOSHH
AGH!
UNGRATEFUL BRAT. I GAVE YOU THE GREATEST GIFT OF ALL!
I GAVE YOU *LIFE!*
AND ALL YOU'VE DONE IS *WASTE IT!*

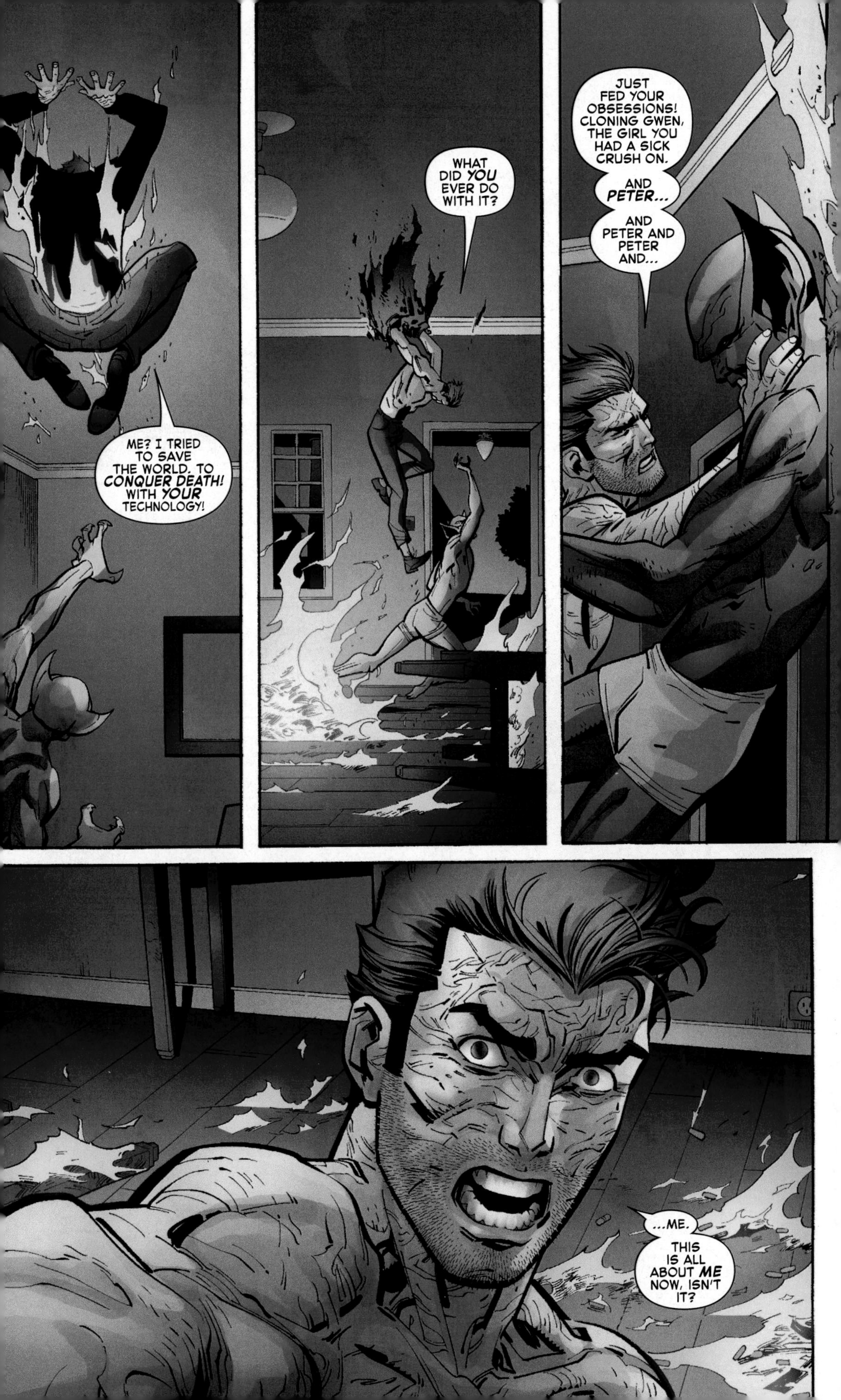
ME? I TRIED TO SAVE THE WORLD. TO CONQUER DEATH! WITH YOUR TECHNOLOGY!
WHAT DID YOU EVER DO WITH IT?
JUST FED YOUR OBSESSIONS! CLONING GWEN, THE GIRL YOU HAD A SICK CRUSH ON.
AND PETER...
AND PETER AND PETER AND...
...ME.
THIS IS ALL ABOUT ME NOW, ISN'T IT?

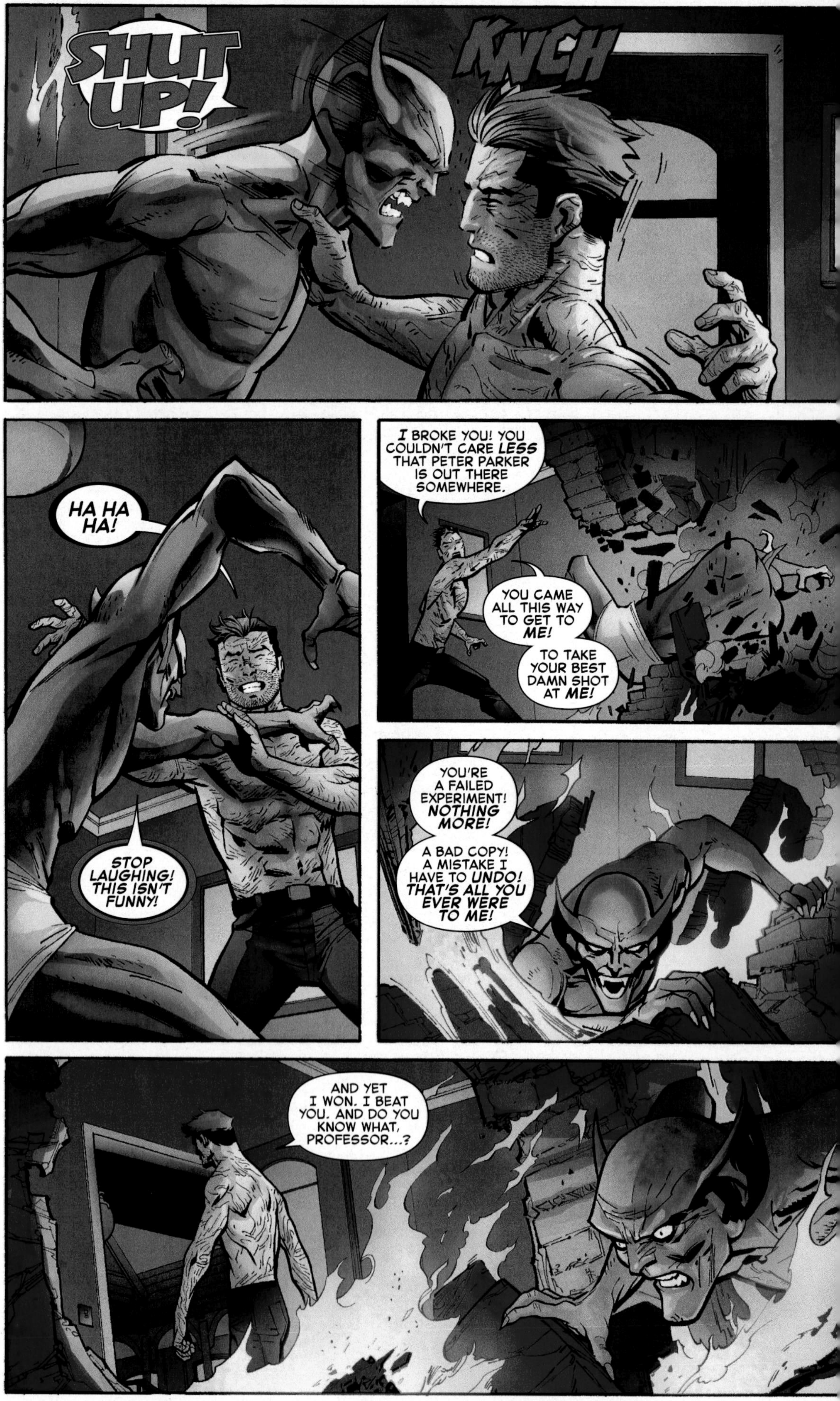
SHUT UP!
KNCH
HA HA HA!
STOP LAUGHING! THIS ISN'T FUNNY!
I BROKE YOU! YOU COULDN'T CARE LESS THAT PETER PARKER IS OUT THERE SOMEWHERE.
YOU CAME ALL THIS WAY TO GET TO ME!
TO TAKE YOUR BEST DAMN SHOT AT ME!
YOU'RE A FAILED EXPERIMENT! NOTHING MORE!
A BAD COPY! A MISTAKE I HAVE TO UNDO! THAT'S ALL YOU EVER WERE TO ME!
AND YET I WON. I BEAT YOU. AND DO YOU KNOW WHAT, PROFESSOR...?

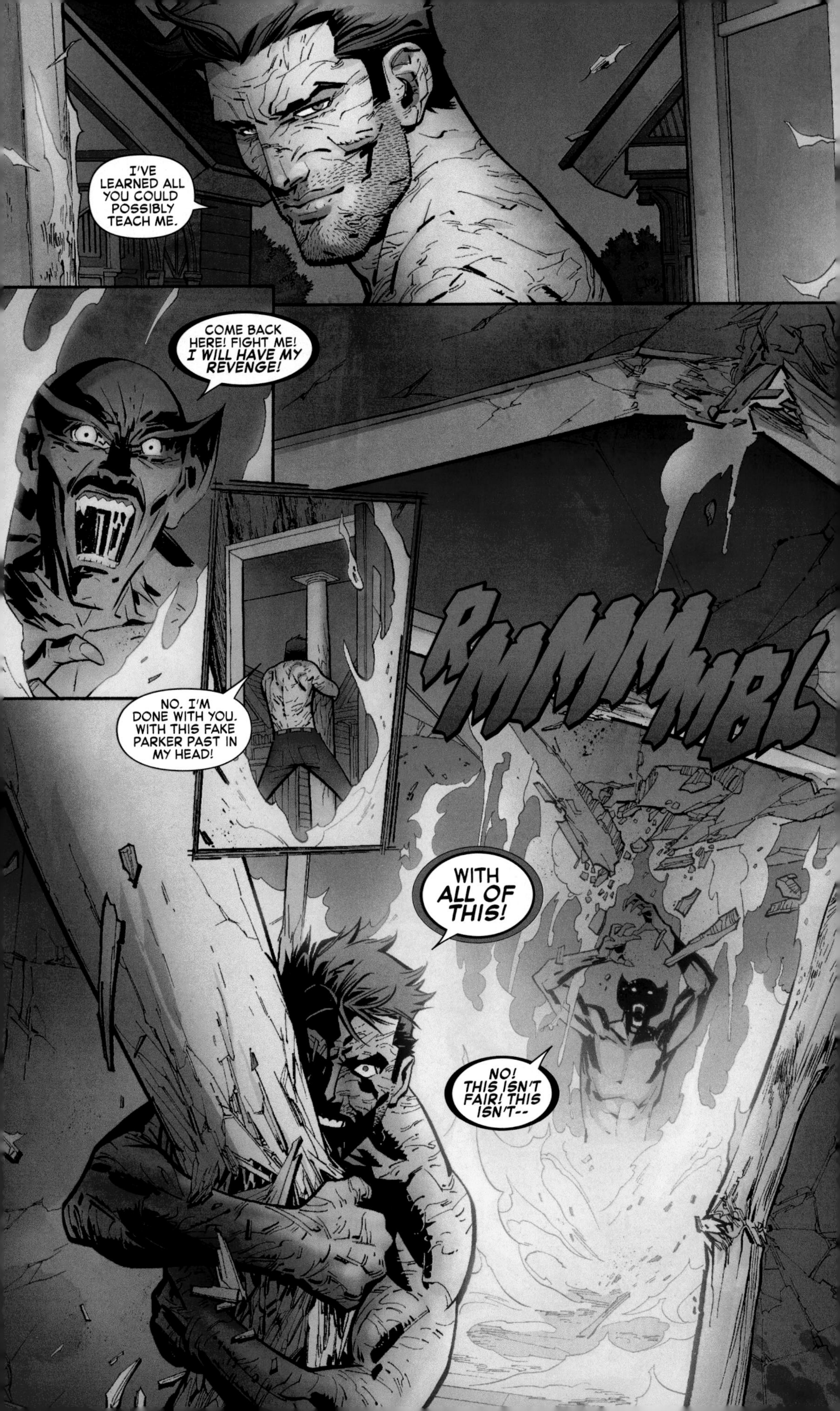
I'VE LEARNED ALL YOU COULD POSSIBLY TEACH ME.
COME BACK HERE! FIGHT ME! *I WILL HAVE MY REVENGE!*
NO. I'M DONE WITH YOU. WITH THIS FAKE PARKER PAST IN MY HEAD!
RMMMMMBL
WITH **ALL OF THIS!**
NO! THIS ISN'T FAIR! THIS ISN'T--

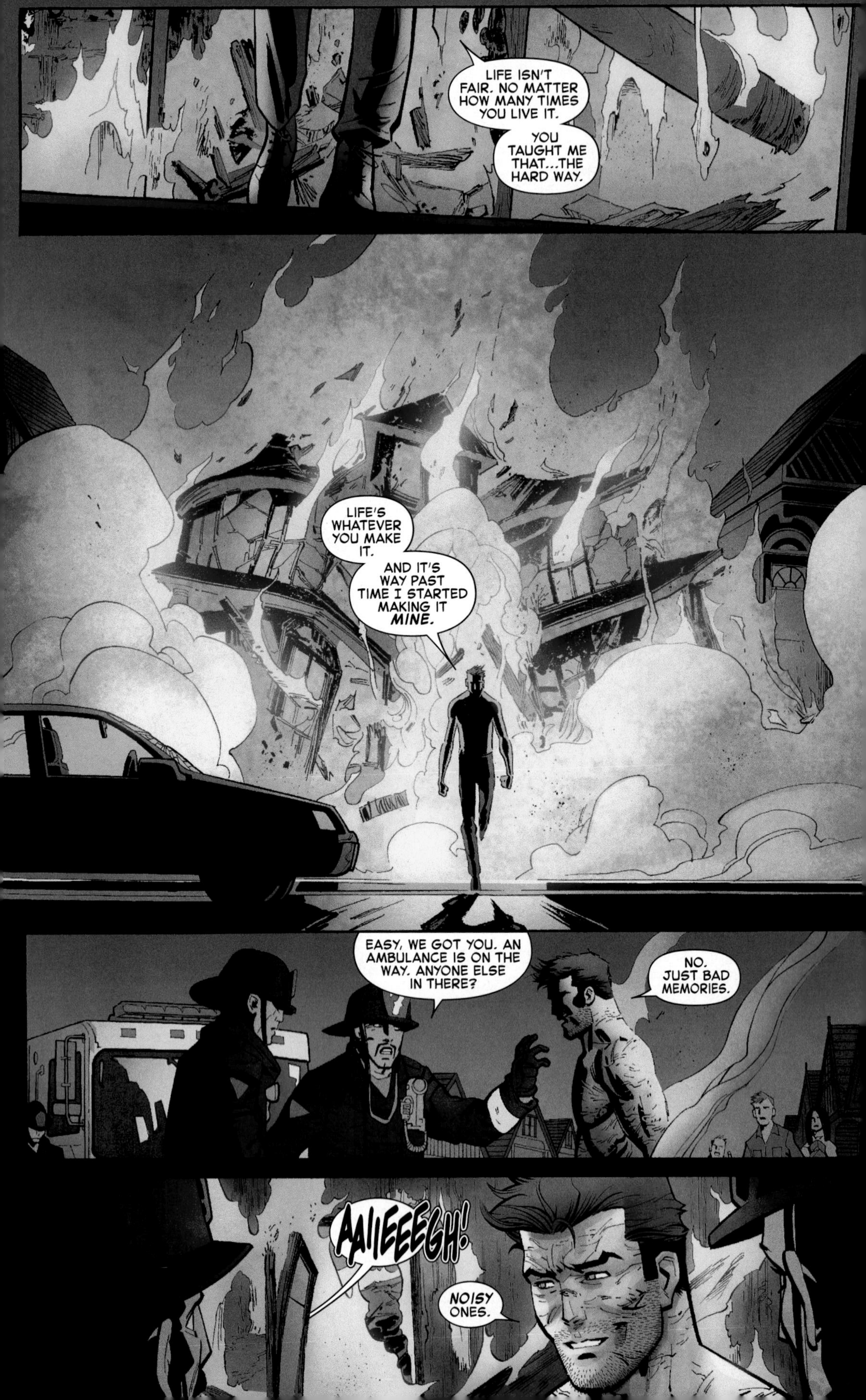
LIFE ISN'T FAIR. NO MATTER HOW MANY TIMES YOU LIVE IT.
YOU TAUGHT ME THAT...THE HARD WAY.
LIFE'S WHATEVER YOU MAKE IT.
AND IT'S WAY PAST TIME I STARTED MAKING IT MINE.
EASY, WE GOT YOU. AN AMBULANCE IS ON THE WAY. ANYONE ELSE IN THERE?
NO. JUST BAD MEMORIES.
AAIIEEEGH!
NOISY ONES.

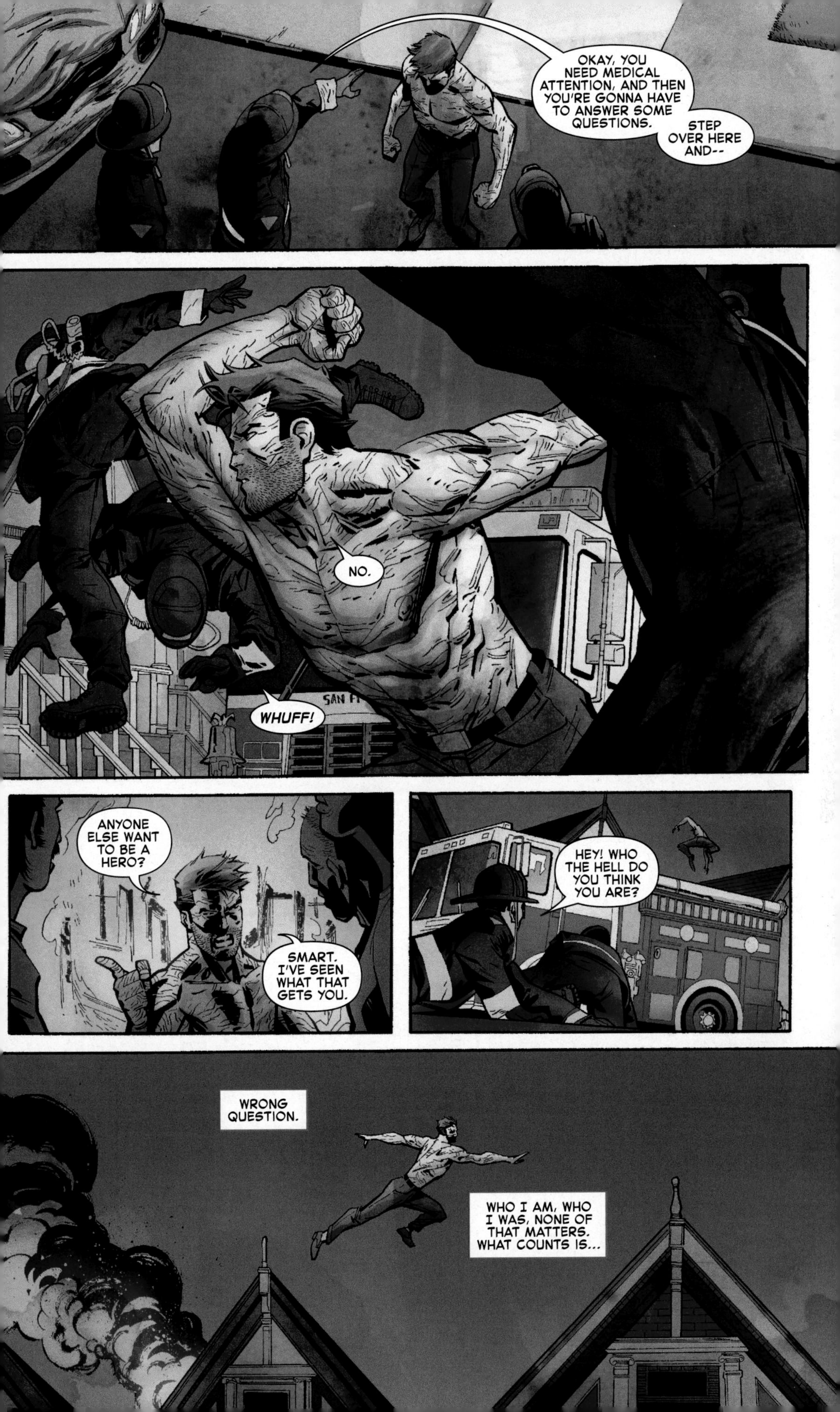
OKAY, YOU NEED MEDICAL ATTENTION, AND THEN YOU'RE GONNA HAVE TO ANSWER SOME QUESTIONS.
STEP OVER HERE AND--
NO.
WHUFF!
SAN FR
ANYONE ELSE WANT TO BE A HERO?
SMART. I'VE SEEN WHAT THAT GETS YOU.
HEY! WHO THE HELL DO YOU THINK YOU ARE?
WRONG QUESTION.
WHO I AM, WHO I WAS, NONE OF THAT MATTERS. WHAT COUNTS IS...

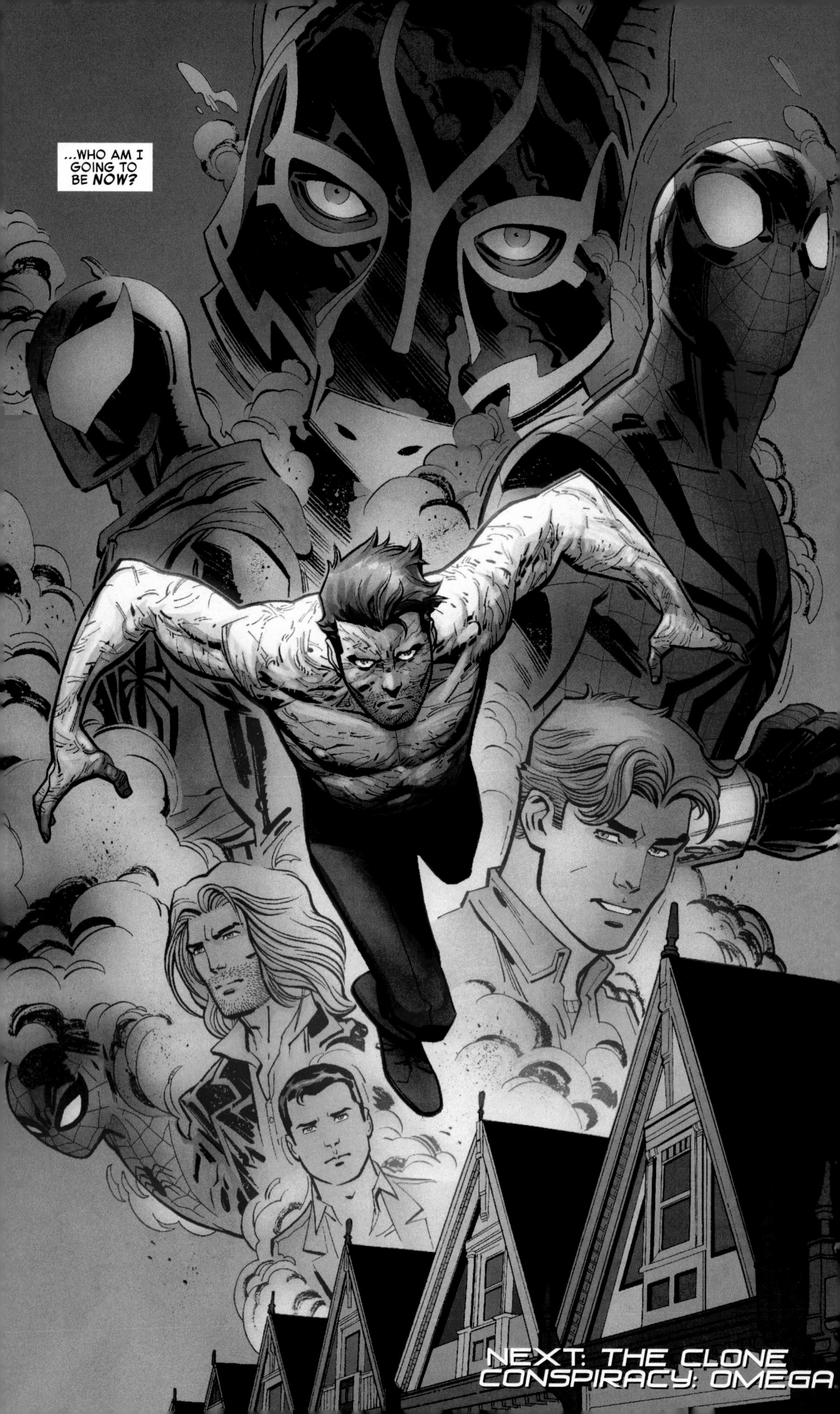
...WHO AM I GOING TO BE NOW?
NEXT: THE CLONE CONSPIRACY: OMEGA

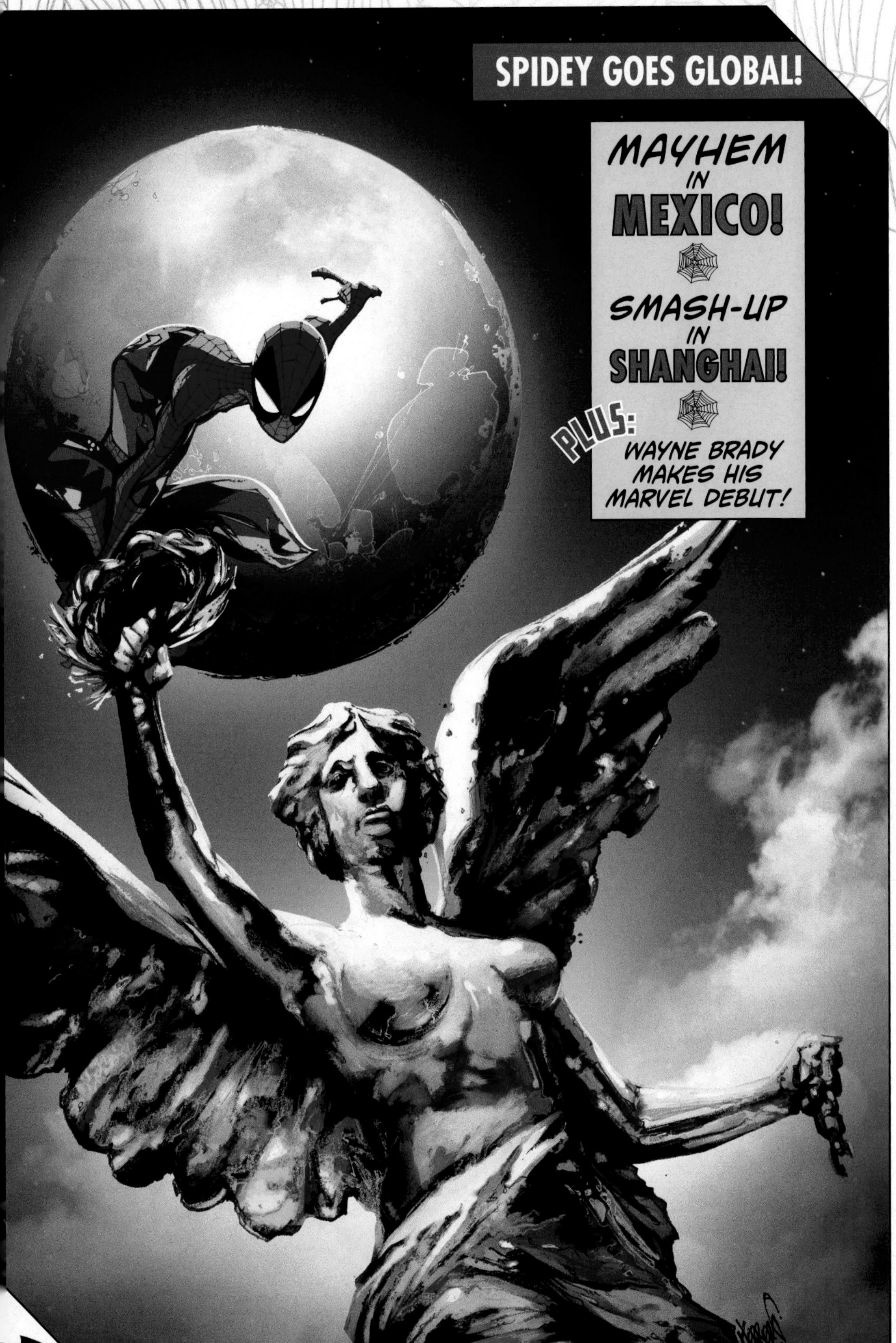
SPIDEY GOES GLOBAL!
MAYHEM IN MEXICO!
SMASH-UP IN SHANGHAI!
PLUS:
WAYNE BRADY MAKES HIS MARVEL DEBUT!

AMAZING SPIDER-MAN ANNUAL 1

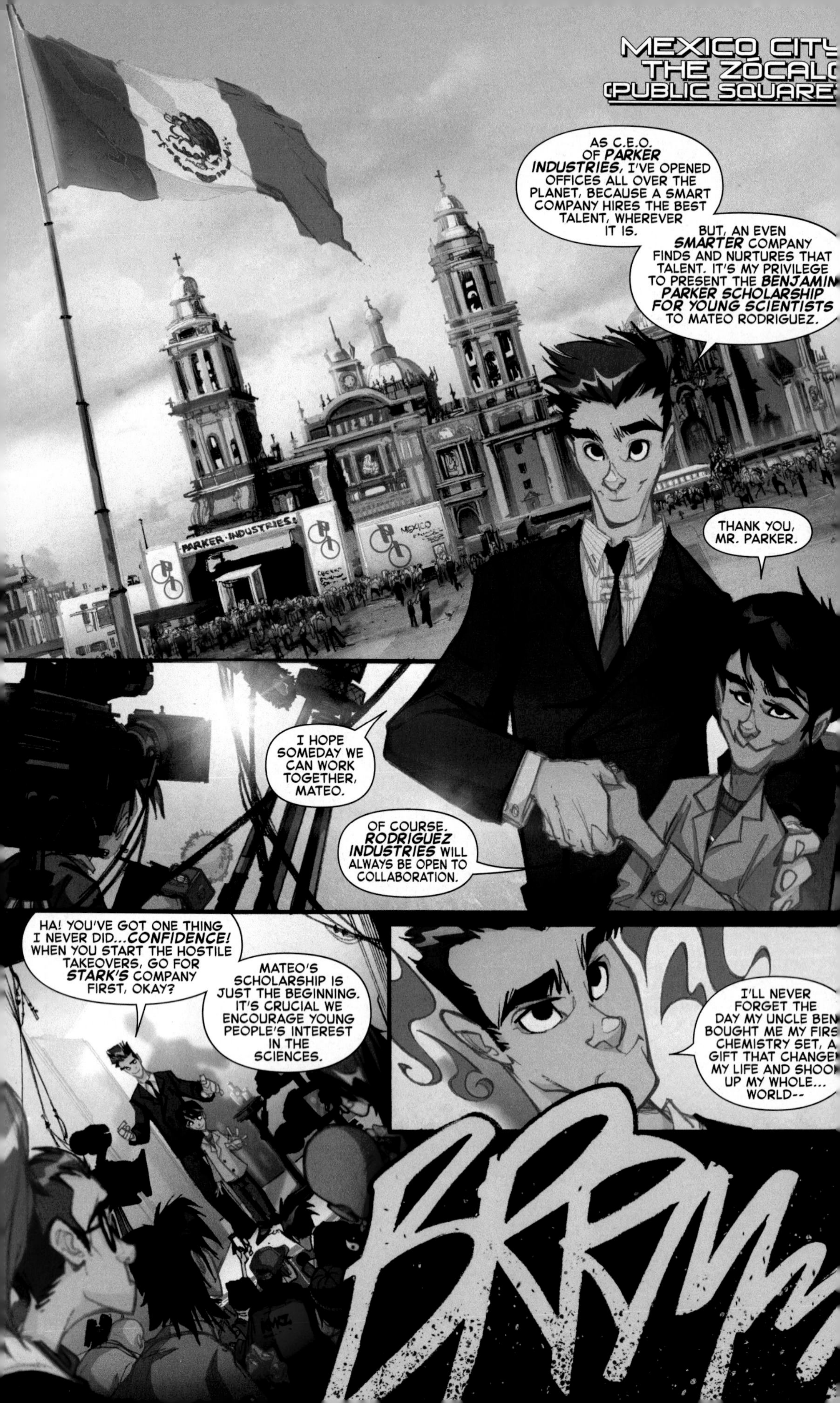
MEXICO CITY THE ZÓCALO (PUBLIC SQUARE)
AS C.E.O. OF PARKER INDUSTRIES, I'VE OPENED OFFICES ALL OVER THE PLANET, BECAUSE A SMART COMPANY HIRES THE BEST TALENT, WHEREVER IT IS.
BUT, AN EVEN SMARTER COMPANY FINDS AND NURTURES THAT TALENT. IT'S MY PRIVILEGE TO PRESENT THE BENJAMIN PARKER SCHOLARSHIP FOR YOUNG SCIENTISTS TO MATEO RODRIGUEZ.
PARKER INDUSTRIES
THANK YOU, MR. PARKER.
I HOPE SOMEDAY WE CAN WORK TOGETHER, MATEO.
OF COURSE. RODRIGUEZ INDUSTRIES WILL ALWAYS BE OPEN TO COLLABORATION.
HA! YOU'VE GOT ONE THING I NEVER DID...CONFIDENCE! WHEN YOU START THE HOSTILE TAKEOVERS, GO FOR STARK'S COMPANY FIRST, OKAY?
MATEO'S SCHOLARSHIP IS JUST THE BEGINNING. IT'S CRUCIAL WE ENCOURAGE YOUNG PEOPLE'S INTEREST IN THE SCIENCES.
I'LL NEVER FORGET THE DAY MY UNCLE BEN BOUGHT ME MY FIRST CHEMISTRY SET, A GIFT THAT CHANGED MY LIFE AND SHOOK UP MY WHOLE... WORLD--

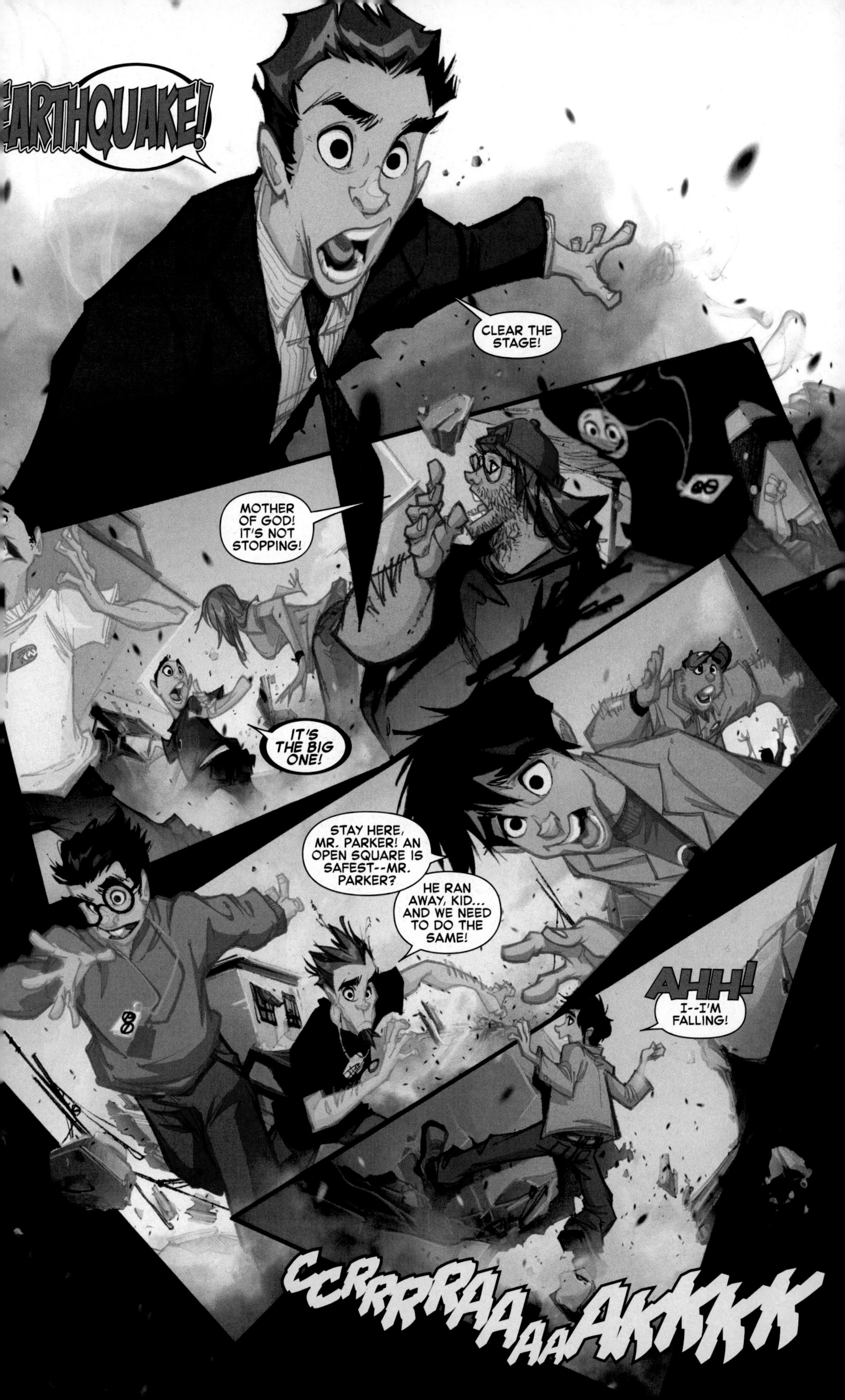
EARTHQUAKE!
CLEAR THE STAGE!
MOTHER OF GOD! IT'S NOT STOPPING!
IT'S THE BIG ONE!
STAY HERE, MR. PARKER! AN OPEN SQUARE IS SAFEST--MR. PARKER?
HE RAN AWAY, KID... AND WE NEED TO DO THE SAME!
AHH!
I--I'M FALLING!
CCRRRRRAAAAAKKKKK

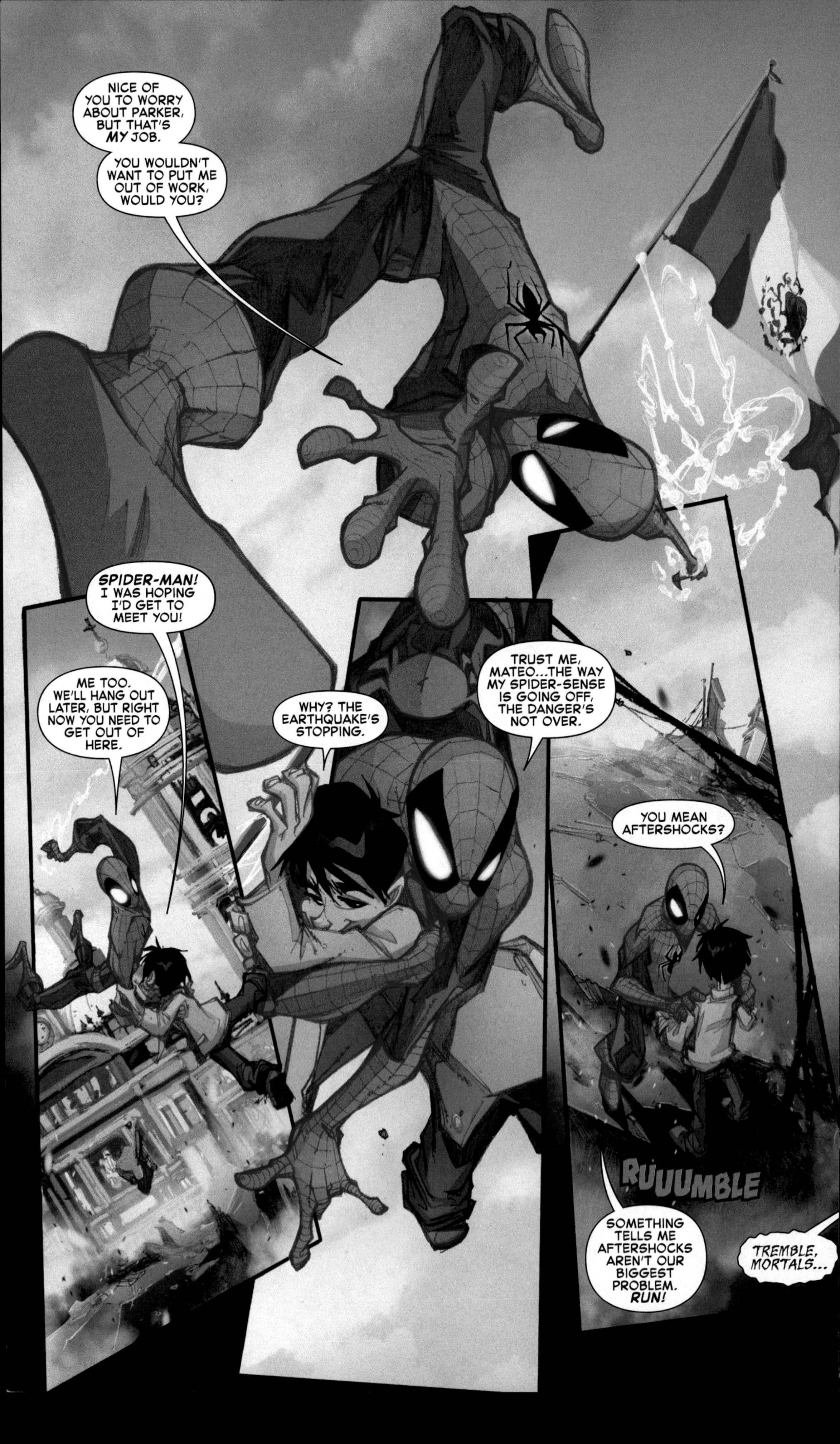
NICE OF YOU TO WORRY ABOUT PARKER, BUT THAT'S *MY* JOB.
YOU WOULDN'T WANT TO PUT ME OUT OF WORK, WOULD YOU?
SPIDER-MAN! I WAS HOPING I'D GET TO MEET YOU!
ME TOO. WE'LL HANG OUT LATER, BUT RIGHT NOW YOU NEED TO GET OUT OF HERE.
WHY? THE EARTHQUAKE'S STOPPING.
TRUST ME, MATEO...THE WAY MY SPIDER-SENSE IS GOING OFF, THE DANGER'S NOT OVER.
YOU MEAN AFTERSHOCKS?
RUUUMBLE
SOMETHING TELLS ME AFTERSHOCKS AREN'T OUR BIGGEST PROBLEM. *RUN!*
TREMBLE, MORTALS...

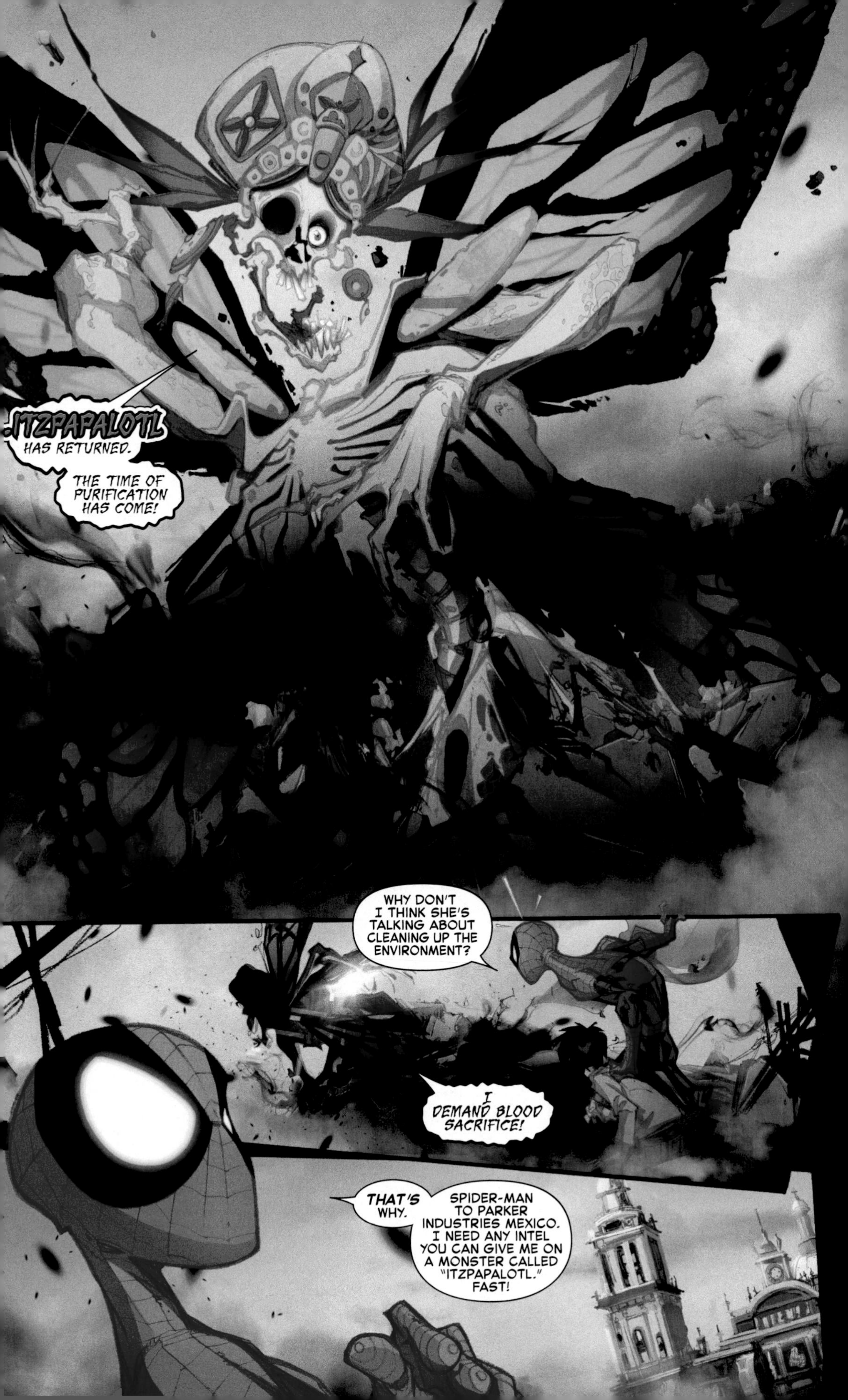
...ITZPAPALOTL HAS RETURNED.
THE TIME OF PURIFICATION HAS COME!
WHY DON'T I THINK SHE'S TALKING ABOUT CLEANING UP THE ENVIRONMENT?
I DEMAND BLOOD SACRIFICE!
THAT'S WHY.
SPIDER-MAN TO PARKER INDUSTRIES MEXICO. I NEED ANY INTEL YOU CAN GIVE ME ON A MONSTER CALLED "ITZPAPALOTL." FAST!

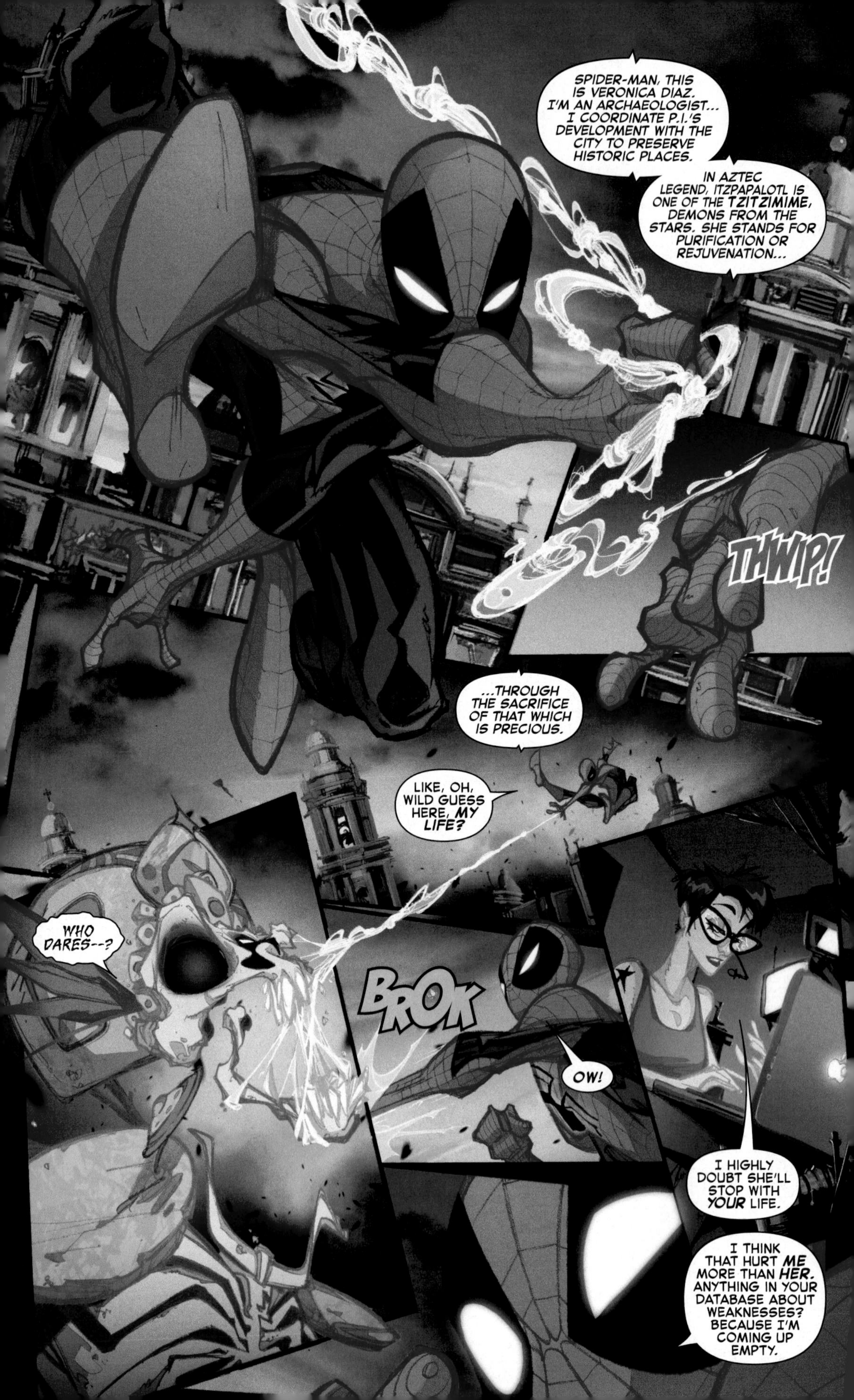
SPIDER-MAN, THIS IS VERONICA DIAZ. I'M AN ARCHAEOLOGIST... I COORDINATE P.I.'S DEVELOPMENT WITH THE CITY TO PRESERVE HISTORIC PLACES.
IN AZTEC LEGEND, ITZPAPALOTL IS ONE OF THE TZITZIMIME, DEMONS FROM THE STARS. SHE STANDS FOR PURIFICATION OR REJUVENATION...
THWIP!
...THROUGH THE SACRIFICE OF THAT WHICH IS PRECIOUS.
LIKE, OH, WILD GUESS HERE, MY LIFE?
WHO DARES--?
BROK
OW!
I HIGHLY DOUBT SHE'LL STOP WITH YOUR LIFE.
I THINK THAT HURT ME MORE THAN HER. ANYTHING IN YOUR DATABASE ABOUT WEAKNESSES? BECAUSE I'M COMING UP EMPTY.

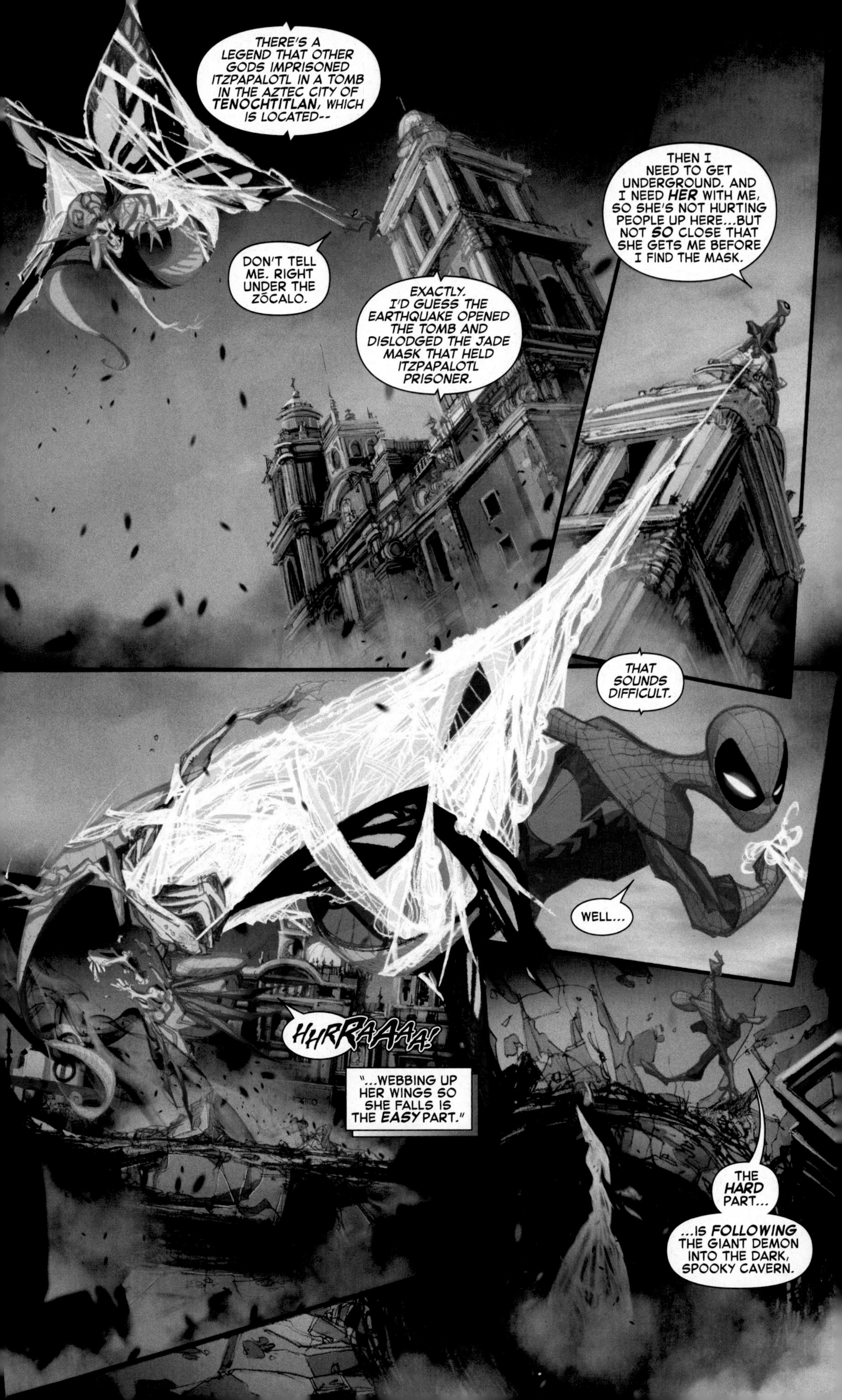

THERE'S A LEGEND THAT OTHER GODS IMPRISONED ITZPAPALOTL IN A TOMB IN THE AZTEC CITY OF TENOCHTITLAN, WHICH IS LOCATED--
DON'T TELL ME. RIGHT UNDER THE ZÓCALO.
EXACTLY. I'D GUESS THE EARTHQUAKE OPENED THE TOMB AND DISLODGED THE JADE MASK THAT HELD ITZPAPALOTL PRISONER.
THEN I NEED TO GET UNDERGROUND. AND I NEED HER WITH ME, SO SHE'S NOT HURTING PEOPLE UP HERE...BUT NOT SO CLOSE THAT SHE GETS ME BEFORE I FIND THE MASK.
THAT SOUNDS DIFFICULT.
WELL...
HHRRAAAAA!
"...WEBBING UP HER WINGS SO SHE FALLS IS THE EASY PART."
THE HARD PART...
...IS FOLLOWING THE GIANT DEMON INTO THE DARK, SPOOKY CAVERN.

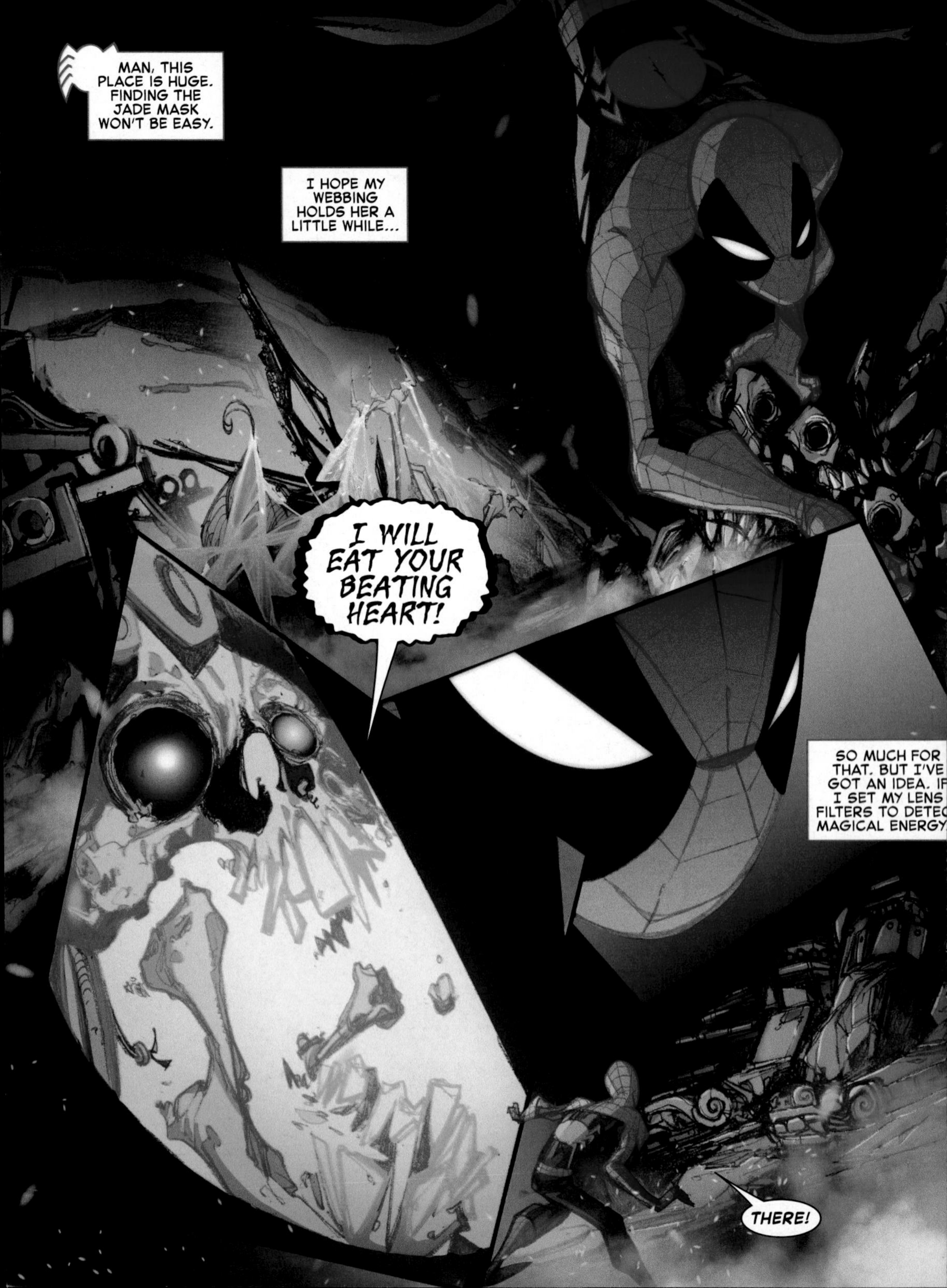
MAN, THIS PLACE IS HUGE. FINDING THE JADE MASK WON'T BE EASY.
I HOPE MY WEBBING HOLDS HER A LITTLE WHILE...
I WILL EAT YOUR BEATING HEART!
SO MUCH FOR THAT. BUT I'VE GOT AN IDEA. IF I SET MY LENS FILTERS TO DETEC MAGICAL ENERGY
THERE!

FOUND IT. NOW ALL I HAVE TO DO IS PUT THE MASK BACK ON HER.
BUT I'VE SEEN ENOUGH MOVIES TO KNOW YOU DON'T JUST GRAB ANCIENT ARTIFACTS WITHOUT EXPECTING BOOBY TRAPS.
SO, WITH A BAG FULL OF DEBRIS, AND APOLOGIES TO INDIANA JONES!
THE MASK? YOU FANCY YOURSELF EQUAL TO THE GODS OF OLD?
APPROACH, THEN! LET US SEE IF YOU CAN SURVIVE MY ATTENTIONS!
THWIP
SORRY. YOU'RE TOO MUCH WOMAN FOR ME. I'LL JUST ADMIRE YOU FROM AFAR...
...AND SEND GIFTS.

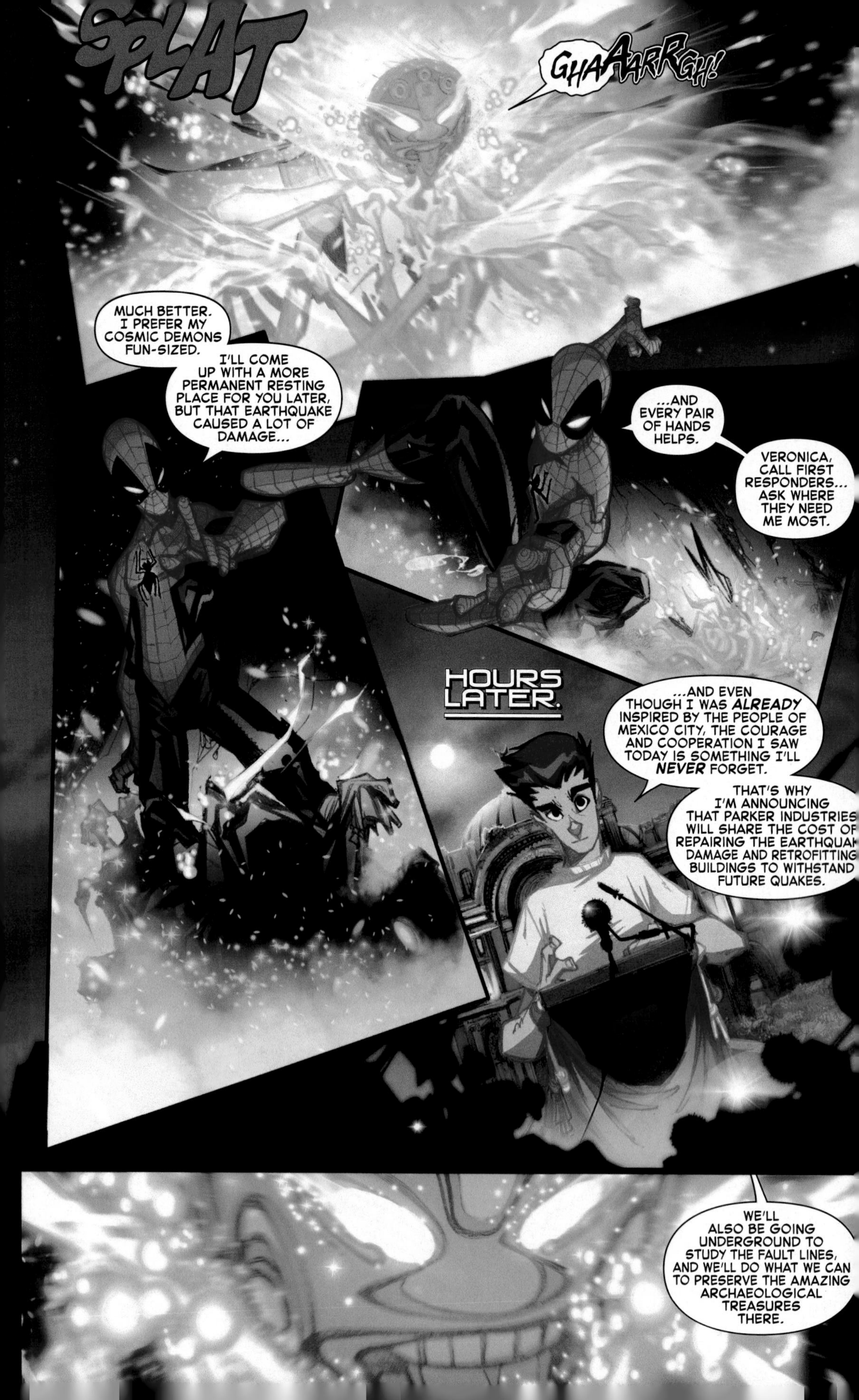
SPLAT
GHAAARRGH!
MUCH BETTER. I PREFER MY COSMIC DEMONS FUN-SIZED.
I'LL COME UP WITH A MORE PERMANENT RESTING PLACE FOR YOU LATER, BUT THAT EARTHQUAKE CAUSED A LOT OF DAMAGE...
...AND EVERY PAIR OF HANDS HELPS.
VERONICA, CALL FIRST RESPONDERS... ASK WHERE THEY NEED ME MOST.
HOURS LATER.
...AND EVEN THOUGH I WAS ALREADY INSPIRED BY THE PEOPLE OF MEXICO CITY, THE COURAGE AND COOPERATION I SAW TODAY IS SOMETHING I'LL NEVER FORGET.
THAT'S WHY I'M ANNOUNCING THAT PARKER INDUSTRIES WILL SHARE THE COST OF REPAIRING THE EARTHQUAK DAMAGE AND RETROFITTING BUILDINGS TO WITHSTAND FUTURE QUAKES.
WE'LL ALSO BE GOING UNDERGROUND TO STUDY THE FAULT LINES, AND WE'LL DO WHAT WE CAN TO PRESERVE THE AMAZING ARCHAEOLOGICAL TREASURES THERE.

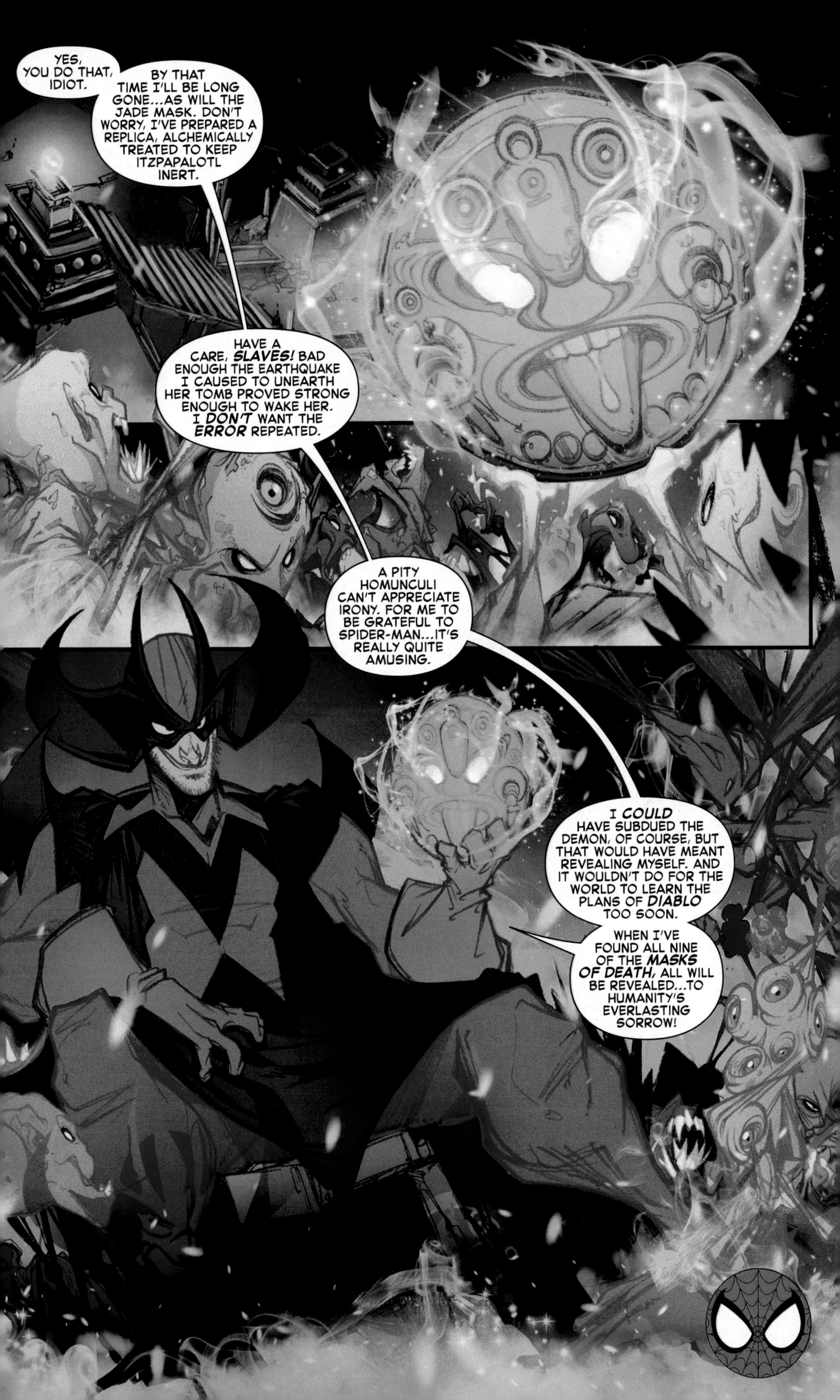

YES, YOU DO THAT, IDIOT.
BY THAT TIME I'LL BE LONG GONE...AS WILL THE JADE MASK. DON'T WORRY, I'VE PREPARED A REPLICA, ALCHEMICALLY TREATED TO KEEP ITZPAPALOTL INERT.
HAVE A CARE, SLAVES! BAD ENOUGH THE EARTHQUAKE I CAUSED TO UNEARTH HER TOMB PROVED STRONG ENOUGH TO WAKE HER. I DON'T WANT THE ERROR REPEATED.
A PITY HOMUNCULI CAN'T APPRECIATE IRONY. FOR ME TO BE GRATEFUL TO SPIDER-MAN...IT'S REALLY QUITE AMUSING.
I COULD HAVE SUBDUED THE DEMON, OF COURSE, BUT THAT WOULD HAVE MEANT REVEALING MYSELF. AND IT WOULDN'T DO FOR THE WORLD TO LEARN THE PLANS OF DIABLO TOO SOON.
WHEN I'VE FOUND ALL NINE OF THE MASKS OF DEATH, ALL WILL BE REVEALED...TO HUMANITY'S EVERLASTING SORROW!

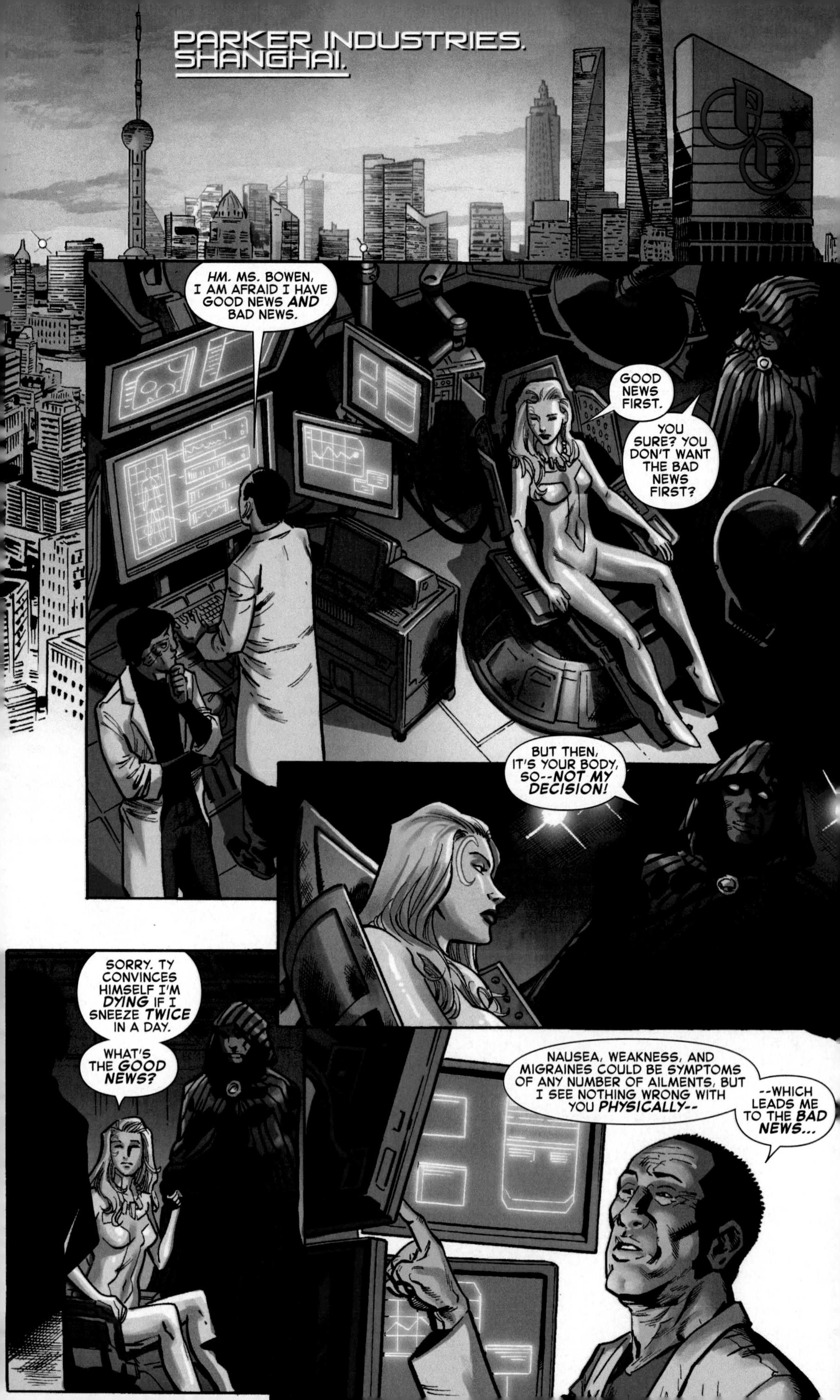
PARKER INDUSTRIES. SHANGHAI.
HM. MS. BOWEN, I AM AFRAID I HAVE GOOD NEWS AND BAD NEWS.
GOOD NEWS FIRST.
YOU SURE? YOU DON'T WANT THE BAD NEWS FIRST?
BUT THEN, IT'S YOUR BODY, SO--NOT MY DECISION!
SORRY. TY CONVINCES HIMSELF I'M DYING IF I SNEEZE TWICE IN A DAY.
WHAT'S THE GOOD NEWS?
NAUSEA, WEAKNESS, AND MIGRAINES COULD BE SYMPTOMS OF ANY NUMBER OF AILMENTS, BUT I SEE NOTHING WRONG WITH YOU PHYSICALLY--
--WHICH LEADS ME TO THE BAD NEWS...

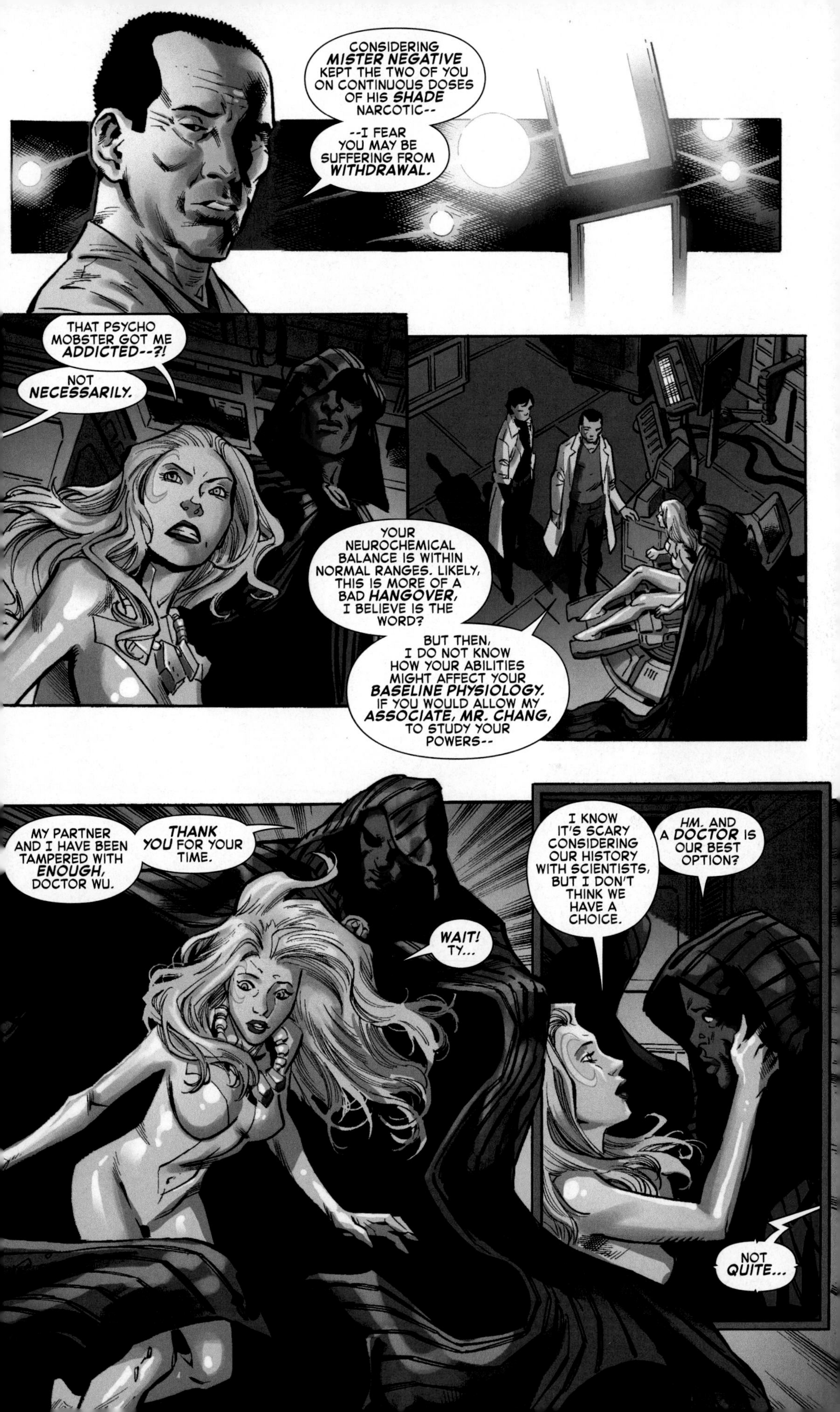
CONSIDERING MISTER NEGATIVE KEPT THE TWO OF YOU ON CONTINUOUS DOSES OF HIS SHADE NARCOTIC--
--I FEAR YOU MAY BE SUFFERING FROM WITHDRAWAL.
THAT PSYCHO MOBSTER GOT ME ADDICTED--?!
NOT NECESSARILY.
YOUR NEUROCHEMICAL BALANCE IS WITHIN NORMAL RANGES. LIKELY, THIS IS MORE OF A BAD HANGOVER, I BELIEVE IS THE WORD?
BUT THEN, I DO NOT KNOW HOW YOUR ABILITIES MIGHT AFFECT YOUR BASELINE PHYSIOLOGY. IF YOU WOULD ALLOW MY ASSOCIATE, MR. CHANG, TO STUDY YOUR POWERS--
MY PARTNER AND I HAVE BEEN TAMPERED WITH ENOUGH, DOCTOR WU.
THANK YOU FOR YOUR TIME.
WAIT! TY...
I KNOW IT'S SCARY CONSIDERING OUR HISTORY WITH SCIENTISTS, BUT I DON'T THINK WE HAVE A CHOICE.
HM. AND A DOCTOR IS OUR BEST OPTION?
NOT QUITE...

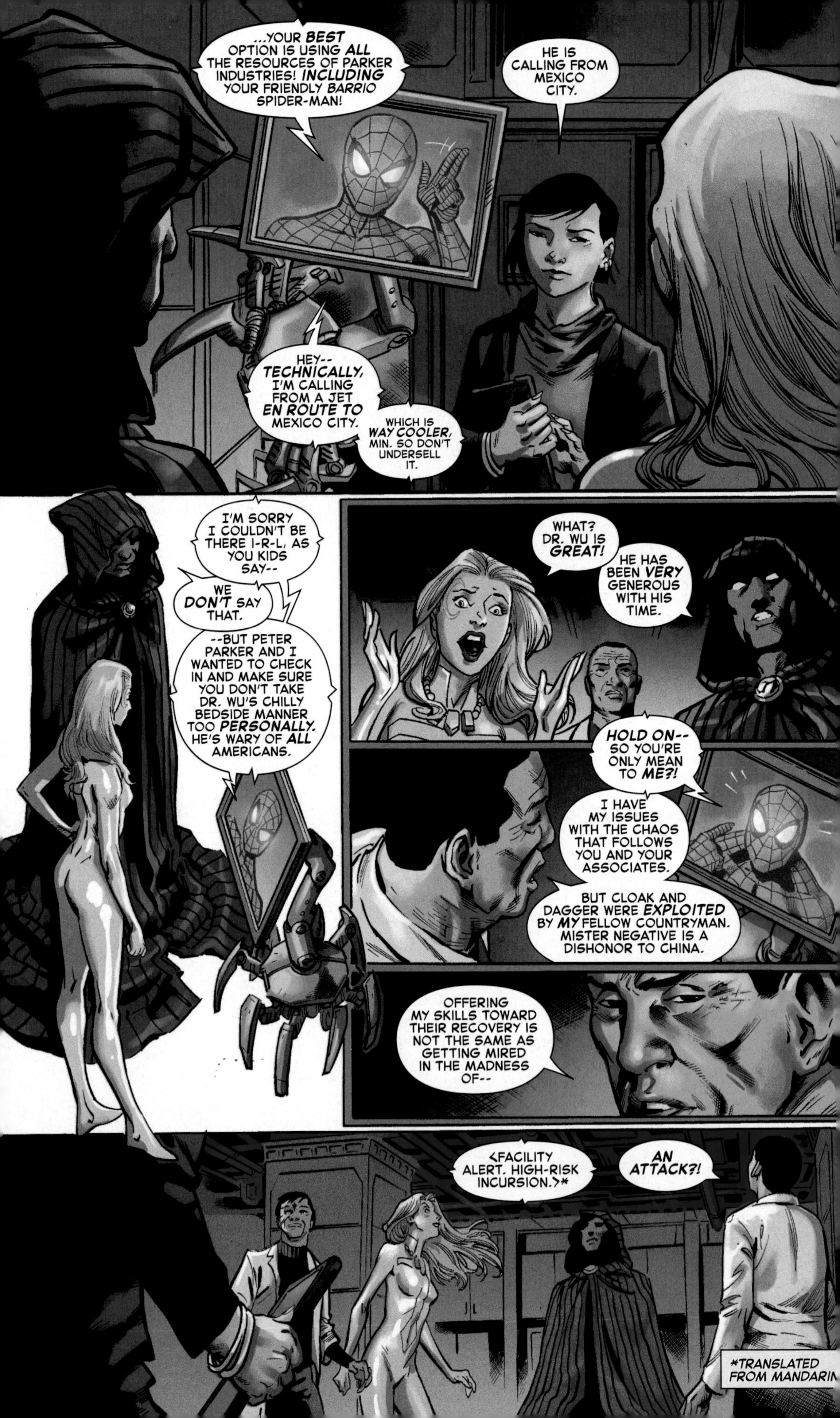
...YOUR BEST OPTION IS USING ALL THE RESOURCES OF PARKER INDUSTRIES! INCLUDING YOUR FRIENDLY BARRIO SPIDER-MAN!
HE IS CALLING FROM MEXICO CITY.
HEY-- TECHNICALLY, I'M CALLING FROM A JET EN ROUTE TO MEXICO CITY.
WHICH IS WAY COOLER, MIN. SO DON'T UNDERSELL IT.
I'M SORRY I COULDN'T BE THERE I-R-L, AS YOU KIDS SAY--
WE DON'T SAY THAT.
--BUT PETER PARKER AND I WANTED TO CHECK IN AND MAKE SURE YOU DON'T TAKE DR. WU'S CHILLY BEDSIDE MANNER TOO PERSONALLY. HE'S WARY OF ALL AMERICANS.
WHAT? DR. WU IS GREAT!
HE HAS BEEN VERY GENEROUS WITH HIS TIME.
HOLD ON-- SO YOU'RE ONLY MEAN TO ME?!
I HAVE MY ISSUES WITH THE CHAOS THAT FOLLOWS YOU AND YOUR ASSOCIATES.
BUT CLOAK AND DAGGER WERE EXPLOITED BY MY FELLOW COUNTRYMAN. MISTER NEGATIVE IS A DISHONOR TO CHINA.
OFFERING MY SKILLS TOWARD THEIR RECOVERY IS NOT THE SAME AS GETTING MIRED IN THE MADNESS OF--
<FACILITY ALERT. HIGH-RISK INCURSION.>*
AN ATTACK?!
*TRANSLATED FROM MANDARIN

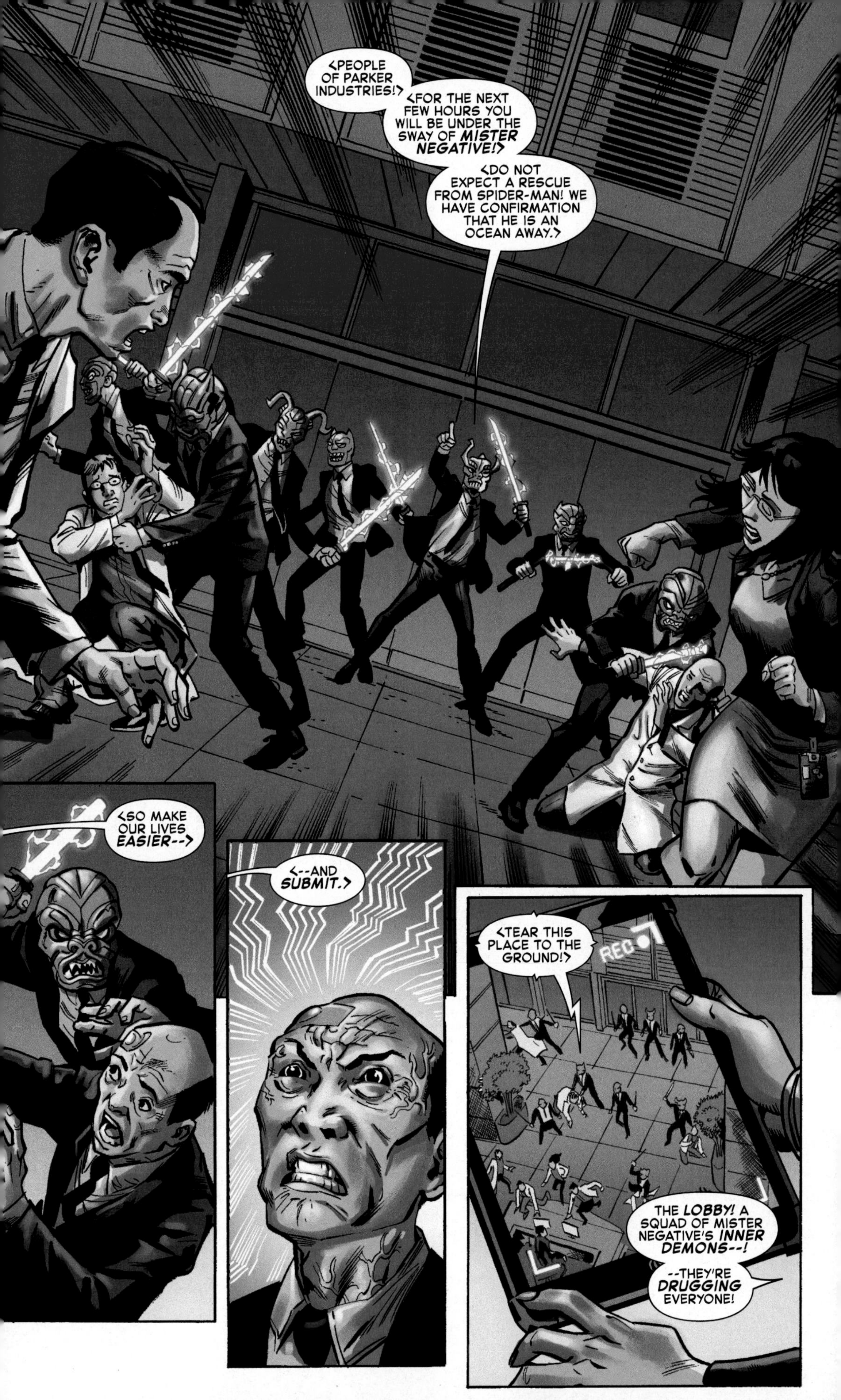
<PEOPLE OF PARKER INDUSTRIES!>
<FOR THE NEXT FEW HOURS YOU WILL BE UNDER THE SWAY OF MISTER NEGATIVE!>
<DO NOT EXPECT A RESCUE FROM SPIDER-MAN! WE HAVE CONFIRMATION THAT HE IS AN OCEAN AWAY.>
<SO MAKE OUR LIVES EASIER-->
<--AND SUBMIT.>
<TEAR THIS PLACE TO THE GROUND!>
REC
THE LOBBY! A SQUAD OF MISTER NEGATIVE'S INNER DEMONS--!
--THEY'RE DRUGGING EVERYONE!

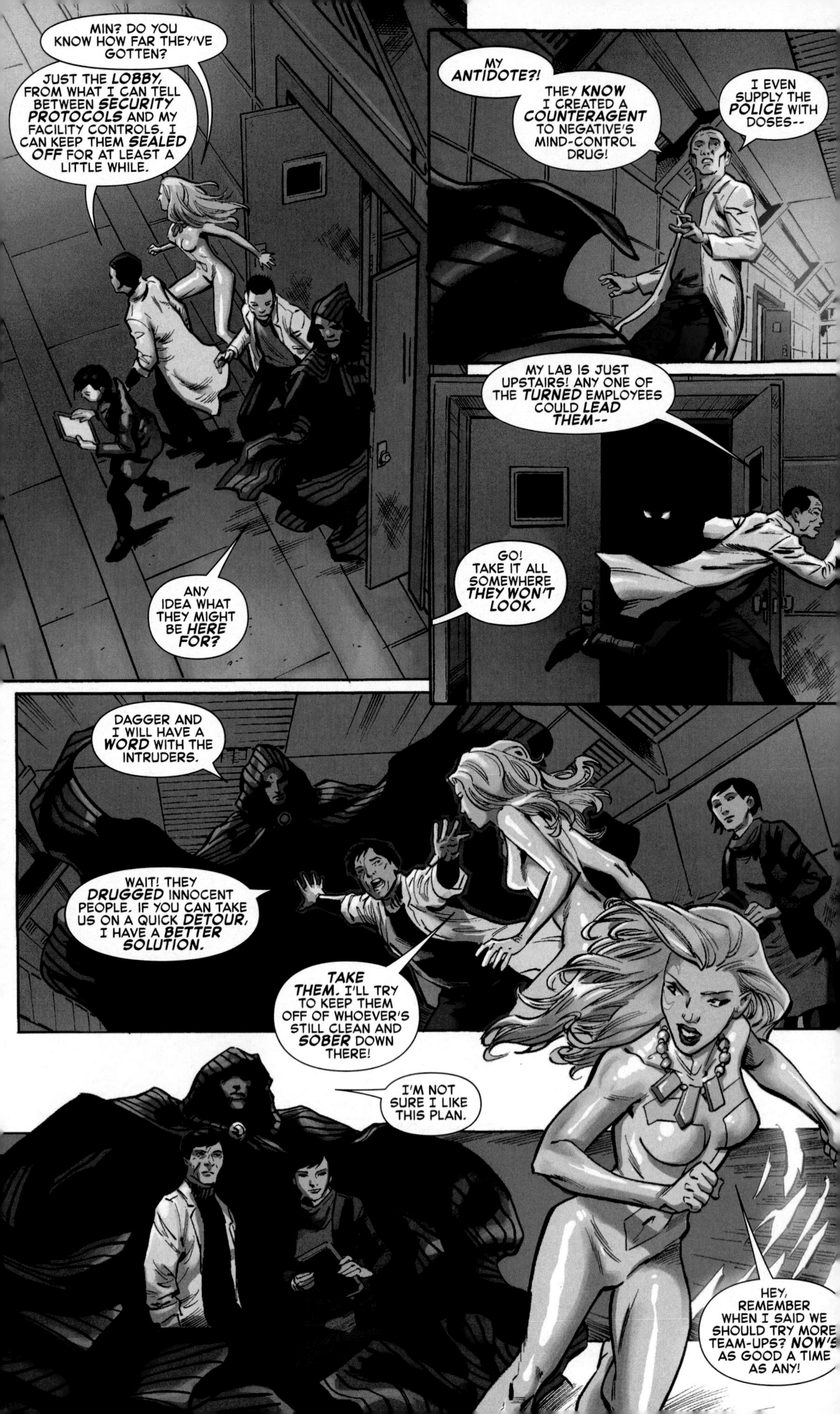
MIN? DO YOU KNOW HOW FAR THEY'VE GOTTEN?
JUST THE LOBBY, FROM WHAT I CAN TELL BETWEEN SECURITY PROTOCOLS AND MY FACILITY CONTROLS. I CAN KEEP THEM SEALED OFF FOR AT LEAST A LITTLE WHILE.
ANY IDEA WHAT THEY MIGHT BE HERE FOR?
MY ANTIDOTE?!
THEY KNOW I CREATED A COUNTERAGENT TO NEGATIVE'S MIND-CONTROL DRUG!
I EVEN SUPPLY THE POLICE WITH DOSES--
MY LAB IS JUST UPSTAIRS! ANY ONE OF THE TURNED EMPLOYEES COULD LEAD THEM--
GO! TAKE IT ALL SOMEWHERE THEY WON'T LOOK.
DAGGER AND I WILL HAVE A WORD WITH THE INTRUDERS.
WAIT! THEY DRUGGED INNOCENT PEOPLE. IF YOU CAN TAKE US ON A QUICK DETOUR, I HAVE A BETTER SOLUTION.
TAKE THEM. I'LL TRY TO KEEP THEM OFF OF WHOEVER'S STILL CLEAN AND SOBER DOWN THERE!
I'M NOT SURE I LIKE THIS PLAN.
HEY, REMEMBER WHEN I SAID WE SHOULD TRY MORE TEAM-UPS? NOW'S AS GOOD A TIME AS ANY!

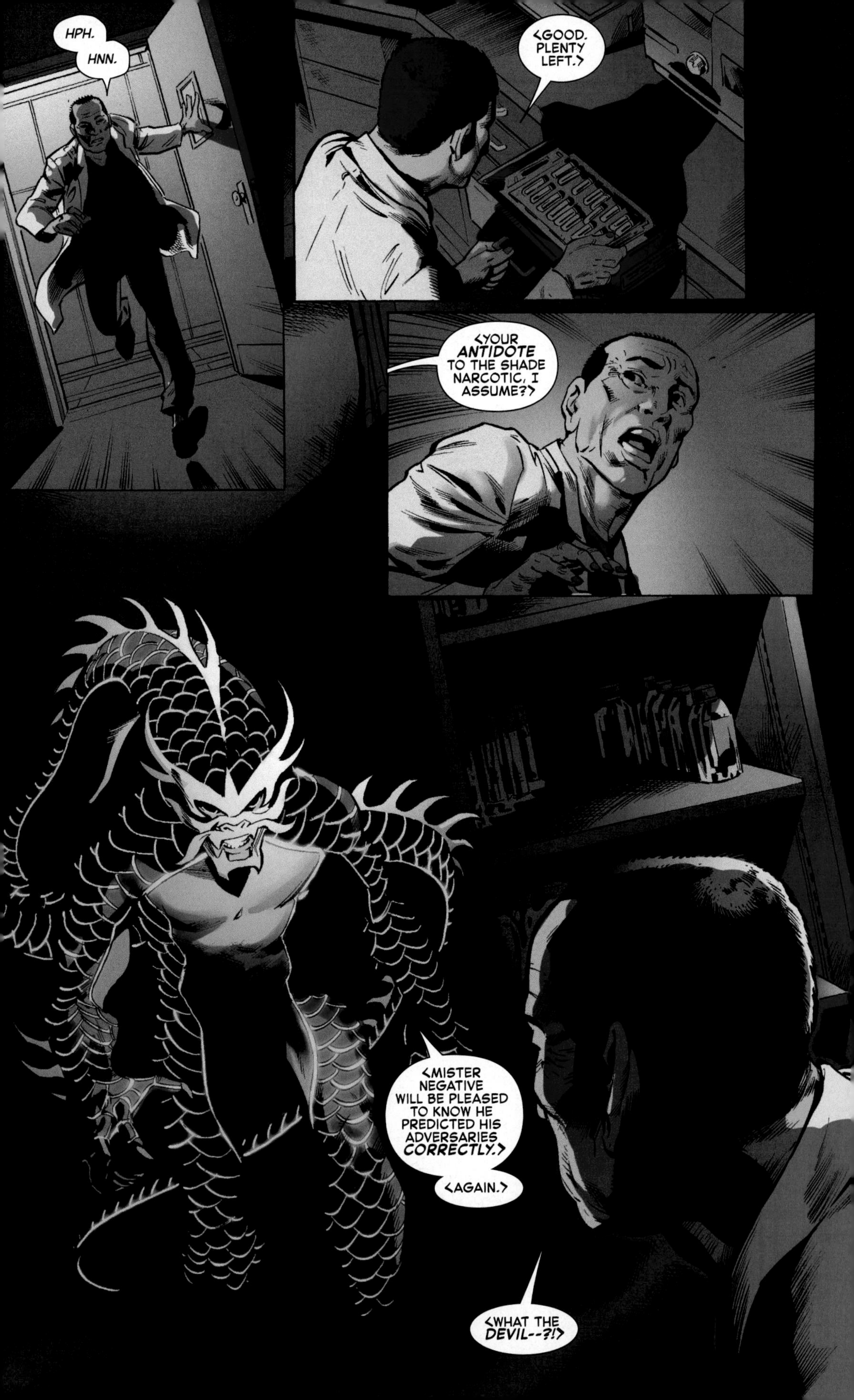
HPH.
HNN.
<GOOD. PLENTY LEFT.>
<YOUR ANTIDOTE TO THE SHADE NARCOTIC, I ASSUME?>
<MISTER NEGATIVE WILL BE PLEASED TO KNOW HE PREDICTED HIS ADVERSARIES CORRECTLY.>
<AGAIN.>
<WHAT THE DEVIL--?!>

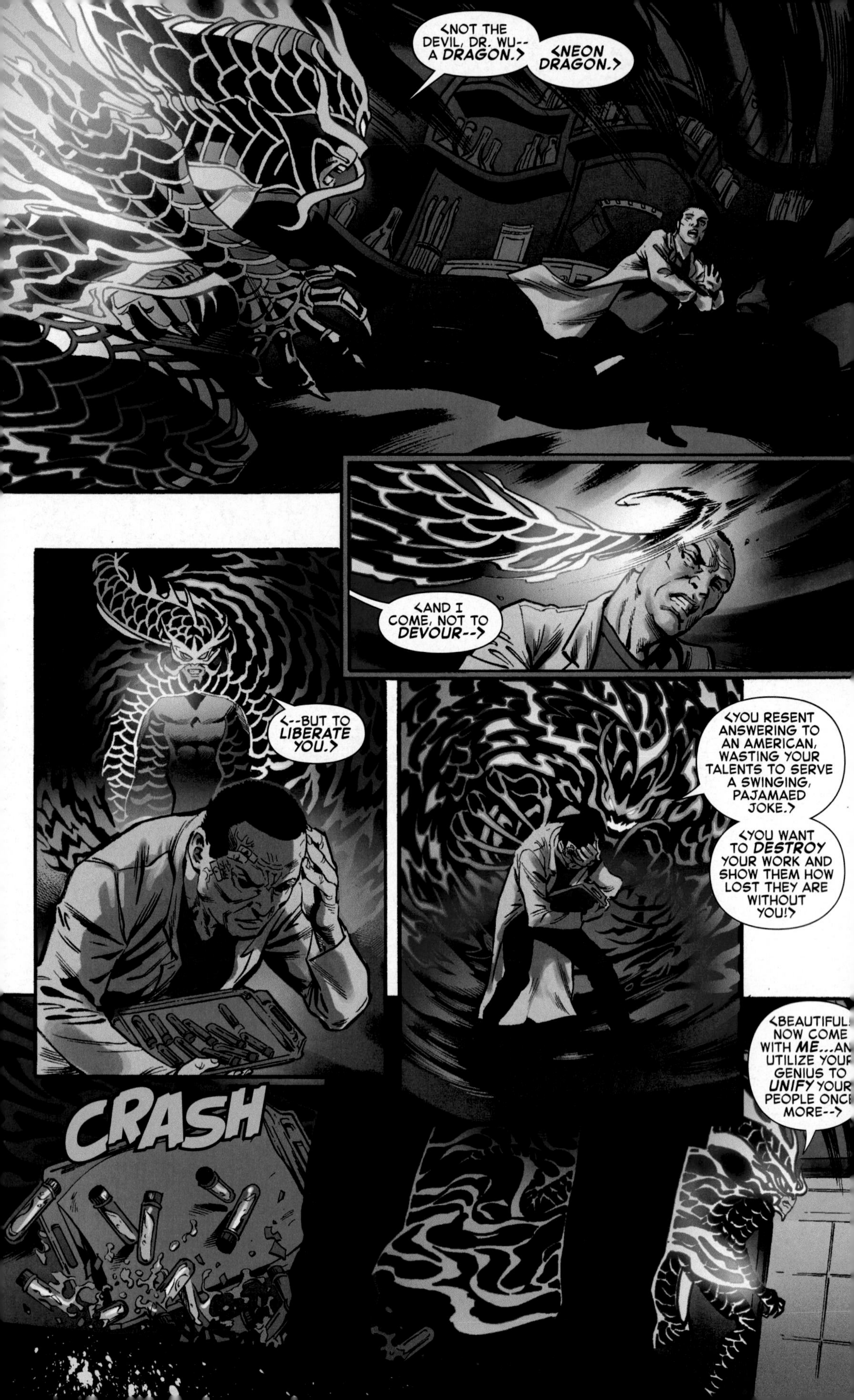

<NOT THE DEVIL, DR. WU-- A DRAGON.>
<NEON DRAGON.>
<AND I COME, NOT TO DEVOUR-->
<--BUT TO LIBERATE YOU.>
<YOU RESENT ANSWERING TO AN AMERICAN, WASTING YOUR TALENTS TO SERVE A SWINGING, PAJAMAED JOKE.>
<YOU WANT TO DESTROY YOUR WORK AND SHOW THEM HOW LOST THEY ARE WITHOUT YOU!>
CRASH
<BEAUTIFUL! NOW COME WITH ME...AN UTILIZE YOUR GENIUS TO UNIFY YOUR PEOPLE ONCE MORE-->

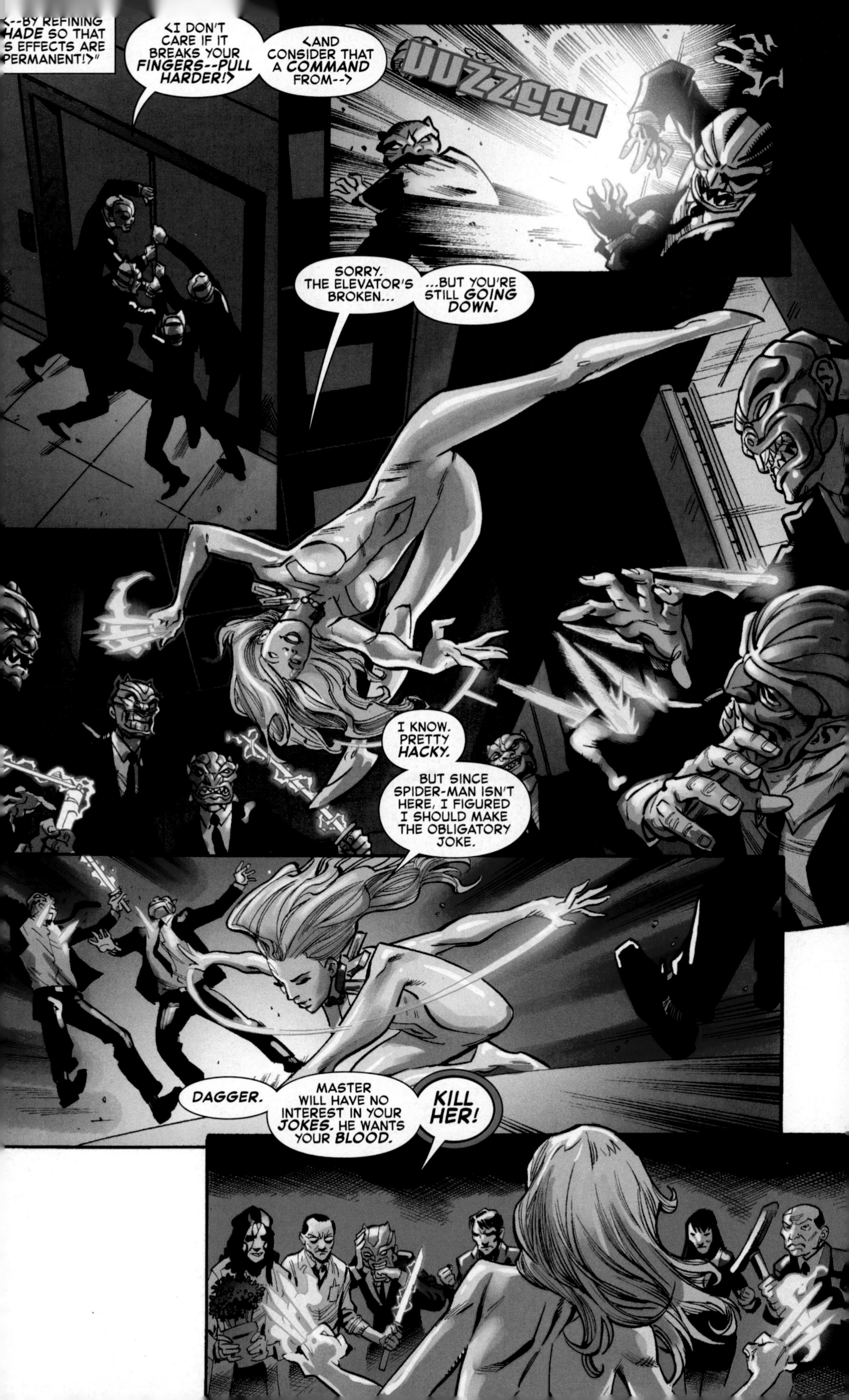
<--BY REFINING HADE SO THAT S EFFECTS ARE PERMANENT!>"
<I DON'T CARE IF IT BREAKS YOUR FINGERS--PULL HARDER!>
<AND CONSIDER THAT A COMMAND FROM-->
VVZZSSH
SORRY. THE ELEVATOR'S BROKEN...
...BUT YOU'RE STILL GOING DOWN.
I KNOW. PRETTY HACKY.
BUT SINCE SPIDER-MAN ISN'T HERE, I FIGURED I SHOULD MAKE THE OBLIGATORY JOKE.
DAGGER.
MASTER WILL HAVE NO INTEREST IN YOUR JOKES. HE WANTS YOUR BLOOD.
KILL HER!

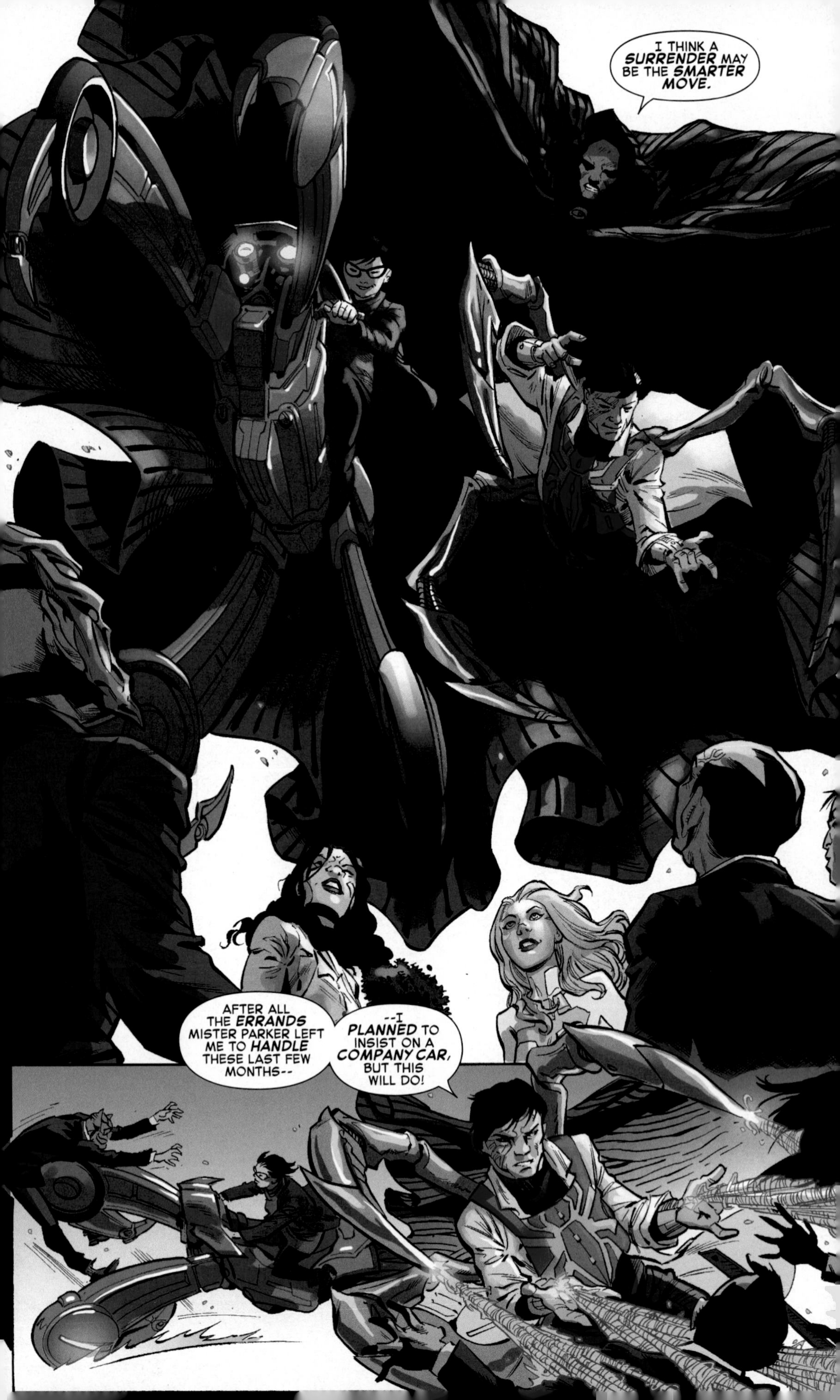

I THINK A SURRENDER MAY BE THE SMARTER MOVE.
AFTER ALL THE ERRANDS MISTER PARKER LEFT ME TO HANDLE THESE LAST FEW MONTHS--
--I PLANNED TO INSIST ON A COMPANY CAR, BUT THIS WILL DO!

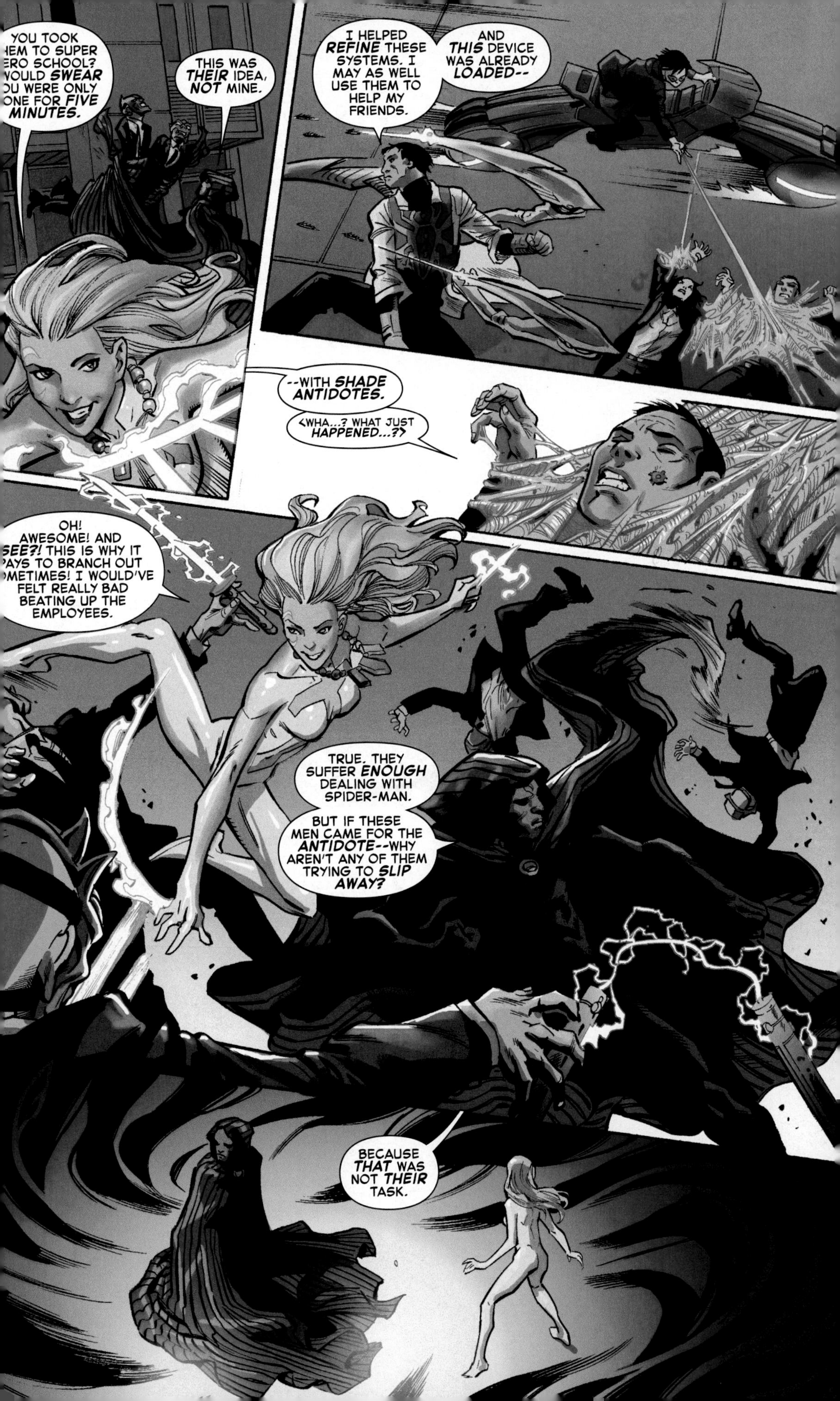

YOU TOOK HEM TO SUPER ERO SCHOOL? WOULD SWEAR OU WERE ONLY ONE FOR FIVE MINUTES.
THIS WAS THEIR IDEA, NOT MINE.
I HELPED REFINE THESE SYSTEMS. I MAY AS WELL USE THEM TO HELP MY FRIENDS.
AND THIS DEVICE WAS ALREADY LOADED--
--WITH SHADE ANTIDOTES.
<WHA...? WHAT JUST HAPPENED...?>
OH! AWESOME! AND SEE?! THIS IS WHY IT AYS TO BRANCH OUT OMETIMES! I WOULD'VE FELT REALLY BAD BEATING UP THE EMPLOYEES.
TRUE. THEY SUFFER ENOUGH DEALING WITH SPIDER-MAN.
BUT IF THESE MEN CAME FOR THE ANTIDOTE--WHY AREN'T ANY OF THEM TRYING TO SLIP AWAY?
BECAUSE THAT WAS NOT THEIR TASK.

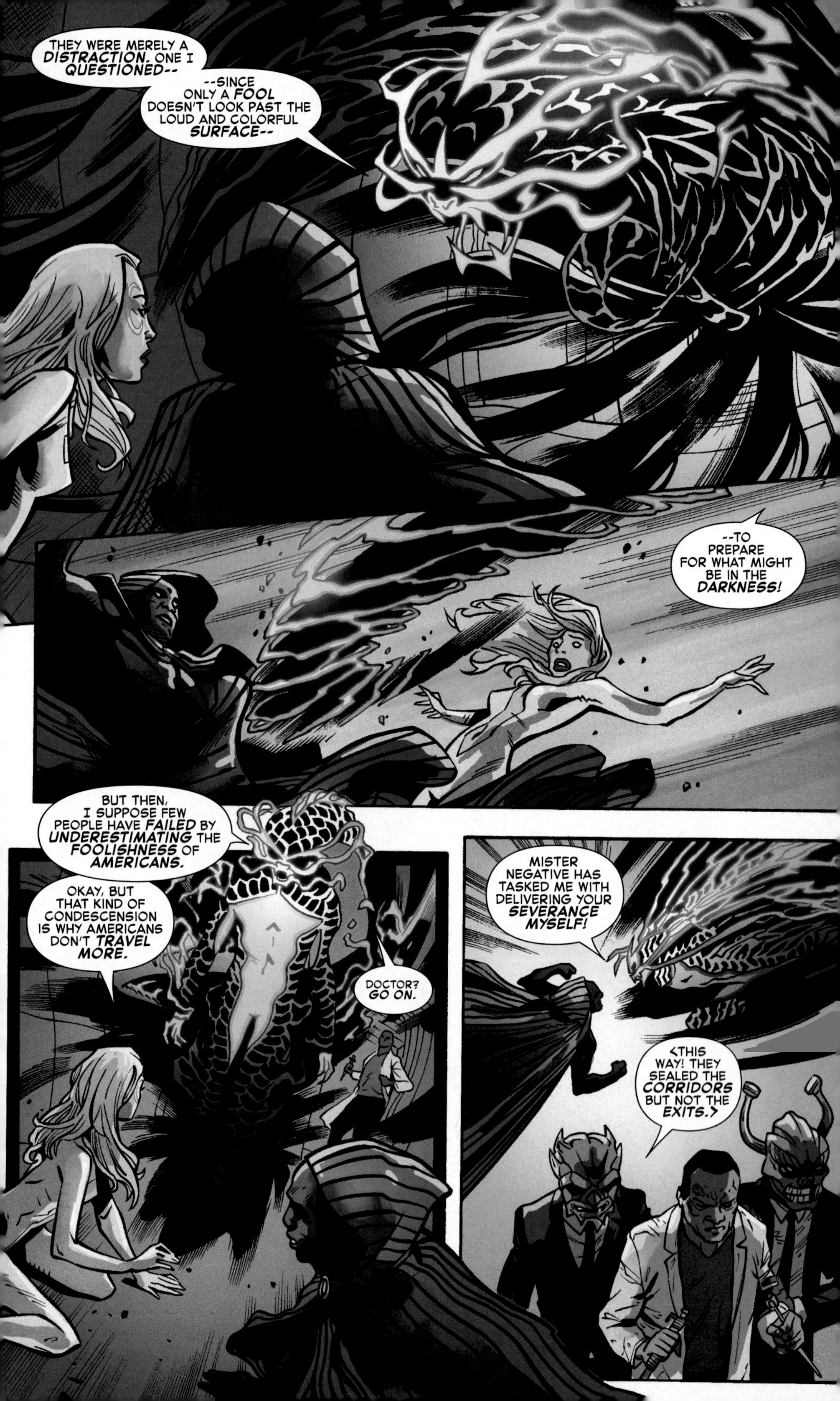
THEY WERE MERELY A DISTRACTION. ONE I QUESTIONED--
--SINCE ONLY A FOOL DOESN'T LOOK PAST THE LOUD AND COLORFUL SURFACE--
--TO PREPARE FOR WHAT MIGHT BE IN THE DARKNESS!
BUT THEN, I SUPPOSE FEW PEOPLE HAVE FAILED BY UNDERESTIMATING THE FOOLISHNESS OF AMERICANS.
OKAY, BUT THAT KIND OF CONDESCENSION IS WHY AMERICANS DON'T TRAVEL MORE.
DOCTOR? GO ON.
MISTER NEGATIVE HAS TASKED ME WITH DELIVERING YOUR SEVERANCE MYSELF!
<THIS WAY! THEY SEALED THE CORRIDORS BUT NOT THE EXITS.>

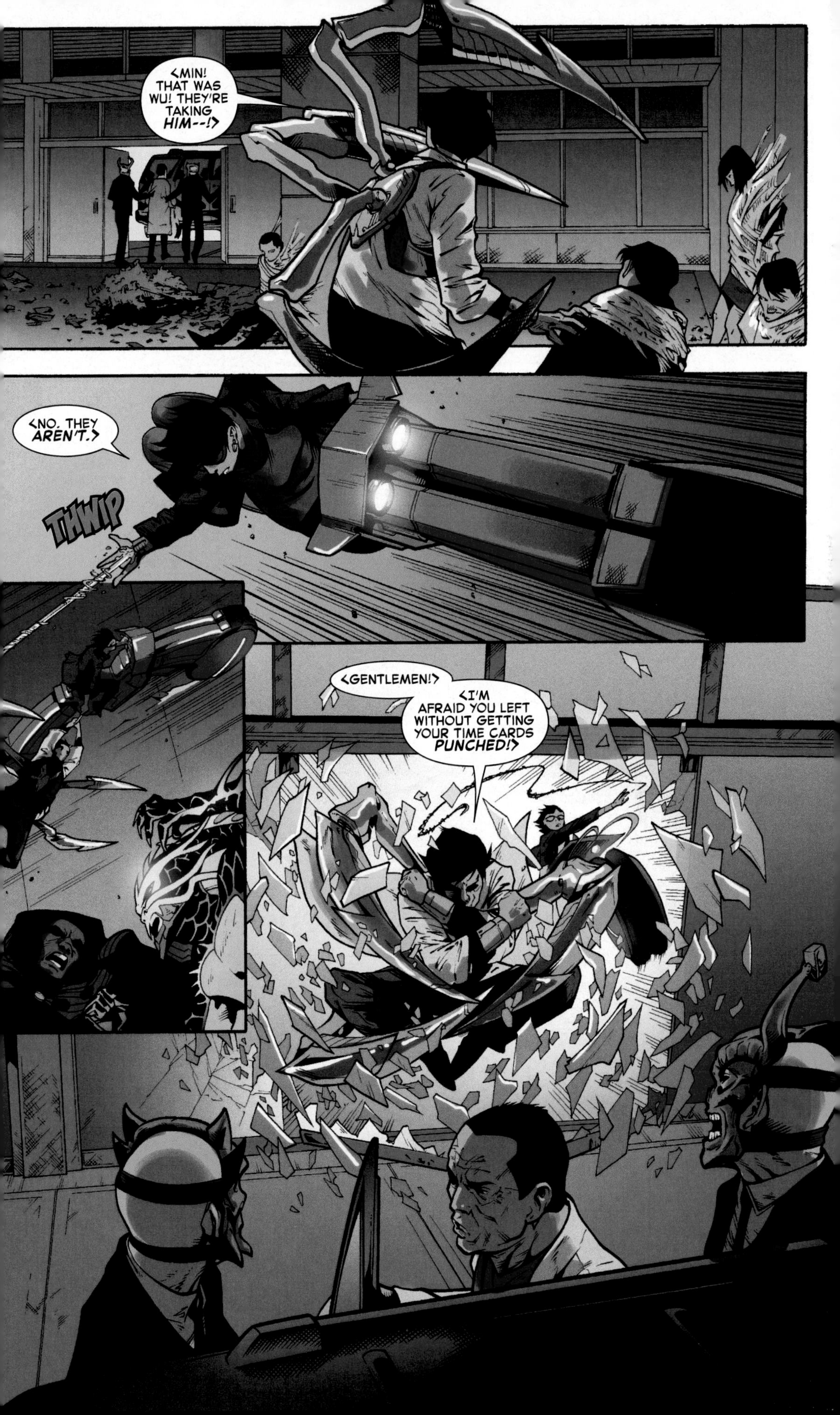
<MIN! THAT WAS WU! THEY'RE TAKING HIM--!>
<NO. THEY AREN'T.>
THWIP
<GENTLEMEN!>
<I'M AFRAID YOU LEFT WITHOUT GETTING YOUR TIME CARDS PUNCHED!>

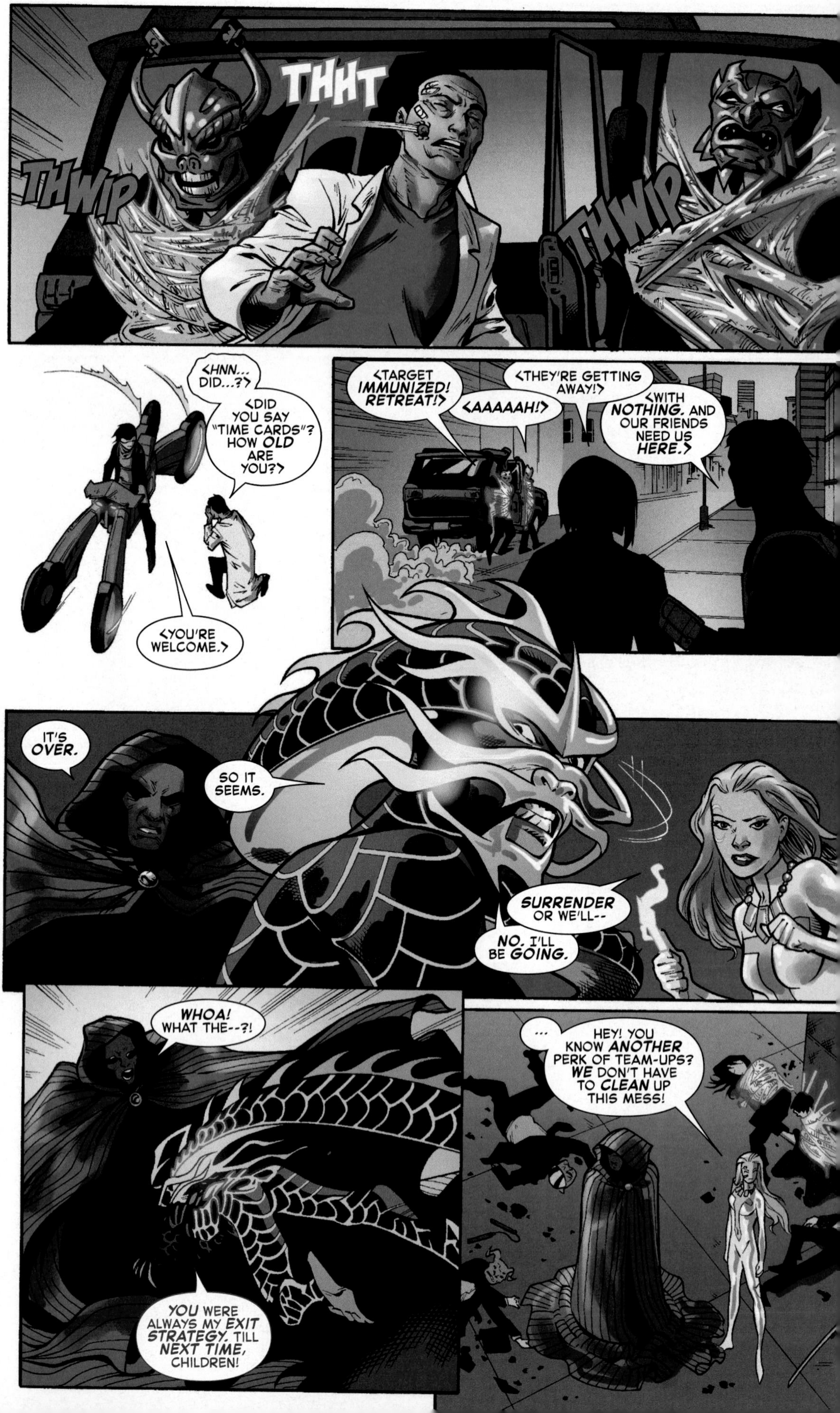
THWIP
THHT
THWIP
<HNN... DID...?>
<DID YOU SAY "TIME CARDS"? HOW OLD ARE YOU?>
<YOU'RE WELCOME.>
<TARGET IMMUNIZED! RETREAT!>
<AAAAAH!>
<THEY'RE GETTING AWAY!>
<WITH NOTHING. AND OUR FRIENDS NEED US HERE.>
IT'S OVER.
SO IT SEEMS.
SURRENDER OR WE'LL--
NO. I'LL BE GOING.
WHOA! WHAT THE--?!
YOU WERE ALWAYS MY EXIT STRATEGY. TILL NEXT TIME, CHILDREN!
...
HEY! YOU KNOW ANOTHER PERK OF TEAM-UPS? WE DON'T HAVE TO CLEAN UP THIS MESS!

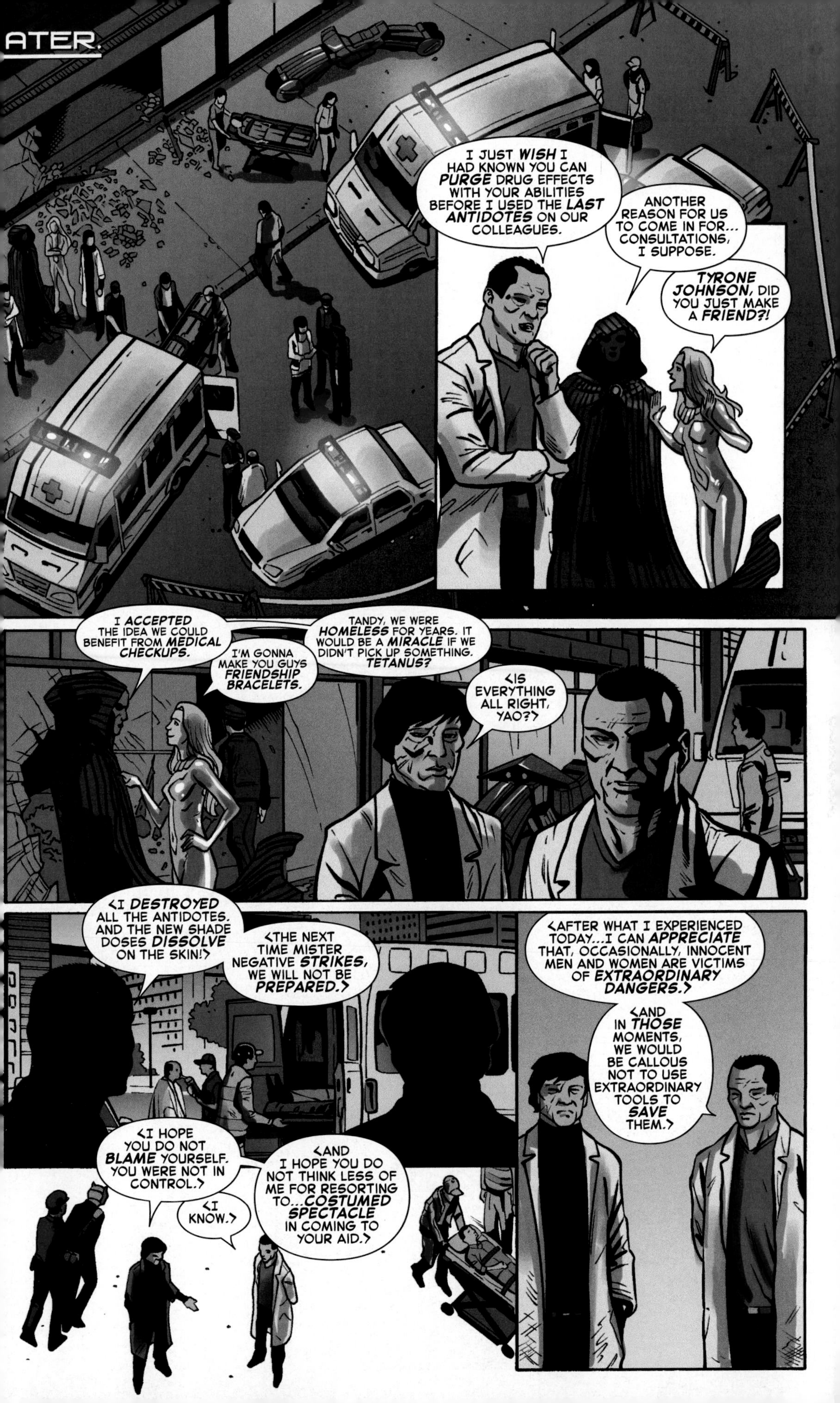

ATER.
I JUST WISH I HAD KNOWN YOU CAN PURGE DRUG EFFECTS WITH YOUR ABILITIES BEFORE I USED THE LAST ANTIDOTES ON OUR COLLEAGUES.
ANOTHER REASON FOR US TO COME IN FOR... CONSULTATIONS, I SUPPOSE.
TYRONE JOHNSON, DID YOU JUST MAKE A FRIEND?!
I ACCEPTED THE IDEA WE COULD BENEFIT FROM MEDICAL CHECKUPS.
I'M GONNA MAKE YOU GUYS FRIENDSHIP BRACELETS.
TANDY, WE WERE HOMELESS FOR YEARS. IT WOULD BE A MIRACLE IF WE DIDN'T PICK UP SOMETHING. TETANUS?
<IS EVERYTHING ALL RIGHT, YAO?>
<I DESTROYED ALL THE ANTIDOTES. AND THE NEW SHADE DOSES DISSOLVE ON THE SKIN!>
<THE NEXT TIME MISTER NEGATIVE STRIKES, WE WILL NOT BE PREPARED.>
<AFTER WHAT I EXPERIENCED TODAY...I CAN APPRECIATE THAT, OCCASIONALLY, INNOCENT MEN AND WOMEN ARE VICTIMS OF EXTRAORDINARY DANGERS.>
<AND IN THOSE MOMENTS, WE WOULD BE CALLOUS NOT TO USE EXTRAORDINARY TOOLS TO SAVE THEM.>
<I HOPE YOU DO NOT BLAME YOURSELF. YOU WERE NOT IN CONTROL.>
<I KNOW.>
<AND I HOPE YOU DO NOT THINK LESS OF ME FOR RESORTING TO...COSTUMED SPECTACLE IN COMING TO YOUR AID.>

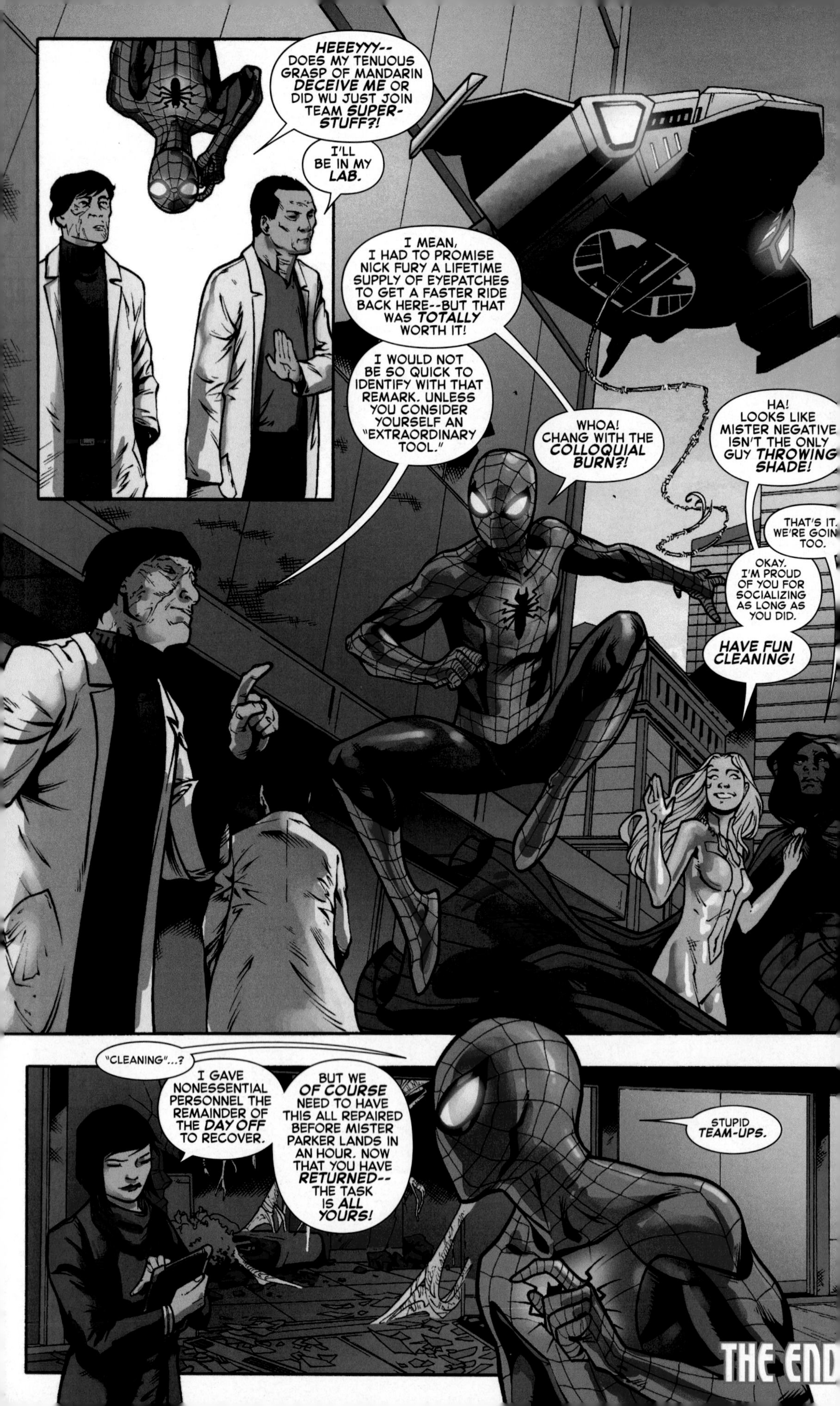
HEEEYYY-- DOES MY TENUOUS GRASP OF MANDARIN DECEIVE ME OR DID WU JUST JOIN TEAM SUPER-STUFF?!
I'LL BE IN MY LAB.
I MEAN, I HAD TO PROMISE NICK FURY A LIFETIME SUPPLY OF EYEPATCHES TO GET A FASTER RIDE BACK HERE--BUT THAT WAS TOTALLY WORTH IT!
I WOULD NOT BE SO QUICK TO IDENTIFY WITH THAT REMARK. UNLESS YOU CONSIDER YOURSELF AN "EXTRAORDINARY TOOL."
WHOA! CHANG WITH THE COLLOQUIAL BURN?!
HA! LOOKS LIKE MISTER NEGATIVE ISN'T THE ONLY GUY THROWING SHADE!
THAT'S IT. WE'RE GOIN TOO.
OKAY. I'M PROUD OF YOU FOR SOCIALIZING AS LONG AS YOU DID.
HAVE FUN CLEANING!
"CLEANING"...?
I GAVE NONESSENTIAL PERSONNEL THE REMAINDER OF THE DAY OFF TO RECOVER.
BUT WE OF COURSE NEED TO HAVE THIS ALL REPAIRED BEFORE MISTER PARKER LANDS IN AN HOUR. NOW THAT YOU HAVE RETURNED-- THE TASK IS ALL YOURS!
STUPID TEAM-UPS.
THE END

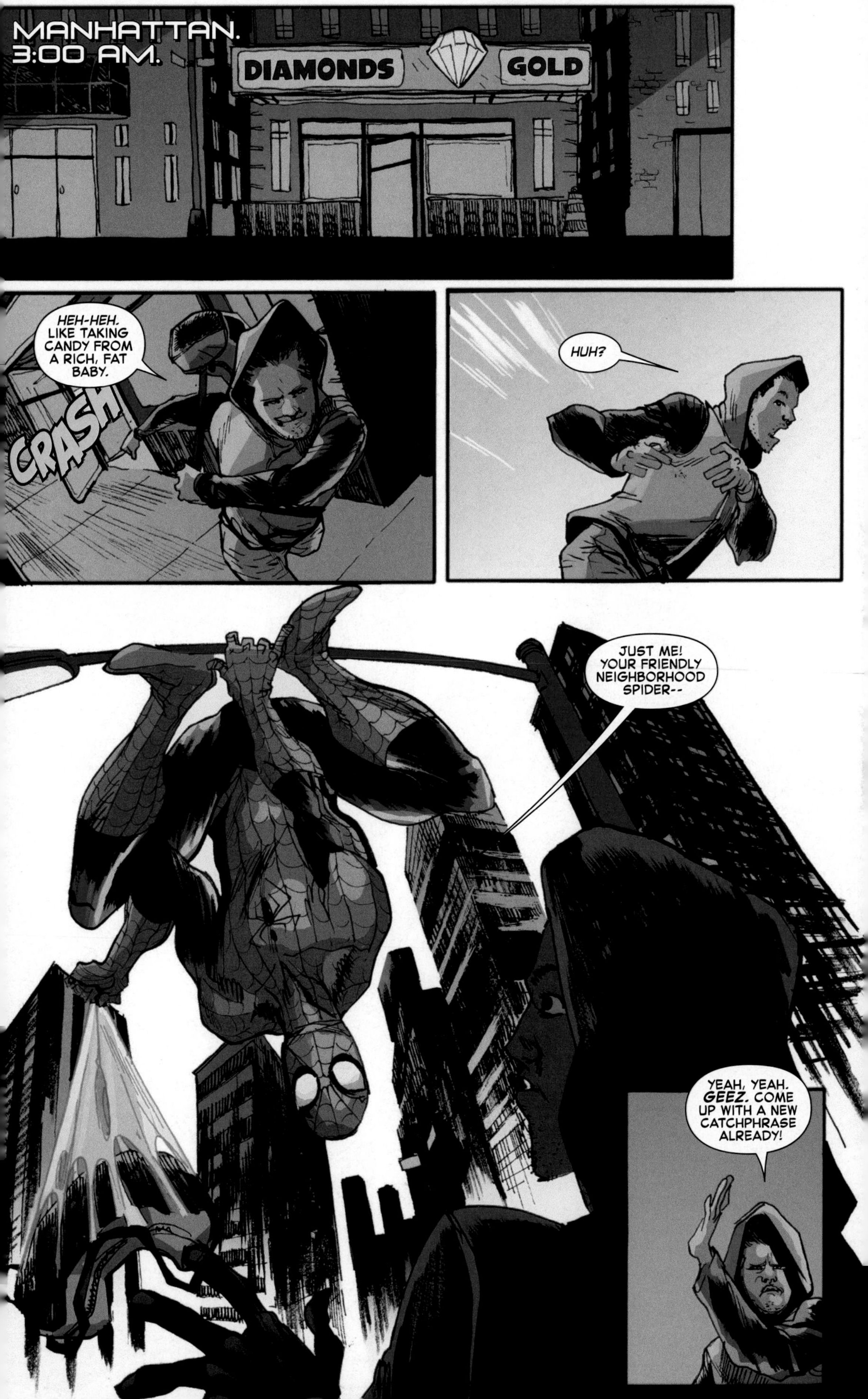
MANHATTAN.
3:00 AM.
DIAMONDS
GOLD
HEH-HEH. LIKE TAKING CANDY FROM A RICH, FAT BABY.
CRASH
HUH?
JUST ME! YOUR FRIENDLY NEIGHBORHOOD SPIDER--
YEAH, YEAH. GEEZ. COME UP WITH A NEW CATCHPHRASE ALREADY!

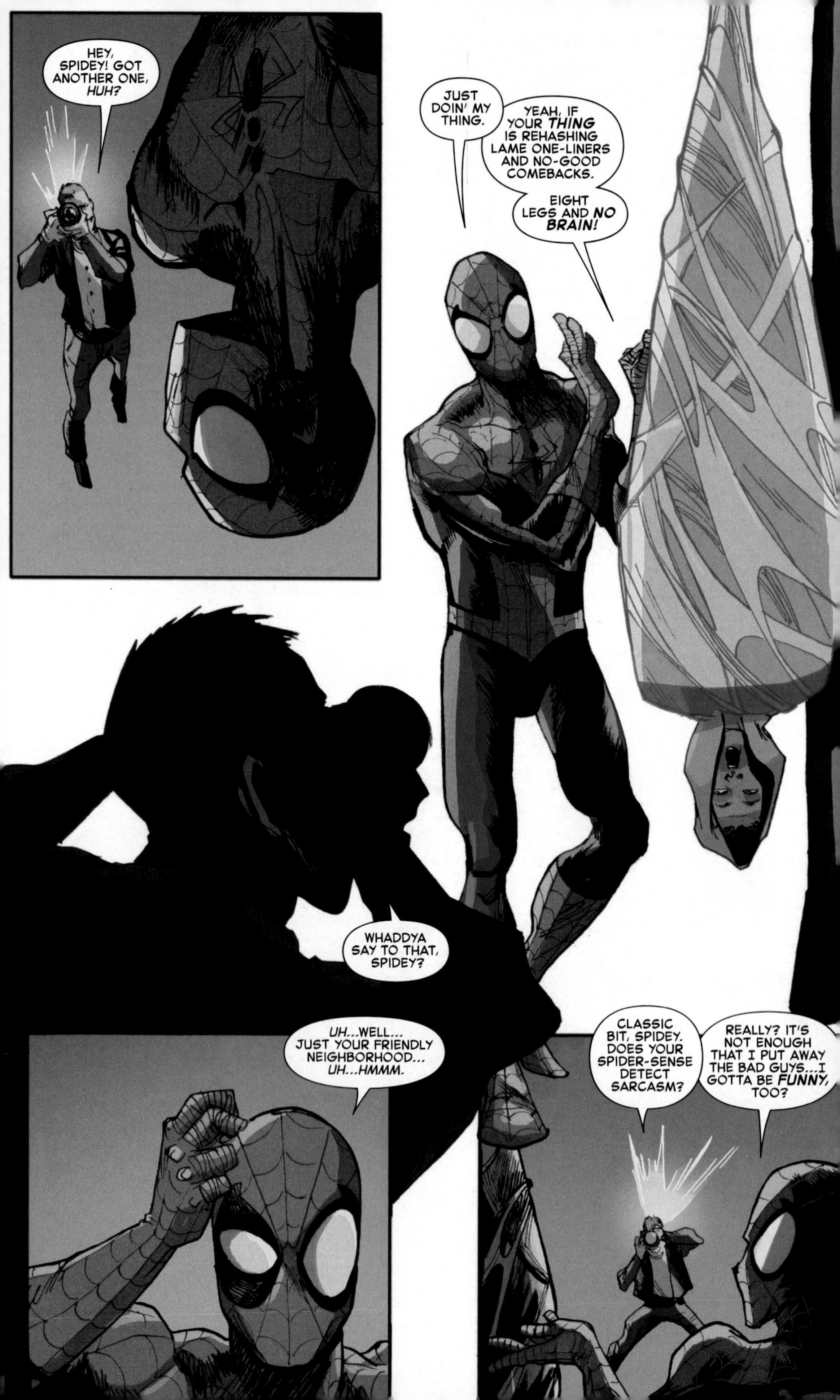

HEY, SPIDEY! GOT ANOTHER ONE, *HUH?*
JUST DOIN' MY THING.
YEAH, IF YOUR *THING* IS REHASHING LAME ONE-LINERS AND NO-GOOD COMEBACKS.
EIGHT LEGS AND ***NO BRAIN!***
WHADDYA SAY TO THAT, SPIDEY?
*UH...*WELL... JUST YOUR FRIENDLY NEIGHBORHOOD... *UH...*HMMM.
CLASSIC BIT, SPIDEY. DOES YOUR SPIDER-SENSE DETECT SARCASM?
REALLY? IT'S NOT ENOUGH THAT I PUT AWAY THE BAD GUYS...I GOTTA BE ***FUNNY,*** TOO?

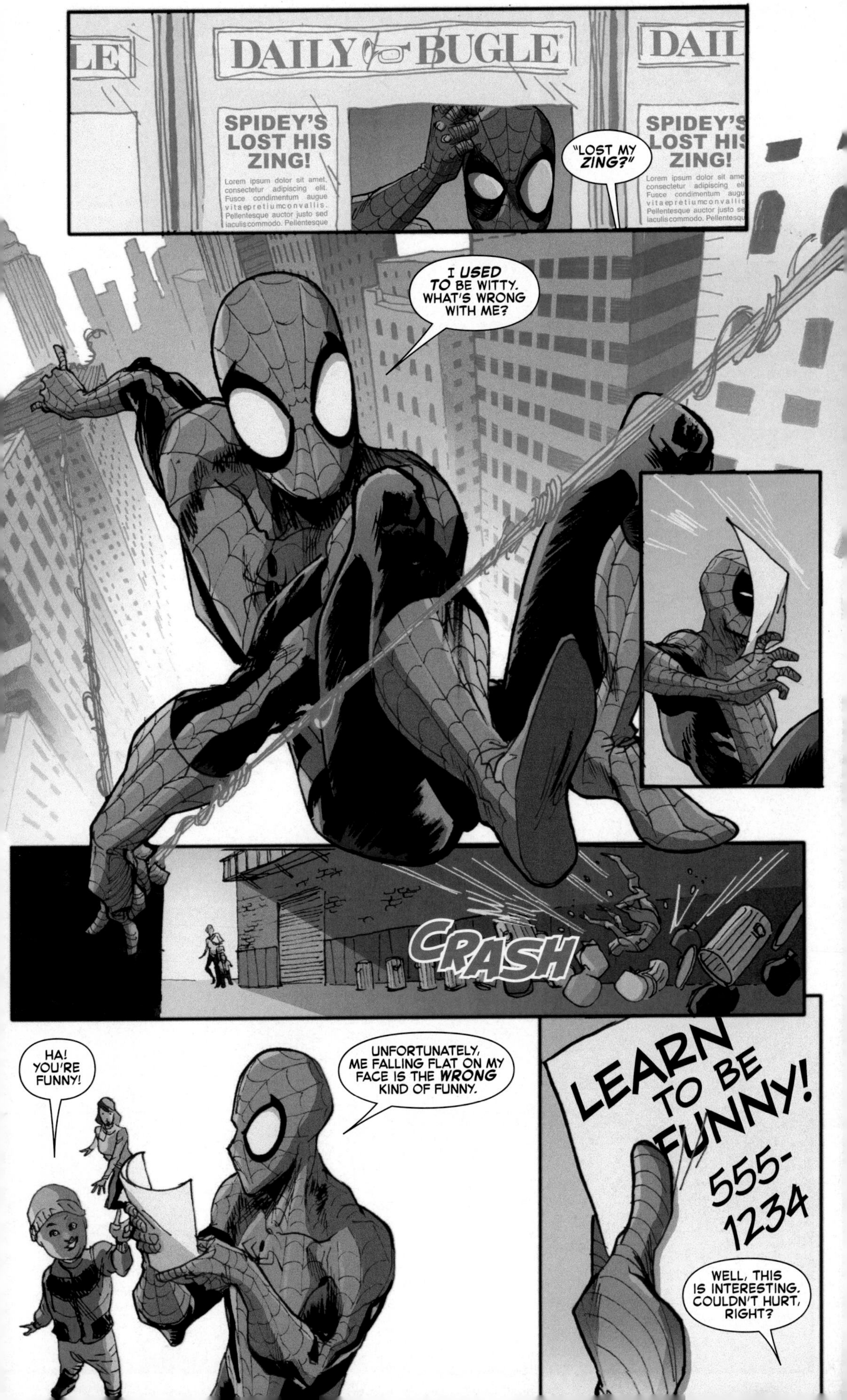
DAILY BUGLE
SPIDEY'S LOST HIS ZING!
Lorem ipsum dolor sit amet, consectetur adipiscing elit. Fusce condimentum augue vitae pretium convallis. Pellentesque auctor justo sed iaculis commodo. Pellentesque
"LOST MY ZING?"
I USED TO BE WITTY. WHAT'S WRONG WITH ME?
CRASH
HA! YOU'RE FUNNY!
UNFORTUNATELY, ME FALLING FLAT ON MY FACE IS THE WRONG KIND OF FUNNY.
LEARN TO BE FUNNY!
555-1234
WELL, THIS IS INTERESTING. COULDN'T HURT, RIGHT?

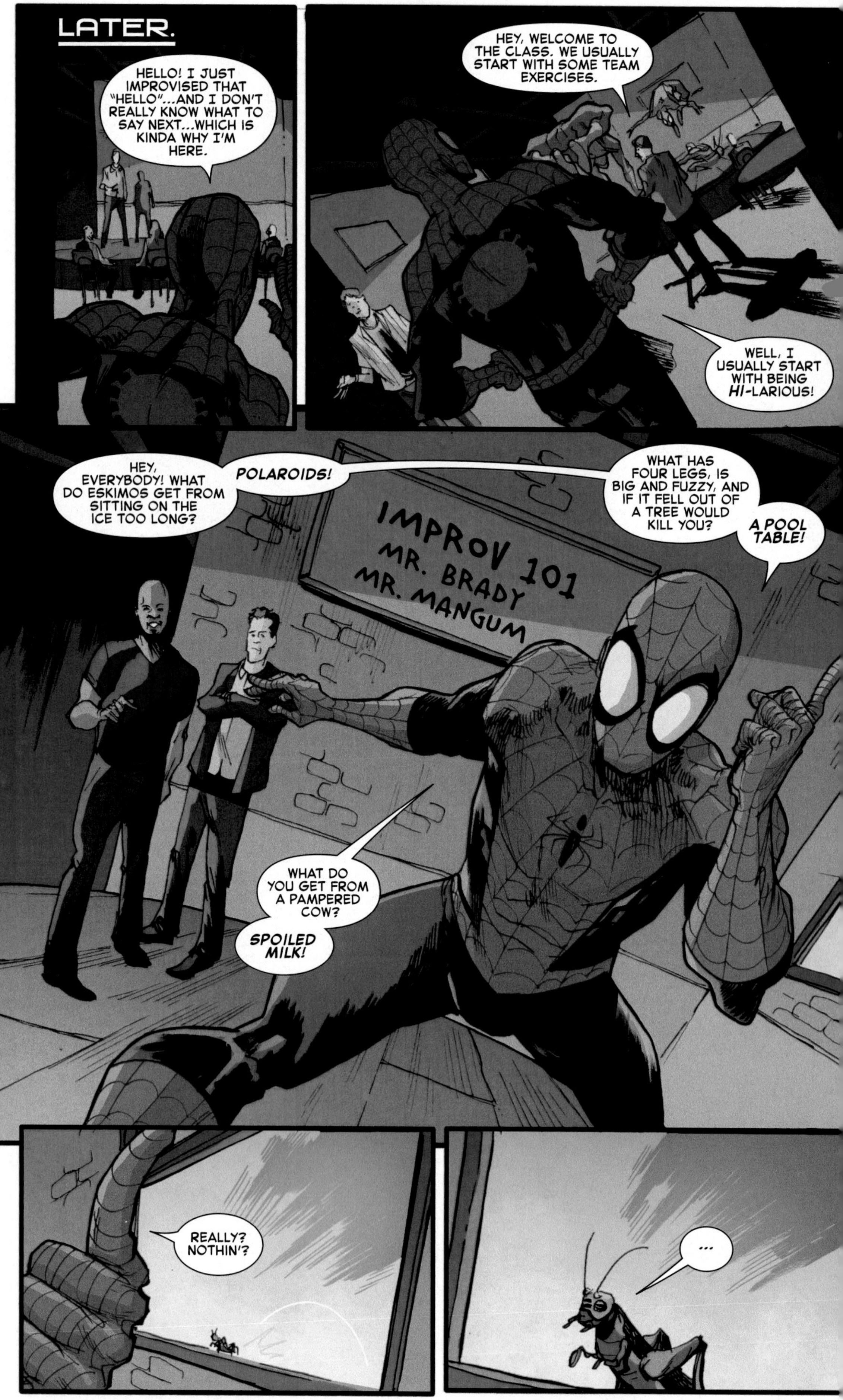
LATER.
HELLO! I JUST IMPROVISED THAT "HELLO"...AND I DON'T REALLY KNOW WHAT TO SAY NEXT...WHICH IS KINDA WHY I'M HERE.
HEY, WELCOME TO THE CLASS. WE USUALLY START WITH SOME TEAM EXERCISES.
WELL, I USUALLY START WITH BEING HI-LARIOUS!
HEY, EVERYBODY! WHAT DO ESKIMOS GET FROM SITTING ON THE ICE TOO LONG?
POLAROIDS!
WHAT HAS FOUR LEGS, IS BIG AND FUZZY, AND IF IT FELL OUT OF A TREE WOULD KILL YOU?
A POOL TABLE!
IMPROV 101
MR. BRADY
MR. MANGUM
WHAT DO YOU GET FROM A PAMPERED COW?
SPOILED MILK!
REALLY? NOTHIN'?
...

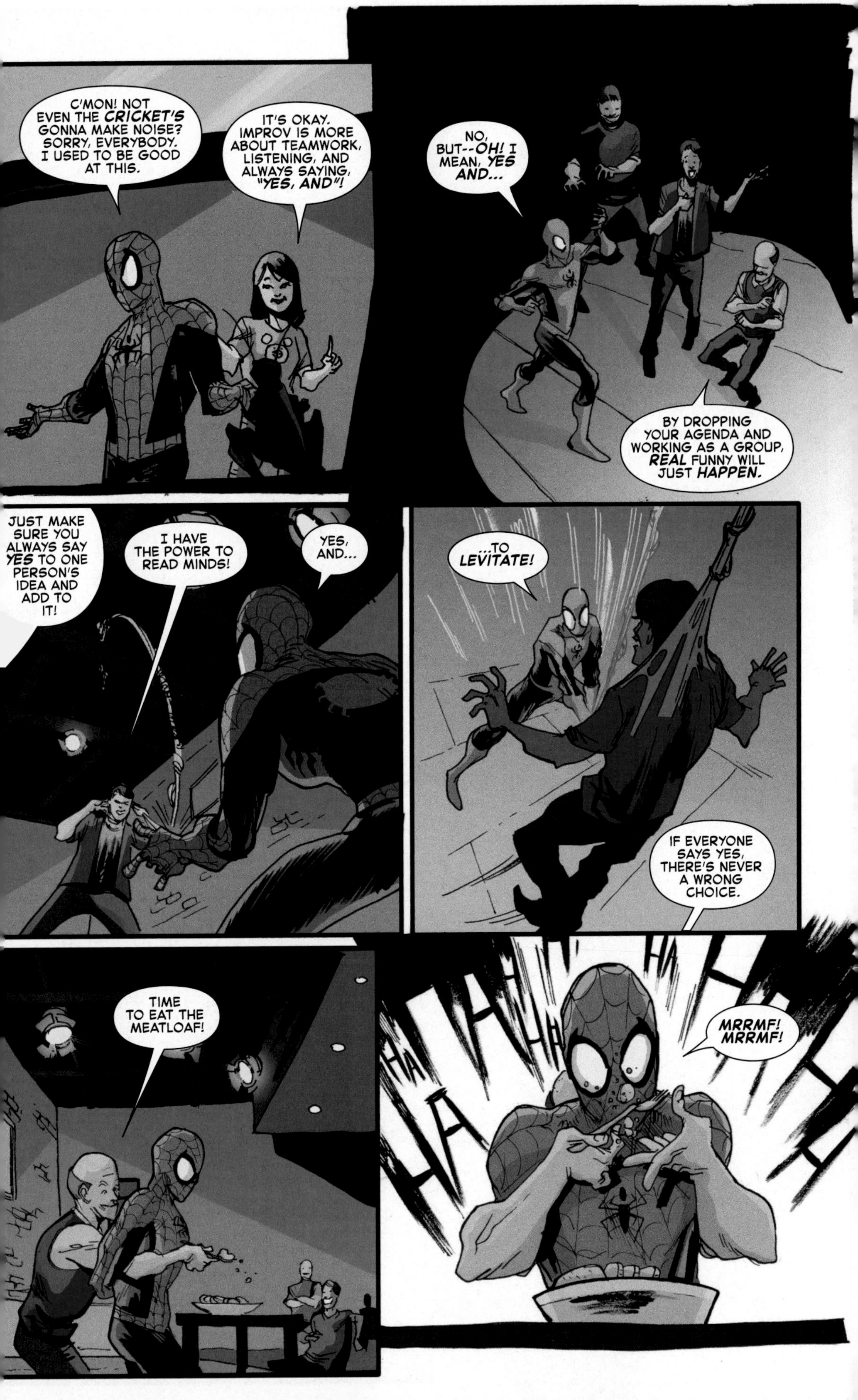
C'MON! NOT EVEN THE CRICKET'S GONNA MAKE NOISE? SORRY, EVERYBODY. I USED TO BE GOOD AT THIS.
IT'S OKAY. IMPROV IS MORE ABOUT TEAMWORK, LISTENING, AND ALWAYS SAYING, "YES, AND"!
NO, BUT--OH! I MEAN, YES AND...
BY DROPPING YOUR AGENDA AND WORKING AS A GROUP, REAL FUNNY WILL JUST HAPPEN.
JUST MAKE SURE YOU ALWAYS SAY YES TO ONE PERSON'S IDEA AND ADD TO IT!
I HAVE THE POWER TO READ MINDS!
YES, AND...
...TO LEVITATE!
IF EVERYONE SAYS YES, THERE'S NEVER A WRONG CHOICE.
TIME TO EAT THE MEATLOAF!
MRRMF! MRRMF!

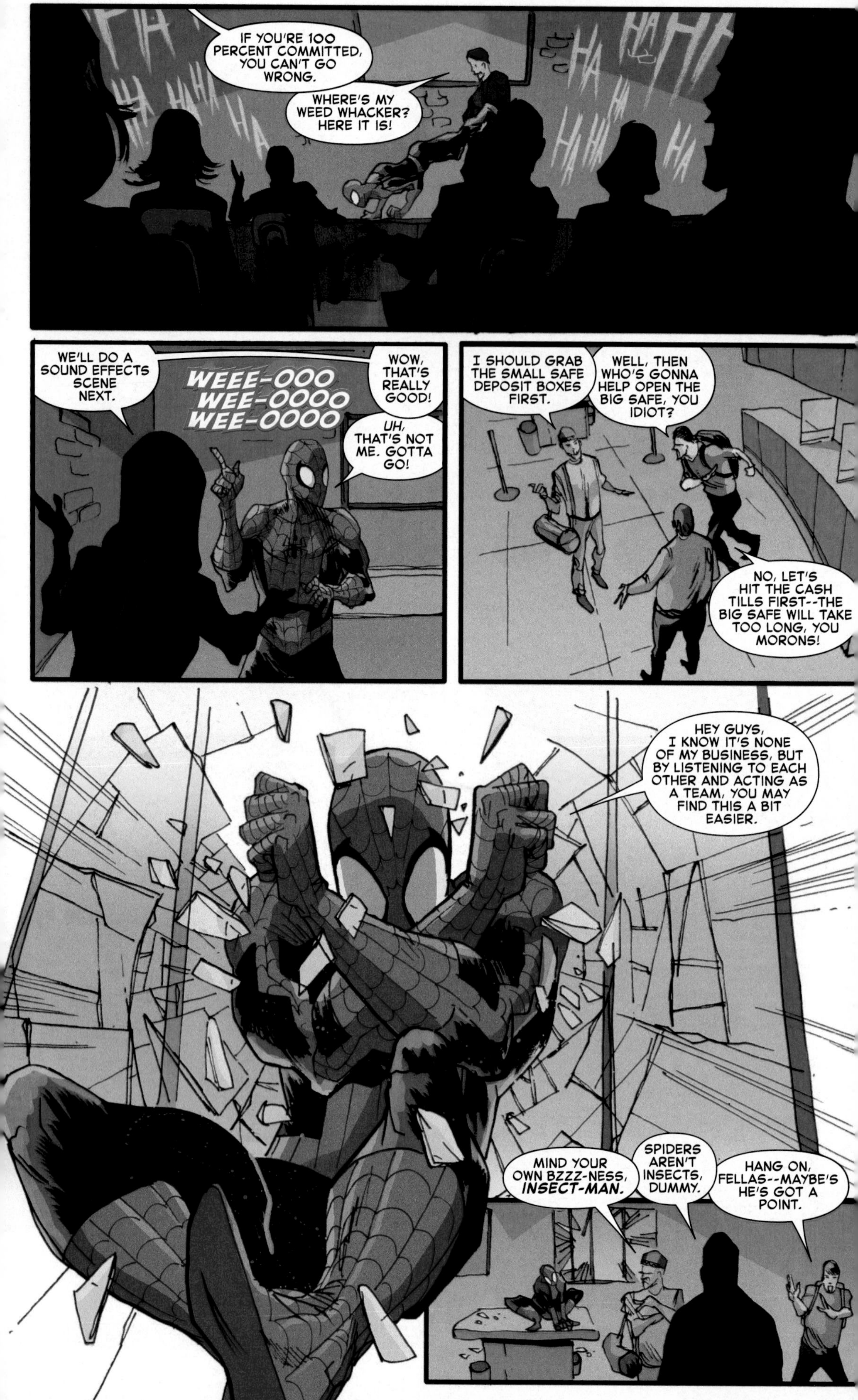
IF YOU'RE 100 PERCENT COMMITTED, YOU CAN'T GO WRONG.
WHERE'S MY WEED WHACKER? HERE IT IS!
HA HA HA HA HA
WE'LL DO A SOUND EFFECTS SCENE NEXT.
WEEE-OOO WEE-OOOO WEE-OOOO
WOW, THAT'S REALLY GOOD!
UH, THAT'S NOT ME. GOTTA GO!
I SHOULD GRAB THE SMALL SAFE DEPOSIT BOXES FIRST.
WELL, THEN WHO'S GONNA HELP OPEN THE BIG SAFE, YOU IDIOT?
NO, LET'S HIT THE CASH TILLS FIRST--THE BIG SAFE WILL TAKE TOO LONG, YOU MORONS!
HEY GUYS, I KNOW IT'S NONE OF MY BUSINESS, BUT BY LISTENING TO EACH OTHER AND ACTING AS A TEAM, YOU MAY FIND THIS A BIT EASIER.
MIND YOUR OWN BZZZ-NESS, INSECT-MAN.
SPIDERS AREN'T INSECTS, DUMMY.
HANG ON, FELLAS--MAYBE'S HE'S GOT A POINT.

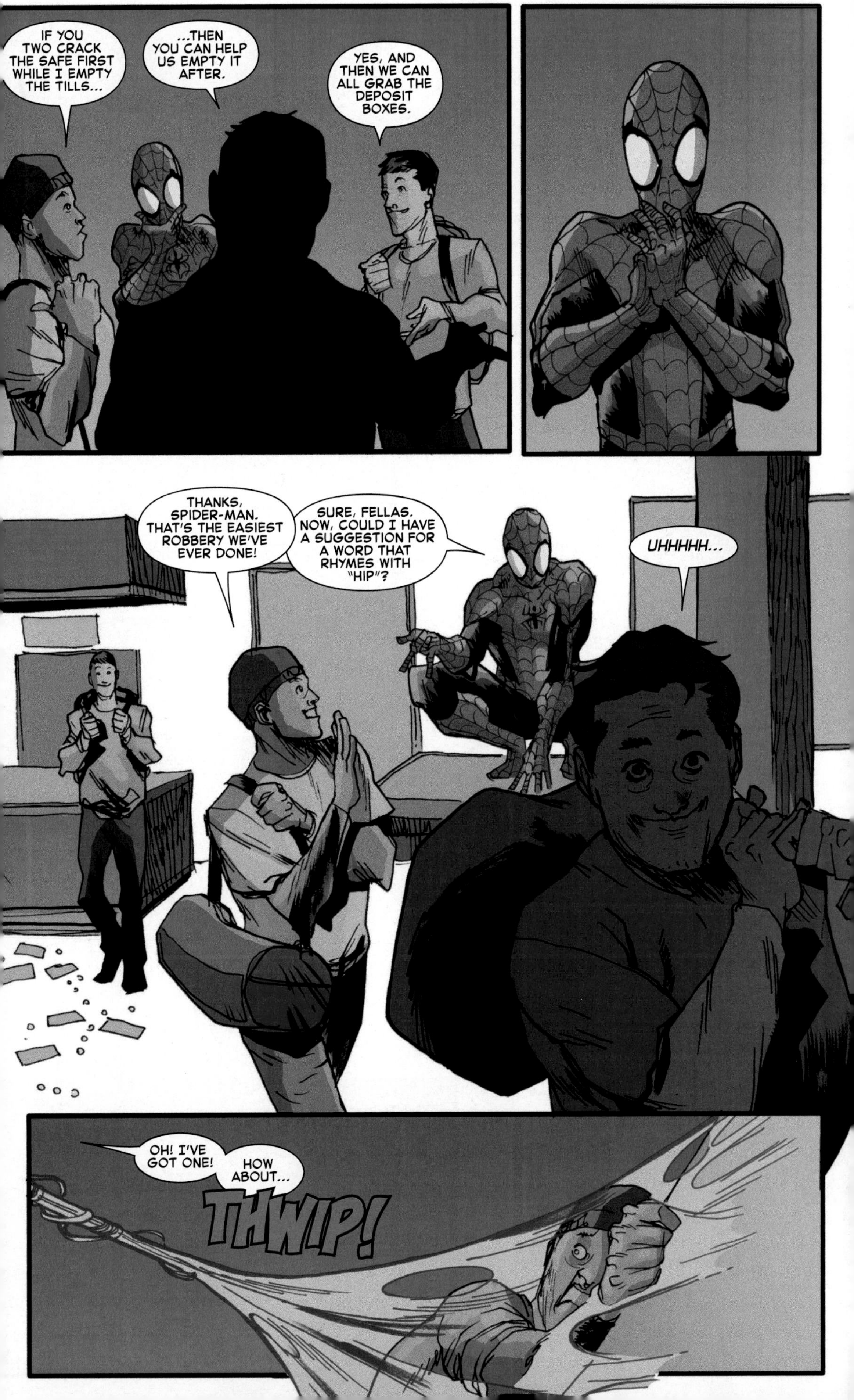
IF YOU TWO CRACK THE SAFE FIRST WHILE I EMPTY THE TILLS...
...THEN YOU CAN HELP US EMPTY IT AFTER.
YES, AND THEN WE CAN ALL GRAB THE DEPOSIT BOXES.
THANKS, SPIDER-MAN. THAT'S THE EASIEST ROBBERY WE'VE EVER DONE!
SURE, FELLAS. NOW, COULD I HAVE A SUGGESTION FOR A WORD THAT RHYMES WITH "HIP"?
UHHHHH...
OH! I'VE GOT ONE!
HOW ABOUT...
THWIP!

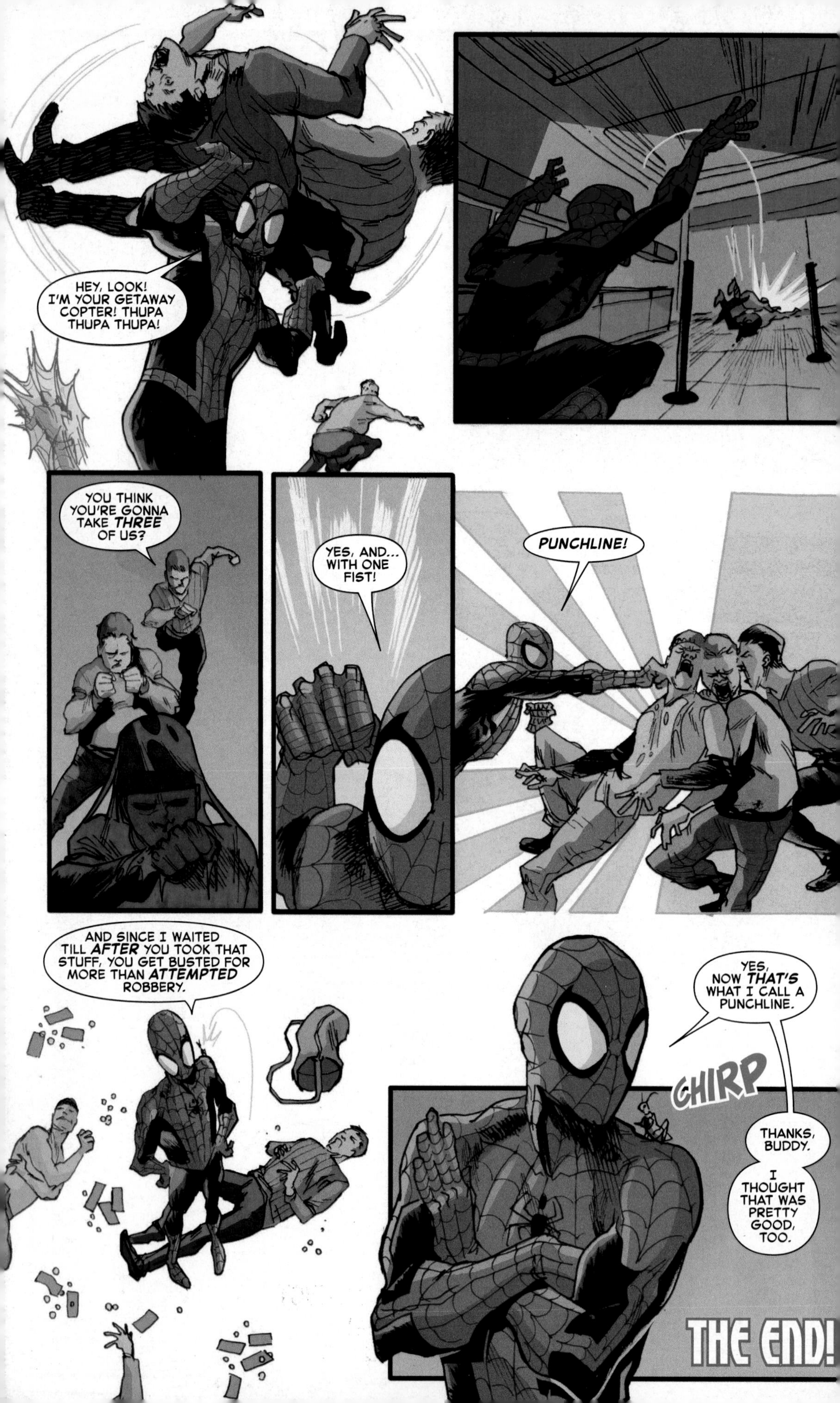
HEY, LOOK! I'M YOUR GETAWAY COPTER! THUPA THUPA THUPA!
YOU THINK YOU'RE GONNA TAKE THREE OF US?
YES, AND... WITH ONE FIST!
PUNCHLINE!
AND SINCE I WAITED TILL AFTER YOU TOOK THAT STUFF, YOU GET BUSTED FOR MORE THAN ATTEMPTED ROBBERY.
YES, NOW THAT'S WHAT I CALL A PUNCHLINE.
CHIRP
THANKS, BUDDY.
I THOUGHT THAT WAS PRETTY GOOD, TOO.
THE END!